INNOVATIONS in INTERNATIONAL and CROSS-CULTURAL MANAGEMENT

INNOVATIONS in INTERNATIONAL and CROSS-CULTURAL MANAGEMENT

Edited by

P. Christopher Earley
Harbir Singh

Sage Publications, Inc.
International Educational and Professional Publisher
Thousand Oaks ▪ London ▪ New Delhi

For information:

Sage Publications, Inc.
2455 Teller Road
Thousand Oaks, California 91320
E-mail: order@sagepub.com

Sage Publications Ltd.
6 Bonhill Street
London EC2A 4PU
United Kingdom

Sage Publications India Pvt. Ltd.
M-32 Market
Greater Kailash I
New Delhi 110 048 India

Printed in the United States of America

Library of Congress Cataloging-in-Publication Data

Earley, P. Christopher
    Innovations in international and cross-cultural management /
by P. Christopher Earley and Harbir Singh.
      p. cm.
    Includes bibliographical references and index.
    ISBN 0-7619-1234-7 (cloth: alk. paper)
    ISBN 0-7619-1235-5 (pbk.: alk. paper)
    1. International business enterprise—Management—Research.
    2. Management—Cross-cultural studies. I. Singh, Harbir. II. Title.
HD62.4 .E238   2000
658.'049'—dc21   00-008094

This book is printed on acid-free paper.

00 01 02 03 04 05 06 7 6 5 4 3 2 1

Acquiring Editor:	Harry Briggs/Marquita Flemming
Editorial Assistant:	Mary Ann Vail
Production Editor:	Astrid Virding
Editorial Assistant:	Victoria Cheng
Typesetter:	Lynn Miyata
Cover Designer:	Candice Harman/Michelle Lee

Contents

Preface   vii

1. Introduction: New Approaches to International and
   Cross-Cultural Management Research   1
   P. Christopher Earley and Harbir Singh

PART I. Micro-Organizational Approaches

2. Beliefs About Values, Status, and Legitimacy
   in Multicultural Groups: Influences on Intragroup Conflict   17
   Elizabeth C. Ravlin, David C. Thomas, and Arzu Ilsev

3. Missing Relations: Incorporating Relational Constructs
   Into Models of Culture   52
   Michael W. Morris, Joel M. Podolny, and Sheira Ariel

4. The Cultural Metaphor: A Grounded Method
   for Analyzing National Cultures   91
   Martin J. Gannon and Pino G. Audia

5. Strategic Human Resource Management in
   International Joint Ventures   107
   J. Michael Geringer and Colette A. Frayne

PART II. Meso-Organizational Approaches

6. Extending Agency Theory With Event Management and
   Foreign Direct Investment Theories:
   U.S. Investments in Brazilian Banks   131
   Mark F. Peterson, Carlos L. Rodriguez, and Peter B. Smith

7. Strategic Social Partnerships for Change:
   A Framework for Building Sustainable Growth
   in Developing Countries   183
   Cathy A. Enz, Crist Inman, and Melenie J. Lankau

PART III. Macro-Organizational Approaches

8. Examining Interfirm Trust and Relationships
   in a Cross-National Setting   215
   Jeffrey H. Dyer

9. Replication of *Keiretsu* in the United States:
   Transfer of Interorganizational Network
   Through Direct Investment   245
   Sea Jin Chang

10. Toward a Model of Accelerating Organizational Change:
    Evidence From the Globalization Process   267
    Thomas W. Malnight

11. Strategic Colonialism in Unfamiliar Cultures:
    Overcoming Extreme Forms of Causal Ambiguity Internationally   311
    Elaine Mosakowski

12. Time Zone Economies and Managerial Work in a Global World   339
    Srilata Zaheer

Author Index   355

Subject Index   359

About the Editors   367

About the Contributors   369

Preface

An ever-increasing internationalization occurring in the workplace and its concomitant demands placed on researchers acted as an impetus for this volume. Despite an obvious need to map the limits of generalization of our theories and frameworks, there seems to be a lack of understanding concerning the theoretical and practical limits of current organizational research. Despite the seemingly obvious constraint that an international setting places on research paradigms, research proliferates with findings based on single cultural contexts without asking the critical question concerning generalizability. In this sense, the research literature is plagued by a single blind man's description of an elephant or an incomplete view of the entire phenomenon under observation. Our purpose in collecting the chapters for this book is to provide interested readers with divergent perspectives concerning a wide variety of international and cross-cultural research topics.

For a number of years, evidence emerged demonstrating that various organizational interventions were differentially effective in various cultures, but researchers could only speculate why such differentiation occurred. It has been dissatisfying to rely on panacea explanations such as those that comparative approaches often provide. It is our belief, and our hope, that the approaches presented in this book will enhance our understanding of the role that nations and culture play in shaping organizational practices and will enable us to predict those practices that will be most effective in a given context.

We began this book after the first author was contacted by Marquita Flemming at Sage Publications concerning the possible development of a volume that would complement our 1995 special research forum in the *Academy of Management Journal* on innovative methods used for international and cross-cultural research. Sage was interested in publishing an edited book complementing the emphasis in our special issue but with a focus on theory development and presentation. After discussing the preliminaries with Sage, I contacted my coeditor and asked him whether he was interested in the project.

One of our greatest challenges for this book has been to identify both new and established international and cross-cultural management scholars. We wanted a mix of well-established scholars and veteran researchers who had only begun conducting international work within the past 3 or 4 years. We believe that our book provides a nice mix of both perspectives for the purpose of stimulating new questioning of old propositions. What all of the contributors have in common is a passion for international work despite very different conceptual starting points.

Many individuals contributed to the creation of this book. Needless to say, our collection of chapters reflects the accumulation of many scholars' efforts. In developing the core concept behind this volume, our thinking was influenced by a number of people including Miriam Erez, Elaine Mosakowski, and Harry Triandis, to name just a few individuals. We are grateful to our home institutions and colleagues for their continued support as we worked on this book. The first author thanks the Randall L. Tobias Chair of Global Leadership, Indiana University, and the London Business School for their support. The second author thanks the Wharton School at the University of Pennsylvania for its support. We are particularly grateful to Flemming, our editor at Sage, for her guidance and assistance during the development of this project.

We also thank the editorial staff at Sage for their patience and help in shaping our volume into a rigorous presentation. We thank the various contributors to this volume; their responsiveness to deadlines varied dramatically, so a number of authors bore the brunt of awaiting the responses of their co-contributors. Ultimately, as the editors, we are to blame for the time line in this book, and we appreciate the patience of our contributors and the staff at Sage.

Finally, we thank our doctoral students who have stimulated our thinking about international, cross-cultural, and intercultural issues. We continue to develop, in part, because our students never cease in asking what scholars mean by international and cross-cultural organizational research.

P. Christopher Earley
Harbir Singh

chapter 1

Introduction

New Approaches to International and Cross-Cultural Management Research

P. CHRISTOPHER EARLEY
HARBIR SINGH

I recall that on a foggy night a short number of years ago, I found myself driving with a physicist along the mountainous stretch of Route 17 between Santa Cruz and San Jose. Both of us felt anxious about the weather and somewhat bored, so we began to discuss our respective fields. My companion opened by asking me, as only a physicist could, what anthropologists had discovered.

"Discovered?" I asked, pretending to be puzzled. I was stalling for time. Perhaps something would come to me.

"Yes, you know, something like the properties or the laws of other cultures."

"Do you mean something like $E = mc^2$?"

"Yes," he said. (Rosaldo, 1989, p. 33)

There are both scientific and practical reasons for this book to emerge at this time. From a scientific perspective, cultural and international research in the fields of anthropology, psychology, and sociology, among others, has come to a crossroads of generalizability that cannot be addressed using existing Western models of management thought (Earley & Erez, 1997; Hofstede, 1991; Rosaldo, 1989). This concern is particularly salient for management research inasmuch as we adopted an international and cross-cultural research agenda quite recently. Conceptualizations of the self, work team, and

1

organization in management research suffer from the myopia of a Western lens. Although such a perspective is not inherently weak or inappropriate, we are left wonting. Are these various theories and perspectives generalizable across national and cultural boundaries? Do theories derived by Western researchers inform their counterparts in the East and Middle East? Certainly, the cry for our research models to be decoupled from Western civilization is not new by any means. It has been two decades since Hofstede (1980) questioned the crossnational utility of American management theory, and it has been more than three decades since Haire, Ghiselli, and Porter (1966) highlighted the divergent values underlying managers' psyches across nations. Despite this lapsed time and the clear proliferation of cross-national and cross-cultural management research, are we closer to understanding the generality of management theory in the face of national and cultural variance?

From a practical perspective, businesses are increasing their international exposure and penetration, and this shift seems to have few limits at the moment. With international expansion comes a myriad of difficulties including issues surrounding human resource management (HRM) practices for multinational and transnational companies, parent-subsidiary governance and control, investment decisions and practices, organization formation and structure in a transnational context, and reconciling the diversity of action underlying employees drawn from diverse cultures, to name but a few difficulties. This trend also is reflected in business school hiring, with a scramble of many institutions to "internationalize" their faculties and curricula. The popular press decries the need for management education to reflect the complexity of a "global village" just as managers condemn us for failing to keep pace with the rapid changes that they face each and every day.

Despite these academic and practical demands on us as scholars and researchers, there is a paucity of theory that can be drawn on concerning the conduct of sophisticated international research in management. Of course, there are notable exceptions including work by industry- and organization-level researchers such as Dyer, Ghosal, Hennart, Kobrin, Kogut, and Zaheer. Likewise, organization behavior and theory scholars such as Adler, Bond, Brett, Brewer, Brislin, Child, Erez, Gannon, Hofstede, House, Miller, Porter, Schuler, Schneider, Steers, Triandis, and Westney, as well as the contributors to this volume, have begun the arduous task of laying down the conceptual foundation for management research in an international context. Despite these efforts, the field continues to suffer from a lack of conceptual frameworks, and much of the research attention continues to be an extrapolation of Hofstede's values system.

It is not possible to review even this literature to which we refer, but we refer to some of the work for illustrative purposes. For example, the significant foundation of international and cross-cultural research in management can be traced to early comparative work such as Haire et al.'s (1966) study of managerial values. The focus of these studies was to uncover the nature of values and beliefs that exist in a number of different countries. An important variation on this approach is the now classic study of Hofstede (1980, 1991) in which he sampled the values of organizational members from more than 40 countries. His initial empirical analysis showed a four-part typology of cultural dimensions, and his subsequent research (Hofstede, 1991; Hofstede & Bond, 1988) yielded an additional characteristic denoting time and fate in society. Values research also is the focus of other management gurus such as Trompenaars (1997). This work is complemented by that of scholars from psychology such as Schwartz's (1993) elaboration on values (providing an additional perspective on the Hofstede type of approach), Markus and Kitayama's (1991) modern classic on the self in a cultural context, and Ting-Toomey and Gudykunst's (1988) contributions to intercultural communication and negotiation theory.

There is a large body of work on patterns of foreign direct investment (FDI) by multinational corporations (MNCs) beginning with Hymer (1976) and followed by work on oligopolistic competition between firms by Caves (1982), Kindleberger (1969), and Knickerbocker (1973) as well as Vernon's (1966) work on the international product cycle. Theoretical explanations for the existence of the MNC have been discussed by scholars such as Buckley and Casson (1976), Hennart (1982), and Rugman (1981). Work by Kogut (1983) presented an options view of FDI. His approach characterizes the investments made by MNCs as a series of sequential decisions that determine the flow of their resources across countries. This approach emphasizes a learning-based perspective on the evolution of the MNC and has resulted in several important contributions to the literature including those of Kogut and Chang (1991, 1996). This style of research also is reflected in the chapter by Chang in this book (Chapter 9).

Another area of work in an international and cross-cultural context is the study of administrative processes within MNCs (Franko, 1976; Stopford & Wells, 1972; see also Perlmutter, 1969, for challenges to the evolution of MNCs). More recently, scholars have examined issues including choices in strategy, structure and administration, and HRM practices and policies (Arvey, Bhagat, & Sales, 1991; Bartlett & Goshal, 1989; Black, Gregerson, & Mendenhall, 1992; Boyacigiller, 1990; Doz, 1976; Hedlund, 1986; Prahalad, 1976; Schuler, Dowling, & DeCieri, 1993; Tung, 1981). These works have addressed choices in structure and administrative process, explicitly recognizing the pressure faced by them in responding to local (national) pressures while pursuing strategies that leverage corporate capabilities across national borders. Recent work on the process of globalization extends this line of research. In a related vein, research has examined the pressures for local isomorphism versus parent corporation influences on managerial practices in various subsidiaries (Goshal & Nohria, 1987; Rosenzweig & Nohria, 1994; Westney, 1993).

Whereas interest in understanding the practical and comparative aspects of international and cross-cultural research has stimulated a movement having tremendous momentum, it is the desire to enhance our knowledge of fundamental theory that will fuel the sustained contribution of international and cross-cultural research in the field of management. The focus of this volume is to highlight new research frameworks on international and cross-cultural management. In one sense, this book is the logical follow-up to our earlier special issue in the *Academy of Management Journal* (*AMJ*) on novel methods used in international and cross-cultural research. We invited a number of both established and new scholars who are using novel conceptualizations of international and cross-cultural research to highlight new approaches to this work. We sought contributors who had new ways of viewing existing research streams to create the basis for future research. We present these frameworks as examples for researchers who generally work on questions defined in a domestic context and who intend to begin working on issues in an international and cross-cultural context. Research in the area of international management, broadly defined, has explored many issues related to comparative management, FDI, and competitiveness of firms across national borders. By highlighting the research contained in this book, we hope that readers will have an opportunity to see how these frameworks hold true to their particular international contexts while linking to the mainstream literatures from which they are derived.

Our introductory comments are divided into three sections. In the first section, we describe a general framework through which to understand and classify international and cross-cultural management research that we developed in our earlier special issue of *AMJ*. We use this framework as a way of describing the various approaches used in theory building for international and cross-cultural research. In the second section, we describe the potential limitations of various types of theory building. In the final section, we introduce the various chapters presented by our contributors in relation to our framework.

GENERAL FRAMEWORK
FOR CULTURAL RESEARCH

We begin our discussion with a typology that we introduced in our special issue of *AMJ*. This typology generates four general forms of research styles based on two dimensions, relevance to international management, and relevance to cross-cultural management. The differences between these two dimensions often are attributed to the level of analysis, but we suggest that the differences can be thought of as examining a system versus component elements of a system. In our use, a *system* refers to a naturally occurring set of individuals, organizations, and institutions that coexist and are interdependent. The international dimension reflects an examination of a cultural or national system as a singular entity, whereas the cross-cultural dimension reflects atomized, or component, relationships within a cultural system. Using our categorization scheme, we propose four basic types of research approaches that might classify existing research and guide future work.

Unitary Form

In a unitary form, a researcher places an emphasis on understanding a given phenomenon in a particular circumstance on its own terms. That is, the emphasis is on the emic (Berry, 1990) or pseudo-emic (Earley & Mosakowski, 1995) nature of a phenomenon. An emic approach refers to understanding a single cultural group and its endogenous characteristics on their own terms. For example, the concept of "face" has a unique meaning and interpretation in China that is not shared in the United States. Anthropological fieldwork often is cited as an example of what we label a unitary form (e.g., Mead's [1928] classic assessment of Samoan culture), whereas in an organizational context, exemplary work of this type was presented by Barley (1990) in his assessment of the technology industry. Although this type of research is very important for understanding a given group, it does not provide the opportunity for establishing universal principles afforded by other research paradigms, assuming that such universals exist. In the context of our book, the unitary form is limited because it does not provide an adequate platform for comparative work unless it is done with the purpose of trying to uncover overlapping emics.

Gestalt Form

A gestalt approach requires a researcher to examine a system as an intact whole rather than breaking it apart. The gestalt form has several important features. First, relationships among variables can be examined as they occur across different cultural or national systems. Second, constructs and hypothesized relationships are derived from general principles rather than from within the systems themselves. Third, interpretations of findings from a given cultural or national system must be developed with reference to specifics of the system. These interpretations inform the researcher as to the universality of a given principle.

One example of this research is presented in Erez's (1986) study of three industry sectors within Israel. In her study, she examined the relationship of performance and several goal-setting strategies in the Kibbutz, Histradrut, and private sectors within Israel. Her conceptual framework was based on an imported motivation model (goal setting), but her interpretation of various findings was based on an examination of each of these three sectors with reference to one another as well as the United States. Another example is presented in Lincoln, Hanada, and McBride's (1986) discussion of organizational structures in Japan. They used American organizational structure as a comparator for interpreting many of their observations. Although their focus was primarily on Japanese organizations, their conceptual orientation reflected organizational theory (OT) evolved from other cultural systems (predominantly the United States) so as to understand their observations concerning Japan. Also, they interpreted a number of their findings (e.g., relationships among interdependent companies within a *keiretsu*) within the context of how organizations operate in Japan.

Although the gestalt form shares features in common with the unitary form, there are several key differences. For example, constructs used in the gestalt form are not necessarily created or discovered as a consequence of the researcher's interaction within the system. A gestalt form does not assume that the system can be understood only on its own terms. With the gestalt form, understanding comes from explicit comparisons with similar systems in different larger contexts (e.g., nations). It is important to emphasize this comparative aspect of the gestalt form because the unitary form also examines gestalt but without the comparative dimension.

Reduced Form

The reduced form emphasizes breaking down a system into component parts to understand process functioning within the system. The reduced form assumes that a cultural system is divisible and that any given facet of the system can be examined independently of other facets. The characteristics of this form include several other features. Constructs and hypothesized relationships typically are derived from other systems, cultures, or nations. Relationships are not interpreted in terms of the overall system in which they are embedded; rather, they are interpreted using specific aspects of the system. Relationships in the system can be studied independently from other relationships in the cultural system.

The reduced form of research is exemplified in a number of studies in the organizations literature. This style of research is one of the most frequently employed approaches by researchers seeking to integrate specific cultural accounts in their descriptions of organizational phenomena. For example, Earley (1989) examined the role of individualism-collectivism in the display of social loafing in an organizational context. In his article, a single dimension of culture was used as a moderator in the relation of social context to the display of loafing. Tornblom, Jonssons, and Foa (1985) examined the reward allocation preferences of Americans and Swedes using this form as well. They hypothesized that the strong collectivist orientation characteristic of Sweden would result in a preference in favor of an equality-based preference rule and that the strong individualist orientation of the United States would favor an equity-based rule. Their findings strongly supported their hypotheses. From our perspective, their study illustrates the reduced form because they examined a specific process (reward allocation) with regard to a specific feature of the system (individualism vs. collectivism). In this case, the cultural dimension of individualism and collectivism functioned as a moderator variable in determining reward allocation preferences.

There are several differences and similarities among the reduced form as well as the unitary and gestalt forms. First, the reduced approach assumes that individual relationships are meaningful taken out of context. By "taking out of context," it is meant that a given cultural dimension operates independently of other dimensions such that its unique effects can be isolated. Second, this approach assumes that relationships taken out of context can be placed back into a cultural system without the loss of meaning. That is, on finding a moderating effect for individualism-collectivism (Earley, 1989) on the display of social loafing, this finding can be imposed back onto the originating samples. Finally, theoretical relationships typically are arrived at deductively based on general principles observed across various cultural systems.

Hybrid Form

The hybrid form refers to an approach that uses aspects of both a gestalt and a reduced perspective. In a hybrid form, research questions are studied as a complete system to identify important aspects of the systems. Hypothesized relationships are derived across systems, and they are not necessarily unique to a given system. Furthermore, constructs and relationships are assumed to be separable from the system in which they are embedded, but mapping back isolated relationships to an existing system might not be straightforward. Specific relationships are interpreted using reduced parts of the system but with reference to the general system. These interpretations can, in turn, lead to a further refinement of general principles.

An interesting example of this style of research is Van Maanen and Barley's (1984) assessment of occupational communities. Although their work is primarily conceptual, the inferences drawn from prior empirical work illustrate the complementary mixing of ethnographic observation, conceptualizations derived from within a given system extended onto other systems, and the development of a general theoretical model that captures general principles across many systems. For example, they examine a number of occupational systems through an intensive immersion to understand why individuals within the system behave as they do and the nature of each community's social structure. Next, they take these observations and combine them so as to understand the patterns of actions across multiple communities using several theoretical perspectives as a means of discussing these observations. An additional example is the Schwartz and Bilsky (1987) study of values in which they developed a typology of cultural values. In their study, they used a conceptual model of values, motives, and beliefs derived from existing research on personality theory in a number of countries that is applied to the derivation of universal dimensions of culture. They used this model as a way of establishing universal types of values by viewing the values as cognitive representations of three universal requirements (biological needs, interactional requirements for interpersonal coordination, and social demands for group survival) consistent with the hybrid assumption of separability. This model was used to generate categories of universal values that, in turn, are assessed in Germany and Israel. Schwartz's (1993) follow-up work extended the framework to test the typology at both a national and an individual level of analysis in more than 40 countries. In addition, some of the work on FDI and strategy and structure in multinational corporations (or MNCs) has the characteristics of the hybrid form.

Our four-part classification of research approaches is not meant to imply a universal rank-ordering or preference structure. Each form has its own unique strengths and should not be viewed as inherently superior to any other form. However, the hybrid form appears to be the best general style for conducting international and cross-cultural research, in our view. Work conducted using a hybrid approach has the advantage of building etic, or universal, relationships from emic analyses (or what Berry, 1990, referred to as the "pseudo-etic") without falling into a trap of idiosyncrasy. That is, by building a theory using the observed principles that cross over national and cultural borders, a researcher can gain insights concerning universals that are appropriate for application to additional societies.

MOVING INTERNATIONAL AND CROSS-CULTURAL RESEARCH FORWARD: NEW THEORY

There are several important challenges for international and cross-cultural management research according to our proposed framework. First, the impetus for many international and cross-cultural studies is the desire to make accurate outcome predictions based on a given theory in various countries or cultural settings. In the gestalt form of research, conducted at the level of culture or nation, a study is conducted capturing the potential for generalizability. By using a model in various nations, a researcher assesses when the models do and do not enable us to make good predictions. But outcome prediction and generalizability are not the only criteria of good theories. As researchers continue to generalize their models, they also need to provide explanations for observed phenomena. Thus, the critical question shifts from "Will it work here?" to "How and why does it work?"

Second, we argued in our article in the special issue of *AMJ* (Earley & Singh, 1995) that a finer distinction of the constructs of nation and culture is necessary. This argument remains salient and critical. The distinction between nation and culture is critical to understanding many of the present deficiencies in management research. As suggested earlier, some studies seek to identify differences of organizational practices among nations in a simple comparative or holistic fashion. A comparative approach seeks to directly contrast the practices used in various countries and provide a post hoc explanation concerning the occurrences of various practices. On finding differences, explanations using political, economic, or cultural dimensions are offered using a reductionist interpretation. Take, for example, a researcher who conducts a comparative study of negotiation behavior and uses country of origin as an explanatory device (e.g., Americans use a confrontational style of negotiation, whereas Japanese use a cooperative style). We would categorize this approach as a reduced form. However, researchers seek to identify underlying processes of organizational phenomena as well as to identify whether or not differences exist. National, political, economic, or cultural explanations of why similarities or differences exist enable researchers to better understand phenomena only if they are an integrated aspect of the researchers' theoretical frameworks. With a hybrid form, the key to developing a meaningful model is in understanding how and why differences exist vis-à-vis nation or culture rather than just their identification. A hybrid form attempts to identify and isolate which of various alternative explanations accurately captures a given phenomenon by identifying specific aspects of nation or culture that are related to a given explanation. The reliance on nation or culture as a "black box" is abandoned in favor of a more precise specification of theoretical relationships. Although a hybrid approach to studying international and cross-cultural issues can be useful, it is by no means a mandated research style. In many cases, research questions preclude such a style. For example, researchers examining the "M-form" of organizational structure cannot necessarily reduce their use of a national context to a single dimension of culture or a legalistic parameter of corporate law.

WHERE DOES THE PATH OF INTERNATIONAL AND CROSS-CULTURAL THEORY LEAD US?

We describe four paths that a researcher may follow to conduct international and cross-cultural research. Our general argument is that the hybrid form is the most useful overall because it provides the insights of an in-depth analysis with the richness of a general context. It is in this spirit that we turn our discussion to the various theoretical perspectives offered in this volume. We have a number of contributions to this volume ranging from micro-organizational behavior approaches (e.g., Ravlin, Thomas, and Ilsev's work on transnational teams [Chapter 2]) to strategy (e.g., Dyer's work on trust in interfirm supplier relationships [Chapter 8], Mosakowski's work on the transfer of strategic rules across national boundaries [Chapter 11]). There are a number of threads that connect these various chapters to one another.

First, the contributors to the volume were asked to "push the envelope" and to create new ways of thinking about existing topics within international and cross-cultural management. We urged contributors to take some risks and propose ideas that they thought were innovative and novel. As the reader will see, there are a number of interesting and new ideas proposed in these various chapters as opposed to a more traditional review of existing literatures.

Second, the theories and models proposed in these chapters take on a hybrid spirit in that they derive general predictions and principles from specific settings. We think that this style of thinking holds great promise for the literature because it avoids the emic trap of idiosyncrasy as well as the pseudo-etic trap of apparent, but not real, universality. The various authors are taking perspectives drawn from one literature and applying them to other literatures. For example, the chapter by Peterson, Rodriguez, and Smith (Chapter 6) uses agency theory predictions and integrates them into an organizational perspective to understand South American banking. This effort uses the general model of agency to inform the specifics of Brazilian banking integrating these insights into Peterson and Smith's prior work on event management methods. Thus, their work integrates several different theories across a variety of organizational levels. Likewise, the work of Dyer (Chapter 8) links the research on trust building at the individual level, with the strategic incentives for firms to appoint suppliers based on their resources and competitive imperatives.

Finally, these chapters provide each of their respective fields with a new approach to examining a core idea in an international context. For example, Enz, Inman, and Lankau (Chapter 7) introduce a new understanding of social partnerships. What is particularly interesting about their work is that it explains these partnerships in a developing nation context, and they provide a number of key insights concerning the differences between a developed and a developing national context. In their chapter, they explore four different models for building strategic partnerships and illustrate the types of business relations that emerge under each with an emphasis on development in Central America.

OVERVIEW OF THE CHAPTERS

This book consists of 11 chapters, in addition to this introductory chapter, ranging from micro- to macro-organizational behavior, OT, and strategy. We have organized our chapters using a simplistic algorithm, namely, from the micro to the macro. In Part I, we have four chapters. Ravlin and colleagues (Chapter 2) focus their discussion on the nature of multicultural groups and teams using a variety of perspectives drawn from social psychology and sociology. Morris (Chapter 3) examines the nature of social networks and cultural values to understand how process versus structure influences work context. In the chapter by Gannon and Audia (Chapter 4), the role of the cultural metaphor is explored as a tool for understanding the nature of how culture influences organizational functioning. This work is an extension and elaboration of Gannon's earlier work and provides some new integrations of the metaphor approach with organizational functioning. The final chapter in this first part, by Geringer and Frayne (Chapter 5), concerns the role of HRM practices.

Part II consists of two chapters that cross over the micro and macro levels of analysis and focus on a somewhat more contextual style. The work by Peterson and colleagues (Chapter 6) exemplifies such a crossover of theory and level, as we described earlier. The contribution by Enz and colleagues (Chapter 7) illustrates such a crossover approach as well in their description of social partnerships in developing nations.

Part III consists of chapters dealing with largely macro and strategic topics. The work of Dyer (Chapter 8) examines the development of trust in a crossnational setting. The building of trust, as an essential driver of success in strategic alliances, has remained one of the more central challenges in cross-national alliances. Dyer shows how the issue of trust building can be effectively researched cross-nationally in the United States, Japan, and Korea. This work is particularly exemplary in its development of research design by exploring a very well-specified model in multiple national and cultural settings. The work shows how a multination research design offers significant advantages over a singlenation study. In Chapter 9, Chang explores the FDI strategies of keiretsu member firms in the United States. He notes that firms that are members of keiretsu invest to help keiretsu member firms, particularly in the context of horizontal member. This work illustrates the influence of keiretsu membership on investment activities and the additional role that such membership plays in influencing investment behavior. Malnight, in Chapter 10, explores the process of fundamental organizational change in the context of globalization. He shows how such a question can be examined to advantage by in-depth historical and comparative research on two pharmaceutical MNCs. He finds that the firms tend to make initial informal adjustments to their structures, to minimize disruptions, before engaging in the more dramatic adjustments needed to respond to the rapidly changing global environment. In Chapter 11, Mosakowski discusses the use of transfer of strategic rules of the game in new markets as a way for firms to develop competitive advantage across borders and international cultures. The chapter illustrates the use of a new conceptual lens on foreign market entry and postentry competitive dynamics. Finally, Zaheer (Chapter 12) examines the nature of time zones in relation to conducting business across national boundaries. In this chapter, Zaheer emphasizes the nature of managerial coordination and temporal rhythms as underpinnings of efficiency and information benefits.

All of the chapters presented in the book serve as exemplars of strong research conducted on theories that are developed in an international and cross-cultural setting, and all use research designs that take particular advantage of their cross-cultural setting. This research shows that our most interesting and challenging ideas emerge when conceived in a cross-national and cross-cultural setting and when implemented to test their applicability across national borders.

CONCLUSION

There has been debate concerning the role of culture versus national context in management research. The intent of this book is to provide a number of theoretical perspectives that enable us to understand these differences. Effective hybrid research emphasizes an understanding of all systems (e.g., political, socioeconomic, legal) within a given nation rather than a focus on isolated ones. In taking such an approach, we believe that the chapters in this book illustrate a synthesis of nation and culture.

REFERENCES

Arvey, R. D., Bhagat, R. S., & Sales, E. (1991). Cross-cultural and national issues in personnel and human resource management: Where do we go from here? In G. R. Ferris & K. M. Rowland (Eds.), *Research in personnel and human resource management: A research annual* (Vol. 9, pp. 367-407). Greenwich, CT: JAI.

Barley, S. R. (1990). The alignment of technology and structure through roles and networks. *Administrative Science Quarterly, 33,* 24-60.

Bartlett, C. A., & Goshal, S. (1989). *Managing across borders: The transnational solution.* Boston: Harvard Business School Press.

Berry, J. W. (1990). Imposed etics, emics, and derived etics: Their conceptual and operational status in cross-cultural psychology. In T. N. Headland, K. L. Pike, & M. Harris (Eds.), *Emics and etics: The insider/outsider debate* (pp. 84-99). Newbury Park, CA: Sage.

Black, J. S., Gregerson, H. B., & Mendenhall, M. (1992). *Global assignments.* San Francisco: Jossey-Bass.

Boyacigiller, N. (1990). The role of expatriates in the management of interdependence, complexity, and risk in multinational corporations. *Journal of International Business Studies, 21,* 357-381.

Buckley, P., & Casson, M. (1976). *The future of multinational enterprise.* London: Macmillan.

Caves, R. E. (1982). *Multinational enterprise and economic analysis.* New York: Cambridge University Press.

Doz, Y. (1976). *National policies and multinational management.* Unpublished doctoral dissertation, Harvard University, Graduate School of Business Administration.

Earley, P. C. (1989). Social loafing and collectivism: A comparison of United States and the People's Republic of China. *Administrative Science Quarterly, 34,* 565-581.

Earley, P. C., & Erez, M. (1997). *The transplanted executive.* New York: Oxford University Press.

Earley, P. C., & Mosakowski, E. M. (1995). A framework for understanding experimental research in an international and intercultural context. In B. J. Punnet & O. Shenkar (Eds.), *Handbook of international management research* (pp. 83-114). London: Blackwell.

Earley, P.C., & Singh, H. (1995). International and intercultural research: What's next? *Academy of Management Journal, 38,* 1-14.

Erez, M. (1986). The congruence of goal-setting strategies with socio-cultural values and its effect on performance. *Journal of Management, 12,* 83-90.

Franko, L. G. (1976). *The European multinationals: A renewed challenge to American and British big business.* Stamford, CT: Greylock.

Goshal, S., & Nohria, N. (1987). Internal differentiation within multinational corporations. *Strategic Management Journal, 10,* 323-337.

Gudykunst, W. B., Ting-Toomey, S., & Chua, E. (1988). *Culture and interpersonal communication.* Newbury Park, CA: Sage.

Haire, M., Ghiselli, E. E., & Porter, L. (1966). *Managerial thinking: An international study.* New York: John Wiley.

Hedlund, G. (1986, Spring). The hypermodern MNC: A heterarchy? *Human Resource Management, 25*(1), 9-35.

Hennart, J. F. (1982). *A theory of multinational enterprise.* Ann Arbor: University of Michigan Press.

Hofstede, G. (1980). *Culture's consequences: International differences in work-related values.* Beverly Hills, CA: Sage.

Hofstede, G. (1991). *Culture and organizations: Software of the mind.* New York: McGraw-Hill.

Hofstede, G. (1993). Cultural constraints in management theories. *Academy of Management Executive, 7,* 81-94.

Hofstede, G., & Bond, M. H. (1988, Spring). The Confucius connection: From cultural roots to economic growth. *Organizational Dynamics, 16,* 4-21.

Hymer, S. H. (1976). *The international operations of national firms: A study of direct foreign investment.* Cambridge, MA: MIT Press.

Kindleberger, C. P. (1969). *American business abroad: Six lectures on direct investment.* New Haven, CT: Yale University Press.

Knickerbocker, F. T. (1973). *Oligopolistic reaction and multinational enterprise.* Cambridge, MA: Harvard University Press.

Kogut, B. (1983). Foreign direct investment as a sequential process. In C. P. Kindleberger & D. Autretsch (Eds.), *The multinational corporation in the 1980s* (pp. 35-86). Cambridge, MA: MIT Press.

Kogut, B., & Chang, S. (1991). Technological capabilities and Japanese foreign direct investment in the United States. *Review of Economics and Statistics, 73,* 401-413.

Kogut, B., & Chang, S. (1996). Platform investment and volatile exchange rates. *Review of Economics and Statistics, 78,* 221-231.

Lincoln, J. R., Hanada, M., & McBride, K. (1986). Organization structures in Japanese and U.S. manufacturing. *Administrative Science Quarterly, 31,* 338-364.

Markus, H. R., & Kitayama, S. (1991). Culture and self: Implication for cognition, emotion, and motivation. *Psychological Review, 98,* 224-253.

Mead, M. (1928). *Coming of age in Samoa.* Chicago: University of Chicago Press.

Perlmutter, H. V. (1969). The tortuous evolution of the multinational corporation. *Columbia Journal of World Business, 10*(1), 9-18.

Prahalad, C. K. (1976). *The strategic process in a multinational corporation.* Unpublished doctoral dissertation, Harvard University, Graduate School of Business Administration.

Rosaldo, R. (1989). *Culture and truth.* Boston: Beacon.

Rosenzweig, P., & Nohria, N. (1994). Influences of human resource management practices in multinational firms. *Journal of International Business Studies, 20,* 229-252.

Rugman, A. M. (1981). *Inside the multinationals: The economics of internal markets.* New York: Columbia University Press.

Schuler, R. S., Dowling, P. J., & DeCieri, H. (1993). An integrative framework of strategic international human resource management. *Journal of Management, 19,* 419-459.

Schwartz, S. H. (1993). Universals in context and structure of values: Theoretical advances and empirical tests in two countries. In L. Berkowitz (Ed.), *Advances in experimental and social psychology.* San Diego: Academic Press.

Schwartz, S. H., & Bilsky, W. (1987). Toward a universal psychological structure of human values. *Journal of Personality and Social Psychology, 53,* 550-620.

Stopford, J., & Wells, L. T., Jr. (1972). *Managing the multinational enterprise: Organization of the firm and its subsidiaries.* New York: Basic Books.

Tornblom, K. Y., Jonssons, D., & Foa, U. G. (1985). Nationality, resource, class, and preferences among three allocation rules: Sweden vs. USA. *International Journal of Intercultural Relations, 9,* 51-77.

Trompenaars, F. (1997). *Riding the waves of culture.* London: Nicholas Brealey.

Tung, R. (1981). Selection and training of personnel for overseas assignments. *Columbia Journal of World Business, 16,* 74-80.

Van Maanen, J., & Barley, S. R. (1984). Occupational communities: Culture and control in organizations. In B. M. Staw & L. L. Cummings (Eds.), *Research in organizational behavior* (pp. 287-356). Greenwich, CT: JAI.

Vernon, R. (1966, May). International investment and international trade in the product cycle. *Quarterly Journal of Economics, 80,* 190-207.

Westney, D. E. (1993). Institutionalization theory and the multinational corporation. In S. Goshal & D. Eleanor Westney (Eds.), *Organization theory and the multinational corporation* (pp. 53-76). New York: St. Martin's.

PART I

Micro-Organizational Approaches

Beliefs About Values, Status, and Legitimacy in Multicultural Groups

Influences on Intragroup Conflict

ELIZABETH C. RAVLIN
DAVID C. THOMAS
ARZU ILSEV

It is a truism today that the economic and social forces associated with globalization have altered the cultural composition of the workforce and that many organizations are experiencing a difficult transition with regard to managing workforce diversity as a result. Nowhere is this evolution more apparent than in the case of multinational corporations, which are faced with increasingly multicultural workforces (Adler & Ghadar, 1990). Accompanying these changes in the workforce is a move toward work group or team structures in organizations. These structural changes are driven by the growing complexity of organizational work, the difficulties in fostering workforce commitment, and the need to draw on all available employee skills and resources (Hoerr, 1989; Sundstrom, DeMeuse, & Futrell, 1990). In the current environment, the requirements for coordination, cooperation, and communication make the management of multicultural interactions an issue of primary importance. In particular, the effective management of intragroup conflict generated by cultural differences is a central concern for groups and their leadership.

This chapter draws on prior theory in a number of areas including social psychology (Fiske & Taylor, 1984), sociology (Berger, Norman, Balkwell, & Smith, 1992), and organizational science (Tajfel & Turner, 1986) to specify the processes whereby multiculturalism generates conflict and those processes involved in its resolution. First, we define multiculturalism, conflict, and group effectiveness, and we provide a preliminary look at their linkages. Second, we use a legitimacy perspective to integrate the mechanisms leading from multicultural group composition to conflict. Finally, we suggest how such conflicts can be resolved over time and the impact that resolution has on group effectiveness.

Multiculturalism

Prior to discussing the relationship between multiculturalism and intragroup conflict, we must clarify our perspective on culture. Kroeber and Kluckhohn's (1952) widely accepted definition noted that culture consists of traditional values and other ideas and that it emphasizes its patterned nature as both a result of prior action and a determinant of future action (p. 181). Other definitional statements consistent with the perspective taken here are conceptualizations of culture as (a) the collective programming of the mind that distinguishes one human group from another (Hofstede, 1980), (b) important sets of assumptions that are shared by members of a community (Sathe, 1985), and (c) a group's characteristic way of perceiving its environment (Triandis, 1972). Certain characteristics of culture as a construct are particularly important to consider here. A concise statement of these characteristics is that culture is something that is shared by members of a social group, something that is passed on from one generation of group members to another, and something that shapes members' behavior. It is, therefore, appropriate to define culture as those values, attitudes, beliefs, and behavior patterns (scripts) that are shared by members of a social group. This definition of culture can be applied to any social group with which an individual identifies, such as a gender group, a racial/ethnic group, a religious group, or a national group (Cox, 1993; Ferraro, 1994).

Because international business is, by definition, conducted across national boundaries, it seems particularly appropriate to consider national cultural groups in discussing the influence of culture in work groups. A number of studies suggest that when individuals are confronted with members of other national or cultural groups, they regard the others, and themselves, primarily in terms of national or cultural orientations (Bochner & Ohsako, 1977; Bochner & Perks, 1971; Hartley & Thompson, 1967). Encountering those of a different culture makes culture a salient factor in the interaction. Furthermore, research suggests that if one characteristic is activated as an organizing dimension, then other potential dimensions are suppressed (Macrae, Bodenhausen, & Milne, 1995). Based on these findings, we suggest that culture is a dominant factor in multicultural interactions and is particularly important for our purposes here because national culture is associated with differences in value priorities (Hofstede, 1980). These differences in values are proposed to play an important role in the conflict generation process.

Core values in culture are defined here as the internalized beliefs that people hold, as conveyed by the context in which they exist, regarding what they should or ought to do and what they should strive for (Ott, 1989; Ravlin & Meglino, 1987; Rokeach, 1973). We chose values as our primary focus (although they do not encompass all aspects of culture) because of their particular links to conflict and national culture. Values are learned early in life and, as such, are relatively stable over time. When individuals are confronted with an opposing set of values, they do not readily adapt to them (Rokeach, 1973). Values are representations of societal motives (i.e., what behavior is good for society rather than for the individual per se (Kluckhohn, 1951; Williams, 1968) and, therefore, are powerful representations of national culture. They are central core beliefs that form an important part of the self schema or the ideal self (Markus & Wurf, 1987). From such beliefs come many other elements of culture—beliefs about the desirability of specific modes of behavior (norms), specific attitudes and interests (Rokeach, 1973), conceptions of the value of objects (Prentice, 1987), and elements of cognitive organization that affect processing of new stimuli (Postman, Bruner, & McGinnies, 1948; Ravlin & Meglino, 1987). All of these elements are subject to threat when individuals encounter alternative value systems. In addition, values are used to legitimate past action (Meglino & Ravlin, 1998; Nord, Brief, Atieh, & Doherty, 1988; Williams, 1979), and this raises the issue of whether a past action is legitimate when the value system used to justify it is challenged.

Prior research also suggests a central role for values in our understanding of multicultural interactions. Hofstede's (1980) research on cultural value dimensions has provided a common framework for many authors in international management and is familiar to most people with an interest in this area. Subsequent work has largely sustained and amplified Hofstede's findings (Smith & Bond, 1999). Thus, the best conceptual frameworks presently available to guide research in this area are those dealing with value differences across cultures. In sum, this literature indicates that values influence varied aspects of cultural phenomena and, therefore, play a substantive role in defining what interests might be threatened in a conflict situation.

Conflict

Regardless of group composition, conflict is an important part of group process (Argote & McGrath, 1993). Wall and Callister (1995) defined conflict generally as "a process in which one party perceives that its interests are being opposed or negatively affected by another party" (p. 517). Key aspects are the process-based and perceptual nature of the construct, the involvement of more than one entity, and the element of opposition. Interests include values and other value-related phenomena such as goals, behavior, attitudes, and possessions (Deutsch, 1980; Putnam & Poole, 1987). As noted earlier, given the central role of values in the self-schema, challenges to values are powerful bases for the development of conflict, particularly in multicultural groups in which cultural values are likely to be salient.

As noted by Pondy (1967), conflict occurs in stages. Latent conflict, in the current context, occurs because differing values specify different goals, modes of behavior, attitudes, and preferences for culturally different group members. Latent conflict is not recognized but can create group process problems anyway, as described later. Perceived conflict indicates that individuals do perceive a con- flict in goals or other value-related phenomena. Pondy pointed out that many conflicts are suppressed out of awareness but that this is unlikely to happen when the "conflicts relate to values central to the individual's personality" (p. 301). Conflict is not always felt; there may be an awareness of a conflict of interests that does not generate a tension in the parties. Personalization may be one cause of escalation to the felt conflict stage, as may the characteristics of the parties involved such as their relative status or their similarity to one another. Manifest conflict, in this model, indicates that conflict-oriented behavior occurs between the two entities.

Conflict and Multiculturalism

Reviews of the literature on groups and teams (Bettenhausen, 1991; Cohen & Bailey, 1997; Gist, Locke, & Taylor, 1987; Goodman, Ravlin, & Argote, 1986; McGrath & Kravitz, 1982; Milliken & Martins, 1996) consistently show rather minimal work in the area of cultural composition (for recent exceptions, see Cox, Lobel, & McLeod, 1991; Thomas, Ravlin, & Wallace, 1996; Watson, Kumar, & Michaelsen, 1993). Such research still is preliminary, tends to be somewhat atheoretical, and (for the most part) touches on conflict and conflict generation processes peripherally or not at all. However, recent authors have begun to address the role of cultural influences in generating interpersonal conflict (Weisinger & Salipante, 1995; Yu, 1995) and differences in conflict manage- ment styles (Henderson & Argyle, 1986; Kozan, 1989; Ohbuchi & Takahashi, 1994; Rossi & Todd-Mancillas, 1985; Westwood, Tang, & Kirkbride, 1992).

This body of literature typically discusses cultural values (e.g., individualism, collectivism) that collide in practice in the multicultural group and does not specify the processes underlying the generation of intragroup conflict in multicultural groups (for an exception, see Ting-Toomey et al., 1991, for their face mainte- nance approach to differing conflict handling styles). Weldon and Jehn (1995) suggested that some possible reasons for the slow rate of progress in this area include the application of Western management theories to non-Western cultures, a failure to systematically explore the potential existence of non-Western constructs that might be essential in understanding conflict perceptions of non-Western individuals (to the extent that non-Western cultures are represented in the multicultural group), and the prevalent lack of tests for equivalence of constructs and measures across the cultures under study. We would argue that the neglect of the process whereby multiculturalism generates conflict, and in turn affects group effectiveness, has impeded our understanding as well and has broad applicability to all multicultural groups.

Group Effectiveness

Ultimately, our concern must be with the effectiveness of groups or teams and the influence that conflict and multiculturalism have on effectiveness outcomes. Hackman's (1987) group effectiveness model provides a commonly accepted way of thinking about the dimensions of effectiveness in groups or teams. To be effective, a group must (a) provide output that meets or exceeds the expectations of its constituents, (b) maintain the capability of working together over time, and (c) provide experiences for group members that are, on balance, more satisfying than dissatisfying. This last component includes both short-term satisfaction and longer term developmental experiences. How conflict and multicultural composition are thought to affect these three dimensions is detailed in what follows.

Group Effectiveness and Conflict

Early approaches to conflict in the organizational and management literatures tended to treat conflict as a negative influence on effectiveness—to be avoided, if possible, through structural devices such as departmentalization and the scalar chain, and otherwise suppressed quickly through the hierarchical power of the organization (Fayol, 1949; Weber, 1948). Current views recognize conflict as being a multifaceted and unavoidable process as well as a positive influence on effectiveness under some conditions (Amason, 1996; Jehn, 1995). At least two types of conflict usually are specified: functional (or task-oriented) and dysfunctional (or relational) conflict. Functional conflict is viewed as a way of surfacing more ideas, criticisms, and opinions of group members regarding task performance and can make a positive contribution to group performance, whereas relational conflict focuses on interpersonal relationships and personalities and is detrimental to the group. Clearly, virtually all positive effects of conflict should be observed on the first dimension of group effectiveness, providing acceptable output. It generally is considered to be a deterrent to group maintenance functions (Jehn, 1995; Williams & O'Reilly, 1998), although functional conflict could potentially have positive developmental influences on individual group members.

Group Effectiveness and Composition

Group performance is undeniably related to properties of group members. Membership composition in general has been studied for many years in an effort to find ways in which to create more effective groups. The seminal work of Steiner (1972) summed up the complexity of group composition effects by illustrating that both the group task and the dimension of heterogeneity observed are important factors in determining outcomes. As Steiner suggested, "A theory of composition effects should deal with . . . the identification of variables on which homogeneity-heterogeneity really matters, and it should relate heterogeneity-homogeneity on these variables to the consequences they are likely to promote" (p. 108).

In the context of McGrath's (1984) typology of group tasks, Jackson (1992) presented a summary of group composition research in which she disaggregated group heterogeneity into two fundamental types: heterogeneity in personal attributes and heterogeneity in skills and abilities. Our concern here is with personal attributes, in particular, values associated with national culture. Empirically, heterogeneity on personal attributes generally has been positively related to performance on creative idea generation and decision-making tasks. Heterogeneity in personal attributes such as attitudes (Hoffman, Harburg, & Maier, 1962; Triandis, Hall, & Evans, 1965), personality (Hoffman & Maier, 1961), and prior career socialization (Pelz, 1956) has been related to higher quality decisions. However, the effect of personal attribute heterogeneity on group performance on other types of tasks still is somewhat unclear. For the most part, the studies just cited do not examine the role of conflict in either facilitating or diminishing performance (for an exception, see Jehn, Northcraft, & Neale, 1999).

In addition to studies of group performance, other research has noted the implications of composition for group processes. For example, attitude homogeneity and demographic homogeneity generally have been shown to be positively related to group cohesiveness (Jackson, 1992). Also, members of demographically homogeneous groups tend to exhibit higher satisfaction and lower absenteeism and turnover (Jackson et al., 1991). These findings are consistent with the well-established principle that people are attracted to similar others (Byrne, 1971) and the converse notion that heterogeneous groups experience more conflict (Jehn et al., 1999).

Taken as a whole, prior research indicates that multicultural composition should generate more conflict, which in turn will reduce the ability of a group to maintain itself over time and to provide satisfying experiences for its members.

The effect of cultural composition on acceptable output should be determined by the group's task. Nonroutine task performance can be facilitated by multiculturalism, whereas performance on routine tasks should be unaffected or possibly even negatively affected. Positive effects are anticipated only when the group has learned to manage its conflict and when the dimension of diversity is relevant to the task at hand (Thomas et al., 1996).

Although the literature relating multicultural composition, conflict, and group effectiveness is limited, the social psychology and cognition literatures provide insights into this issue by way of the similarity-attraction paradigm (Byrne, 1971) and social information processing theories of person perception (Brewer, Weber, & Carini, 1995; Fiske & Taylor, 1984; Higgins & Bargh, 1987; Srull & Wyer, 1979). Other research from sociology offering contributions to theory on multicultural group conflict includes status characteristics theory (Berger, et al., 1992; Ridgeway & Diekema, 1989; Skvoretz & Fararo, 1996) and developing theories of legitimacy (Brown, 1997; Suchman, 1995). General research on group composition from the organizational sciences has gone much further to establish process theories that are relevant to understanding interpersonal conflict in diverse groups (see, e.g., Jackson, May, & Whitney, 1994). In addition, processes that help us to understand what happens when values conflict are specified in theories of values (Kluckhohn, 1951; Meglino & Ravlin, 1998; Rokeach, 1973). We draw on all of these areas in developing propositions regarding the influence of cultural composition.

THE INFLUENCE OF CULTURAL COMPOSITION ON CONFLICT

Overview

As noted earlier, our approach to understanding cultural composition effects is based on multiple lines of theory. Figure 2.1 organizes the central constructs drawn from each paradigm for the model presented here. The reader should note that, given our focus on the collision of different cultural value systems, the model is not intended to be all-inclusive. As shown, we propose that individuals in multicultural groups initially make distinctions among members' belief systems, resulting in judgments of similarity or difference. As is typical in groups, an assessment of these differences is made that results in a perceived status hierarchy of members based on comparative evaluations (Sidanius, Pratto, & Rabinowitz, 1994). Because values are a core part of the self-schema (Markus & Wurf, 1987) and have implications for many aspects of perception and behavior (Ravlin & Meglino, 1987), perceived differences on value and value-related dimensions can challenge an individual's feelings of legitimacy. These chal-

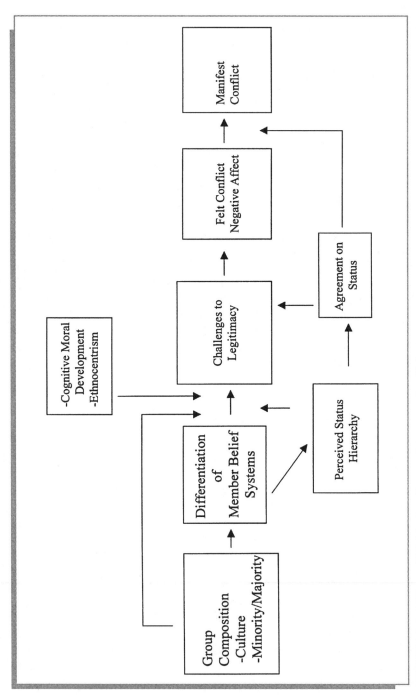

FIGURE 2.1. Effects of Multiculturalism on Intragroup Conflict

lenges to legitimacy tend to lead to overt functional and relational conflict when there is a lack of agreement on the group's status ordering. The process is moderated by several factors including an individual's interpretation of legitimacy (ethnocentrism), his or her perceived place in the status hierarchy, level of cognitive moral development, and whether he or she is in the minority or majority on the dimension of interest. Theoretical processes involved in the model are described in what follows.

Consistent with prior treatments of composition effects (Jackson et al., 1994; Thomas et al., 1996), both cognitive and motivational influences deriving from composition are identified on group interaction processes. For example, cognitive influences typically relate to the need to reduce cognitive load through the organizing and simplifying functions of stereotypes and other types of cognitive structures (Fiske & Taylor, 1984). Motivational influences include the desire to be with attractive and self-validating others (Byrne, 1971) and social identity processes, which motivate affiliation with high-status groups (Tajfel & Turner, 1986). Both cognitive and motivational influences are important in understanding multicultural interactions in group contexts and are referred to throughout our discussion.

An additional distinction that might be useful in this context relates to the differentiation and evaluation processes in interpersonal perception. A social information processing perspective on interpersonal perception suggests that a heuristic for examining the interaction between two culturally different others might be to explore the initial process, differentiation of belief systems, followed by evaluative judgments of these differences. In other words, individuals gather information and then see how it fits into their cognitive organization, which typically includes affectively toned "good" versus "bad" or "better" versus "worse" judgments (Wyer & Gordon, 1982). In reality, it might be that this distinction cannot be maintained, and certainly, theories cross over these categories. However, we use the differentiation/evaluative judgment distinction as an organizing device here to discuss the process whereby group members develop beliefs as to the similarities and differences among them (differentiation) and attributions of status (evaluation).

Differentiation of Member Belief Systems on the Basis of Culture

Individuals in organizational groups generally have prior or virtually immediate knowledge of the nationalities of their interaction partners, and this in and of itself triggers a categorization process among group members (Bochner & Ohsako, 1977; Bochner & Perks, 1971). In general, traits that make an individual distinctive within a given context are used as a basis for organization (Fisek,

Berger, & Norman, 1995; Nelson & Miller, 1995; Wyer & Gordon, 1982). In the United States, Zarate and Smith (1990) argued that culture is based on a white male norm and that what differentiates group members from this norm will be the dimension(s) of categorization. Some authors have argued that the default preference is to select one category from which to generate predictions. Unselected categories (e.g., age instead of culture) may be actively inhibited to avoid potential interference or inconsistencies in forecasts of future behavior (Macrae et al., 1995). Information processing researchers have argued that category salience or accessibility (Srull & Wyer, 1979) and fit (Oakes, 1994) determine which dimension will be selected. Research clearly indicates that the presence of culturally different others makes culture a salient dimension (Bochner & Ohsako, 1977; Bochner & Perks, 1971; Mullen, 1983, 1987). In some cases, readily observable differences, such as skin color and facial features, provide primary characteristics on which to differentiate group members (Fiske & Taylor, 1984). At other times, differentiation is triggered by speech patterns, differences in dress, or normative behavior (Wilder, 1986).

Research on information processing provides us with a fairly detailed view of what happens in person perception between subgroups that differ on one or more dimensions. More complex information processing appears to occur with regard to the in-group, leading to impoverished homogeneous views of the out-group. Within-category (subgroup) mistakes as to who did what are more common than between-category errors (Fiske & Taylor, 1984; Hastie, Park, & Weber, 1984). The cognitive (as opposed to motivational) nature of this process is emphasized by the finding that when individuals have less information to process, they can and do associate traits with individuals, but as the information load increases, they begin to associate traits with larger aggregates. Under high-load conditions, traits represented by a number of people tend to dominate the impression formed, but the individual member information is missing on recall and the group is described as homogeneous (Biernat & Vescio, 1994; Linville & Jones, 1980).

Information processing approaches also have examined effects of minority/majority composition issues. Kanter's (1977) research on the bias women experience in the work environment, as well as social psychological research on tokenism (Fiske & Taylor, 1984), has argued that this bias stems from the degree to which women or minorities (or culturally different others) tend to stand out or be visible in traditional work contexts. This visibility leads to increased ability to recall the individual's behavior and work record and to an expectation that there should be some generalizations or stereotypes that can be explicitly identified that contrast this individual with the majority.

In sum, social information processing approaches to interaction emphasize the cognitive components of the interaction. The goal is to reduce the quantity of information to a manageable amount. As individuals are sorted into categories, they are subject to more or less processing based on their membership in the in-group or out-group. These processing differences lead to differentially complex schemata regarding both subgroups and their individual members. The ultimate outcomes of these differentiation processes described thus far are (a) a differentiation of other members from the self on central highly valued dimensions and (b) a basis for evaluation of those differences as positive or negative.

Social identity and categorization theories (Tajfel, 1974; Tajfel & Turner, 1986) provide an alternative, motivationally based way of approaching group cultural composition. These theories suggest that people derive an important part of their self-identities from the groups to which they belong (social identity theory) and that actively distinguishing between themselves and other groups is part of the process of affiliation (social categorization theory). Minimal distinctions that are meaningless in the broader social context have been shown to produce reliable affiliation and in-group/out-group effects (Tajfel & Turner, 1986). This body of findings suggests both positive and negative potential for differentiation within work groups. On the positive side, under some conditions, the structural distinction of belonging to a work group can produce identification with the group as individuals seek positive social identities (Tajfel & Turner, 1986), inclusion (Brewer, 1993), or collective action (Kelly, 1993), as discussed later. However, on the negative side, characteristics that "spill over" from the larger context (Gutek, 1985) often are used as categorization devices instead, causing a fractionalization of the group. Ting-Toomey (1993) suggested that the process whereby an identity (based on work group, culture, or other factors) is selected for use in any given context is the product of negotiations between an individual and those who are parties to the interaction.

In one of the more fully developed theoretical approaches to composition effects, Mullen (1983, 1987) combined both cognitive and motivational processes. He focused on the salience of culture in suggesting that the more culturally different an individual is from other group members, the more self-aware he or she becomes. In this process of increasing self-awareness, cultural standards for behavior become more important in guiding responses to culturally different others. This self-awareness leads a person to compare his or her behavior to the perceived behavioral standards of the group and has implications for perceptions regarding ability to adapt and perform (Mullen & Baumeister, 1987). According to Mullen's model, then, interactions within multicultural work groups should enhance the effect of culture on perception and tend to increase the differentiation process.

Taken together, past research and thinking about group member cultural attributes as a component of information processing and affiliation clearly indicates support for our first proposition:

> *Proposition 1:* Individuals in multicultural work groups will use culture as a central dimension in differentiating among members.

In addition to providing evidence that culture is an important element of categorization processes, the social psychology, sociology, and organizational science literatures provide many insights as to how members of multicultural teams evaluate their members (for reviews of some of the relevant literature, see Gudykunst & Bond, 1997; Hastie et al., 1984; Higgins & Bargh, 1987). As members are categorized, status attributions become attached to members based on prior categorical knowledge and comparison with the self. In addition, the individual experiences challenges to his or her legitimacy and the attendant affect, based on the extent to which member beliefs are perceived to differ from those held by the individual. How culture affects these attributions of status and in turn can produce challenges to legitimacy is discussed in what follows.

Evaluation of Member Beliefs: Development of the Status Hierarchy

Sociological and sociobiological perspectives suggest that virtually any group formation will generate a status hierarchy, based on needs for predictability and individual differences (Sidanius et al., 1994). Status perceptions refer to the identification of differences in prestige and deference among group members (Conway, Pizzamiglio, & Mount, 1996; Mayer & Buckley, 1970; Shils, 1975). As differentiating information is categorized as "good" or "bad," the overall hierarchy is created by combining salient dimensions of comparison, weighted for importance (Fisek et al., 1995). The generalized perception of the status hierarchy within the group is expected to be strongly influenced by the evaluation of the characteristics of culturally different others based on culture's relevance to typical sources of status orders identified in the literature.

In general, four sources of status orders are relevant here. First, external status characteristics such as culture, age, and ethnicity generate status evaluations and expectations for the focal individual. For example, a middle-aged white male in U.S. society typically is perceived to be a relatively higher status individual than an elderly African American female. Second, interaction patterns over time also generate status. Cultural differences play a role here as well in that the reactor role is more predominant than the performer role in some cultures (e.g., collectivist cultures) than in others (Triandis, 1995). Third, members will evaluate each other's competence on the current task, as will authorized "evaluators." Competence evaluations may be driven by cultural stereotypical information as well as by actual information about an individual's performance. Fourth, styles of nonverbal behavior or speech are evaluated for status as well. Again, cultural differences are relevant in that language fluency is a status indicator because it tends to have implications for perceptions of competency (Fisek et al., 1995). In addition, literature in linguistics indicates that language affects the self-concept (Pierson

& Bond, 1982). The language of interaction affects the perceptions of both parties and elicits different types of nonverbal behavior (Gudykunst & Bond, 1997).

Status characteristics theory suggests that diffuse status characteristics (e.g., being a white male) become associated with the current task simply because expectations regarding the performance of an individual with these characteristics are activated in conjunction with current task outcomes. Research evidence indicates that these diffuse characteristics contribute, independently of performance, to ascriptions of status (Cohen & Zhou, 1991). Typically, once status orders are formulated, they are difficult to change because they exist, to a great extent, independently of current performance evaluations (Berger, Rosenholtz, & Zelditch, 1980). Once in place, they are the basis for interactions and expectations of participants and, as such, simply self-replicate over time. However, as time passes, status structures derived from the environment external to the group might become less relevant.

It might be argued that social identity and categorization theories predict that individuals will perceive their subgroups as being superior to (higher in status than) other cultural subgroups (given that, in the case of national culture, it is difficult to change subgroup membership), no matter what objective evidence suggests. This would be hypothesized on the basis that social identity must be positive to enhance an individual's sense of identity and that such perceptions are reasonably ambiguous and arbitrary in any event. These theories suggest that the use of multiple dimensions for the ranking of relevant subgroups allows individuals to maintain their self-esteem. At the same time, this process provides an opportunity for groups to develop shared rankings on the dimensions and give some positive evaluations to all subgroups (Berry, Kalin, & Taylor, 1977). On the other hand, there are limitations to the ability of this process to provide a positive view for all group members because people compare their subgroups to others on dimensions of value (Tajfel, 1978) and probably cannot simply select those on which they feel superior to use for comparisons.

Similarly, social information processing and similarity-attraction approaches also suggest that because of the self-validation motive, people who encounter different others should be motivated to rate others' perceived characteristics as less desirable than their own. However, a key aspect of information processing in this context is that any negative information acquired during differentiation is thought to be weighted substantially more heavily than positive information (Fiske & Taylor, 1984). Thus, the potential disconfirming of valued goals and behaviors should receive adequate resources at the attention stage of perception and also be encoded in memory. Source of information (direct vs. indirect) also can be a key factor in processing differentiating information. Second-level stereotyping (i.e., stereotypical information received from a respected or similar other) might not be recognized as stereotypical. Instead, it might be taken as more diagnostic when compared to the actual direct experience of culturally different others because of its less ambiguous nature (e.g., all positive or all negative [LaBianca, Brass, & Gray, 1998]).

Relatedly, although the search for self-confirming evidence is well known as a motive in information processing (Higgins & Bargh, 1987), less recognized is the need for valid information about the environment to enhance its predictability (Doosji, Spears, & Koomen, 1995; Higgins & Bargh, 1987). Individuals do have a tendency to search for and remember information that is consistent with already formed schemata. This is a primary factor leading to the favoring of culturally similar others or the in-group. However, without a drive to attend to environmental information that is inconsistent with current belief structures, not only would people be unable to predict others' behavior, they also would be unable to adapt to changing circumstances. This is interpreted by some as a basis for "fairness" in that it infers the processing of valid positive information about the out-group.

One result of these opposing processes is that stereotypes often are widely shared, even by the stereotyped individuals (Smith & Bond, 1999). Differently categorized individuals often show consensus on relative ranking of the relevant groups on specific dimensions (Ottati & Lee, 1995). This finding suggests that the content of stereotypes is not fully determined by differences in cognitive processing between members and out-groups, nor is it fully a product of self-confirming motives. Instead, cultural comparisons directly influence attributions of status that may or may not be shared throughout the group.

Proposition 2: Cultural characteristics of group members will influence perceptions of the status hierarchy within the group.

Agreement About the Status Hierarchy

Although social identity theory clearly indicates a motive toward the formulation of a positive identity, individuals will not always be successful in generating such identities by affiliation with high-status groups. Consistent with Proposition 2, there might in fact be substantial agreement about rank orderings of subgroups within a group on dimensions of value, and as noted earlier, in any given context it is likely that only one categorization scheme will be activated (Macrae et al., 1995). The literatures on status and culture (Triandis, 1972) and national self-esteem (Luhtanen & Crocker, 1991) clearly illustrate that individuals from some cultures derive less positive social identities than do others. This sometimes can lead to the development of agreement about status in a group. However, it also is the case that although subcultures that coexist in the same general location usually must develop heuristics regarding relative status to promote predictable interaction, such heuristics are less likely to be operational across national boundaries. Therefore, work groups with members representing multiple national cultures might encounter the problem of a lack of agreement about status order more frequently than do culturally homogeneous groups or groups whose members are from the same area.

Disagreement regarding the status hierarchy signals a lack of legitimacy of the current status structure in that it is not accepted as appropriate or proper by all group members. This is a significant issue because when status orders are unstable, conflict is more likely to become manifest (Zelditch & Walker, 1989). The potential for instability and change is further exacerbated by the idea that culturally different others rely on different bases of power (structural incongruence), which also is thought to be a source of conflict (Kabanoff, 1988). Although both differentiation and evaluative judgments of the status of group members are ongoing processes that challenge individuals' perceived legitimacy, we propose that they do not necessarily result in manifest conflict unless there are substantive disagreements regarding the status structure of the group.

Evidence on this point is provided in part by Blalock's (1957) study of race relations in the United States. He argued that as members of a relatively advantaged group become less numerous, and as members of a relatively disadvantaged group become more numerous, the stability of the status hierarchy decreases. The advantaged group feels threatened by its members' perceived inferiors, and it becomes more hostile, thus worsening relations.

In other cases, individuals who have accepted, but not necessarily recognized the legitimacy of, the status hierarchy will use opportunities of instability to acquire the status they believe they deserve. Typically, higher status subgroups feel more secure and positive about all group members maintaining their unique heritages (Moghaddam, 1994). However, if higher status groups decide how evaluative judgments will be made, then lower status subgroups might have trouble valuing their heritages and feeling secure within the context of the current hierarchical structure. Individuals who experience less contact with high-status members, hold lower status, and are in the minority are likely to expect negative outcomes from the current structure (Stephen & Stephen, 1984). This is unlikely to be consistent with maintenance of a positive identity and, therefore, is not likely to be seen as legitimate. Our discussion of status structure agreement leads to the following proposition:

> *Proposition 3:* The extent of multiculturalism within a group will be negatively related to agreement regarding the group's status hierarchy.

The research areas reviewed heretofore suggest an important role for individuals' perceptions of the legitimacy of their beliefs and actions and, in turn, their self-schemata (Byrne, 1971; Kluckhohn, 1951). Whereas social identity processes are a central part of such perceptions, we focus on the social categorization side of this set of theories in examining the role of challenges to legitimacy provided by membership in multicultural work teams. In what follows, we briefly discuss what legitimacy is, how individuals derive legitimacy for their self-identities, how legitimacy is challenged, and implications for the development of conflict.

Legitimacy

What Is Legitimacy?

Most conceptualizations of legitimacy that appear in the organizational literature emphasize the aggregate; that is, they describe how units or structures derive legitimacy in the eyes of their constituents (Dornbusch & Scott, 1975; Zelditch & Walker, 1989). More recently, however, individual-level perceptions of legitimacy have been used to examine the extent to which individuals identify with larger aggregates (Brown, 1997). General definitions of legitimacy include the following: being in compliance with the law, being in accordance with patterns or standards that are somehow established or accepted based on logic or reason, and being genuine (Houghton Mifflin, 1984). Commonly used synonyms from *Roget's Thesaurus* (Lewis, 1969) include words such as the following: logical, reasonable, fair, proper, appropriate, correct, official, justifiable, and rightful.

Focusing on the individual level, we draw on a number of sources (e.g., Brown, 1997; Suchman, 1995) to define legitimacy as the perceived appropriateness of an individual's beliefs, affect, and behavior in the context of a larger reference aggregate. This definition has several important implications relevant to our current purpose. First, some evaluation of "fit" or congruence with the values, norms, and culture of a social system is implied. Second, the reference aggregate might not be the system in which the individual currently exists, although we anticipate that in most cases this system will be an important potential referent. Third, legitimacy in this sense is directly related to the individual's sense of his or her life's meaning and, therefore, is central to feelings of self-esteem.

Legitimation of Self-Identity

Literature on legitimacy has identified three relevant bases or types of legitimacy: the pragmatic, the moral, and the cognitive (Brown, 1997; Suchman, 1995). Pragmatic legitimacy is based on general exchange principles in that outcomes are expected to be positive for the reference aggregate. Such exchanges might not be explicit but are, over the long run, anticipated to be beneficial. Moral legitimacy implies that an individual has the "right" set of beliefs (i.e., the right values) and that he or she responds both affectively and behaviorally in an appropriate way. Cognitive legitimacy implies a "taken-for-grantedness" or plausibility of belief, affect, and behavior. These types, as expressed in the literature, tend to have a substantial amount of overlap (see, e.g., Suchman, 1995).

Here, we focus somewhat more narrowly in part to avoid such overlap. In our approach, individuals can gain legitimacy as adults in primarily two ways: by attaining *mastery* over the current task and offering the reference aggregate positive outcomes or by attaining *morality* (i.e., consistently expressing and conveying the values and norms of the reference aggregate). Our framework has parallels with Earley's (1997) work on face and is consistent with thinking in ethical decision making (see, e.g., Donaldson & Werhane, 1983) that suggests we can interpret the "rightness" of decisions based on whether the outcomes are good (consequentialism) or the principles are good (deontology). This dualistic framework also incorporates cognitive views of legitimacy in that perceivers (the self or others) can interpret either outcomes (mastery) or principles (morality) as consistent with the reference aggregate's socially constructed reality. Such interpretations can produce results that indicate either that the individual could not have behaved in any other way (taken for granted) or that the behavior was a plausible reaction to the situation at hand.

Challenges to Legitimacy

In the context of multicultural groups, many individuals find their legitimacy challenged at some level. The experience of this challenge varies widely. The root of the challenge, as indicated by the literature reviewed heretofore, is that interaction with culturally different others presents us with opposing values and value-related goals, attitudes, and behavior patterns. Both the similarity-attraction paradigm (Byrne, 1971) and social categorization (Tajfel & Turner, 1986) suggest that affiliating oneself with similar others, and taking part of one's identity from a larger aggregate, fulfills a self-validation function for the ego as one's beliefs and values are confirmed and supported by these similar others. The motive is to develop and maintain a positive view of the self through contact with those who support one's belief systems and who presumably also view one in a positive light. Similar others validate and provide legitimacy to one's beliefs, attitudes, and behavior patterns.

Interaction with individuals whose values, self-conceptions, ideas about desirable behavior, and goals are not consistent with one's own is inevitable in the multicultural organizations of today. This experience leads to differing reactions, depending on key variables, but all reactions provide some form of a challenge to legitimacy. A central reason why these value confrontations occur is that cultural values (e.g., individualism/collectivism) are enacted in the work group environment as well as in the broader social context. Theorists and researchers have argued that roles drawn from either the larger context (Gutek, 1985) or other group contexts (Bettenhausen & Murnighan, 1991) "spill over" or are used as appropriate or legitimate approaches to new settings. Core values have such pervasive influences on cognition and behavior that it is difficult to imagine a situation in which an individual would not look to them for guidance either consciously or unconsciously, especially under ambiguous conditions (e.g., entry into a new work group). When these core values are called into question by interaction with others who do not share them, the individual experiences some degree of challenge to his or her personal identity. As noted earlier, multicultural groups also are likely to be particularly prone to disagreements about status among members. Another form of challenge, then, is that culturally different others are more likely to disagree with status beliefs as well.

> *Proposition 4:* Cultural differences between a focal individual and other group members decrease the self-perceived legitimacy of the focal individual's values and related beliefs, affect, and behavior.

The extent to which a challenge to legitimacy is experienced by interacting with culturally different others is affected by several factors. Status perceptions, similarity among team members, minority/majority status, member cognitive moral development, and ethnocentrism all influence how such interactions will be experienced.

Status perceptions. Formation of status perceptions within a multicultural team plays an important role in how encounters with culturally different others are experienced. We would anticipate that the question of whether one's values are right or wrong is more likely to be raised by those who are perceived to be of either equal or greater status on dimensions of value to the group. Therefore, challenges to the legitimacy of one's fundamental beliefs are limited by perceived position in the status hierarchy.

> *Proposition 4a:* The decrease in self-perceived legitimacy will be greater when the culturally different others are perceived to be of greater or equal status relative to the focal individual.

Similarity on other dimensions. We also anticipate that similar others (i.e., those who are similar to the focal person in respects other than the cultural dimension at issue) would be a more important source of disconfirmation than would those who clearly are very different on all dimensions. This thinking is consistent with balance theories (Heider, 1958) and cognitive consistency theories (Festinger, 1954) as well as with the premises of the similarity-attraction paradigm. Thus, we would propose the following:

Proposition 4b: The decrease in self-perceived legitimacy will be greater when the culturally different others are perceived to be more similar to the focal individual on dimensions other than culture.

Majority/minority representation. The extent to which an individual finds himself or herself in the minority in the group context also should influence the extent of the perceived challenge. As mentioned previously with regard to Blalock's (1957) research, individual perceptions of threats to legitimacy can change depending on the proportion of culturally similar others available to bolster feelings of legitimacy. Some authors have included this dimension with other status characteristics, with the implication being that the more of a particular type of person there is in a group, the more status the subgroup has. It is unclear in the present context, however, whether simple minority/majority effects are isomorphic with other status indicators because in many cases numerical majority does not appear to confer status (e.g., groups of employees from less developed countries working for an expatriate manager). However, the presence of culturally similar others, although not necessarily conveying status, should provide support and legitimation in the face of a challenge to values.

Proposition 4c: The decrease in self-perceived legitimacy will be greater to the extent that, numerically, the focal individual is in a cultural minority within the group.

Ethnocentrism. Ethnocentrism also is cast in the literature as an important individual difference moderating relationships between cultural heterogeneity and outcomes. Ethnocentrism infers that what occurs in one's own culture is appropriate and correct (legitimate); that customs, norms, and values should apply universally; and that it is natural and right to favor one's own group (Triandis, 1994). Thus, the more similar to one's own culture another subgroup is, the less negatively its members should be perceived and treated (Brewer & Campbell, 1976). The reverse of ethnocentrism, internationalism (Smith & Bond, 1999), has been examined in the context of increasing recognition of humanity's interdependence. The emergence of this construct is a result of the common dilemma facing people in general: that the systems that support life on earth are at risk (Dawes, 1980). Smith and Bond (1999) called internationalism a "constellation of attitudes towards people of different races, nations, and cultures." It relates to what Sampson and Smith (1957) called "world-mindedness," that is, the use of humans in general (as opposed to nation or culture) as the primary reference group.

This same view has been expressed in other ways as well, for example, as a value of cultural openness versus conservatism (Schwartz, 1992), of social integration versus cultural inwardness (Bond, 1988), and as ideologies of antagonism versus the honoring of other subgroups (Staub, 1990). In our current environment, we might term it "valuing diversity" as well.

The issue resolves itself in an interpretation of what is legitimate and what allows us, as individuals, to be legitimate. Do all others have to propound our values for us to feel legitimate? Or, can we accept the idea that other ideological sets can be legitimate as well? Authors in this area have suggested that a sense of pride in our own values and who we are does not have to be achieved through the denigration of others (e.g., Smith, 1992). Thus, valuing other cultures and valuing our own do not have to be mutually exclusive. Berry (1990) also noted that two motives might exist in this regard: a drive to maintain one's own cultural identity and a valuing of intercultural contact. This leads us to the following proposition:

> *Proposition 4d:* The decrease in self-perceived legitimacy will be greater to the extent that the focal individual is more ethnocentric in his or her understanding of the legitimacy of value systems.

Cognitive moral development. A final individual difference variable to be considered in determining the extent to which individuals will feel challenged by interactions with culturally different others is related to cognitive moral development or the internalization of a value or ethical system (Kohlberg, 1969). Developmentally, the locus of values initially is based in the environment; that is, punishment by significant others will result if values are not followed. Individuals who develop morally internalize a set of standards such that violation of standards is to be avoided not because of fear of punishment but rather to prevent feelings of guilt. In the present context, we would anticipate that because individuals with higher levels of cognitive moral development have internalized their value systems more deeply, they would be more subject to threats to system legitimacy. Individuals with lower levels of cognitive moral development are more likely to adapt when confronted with alternative value systems.

> *Proposition 4e:* The decrease in self-perceived legitimacy will be greater to the extent that the focal individual is higher in cognitive moral development.

Implications for the Development of Conflict

As noted earlier, surprisingly little research has focused on the role of multiculturalism in the development of conflict in organizational work groups. In addition, the process whereby legitimacy is challenged and negative affect occurs has not been subject to empirical testing. However, a vast amount of research has been done that illustrates the negative affective outcomes of interacting with others who differ on personal attribute dimensions. This research is briefly reviewed in what follows with regard to implications for conflict generation.

Affect, Felt Conflict, and Interactions
With Culturally Different Others

Several theoretical approaches provide a wealth of evidence on the development of affect regarding those perceived to be similar or dissimilar. For our current purposes, a central issue is that the differentiation of the values and related phenomena imputed to culturally different others is key to generating negative attitudes toward a group (Esses, Haddock, & Zanna, 1993; Haddock, Zanna, & Esses, 1993; Schwartz & Struch, 1989; Staub, 1990). Information processing (Linville & Jones, 1980), similarity/attraction (Byrne, 1971), social identity and categorization (Tajfel & Turner, 1986), and value theories (Rokeach, 1973) all have contributed evidence on this point.

In general, social information processing research indicates that with regard to perceptions of in-group and out-group members (in this case, culturally similar vs. culturally different), individuals recall more positive behaviors for their in-group and more negative incidents for the out-group. Attributions also differ when made for in-group versus out-group behavior, such that they generally are more favorable and more complex for the in-group (Hewstone, 1990; Weisinger & Salipante, 1995). As noted previously, perceptions of homogeneity of out-group members tend to result from categorization processes, and homogeneous perceptions in turn can lead to extreme judgments, either positive or negative, about the out-group (Biernat & Vescio, 1994; Linville & Jones, 1980). Conflict can potentially be generated at the outset of interaction if members of a group select different dimensions along which to organize the group experiences, members, and activities (Higgins, King, & Mavin, 1982; Korton, 1974).

Generalizations about subgroups produce expectations that also have significant effects on reactions to out-group members. Thomas and Ravlin's (1995) research on the culturally influenced expectations that subordinates have for manager behavior suggests that expectations of differences, in addition to actual differences, are generated by social categorization and stereotyping. These expectations were found to have effects on attraction and other interpersonal outcomes depending on whether or not they were fulfilled and on the causal attribution made for nonstereotypical (counterexpectation) behavior. Thus, it is important to consider not only actual differences among members but also perceptions of differences in examining the effects of team cultural composition.

In addition to social information processing research, social psychology has long investigated the effects of the attraction among similar others (Byrne, 1971). Currently, much of the research on similarity is done under the rubric of relational demography (O'Reilly, Caldwell, & Barnett, 1989; Tsui, Egan, & O'Reilly, 1992; Tsui & O'Reilly, 1989). The similarity-attraction paradigm argues that the more similar group members are to one another, the more attracted they will be to the group. Typically, similarity is considered along dimensions such as attitudes (Byrne, 1971), activity preferences (Jamieson, Lydon, & Zanna, 1987), values (Meglino, Ravlin, & Adkins, 1989), and (more recently) an array of demographic variables (Jackson et al., 1991; Murray, 1989; Wiersema & Bird, 1993; for a recent review, see Williams & O'Reilly, 1998). This body of research has shown very consistently that interpersonal attraction is positively related to similarity on these dimensions. Similarity also has been related to positive outcomes other than attraction. For example, demographic similarity has been related to increased frequency of communication and friendship ties (Lincoln & Miller, 1979), frequency of technical communication (Zenger & Lawrence, 1989), and social integration (O'Reilly et al., 1989). Values similarity has been positively linked to organizational commitment and job satisfaction (Meglino et al., 1989) and has been negatively linked to withdrawal behaviors (Chatman, 1991; O'Reilly, Chatman, & Caldwell, 1991), as is discussed further in what follows.

Typically, value similarity or congruence is assessed based on prior knowledge (stereotypes), interaction, information from others, and generalizations from interactions with similar others (second-level stereotypes). As a group member compares his or her value system to that of other members by way of the everyday interactions of selecting goals and behaviors, expressing attitudes, and exchanging information, similarities or differences emerge. Because values sometimes are unconsciously held (Locke, 1975), it is possible that truly parochial individuals will not recognize the differences that they face in interacting with culturally different others. However, these individuals still will encounter problems of communication, prediction, and (ultimately) lack of coordination that other, more aware members experience simply because they do not share information processing categories, goals, or preferences about behavior. These problems may be identified as relating to latent, rather than manifest, conflict (Pondy, 1967).

Values theory (Kluckhohn, 1951; Rokeach, 1973) suggests that differences in values lead to differences in motivation, information processing, goals, attitudes, and preferences for behaviors. In particular, Schwartz and Bilsky (1990) argued that differences in cultural values are the underlying source of cultural differences in motivation, and Erez and Earley (1993, pp. 97-118) also note that teams composed of very different members are less likely to be commonly motivated. An additional problem is that values, as fundamental cognitive structures, are relatively stable and change resistant (Rokeach, 1973). Therefore, even if members understand their cultural differences, they still might persist in believing that their value systems are the correct ones (ethnocentrism). As noted previously, these effects lead to negative affective responses and withdrawal behavior (O'Reilly et al., 1991), and Jehn and her colleagues (1999) recently identified relationships with conflict as well. Thus, we can infer from the research reviewed here that the results of a challenge to legitimacy are negative affect and felt conflict. We assume that because values influence an extensive network of beliefs, affect, and behaviors, a collision of value systems will produce both functional and relational conflict. This is because values have implications both for task goals and behaviors (functional issues) and for personal identity (relational issues) (for alternative views on the relationship between diversity and functional and relational conflict, see Jehn et al., 1999; Pelled, Eisenhardt, & Xin, 1999).

> *Proposition 5:* The extent to which an individual's self-perceived legitimacy is challenged will increase negative affect and felt conflict.

Manifest Conflict

When will felt conflict, as generated by challenges to legitimacy, develop into manifest conflict? Status characteristics of the group are thought to influence this occurrence. For example, extreme differences in status might limit expressions of conflict. However, most important, based on research on the stability of status hierarchies, we would propose that felt conflict will not become manifest unless the current status hierarchy is of questionable legitimacy itself (Zelditch & Walker, 1989). This lack of stability in the hierarchy can be driven either by prevalent lack of agreement on status internal to the group or external events (e.g., a poor group performance evaluation).

> *Proposition 6:* Felt conflict generated by perceived challenges to legitimacy is more likely to become manifest when the group's current status hierarchy is unstable.

CONFLICT RESOLUTION PROCESSES

Although a complete discussion of conflict resolution processes is beyond the scope of this chapter, we address some key issues related specifically to our legitimacy approach. Because it is not only impossible but also undesirable to eliminate conflict from group processes, individuals operating in multicultural work groups must develop ways of dealing with conflict that enhance or are at least neutral with regard to group effectiveness. Challenges to legitimacy tend to produce unproductive behavior, often in the form of narcissistic forms of ego protection (Brown, 1997). Some considerations, then, are to avoid these types of behavior; maintain a positive sense of ego for group members; and provide for the integration of their beliefs, affect, and behavior. Our intent is not so much to provide a list of actionable strategies to resolve multicultural group conflict as to develop, from the literature and propositions discussed in this chapter, a set of ideas that are consistent with what we know about the interaction processes involved.

Interaction Processes

Watson and his colleagues (1993) provided some of the clearest evidence that allowing the group development time (see also Gersick, 1989; Tuckman, 1965) is extremely valuable in multicultural groups. Multicultural groups need time to understand one another's behavior, to assess one another's capabilities, and to find mutually agreeable ways of working together. Although this is true of any new group, the barriers that culture creates make the process substantially more difficult. Social psychological theory suggests that we typically would expect to see improvement in members' attitudes toward one another based on increased opportunities for interaction over time (Schacter, 1959). Researchers have suggested a role for familiarity with the out-group in mitigating in-group favoritism (Taylor, Fiske, Etcoff, & Ruderman, 1978) or changing behavioral responses to out-groups (Rao & Schmidt, 1995). However, findings have not supported these relationships, suggesting that simply providing opportunities for interaction will not eliminate the negative effects of multiculturalism (see, e.g., Blau, 1977; Katz, Goldston, & Benjamin, 1958). Thomas (1999) suggested that when positive effects of time are observed, these effects are the result of the group receiving process-related feedback, and that in the absence of such feedback, improvement is unlikely to occur.

Thus, the form of interaction and communication within the group over time might be a central component of both the problems of coordination and conflict and the solution to these problems. Use of differing influence strategies with different target subgroups is thought to be a primary method for improving interactions in heterogeneous groups (Rao & Schmidt, 1995). In addition, striving for compromise rather than conversion might result in more positive intermember relationships (Kiesler & Pallak, 1967).

> *Proposition 7:* The extent to which interaction processes over time reflect process-related feedback, the target of influence, and a general compromise-oriented strategy will positively influence the effective management of manifest conflict in multicultural groups; provision of opportunities for interaction by itself will not necessarily have a positive effect.

Dyadic Interaction

In accordance with social identity theory, Tajfel and Turner (1986) argued that enhancing individuals' propensity to interact as individuals rather than as group representatives will significantly improve conflict resolution because it avoids the hardened bargaining positions, based on stereotyping, that develop when groups negotiate. Part of the problem is the inability to process information at a sufficiently complex level to avoid the use of broad categorizations. Ways in which to facilitate this process that are consistent with prior research include reducing members' cognitive load, giving members opportunities to interact with specific individuals (general familiarity with a subgroup does not appear to be effective, as discussed earlier), and allowing members to work in pairs. This process also draws on the positive aspects of mentoring relationships (see, e.g., Thomas, 1993) that can facilitate the integration of culturally diverse others into the aggregate.

> *Proposition 8:* The extent to which dyadic interaction occurs within the multicultural group will positively influence information processing about subgroups and effective management of manifest conflict.

Status of the Group

Also drawing from social identity theory, finding a group identity that enhances social identity for all and in which all can be included should focus members' attention away from cultural divisions and toward the team and accomplishment of its task (Brewer, 1993; Kelly, 1993; Williams & O'Reilly, 1998). Status characteristics of the group as a whole are important to achieving this goal. As discussed previously, it is important that one be able to make a favorable comparison of his or her social category with other groups (Tajfel, 1974; Tajfel & Turner, 1986) because this process helps individuals to achieve and maintain positive self-images (Luhtanen & Crocker, 1991). Status composition of the work group as a whole, derived in part from the overall perceptions of the status of group members, also should influence commitment and satisfaction with the group by providing either a positive or negative group identity for a member (Tajfel & Turner, 1986). The degree to which an individual regards himself or herself as similar to other members of the work group, and the degree to which a positive comparison can be made between this work group and others, has important implications for the extent to which the individual might identify with the group or actively distance himself or herself from other members.

Status of a group as a whole within the organization can be enhanced by way of visible top management support, provision of sufficient resources, management attention to group concerns, and (potentially) some degree of empowerment (Thomas, Ravlin, & Barry, in press). Within the group, a status hierarchy that is based on expertise regarding the task at hand and that is relatively flat and equality based also should help to avoid non-task-oriented political behavior and disagreements about status, and should help to facilitate integration-oriented interaction processes.

Proposition 9: The extent to which group members share in a high-status group identity will positively influence the effective management of manifest conflict in multicultural groups.

Legitimacy and Integration of Multiple Value Systems

Relatedly, another approach to successful conflict resolution should be a move to a relativist view of values and their legitimacy (i.e., that no one value system is superior, or a decrease in ethnocentrism) and development of the group as a source of legitimacy itself through an effort to establish goals that are agreed to be appropriate by group members and promotion of "proper" behaviors. An avenue for pursuing this approach might be to work to clarify the nature of values and members' beliefs about them. In that virtually all values are endorsed by all cultures (Schwartz & Bilsky, 1990), conflicts actually tend to arise over issues of both priorities (which values should be satisfied first [Meglino & Ravlin, 1998]) and behaviors (which behaviors are best for acting consistently with values [Ravlin, Adkins, & Meglino, 1994]). In the clarification process, individuals must not feel that their values are under threat or to be changed or that the meanings of their lives are being challenged; rather, differences and similarities must be clarified with a view toward finding areas of agreement among group members.

Proposition 10: The extent to which group members can learn to value multiple cultural systems and integrate these systems into a group value system will positively influence the effective management of manifest conflict in multicultural groups.

CONCLUSION

The increase in cultural diversity in the workforces of industrialized countries (Adler & Ghadar, 1990), coupled with the popularity of team-based management techniques (Lawler, Mohrman, & Ledford, 1992), has resulted in a need to understand the influence of cultural diversity in work groups. The approach to conflict in culturally diverse groups presented here provides an alternative way of thinking about this problem. Discrimination and evaluative judgment processes are integral parts of person perception (Wyer & Gordon, 1982), and from these processes and their outcomes, we should seek our answers to managing conflict in multicultural groups. An issue important to this process is understanding what it means to an individual to have some of his or her most cherished beliefs challenged (Brown, 1997). This aspect of interactions between culturally different others has received relatively little attention thus far. In addition, how status is perceived in groups, the stability of status hierarchies, and their role in enabling conflict continue to be neglected outside the domain of sociology.

Clearly, the predictions derived here are not specific to a particular culture or cultural belief. Empirical research that examines these propositions in the context of specific cultures and measures cultural differences along specific cultural dimensions is required. Hopefully, the presentation of this framework will lead to the type of detailed empirical study required to understand the influence of cultural diversity on conflict in the organizational work groups that are becoming more representative of today's work environment.

REFERENCES

Adler, N. J., & Ghadar, F. (1990). International strategy from the perspective of people and culture: The North American context. In A. M. Rugman (Ed.), *Research in global strategic management: International business research for the twenty-first century* (pp. 179-205). Greenwich, CT: JAI.

Amason, A. (1996). Distinguishing the effects of functional and dysfunctional conflict on strategic decision making: Resolving a paradox for top management teams. *Academy of Management Journal, 39,* 123-148.

Argote, L., & McGrath, J. E. (1993). Group process in organizations: Continuity and change. *International Review of Industrial and Organizational Psychology, 8,* 333-389.

Berger, J., Norman, R. Z., Balkwell, J. W., & Smith, R. F. (1992). Status inconsistency in task situations: A test of four status processing principles. *American Sociological Review, 57,* 843-855.

Berger, J., Rosenholtz, S. J., & Zelditch, M., Jr. (1980). Status organizing processes. *Annual Review of Sociology, 6,* 479-508.

Berry, J. W. (1990). The role of psychology in ethnic studies. *Canadian Ethnic Studies, 22,* 8-21.

Berry, J. W., Kalin, R., & Taylor, D. M. (1977). *Multi-culturalism and ethnic attitudes in Canada.* Ottawa: Ministry of Supplies and Services.

Bettenhausen, K. L. (1991). Five years of group research: What we have learned and what needs to be addressed. *Journal of Management, 17,* 345-381.

Bettenhausen, K. L., & Murnighan, J. K. (1991). The development of an intragroup norm and the effects of interpersonal and structural changes. *Administrative Science Quarterly, 36,* 20-35.

Biernat, M., & Vescio, T. K. (1994). Still another look at the effects of fit and novelty on the salience of social categories. *Journal of Experimental Social Psychology, 30,* 399-406.

Blalock, H. M. (1957). Percent non-white and discrimination in the South. *American Sociological Review, 22,* 677-682.

Blau, P. M. (1977). *Inequality and heterogeneity.* New York: Free Press.

Bochner, S., & Ohsako, T. (1977). Ethnic role salience in racially homogeneous and heterogeneous societies. *Journal of Cross-Cultural Psychology, 8,* 477-492.

Bochner, S., & Perks, R. W. (1971). National role evocation as a function of cross-national interaction. *Journal of Cross-Cultural Psychology, 2,* 157-164.

Bond, M. H. (1988). Finding universal dimensions of individual variation in multicultural studies of values: The Rokeach and Chinese value surveys. *Journal of Personality and Social Psychology, 55,* 1009-1015.

Brewer, M. B. (1993). Social identity, distinctiveness, and ingroup homogeneity. *Social Cognition, 11,* 150-164.

Brewer, M. B., & Campbell, D. T. (1976). *Ethnocentrism and intergroup attitudes.* Beverly Hills, CA: Sage.

Brewer, M. B., Weber, J. G., & Carini, B. (1995). Person memory in intergroup contexts: Categorization versus individuation. *Journal of Personality and Social Psychology, 69,* 29-40.

Brown, A. D. (1997). Narcissism, identity, and legitimacy. *Academy of Management Review, 22,* 643-686.

Byrne, D. (1971). *The attraction paradigm.* New York: Academic Press.

Chatman, J. A. (1991). Matching people and organizations: Selection and socialization in public accounting firms. *Administrative Science Quarterly, 36,* 459-484.

Cohen, B. P., & Zhou, X. (1991). Status processes in enduring work groups. *American Sociological Review, 56,* 179-188.

Cohen, S. G., & Bailey, D. E. (1997). What makes teams work: Group effectiveness research from the shop floor to the executive suite. *Journal of Management, 23,* 239-290.

Conway, M., Pizzamiglio, M. T., & Mount, L. (1996). Status, communality, and agency: Implications for stereotypes of gender and other groups. *Journal of Personality and Social Psychology, 71,* 25-38.

Cox, T. (1993). *Cultural diversity in organizations: Theory, research, and practice.* San Francisco: Berrett-Koehler.

Cox, T., Lobel, S., & McLeod, P. (1991). Effects of ethnic group cultural differences on cooperative and competitive behavior on a group task. *Academy of Management Journal, 34,* 827-847.

Dawes, R. M. (1980). Social dilemmas. *Annual Review of Psychology, 32,* 169-193.

Deutsch, M. (1980). Fifty years of conflict. In L. Festinger (Ed.), *Four decades of social psychology* (pp. 46-77). New York: Oxford University Press.

Donaldson, T., & Werhane, P. H. (Eds.). (1983). *Ethical issues in business: A philosophical approach* (2nd ed.). Englewood Cliffs, NJ: Prentice Hall.

Doosji, B., Spears, R., & Koomen, W. (1995). When bad isn't all bad: Strategic use of sample information in generalization and stereotyping. *Journal of Personality and Social Psychology, 69,* 642-655.

Dornbusch, S. M., & Scott, W. R. (1975). *Evaluation and the exercise of authority.* San Francisco: Jossey-Bass.

Earley, P. C. (1997). *Face, harmony, and social structure.* New York: Oxford University Press.

Erez, M., & Earley, P. C. (1993). *Culture, self-identity, and work.* New York: Oxford University Press.

Esses, V. M., Haddock, G., & Zanna, M. P. (1993). Values, stereotypes, and emotions as determinants of intergroup attitudes. In D. M. Mackie & D. L. Hamilton (Eds.), *Affect, cognition, and stereotyping: Interactive processes in group perception* (pp. 137-166). New York: Academic Press.

Fayol, H. (1949). *General and industrial management.* New York: Pitman.

Ferraro, G. P. (1994). *The cultural dimension of international business.* Englewood Cliffs, NJ: Prentice Hall.

Festinger, L. (1954). A theory of social comparison processes. *Human Relations, 7,* 117-140.

Fisek, M. H., Berger, J., & Norman, R. Z. (1995). Evaluations and the formation of expectations. *American Journal of Sociology, 101,* 721-746.

Fiske, S. T., & Taylor, S. E. (1984). *Social cognition.* Reading, MA: Addison-Wesley.

Gersick, C. J. G. (1989). Time and transition in work teams: Toward a new model of group development. *Academy of Management Journal, 31,* 9-41.

Gist, M. E., Locke, E. A., & Taylor, M. S. (1987). Organizational behavior: Group structure, process, and effectiveness. *Journal of Management, 13,* 237-258.

Goodman, P. S., Ravlin, E. C., & Argote, L. (1986). Current thinking about groups: Setting the stage for new ideas. In P. S. Goodman (Ed.), *Designing effective work groups* (pp. 1-33). San Francisco: Jossey-Bass.

Gudykunst, W. B., & Bond, M. H. (1997). Intergroup relations across cultures. In J. Berry, M. Segall, & C. Kagitcibasi (Eds.), *Handbook of cross-cultural psychology* (Vol. 3, pp. 119-161). Boston: Allyn & Bacon.

Gutek, B. A. (1985). *Sex and the workplace.* San Francisco: Jossey-Bass.

Hackman, J. R. (1987). The design of work teams. In J. W. Lorsch (Ed.), *Handbook of organizational behavior* (pp. 315-342). Englewood Cliffs, NJ: Prentice Hall.

Haddock, G., Zanna, M. P., & Esses, V. M. (1993). Assessing the structure of prejudicial attitudes: The case of attitudes towards homosexuals. *Journal of Personality and Social Psychology, 65,* 1105-1118.

Hartley, E. L., & Thompson, R. (1967). Racial integration and role differentiation. *Journal of the Polynesian Society, 76,* 427-443.

Hastie, R., Park, B., & Weber, R. (1984). Social memory. In R. S. Wyer, Jr., & T. K. Srull (Eds.), *Handbook of social cognition* (Vol. 2, pp. 151-212). Hillsdale, NJ: Lawrence Erlbaum.

Heider, F. (1958). *The psychology of interpersonal relations.* New York: John Wiley.

Henderson, M., & Argyle, M. (1986). The informal rules of working relationships. *Journal of Occupational Behavior, 7,* 259-275.

Hewstone, M. (1990). The ultimate attribution error? A review of the literature on intergroup causal attribution. *European Journal of Social Psychology, 20,* 311-335.

Higgins, E. T., & Bargh, J. A. (1987). Social cognition and social perception. *Annual Review of Psychology, 38,* 369-425.

Higgins, E. T., King, G. A., & Mavin, G. H. (1982). Individual construct accessibility and subjective impressions and recall. *Journal of Personality and Social Psychology, 43,* 35-47.

Hoerr, J. (1989, July 10). The payoff from teamwork. *Business Week,* pp. 55-62.

Hoffman, L. R., Harburg, E., & Maier, N. R. F. (1962). Differences and disagreements as factors in creative group problem solving. *Journal of Abnormal and Social Psychology, 64,* 206-214.

Hoffman, L. R., & Maier, N. R. F. (1961). Quality and acceptance of problem solutions by members of heterogeneous and homogeneous groups. *Journal of Abnormal and Social Psychology, 62,* 401-407.

Hofstede, G. (1980). *Culture's consequences: International differences in work-related values.* Beverly Hills, CA: Sage.

Houghton Mifflin. (1984). *Webster's II: New Riverside university dictionary.* Boston: Author.

Jackson, S. E. (1992). Team composition in organizational settings: Issues in managing an increasingly diverse work force. In S. Worchel, W. Wood, & J. A. Simpson (Eds.), *Group process and productivity* (pp. 138-173). Newbury Park, CA: Sage.

Jackson, S. E., Brett, J. F., Sessa, V. I., Cooper, D. M., Julin, J. A., & Peyronnin, K. (1991). Some differences make a difference: Individual dissimilarity and group heterogeneity as correlates of recruitment, promotions, and turnover. *Journal of Applied Psychology, 76,* 675-689.

Jackson, S. E., May, K. E., & Whitney, K. (1994). Understanding the dynamics of diversity in decision-making teams. In R. Guzzo & E. Salas (Eds.), *Team effectiveness and decision making in organizations* (pp. 204-261). San Francisco: Jossey-Bass.

Jamieson, D. W., Lydon, J. E., & Zanna, M. P. (1987). Attitude and activity preference similarity: Differential bases of interpersonal attraction for low and high self-monitors. *Journal of Personality and Social Psychology, 53,* 1052-1060.

Jehn, K. (1995). A multimethod examination of the benefits and detriments of intragroup conflict. *Administrative Science Quarterly, 40,* 256-282.

Jehn, K., Northcraft, G., & Neale, M. (1999). Why differences make a difference: A field study of diversity, conflict, and performance in work groups. *Administrative Science Quarterly, 44,* 741-763.

Kabanoff, B. (1988). Analyzing organizational conflicts using a model based on structural role theory. *Human Relations, 41,* 841-870.

Kanter, R. M. (1977). *Men and women of the corporation.* New York: Basic Books.

Katz, I., Goldston, J., & Benjamin, L. (1958). Behavior and productivity in bi-racial work groups. *Human Relations, 11,* 123-141.

Kelly, C. (1993). Group identification, intergroup perceptions, and collective action. In W. Stroebe & M. Hewstone (Eds.), *European review of social psychology* (Vol. 4, pp. 59-83). Chichester, UK: Wiley.

Kiesler, C. A., & Pallak, M. S. (1967). Minority influence: The effect of majority reactionaries and defectors, and minority and majority compromisers, upon majority opinion and attraction. *European Journal of Social Psychology, 5,* 237-256.

Kluckhohn, C. (1951). Values and value-orientations in the theory of action. In T. Parsons & E. Shils (Eds.), *Toward a general theory of action* (pp. 388-433). Cambridge, MA: Harvard University Press.

Kohlberg, L. (1969). Stage and sequence: The cognitive-developmental approach to socialization. In D. A. Goslin (Ed.), *Handbook of socialization theory and research* (pp. 347-380). Chicago: Rand McNally.

Korton, F. F. (1974). The influence of culture and sex on the perception of persons. *International Journal of Psychology, 9,* 31-44.

Kozan, M. K. (1989). Cultural influences on styles of handling interpersonal conflicts: Comparisons among Jordanian, Turkish, and U.S. managers. *Human Relations, 42,* 787-799.

Kroeber, A. L., & Kluckhohn, F. (1952). Culture: A critical review of concepts and definitions. In *Peabody Museum Papers* (Vol. 47, No. 1). Cambridge, MA: Harvard University.

LaBianca, G., Brass, D. J., & Gray, B. (1998). Social networks and perceptions of intergroup conflict: The role of negative relationships and third parties. *Academy of Management Journal, 41,* 55-67.

Lawler, E. E., III., Mohrman, S. A., & Ledford, G. E., Jr. (1992). *Employee involvement and total quality management: Practices and results in Fortune 1000 companies.* San Francisco: Jossey-Bass.

Lewis, N. (Ed.). (1969). *Roget's thesaurus.* New York: Washington Square Press.

Lincoln, J. R., & Miller, J. (1979). Work and friendship ties in organizations: A comparative analysis of related networks. *Administrative Science Quarterly, 24,* 181-199.

Linville, P. W., & Jones, E. E. (1980). Polarized appraisals of outgroup members. *Journal of Personality and Social Psychology, 38,* 689-703.

Locke, E. A. (1975). Personal attitudes and motivation. *Annual Review of Psychology, 61,* 457-480.

Luhtanen, R., & Crocker, J. (1991). Self-esteem and intergroup comparisons: Toward a theory of collective self-esteem. In J. Suls & T. A. Wills (Eds.), *Social cognition: Contemporary theory and research* (pp. 211-221). Hillside, NJ: Lawrence Erlbaum.

Macrae, C. N., Bodenhausen, G. V., & Milne, A. B. (1995). The dissection of selection in person perception: Inhibitory processes in social stereotyping. *Journal of Personality and Social Psychology, 69,* 397-407.

Markus, H. R., & Wurf, E. (1987). The dynamic self-concept: A social psychological perspective. *Annual Review of Psychology, 38,* 299-337.

Mayer, K. B., & Buckley, W. (1970). *Class and society* (3rd ed.). New York: Random House.

McGrath, J. E. (1984). *Groups: Interaction and performance.* Englewood Cliffs, NJ: Prentice Hall.

McGrath, J. E., & Kravitz, D. A. (1982). Group research. *Annual Review of Psychology, 33,* 195-230.

Meglino, B. M., & Ravlin, E. C. (1998). Individual values in organizations: Concepts, controversies, and research. *Journal of Management, 24,* 351-389.

Meglino, B. M., Ravlin, E. C., & Adkins, C. A. (1989). A work values approach to corporate culture: A field test of the value congruence process and its relationship to individual outcomes. *Journal of Applied Psychology, 74,* 424-432.

Milliken, F. J., & Martins, L. L. (1996). Searching for common threads: Understanding the multiple effects of diversity in organizational groups. *Academy of Management Review, 21,* 402-433.

Moghaddam, F. M. (1994). Ethnic segregation in a multicultural society: A review of recent trends in Montreal and Toronto and a reconceptualization of causal factors. In

F. Frisken (Ed.), *The changing Canadian metropolis: A public policy perspective* (Vol. 2). Berkeley: University of California Press.

Mullen, B. (1983). Operationalizing the effect of the group on the individual: A self-attention perspective. *Journal of Experimental Social Psychology, 19,* 295-322.

Mullen, B. (1987). Self-attention theory: The effects of group composition on the individual. In B. Mullen & G. R. Goethals (Eds.), *Theories of group behavior* (pp. 125-46). New York: Springer-Verlag.

Mullen, B., & Baumeister, R. F. (1987). Group effects on self-attention and performance: Social loafing, social facilitation, and social impairment. In C. Hendrick (Ed.), *Review of personality and social psychology* (pp. 189-206). Newbury Park, CA: Sage.

Murray, A. (1989). Top management group heterogeneity and firm performance. *Strategic Management Journal, 10,* 125-141.

Nelson, L. J., & Miller, D. T. (1995). The distinctiveness effect in social categorization: You are what makes you unusual. *Psychological Science, 6,* 246-249.

Nord, W. R., Brief, A. P., Atieh, J. M., & Doherty, E. M. (1988). Work values and the conduct of organizational behavior. In B. Staw & L. Cummings (Eds.), *Research in organizational behavior* (Vol. 10, pp. 1-42). Greenwich, CT: JAI.

Oakes, P. J. (1994). The effects of fit versus novelty on the salience of social categories: A response to Biernat and Vescio (1993). *Journal of Experimental Social Psychology, 30,* 390-398.

Ohbuchi, K., & Takahashi, Y. (1994). Cultural styles of conflict management in Japanese and Americans: Passivity, covertness, and effectiveness of strategies. *Journal of Applied Social Psychology, 24,* 1345-1366.

O'Reilly, C. A., III, Caldwell, D. F., & Barnett, W. P. (1989). Work group demography, social integration, and turnover. *Administrative Science Quarterly, 34,* 21-37.

O'Reilly, C. A., III, Chatman, J. A., & Caldwell, D. F. (1991). People and organizational culture: A profile comparison approach to assessing person-organization fit. *Academy of Management Journal, 34,* 487-516.

Ott, J. S. (1989). *The organizational culture perspective.* Chicago: Dorsey.

Ottati, V., & Lee, Y. (1995). Accuracy: A neglected component of stereotype research. In Y. Lee, L. Jussim, & C. R. McCauley (Eds.), *Stereotype accuracy: Toward appreciating group differences* (pp. 29-59). Washington, DC: American Psychological Association.

Pelled, L. H., Eisenhardt, K. M., & Xin, K. R. (1999). Exploring the black box: An analysis of work group diversity, conflict, and performance. *Administrative Science Quarterly, 44,* 1-28.

Pelz, D. C. (1956). Some social factors related to performance in a research organization. *Administrative Science Quarterly, 1,* 310-325.

Pierson, H. D., & Bond, M. H. (1982). How do Chinese bilinguals respond to variations in interviewer language and ethnicity? *Journal of Language and Social Psychology, 1,* 123-139.

Pondy, L. R. (1967). Organizational conflict: Concepts and models. *Administrative Science Quarterly, 12,* 296-320.

Postman, L., Bruner, J. S., & McGinnies, E. (1948). Personal values as selective factors in perception. *Journal of Abnormal and Social Psychology, 43,* 142-154.

Prentice, D. A. (1987). Psychological correspondence of possessions, attitudes, and values. *Journal of Personality and Social Psychology, 53,* 993-1003.

Putnam, L. L., & Poole, M. S. (1987). Conflict and negotiation. In F. M. Jablin, L. L. Putnam, K. H. Roberts, & L. W. Porter (Eds.), *Handbook of organizational communication: An interdisciplinary perspective* (pp. 549-599). Newbury Park, CA: Sage.

Rao, A., & Schmidt, S. M. (1995). Intercultural influence: An Asian perspective. *Advances in Comparative Management, 10,* 79-98.

Ravlin, E. C., Adkins, C. L., & Meglino, B. M. (1994, August). *Organizational definition of performance and individual value orientation: Interactive effects on performance and absence.* Paper presented at the annual meeting of the Academy of Management, Dallas, TX.

Ravlin, E. C., & Meglino, B. M. (1987). The effect of values on perception and decision making: A study of alternative work values measures. *Journal of Applied Psychology, 72,* 666-673.

Ridgeway, C., & Diekema, D. (1989). Dominance and collective hierarchy formation in male and female task groups. *American Sociological Review, 54,* 79-93.

Rokeach, M. (1973). *The nature of human values.* New York: Free Press.

Rossi, A. M., & Todd-Mancillas, W. R. (1985). A comparison of managerial communication strategies between Brazilian and American women. *Communication Research Reports, 2,* 128-134.

Sampson, E. E., & Smith, H. P. (1957). A scale to measure world-minded attitudes. *Journal of Social Psychology, 45,* 99-106.

Sathe, V. (1985). *Culture and related corporate realities.* Homewood, IL: Irwin.

Schacter, S. (1959). *The psychology of affiliation.* Stanford, CA: Stanford University Press.

Schwartz, S. H. (1992). Universals in the content and structure of values: Theoretical advances and empirical tests in 20 countries. *Advances in Experimental Social Psychology, 25,* 1-65.

Schwartz, S. H., & Bilsky, W. (1990). Toward a universal psychological structure of human values. *Journal of Personality and Social Psychology, 53,* 550-562.

Schwartz, S. H., & Struch, N. (1989). Values, stereotypes, and intergroup antagonism. In D. Bar-Tal, C. F. Graumann, A. W. Kruglanski, & W. Stroebe (Eds.), *Stereotyping and prejudice: Changing conceptions* (pp. 151-167). New York: Springer-Verlag.

Shils, E. (1975). *Center and periphery: Essays in macrosociology.* Chicago: University of Chicago Press.

Sidanius, J., Pratto, F., & Rabinowitz, J. L. (1994). Gender, ethnic status, and ideological asymmetry. *Journal of Cross-Cultural Psychology, 25,* 194-216.

Skvoretz, J., & Fararo, T. J. (1996). Status and participation in task groups: A dynamic network model. *American Journal of Sociology, 101,* 1366-1414.

Smith, M. B. (1992). Nationalism, ethnocentrism, and the new world order. *Journal of Humanistic Psychology, 32,* 76-91.

Smith, P. B., & Bond, M. H. (1999). *Social psychology across cultures: Analysis and perspectives.* Boston: Allyn & Bacon.

Srull, T. K., & Wyer, R. S., Jr. (1979). The role of category accessibility in the interpretation of information about persons: Some determinants and implications. *Journal of Personality and Social Psychology, 37,* 1660-1672.

Staub, E. (1990). Moral exclusion, personal goal theory, and extreme destructiveness. *Journal of Social Issues, 46,* 47-64.

Steiner, I. D. (1972). *Group process and productivity.* New York: Academic Press.

Stephen, W. G., & Stephen, C. W. (1984). The role of ignorance in intergroup relations. In N. Miller & M. B. Brewer (Eds.), *Groups in contact: The psychology of desegregation* (pp. 229-256). New York: Academic Press.

Suchman, M. C. (1995). Managing legitimacy: Strategic and institutional perspectives. *Academy of Management Review, 20,* 571-610.

Sundstrom, E., DeMeuse, K. P., & Futrell, D. (1990). Workteams: Applications and effectiveness. *American Psychologist, 45,* 120-133.

Tajfel, H. (1974). Social identity and intergroup behavior. *Social Science Information, 23,* 65-93.

Tajfel, H. (1978). Social categorization, social identity, and social comparison. In H. Tajfel (Ed.), *Differentiation between social groups* (pp. 61-76). London: Academic Press.

Tajfel, H., & Turner, J. C. (1986). The social identity theory of intergroup behavior. In S. Worchel & W. G. Austin (Eds.), *Psychology of intergroup relations* (2nd ed., pp. 7-24). Chicago: Nelson-Hall.

Taylor, S. E., Fiske, S. T., Etcoff, N. L., & Ruderman, A. J. (1978). Categorical and contextual bases of person memory and stereotyping. *Journal of Personality and Social Psychology, 36,* 778-793.

Thomas, D. A. (1993). Racial dynamics in cross-race developmental relationships. *Administrative Science Quarterly, 38,* 169-194.

Thomas, D. C. (1999). Cultural diversity and work group effectiveness: An experimental study. *Journal of Cross-Cultural Psychology, 30,* 242-263.

Thomas, D. C., & Ravlin, E. C. (1995). Responses of employees to cultural adaptation by a foreign manager. *Journal of Applied Psychology, 80,* 133-146.

Thomas, D. C., Ravlin, E. C., & Barry, D. (in press). Creating effective multicultural teams. *University of Auckland Business Review.*

Thomas, D. C., Ravlin, E. C., & Wallace, A. (1996). Effect of cultural diversity in work groups. *Research in the Sociology of Organizations, 14,* 1-33.

Ting-Toomey, S. (1993). Communicative resourcefulness: An identity negotiation perspective. In R. Wiseman & J. Koester (Eds.), *Intercultural communication competence* (pp. 72-110). Newbury Park, CA: Sage.

Ting-Toomey, S., Gao, G., Trubisky, P., Yang, Z., Kim, H. S., Lin, S., & Nishida, T. (1991). Culture, face maintenance, and styles of handling interpersonal conflict: A study in five cultures. *International Journal of Conflict Management, 2,* 275-296.

Triandis, H. C. (1972). *The analysis of subjective culture.* New York: John Wiley.

Triandis, H. C. (1994). *Culture and social behavior.* New York: McGraw-Hill.

Triandis, H. C. (1995). *Individualism and collectivism.* Boulder, CO: Westview.

Triandis, H. C., Hall, E. R., & Evans, R. B. (1965). Member heterogeneity and dyadic creativity. *Human Relations, 18,* 33-55.

Tsui, A. S., Egan, T. D., & O'Reilly, C. A., III. (1992). Being different: Relational demography and organizational attachment. *Administrative Science Quarterly, 37,* 549-579.

Tsui, A. S., & O'Reilly, C. A., III. (1989). Beyond simple demographic effects: The importance of relational demography in superior-subordinate dyads. *Academy of Management Journal, 32*, 402-442.

Tuckman, B. W. (1965). Developmental sequences in small groups. *Psychological Bulletin, 63*, 384-399.

Wall, J. A., Jr., & Callister, R. R. (1995). Conflict and its management. *Journal of Management, 21*, 515-558.

Watson, W. E., Kumar, K., & Michaelsen, L. K. (1993). Cultural diversity's impact on interaction process and performance: Comparing homogeneous and diverse task groups. *Academy of Management Journal, 36*, 590-602.

Weber, M. (1948). *The theory of social and economic organization.* New York: Free Press.

Weisinger, J. Y., & Salipante, P. F. (1995). Toward a method of exposing hidden assumptions in multicultural conflict. *International Journal of Conflict Management, 6*, 147-170.

Weldon, E., & Jehn, K. A. (1995). Examining cross-cultural differences in conflict management behavior: A strategy for future research. *International Journal of Conflict Management, 6*, 387-403.

Westwood, R. I., Tang, S. F. Y., & Kirkbride, P. S. (1992). Chinese conflict behavior: Cultural antecedents and behavioral consequences. *Organization Development Journal, 10*, 13-19.

Wiersema, M., & Bird, A. (1993). Organizational demography in Japanese firms: Group heterogeneity, individual dissimilarity, and top management team turnover. *Academy of Management Journal, 36*, 996-1025.

Wilder, D. A. (1986). Social categorization: Implications for creation and reduction of intergroup bias. *Advances in Experimental Social Psychology, 19*, 291-355.

Williams, K. Y., & O'Reilly, C. A., Jr. (1998). Demography and diversity in organizations: A review of 40 years of research. *Research in Organizational Behavior, 20*, 77-140.

Williams, R. M., Jr. (1968). The concept of values. In D. Sills (Ed.), *International encyclopedia of the social sciences* (pp. 283-287). New York: Macmillan.

Williams, R. M., Jr. (1979). Change and stability in values and value systems: A sociological perspective. In M. Rokeach (Ed.), *Understanding human values* (pp. 15-46). New York: Free Press.

Wyer, R. S., Jr., & Gordon, S. E. (1982). The recall of information about persons and groups. *Journal of Experimental Social Psychology, 18*, 128-164.

Yu, X. (1995). Conflict in a multicultural organization: An ethnographic attempt to discover work-related cultural assumptions between Chinese and American co-workers. *International Journal of Conflict Management, 6*, 211-232.

Zarate, M. A., & Smith, E. R. (1990). Person categorization and stereotyping. *Social Cognition, 8*, 161-185.

Zelditch, M., Jr., & Walker, H. A. (1989). Legitimacy and the stability of authority. *Advances in Group Processes, 1*, 1-25.

Zenger, T. R., & Lawrence, B. S. (1989). Organizational demography: The differential effects of age and tenure on technical communication. *Academy of Management Journal, 32*, 353-376.

chapter 3

Missing Relations

Incorporating Relational Constructs Into Models of Culture

MICHAEL W. MORRIS
JOEL M. PODOLNY
SHEIRA ARIEL

They say you are not you except in terms of relation to other people. . . .
What you do, which is what you are, only has meaning in relation to
other people.

　　　　　　　　　　　　　　—Robert Penn Warren, *All the King's Men*

As an increasing number of organizations reach across national boundaries, organizational research increasingly addresses the question of how national culture influences individual behavior (Erez & Earley, 1993; Hofstede, 1991). Researchers face a choice among numerous definitions of culture and methods for studying it that have been developed in different academic disciplines (Keesing, 1974). As the diversity of chapters in this volume attests, researchers in different subfields of organizational behavior have chosen different methodological paths and have arrived at different insights. The path chosen by most micro-level organizational behavior researchers is to study "subjective culture," that is, to conceptualize culture as existing in an individual's mental representations rather than in external structures and artifacts (Triandis, 1967, 1972, 1995). Cultural differences in values, beliefs, and attitudes are assessed through inventories such as those traditionally used to measure personality differences. Moreover, just as generalizations about personality were made in terms of underlying dimensions such as introversion-extroversion, generalizations about cultural attitudes have been sought in terms of dimensions such as individualism-collectivism (Triandis, McCusker, & Hui, 1990). The individualism-collectivism construct has been enormously popular, in part because it promises a way in which to capture, at the level of individual values, the cultural difference between "loosely knit" and "tightly knit" societies described by classical social theories (Durkheim, 1897/1951; Tonnies, 1887/1957). Although we review many contributions of this *subjectivist* approach to culture, we describe shortcomings that have emerged in the prevailing research program based on individualism-collectivism. Moreover, we argue that, in principle, the subjectivist approach is incapable of fully capturing the influence of culture on individual behavior.

In this chapter, we argue that a better understanding of how individuals are affected by national culture is achieved when the subjectivist analysis of internal attitudes is supplemented with the *structuralist* approach of focusing on the external social relations that constrain behavior.[1] More specifically, we suggest that the concepts developed for studying patterns of social relations are useful in cultural research. Some relevant relational concepts refer to the form or geometry of an individual's relations. Density, for example, refers to the degree of interconnectedness among the other people in one's networks, and density has been linked to the cultural difference between loosely knit and tightly knit societies (Fischer & Shavit, 1995). Other concepts involve both the content and form of relations. Multiplexity, for example, refers to whether or not one exchanges personal friendship and instrumental resources in the same relationship, and this relational dimension has been suggested by several theorists to explain cultural differences in workplace behavior (Dore, 1983; Gluckman, 1967). We review the sparse literature on cross-national differences in relational variables and conclude that there is a great deal of unexplored potential in capturing the differences among cultures in terms of the differing relations in which individuals are embedded. However, we also review theoretical arguments against the notion that culture can be reduced to a purely structural analysis.

The approach to culture that we advocate integrates subjectivist and structuralist analyses. We argue that international differences in interpersonal behavior in the workplace are best understood in terms of systems of norms. In the tradition of Weber (1922/1963) and Parsons (1951), we assume that a norm exists both in the internal subjective attitudes that individuals hold about interpersonal relations and in the external structure of relations. A norm is the basis of the local sociocultural system that organizes the interaction within a circle of employees. Importantly, we do *not* make the assumption that norms are shared and organized at a societywide level, an assumption for which classical theorists have been critiqued (Wrong, 1961). We merely assume that employees in a given workplace context construct and sustain a local pattern of interaction (Giddens, 1984; Swidler, 1986).[2] Moreover, to a large extent, these systems are based on prior forms of sociality such as market, family, legal, and friendship relations (Fiske, 1991). Thus, the role of national culture is indirect; its role lies in shaping which norms are appropriate to organize a local system of interaction in the workplace, and this local system in turn guides individual behavior (Lonner & Adamopoulos, 1997).

By reviewing our own study of North American, Chinese, German, and Spanish employees of a multinational corporation (MNC) (Morris, Podolny, & Ariel, 1997), we illustrate the advantages of a sociocultural-systems analysis over a purely subjectivist or structuralist analysis. Not only does a systems level of analysis help to distinguish between individualist and collectivist societies, it also provides a more fine-grained understanding of qualitatively different forms of collectivism. Traditional unidimensional analyses of collectivism serve well to contrast the English-speaking nations from most of the world's other major cultural traditions, which accord more concern to social collectivities and less to individuals (Hofstede, 1980, 1991). In itself, this contrast comports well with the ethnographic and historical record. Compared to Western Anglophone societies, there seems to be a greater emphasis on social relations and collectivities in the Chinese societies in East Asia, in social democratic nations in Northern Europe, in Southern European nations on the Mediterranean, and in most other large cultural groups. Yet, the ethnographic record also makes it clear that not all of these differing cultural groups emphasize the same types of social relations and collectivities. Simply put, not all collectivist societies are collectivistic in the same way. In this chapter, we make the case that conceptualizing culture in terms of sociocultural systems helps to clarify the qualitatively different forms of collectivist orientation.

TRADITIONAL APPROACHES TO CULTURE

Subjectivist Approach

Historical roots. The approach of accounting for societal differences in terms of subjective psychological characteristics has a long tradition in anthropology. An influential movement in this tradition was the research program linking culture and personality. Ethnographers such as Benedict (1934) and Mead (1935) were impressed by the variation across societies in patterns of social behavior and the stability of those patterns within societies. In keeping with psychoanalytic theories of their day, they explained patterns of behavior in terms of a modal personality type, transmitted across generations through primary societal institutions such as child-rearing practices (Kardiner, 1939; Mead, 1935). The limitations of this approach are most evident in the World War II-era studies of the "national character" of the United States' military adversaries. For example, based on observations of and interviews with Japanese prisoners of war, Gorer (1943) posited that patterns of Japanese behavior reflect an anal-compulsive personality type inculcated through early toilet training. The most obvious empirical shortcoming of this work is that no attempt was made to measure the underlying personality type (Inkeles & Levinson, 1954). Closely related to this empirical shortcoming is the theoretical shortcoming inherent in the simplistic assumption that each society is characterized by a predominant personality type. In the words of Wrong (1961), such an approach implies an "oversocialized" view of individuals and an "overintegrated" view of society.

Later subjectivist approaches were shaped by the critiques of the culture and personality movement. Researchers shifted from the method of unstructured ethnographic observation to surveys of representative samples of different societies. These surveys revealed the considerable heterogeneity of personality within societies (Cantril, 1965). Moreover, the use of quantitative survey measures led researchers away from hypotheses framed in terms of unified broad personality types toward hypotheses articulated in terms of more distinct specific value and attitude variables. The complexity inherent in describing subjective culture led researchers to seek more general, parsimonious constructs through statistical abstraction (Osgood, 1964), in favor of "thick description." (Yet, anthropology soon turned toward rejection of abstract subjectivist models in Geertz, 1976). Two statistical approaches are noteworthy. First, cluster analysis has been used to form cultural groupings of societies with historical, linguistic, and geographic similarities such as the Southern European Latin societies and the East Asian Chinese societies (Ronen, 1986; Ronen & Shenkar, 1985). Second, factor analysis has been used to uncover the underlying dimensions, such as individualism versus collectivism, that account for variance among cultural groups (Triandis, 1967, 1972). The second approach, which promises a more parsimonious account, has been more influential.

Recent contributions. Recent subjectivist research on culture has been largely focused on the cultural dimension of individualism-collectivism. This construct gained prominence in the wake of Hofstede's (1980) worldwide study of IBM employees. Hofstede found that individualism-collectivism captured a substantial fraction of the variance across countries in mean levels of endorsement of basic values about life and work. In addition, Hofstede's findings revealed that the United States and the few other Western Anglophone countries scored extremely high on individualism relative to the other countries in the sample. This finding raised the concern that organizational and social psychological research based almost exclusively on these few hyper-individualist Western societies might not generalize to the more collectivist societies in which most of the world's population resides. As a result, a wave of studies comparing social psychological variables in highly individualist and highly collectivist countries has addressed this question (for a review, see Triandis, 1995).

In attempting to investigate differences between individualist and collectivist cultures, Triandis and colleagues developed inventories to compare several types of social attitudes between the United States and more collectivist Asian or Latin countries (Triandis, Leung, Villareal, & Clark, 1985, Triandis et al., 1990). Others have investigated the consequences of individualism-collectivism in behavior rather than merely in attitudes. Leung and Bond (1984) tested hypotheses about how the collectivism dimension affects how people handle conflict with in-group or out-group members. In a task that required each participant to divide resources with a friend or a stranger, Leung and Bond observed a greater degree of in-group favoritism, or generosity toward friends, among Chinese students than among American students. Likewise, in conflict resolution tasks, researchers have found a greater preference for nonadversarial procedures with in-group members among Chinese and Spanish students than among American students (Leung, 1987; for a review, see Leung, 1997). Earley (1989, 1994) found that Chinese managers, relative to Americans, were less inclined to exhibit social loafing in a group task, apparently because of a concern for group success that rivals their concern for individual success.

Critiques and current directions. Although the construct of individualism-collectivism has been the most fruitful research program within the subjectivist approach, there has been an increasing number of critiques of the construct. First, compelling theoretical and empirical objections have been raised in research on attitudes and values against the notion that individualist and collectivist items can be arrayed on a single bipolar dimension (Kashima et al., 1995). Many different components of collectivism have been distinguished (Ho & Chiu, 1994). Second, studies of social behavior have indicated that not all forms of collectivism are alike. For example, studies of Latin societies have emphasized that social interactions are characterized by outward displays of warm emotion. Even in workplace interactions, a person creates a harmonious feeling through warm and expressive behavior, a tendency referred to as *simpatia* in Latin America (Diaz-Guerrero, 1967; Lindsley & Braithwaite, 1996; Sanchez-Burks, Nisbett, & Ybarra, 1998; Triandis, Marin, Lisansky, & Betancourt, 1984). This obligation of emotional expressivity contrasts sharply with observations about expressive displays in many other highly collectivist societies. For example, in the Chinese virtue of *jen* (Hsu, 1985) and the Japanese tradition of *amae* (Doi, 1962), harmony is created through passivity rather than expressivity. Hence, although the Confucian and Latin traditions both emphasize harmonious relations, they seem to create different types of harmonious relations. Third, scholars of business and diplomatic practices have found a need for more nuanced characterizations. For example, observations of intensely competitive behavior by Chinese negotiators have led researchers to seek constructs other than a generally collectivist value orientation (Pye, 1982). In sum, the promise of a parsimonious reduction of myriad cultural differences to a unitary individualism-collectivism dimension increasingly seems to be false.

Subjectivist researchers have attempted to redress the limitations of the individualism-collectivism construct by proposing more multifaceted models of cultural values. Schwartz (1994) and others have empirically distinguished different strands of individualist and collectivist values along lines much like those drawn by sociologists and intellectual historians who analyzed these values with different methods (Bellah, Madsen, Sullivan, Swidler, & Tipton, 1985; Lukes, 1973). Triandis and colleagues (Triandis, 1995; Triandis & Gelfand, 1998) have developed a measure of social values and attitudes that distinguishes the *economic* aspect of collectivism (sharing resources with the group) from the *expressive* aspect of collectivism (affective involvement with the group) and distinguishes the economic aspect of individualism (belief in achievement through competition) from the self-expressive aspect of individualism (desire to be unique).[3] Although the distinctive consequences of these specific attitude dimensions have not yet been delineated, the first three of these, on face value, seem to capture norms relevant to workplace obligations. With regard to country differences, there is as yet little data. Singelis, Triandis, Bhawuk, and Gelfand (1995) found that American students of an East Asian background are higher on economic collectivism (sharing resources) than are those of a West European background, and they conjectured that this type of collectivism should be highest in a society such as China, where the primary social value has been neither equality nor freedom but rather stability of the social order. In addition, Singelis et al. conjectured that expressive collectivism (affective involvement) should be highest in communal groups such as the Israeli kibbutz, where equality is more highly valued than freedom. By contrast, economic individualism (achievement through competition) should be highest in Western market democratic societies such as the United States, where freedom is valued over equality. We find these more fine-grained constructs promising and will return to them later.

However, in addition to the limits of particular subjectivist constructs, there are objections to the subjectivist approach itself, which by definition reduces culture to a set of factors that exist "inside the individual's head." Although certainly an actor's behavior is greatly determined by internal factors such as values and attitudes, behavior also is greatly determined by the external social situations that the actor faces. Decades of debate by psychologists over dispositional versus situational interpretation has largely concluded that the proximal causes of action are not personality dispositions but rather situational factors and interactions of situational factors and dispositions (Ross & Nisbett, 1991). Because the subjectivist approach to cross-national differences restricts itself to dispositions as causes of behavior, it is limited in much the same way as was traditional personality research. Interestingly, this bias of dwelling on dispositional causes of social behavior might itself reflect the Western cultural orientation of most researchers (Morris & Peng, 1994). In any case, the subjectivist account, by focusing on internal causes of behavior, is limited in principle to capturing only half of the picture.

Structuralist Approach

Historical roots. There is a long scholarly tradition of analyzing behavioral differences across countries in terms of aspects of the social structure. Marx's (1844/1972) arguments concerning alienation suggest that reduced subjective quality of life results from the patterns of relations fostered by capitalist institutions (Lukes, 1967). Durkheim (1893/1933) attributed country and ethnic differences in suicide rates to the tightness of the social fabric. Even Weber (1922/1963), although more known for his contention that subjective values and beliefs can cause changes to the social structure, also maintained that once social structures and positions are established, they shape values, attitudes, and beliefs.

A major research program testing a structuralist analysis of international differences in attitudes and values was Inkeles' (1960) work on what has come to be called the "convergence" thesis. The convergence thesis holds that the spread of industrialization and the resulting exposure to similar social structures in the form of institutions, such as factories and schools, have led people in different countries to hold similar values. In support of this structuralist argument, Inkeles found that country differences in values are substantially reduced when level of industrialization is controlled. Yet, country differences were by no means eliminated in Inkeles' findings. Moreover, increasingly salient counterexamples such as Japan, highly industrialized yet highly distinctive in its cultural values (Pascale & Athos, 1981), led scholars to become disenchanted with the idea that industrialization inevitably is linked with one set of values.

After decades of further work, Inkeles (1978) proposed several valuable recommendations for research on international differences. One was that the impact of macro-level structural variables, such as a country's level of industrialization, should be understood in terms of how these variables shape *micro-level social structures,* which provide the proximal causal influences on the motivations and behavior of individuals. A second recommendation was that the effects of micro-level structures should be understood in conjunction with the *subjective understandings* that guide people's responses to the situations. As we shall see, the first recommendation to focus on micro-level structures is a direction that structuralist researchers have taken. Our approach also takes the second step of incorporating people's subjective constructs as a mechanism in their responses to social structures.

Recent contributions. During recent decades, structuralism has reemerged in sociology. To a greater extent than classical theorists such as Marx (1844/1972) and Durkheim (1893/1933), the new structuralists have tried to reduce the causes of social phenomena to the pure geometry of social relations, removing any reference to subjective factors (Mayhew, 1980; Mayhew & Levinger, 1976). This movement has been aided by advances in the methods of conceptualizing social structure made by the field of *network analysis* (White, Boorman, & Breiger, 1976). Whereas many network analytic studies focus on the structure of macro-level ties among organizations (for a review, see Lincoln, 1982), other studies have focused on the structure of micro-level ties among individual employees within an organization (Burt, 1992). The networks of employees have been linked to several types of organizationally relevant attitudes and behavior (Ibarra, 1997). The most influential accounts of employee networks have focused strictly on the form of relations, that is, on network size and density (Burt, 1992). However, others have argued that the effects of relational form depend on content; for example, the forms that work best in relation to peers might not work in relation to those in power (Emerson, 1962; Podolny & Baron, 1997).

There has been some theoretical and empirical use of relational constructs in accounting for cultural differences. In particular, investigating country differences in the form of individuals' relational networks has been seen as a way in which to capture differences in the micro-level social situations that constrain behavior. The most prominent hypothesis in this work is the highly intuitive argument that collectivist societies with tightly woven social fabrics should be characterized by networks of high density (Gross & Raynor, 1985). This argument is interesting in that density might offer a way in which to measure the basic assumption that collectivist societies are characterized by tight in-groups. Also, it would serve as a basis to question subjectivist explanations for country differences. For example, the greater tendency of Chinese (as compared to American) participants to show generosity toward friends has been ascribed to Chinese collectivist attitudes (Leung & Bond, 1984). It might be that we all are particularly generous toward friends who are interconnected with other friends (many relations are at stake) and that Chinese friendships tend to be embedded in dense cliques.

Although a structuralist approach to collectivism appeals intuitively, empirical findings are mixed on the question of whether individuals in collectivist societies have denser networks. A review of findings from similar network surveys conducted in different countries concluded that density levels are higher in Chinese and Israeli cities than in American and British cities (Fischer & Shavit, 1995). Furthermore, a study of interaction patterns among university students found that Hong Kong students have group interactions more frequently than do North American students (Wheeler, Reis, and Bond, 1989). Although this study did not measure relationships and structural properties such as density, the finding that students in a collectivist society tend toward group interactions is consistent with a picture of a clique-like social structure in which a person's friends are friends with one another. Yet, the only previous study (to our knowledge) that made a controlled cross-cultural comparison of network density did not observe the predicted pattern of lower density in the friendship networks of North Americans compared to those of East Asians (Kashima et al., 1995). In sum, the most promising operationalization of a purely structuralist analysis of cultural collectivism has not received consistent support.[4]

Critiques and current directions. Despite the face validity of the idea that individuals in collectivist societies have denser networks, comparisons of the average density of relations have not uncovered a clear pattern. More important, there also have been theoretical objections to accounts that explain action in terms of the pure form or geometry of social relations without reference to their content or meaning. One objection is that this account fails to provide a role for individual agency in creating and perpetuating these structures of social relations (Giddens, 1984). Another objection is that the effects of structural positions on behavior are mediated by subjective beliefs and normative commitments, and that might well differ across cultures and yet the crucial role of subjective elements is unspecified in structuralist accounts (Brint, 1992; Emirbayer & Goodwin, 1994). These critiques do not dispute that relational measures and network analysis, in particular, offer powerful tools for conceptualizing social situations; they merely reject the notion that a nuanced account of culture and action can be framed purely in terms of the structure, rather than the content or meaning, of social relations.

Although we have seen that purely structural approaches to capturing cultural differences can be critiqued on empirical and theoretical grounds, there are other relational analyses that incorporate both the form and content of relations.[5] For example, many ethnographic scholars have characterized collectivist societies in terms of the *multiplexity* of relations, that is, the tendency to have two types of relationships with the same person such as a coworker who also is a relative. Studies of organizations in collectivist societies have pointed to the importance of relations that combine sentimental socioemotional content with pragmatic exchange of resources. For example, multiplexity has been noted in studies of relations among Japanese buyers and suppliers (Dore, 1983), in relations of Japanese employees with their supervisors (Rohlen, 1974), and in peer relations of African workers (Gluckman, 1967; Kapferer, 1969). Although these scholars have asserted that the multiplexity they observed is greater than that which would be found in comparable Western settings, we know of no previous studies that have rigorously tested whether multiplexity is higher in collectivist societies.

Another content-oriented area of relationship research focuses on the *affective* closeness or socio-emotional intensity of social relations. As noted earlier, studies of Latin cultural settings have stressed the high level of affectivity in relations

(Triandis et al., 1984). However, there are theoretical reasons to believe that affectivity is not always associated with collectivism. The classic comparison of the United States and Germany by Lewin (1948) argued that the more individualist North American cultural context allows closeness in friendships to be achieved more rapidly than in the German cultural context.

Yet another approach focuses on the duration of relations, linking collectivism to relations of high longevity. Comparative studies have found that North American respondents tend to have briefer friendships than those reported by Chinese respondents (Gudykunst, 1983). Although for a given individual the duration of relations might be associated with their affective closeness, model levels of duration and affectivity may not be associated across countries. Indeed, North American relations may become affectively close in part because norms permit one to exit quickly. Consistent with this picture of superficial or nonbinding friendship in the North American setting, studies have found that American students engage in briefer and more frequent social interactions (Wheeler et al., 1989).

In sum, although cultural differences cannot be reduced purely to the structure of social relations, analyses incorporating the form and content of relations may offer new insights into how individual behavior differs across cultures. Most likely, different relational constructs will be useful for distinguishing different cultures. What is needed is a level of analysis for conceptualizing culture that integrates the causal roles played by the external press of social relations and their subjective meanings.

AN INTEGRATED APPROACH: SOCIOCULTURAL SYSTEMS

Organizational scholars traditionally have approached the topic of culture carrying the biases of their academic disciplines, with psychologists tending to reduce culture to the subjective contents of individual thinking and sociologists tending to reduce culture to the properties of social structures and institutions. Increasingly, however, social scientists concerned with culture have called for a level of analysis that encompasses the imprint of a culture in the individual's thoughts as well as in the social structures surrounding the individual. On topics as diverse as social behavior, mental health, and education, researchers have looked for ways in which to frame hypotheses that integrate the roles of subjective and structural factors (for reviews, see Fiske, Kitayama, Markus, & Nisbett, 1998; Wertsh, del Rio, & Alvarez, 1995). Our own research attempts to integrate subjective and structural elements in an analysis of cultural influences on workplace interaction (Morris, Podolny, & Ariel, 1997, 1998a, 1998b). Our point of departure in developing this analysis was the work of Parsons (1951) on how social action is structured by systems of shared values and norms, although our assumptions, constructs, and methods are influenced by recent work in both the subjectivist and network structuralist traditions.

Before recounting the points made by Parsons (1951) on which we will draw, it is worth addressing the question of "Why Parsons?" Critiques of Parsons' project are well known, and by invoking selected Parsonsian constructs as a point of departure, we do not wish to imply an endorsement of all the features of Parsons' stance. Much like the culture and personality theorists, Parsons conceptualized values as internalized in childhood and as shared on a societywide basis. Not an empiricist, Parsons presented only illustrative anecdotes rather than systematic evidence for his claims. For decades, Parsons' work has been criticized for its highly consensual and functionalist view of values and for its lack of empirical underpinnings.[6] In our view, however, such objectionable aspects of the Parsons project do not undermine its singular contributions. To a greater extent than prior or subsequent theorists Parsons delineated the role of norms in interpersonal conduct. For Parsons, norms are standards that an individual, or "ego," relies on in judging how to act toward a given other person, or "alter." Proposals at this level of analysis can generate hypotheses about both specific subjective social values and specific features of social relations (although Parsons himself did not draw or test such predictions). Second, some of Parsons' descriptive claims about particular cultures strike us as promising ways in which to integrate observations by ethnographers and cross-cultural researchers.

Parsons' proposals about particular norms were framed within a pattern typology that results from answers to two dilemmas. The first dilemma, termed *universalism versus particularism,* centers on whether an ego should make decisions on the basis of general principles (i.e., criteria all actors would be expected to use in the situation) or on the basis of idiosyncratic aspects of the situation including aspects with meaning or relevance specific to an ego, an alter, and the web of surrounding relations. The second dilemma, termed *ascription versus achievement,* concerns whether to judge alters on the basis of who they are (i.e., the groups and categories to which they belong) or on the basis of what they do (i.e., their performances). Importantly, Parsons argued that answers to one dilemma are reached only in combination with answers to the other dilemma.[7] Four qualitatively different resolutions of these dilemmas were illustrated by Parsons in terms of four major cultural traditions, as follows:

1. The universalist-achievement orientation is exemplified by the prevailing normative standards for interpersonal conduct and pattern of behavior in the United States. Relative to other systems, an ego is expected to conduct behavior toward an alter in the way that serves the ego's interests without being greatly constrained by

the presence or absence of prior relations to the alter or by the social categories to which the alter belongs. In Parsons' (1951) idiom, treatment of another person is based on "performances independent of relational foci" (p. 183).

2. The particularistic-achievement orientation is exemplified by Chinese society. In contrast to scholars who have portrayed American and Chinese societies as cultural antipodes, Parsons (1951) regarded the two societies as similar in their orientation toward achievement. In both systems, an ego is strongly motivated to achieve success. However, unlike the American tradition of getting ahead by leaving or overturning the social order, the Confucian tradition requires achievement within a stable ordering of power relations: "achievement should . . . be focused on certain points of reference within the relational system of superiority-inferiority" (p. 195). A key determinant of an ego's action toward an alter, then, is whether the ego has an established hierarchical relation to the alter.

3. For Parsons (1951), German society served to illustrate a universalist-ascriptive system. In this system, an ego's treatment of an alter depends not so much on a direct relation to the alter as on the alter's formal position within an impersonal system of classification, that is, "on classificatory qualities, . . . on status rather than on specific achievements" (p. 192). Parsons argued that this type of system also involves a type of collectivist orientation, but the concern is for broader collectives that are defined universalistically (e.g., categories of occupation or nationality) rather than particularistically (e.g., the handful of alters with whom the ego has a relationship).

4. Finally, for Parsons (1951), Spanish culture exemplified the particularist-ascriptive social system. In this system, an actor's treatment of another is not structured by instrumental purposes or by bureaucratic categories; sociality is pursued as an end in itself. That is, "emphasis is thrown in the expressive direction" (p. 199). In short, this final cultural system centers on concern for a particularistically defined collective (e.g., one's circle of friends) that carries with it a social system of affectively close relationships.

The forgoing review of Parsons' (1951) descriptions of interpersonal interaction in North American, Chinese, German, and Spanish settings illustrates the level of analysis at which we wish to work. Although Parsonsian ideas have been out of favor during the past several decades, there are a few scholars who have worked to refine this level of analysis. Contrary to Parsons' emphasis on abstract values, Garfinkel (1967) argued that, although abstract cultural values might exist, they are not the proximal causes of social behavior; more specific, concrete subjective rules are at work. Indeed, what we find most valuable in Parsons are the more concrete norms or standards for behavior. Contrary to Parsons' notion that normative systems are internalized in childhood and exist in a societywide equilibrium, Swidler (1986) argued that consensus of values and patterns of relations arise and exist within delimited contexts of adult life. This argument is in keeping with the Parsonsian assumption that systematicity arises not through the pressure for cognitive consistency in an individual's beliefs but rather through the pressure for complementarity of interaction within a social circle.

How are norms developed within a specific social context? Fiske (1991) argued that, across cultures, the norms governing particular social contexts can be seen as constructed from the elements of basic models of social relations such as those characterizing markets, hierarchies, and friendships. For a given social context such as the workplace, cultural traditions dictate how these more basic norms are enacted. This is not to say that all of the workplaces in a given society will develop an identical normative system. On the contrary, these systems will vary depending on particular aspects of the social context such as the organizational structure and the nature of the work. In addition, it is likely that certain norms will prevail in certain types of workplaces regardless of the country; for example, authority norms are more likely to prevail in a military regiment than in an artist's cooperative. Nevertheless, it still is possible that country differences exist when other factors are held constant. In the next section, we state predictions about ceteris paribus country differences. We report tests of these predictions in an international organization that deliberately holds formal structure and work tasks constant across different countries of operation.

A FOURFOLD PROPOSAL

Our level of analysis reflects revised conceptions of the relations among culture, norms, and behavior. We suggest that coordinated workplace interaction requires a system of norms governing interpersonal behavior and that national culture determines which norms are carried into the workplace. Depending on the normative system that is established, workplace relations resemble those in a market, a family, or another basic arena of social interaction. Importantly, these normative systems should be manifest both in subjective *social values* about self and others at work and in the properties of *social relations* in the workplace. We follow Parsons in offering a comparative description of North American, Chinese, German, and Spanish systems. Unlike Parsons, we do not regard these cultural settings as exemplifying four basic types of social systems. They are merely four of many cultural traditions that differ in the norms enacted in the workplace. Accordingly, we label each proposed system in terms of its historical grounding.

In developing the four proposals, we start with ethnographic findings to substantiate our description of the norms emphasized in each system. Then, we state predictions in terms of specific social values identified in recent work on subjective culture (Triandis & Gelfand, 1998) and in terms of the properties of social relations. These are ceteris paribus predictions about the norms that characterize work relations within particular cultural traditions. As we shall see, these predictions depart from those of the traditional subjectivist argument that countries can be arrayed on a unidimensional individualism-collectivism dimension. These predictions also depart from those of the structuralist argument that countries vary chiefly in terms of the pure form of social networks.

North American Work Relationships: Market Orientation

A feature of North American culture noted by many social observers and critics is the tendency for people to enter or exit social ties according to the market standard of whether it profits their individual achievement goals. The popular conception of "networking" captures how this norm plays out in the context of work organizations; one manages one's portfolio of relations toward the goal of upward mobility, seeking instrumental relations and necessarily making room for them by discarding old ones that have outlived their instrumental value (Baker, 1993). This view of networks as serving achievement goals is made explicit in a leading network theory of performance in organizations (Burt, 1992). From de Toqueville (1848/1945) onward, observers of American individualism have described the relative ease with which instrumental work relations can be established without the prior basis of friendship or family connection. Yet, individuals also are relatively willing to break ties to achieve success. From the time of the expanding frontier onward, the paragon of the successful American has been the person who leaves the group or disrupts the social order, and Americans remain relatively willing to reshape their social networks to pursue their professional goals (Bellah et al., 1985). The values that support these actions have been linked to the individualist Anglo-American economic, legal, and philosophical traditions (Lukes, 1973).

Now, let us consider what predictions follow from the proposal that North American employees tend to conduct their interpersonal relations according to a market norm. Which dimensions of social values and relations will be the ones on which North American employees stand out relative to those in other countries? With regard to social values, we can predict that economic individualism (i.e., the belief in achievement through social competition) should be highly endorsed by adherents of a market orientation. With regard to social relations, we can predict that the distinguishing features of a market system would be relations low in multiplexity (because instrumental exchange does not require a base of socioemotional connection) and low in duration (because people are free to exit relations).

Chinese Work Relationships: Familial Orientation

The norms of social interaction in Chinese organizations have been described as familial collectivism (Bond & Hwang, 1986). As in a family, employees make sacrifices for the group. Interestingly, however, this Confucian concern for harmony within the group does not preclude placing a strong value on achievement in competitive arenas (Hsu, 1953). Rather, it allows for achievement in part through relationships, such as filial relations to powerful members of the organization (Ho, 1976, 1998), and through the connections (or *guanxi*) that result from these ties (King, 1991). The structural manifestation of filial values in the workplace is suggested by research on Japanese organizations that have developed under similar Confucian influence. Compared to American employees who prefer same-status friends, Japanese managers seek higher status friends (Nakane, 1970; Nakao 1987). Studies of Chinese organizations have noted the care with which employees cultivate relations to those in power (Redding & Wong, 1986).

The predictions that follow from this Chinese familial orientation can be stated in contrast to those of the American market orientation. With regard to social values, Chinese employees may endorse achievement through competition in general; however, Chinese employees should not condone competition within the in-group. Rather, Chinese should endorse the sharing of resources within the in-group (i.e., economic collectivism). Finally, attitudes toward superordinates should be characterized by a filial loyalty and deference. With regard to properties of social relations, there should be a higher level of multiplexity and duration of relations because achievement is sought through a stable social structure. Also, filial patterns of interaction should be evident in close socioemotional ties to more highly ranked coworkers. These differences notwithstanding, it is important to note that the American and Chinese orientations have as much in common as they have in contrast. Both systems involve a concern with achievement and condone instrumental use of relations.

German Work Relationships: Legal-Bureaucratic Orientation

Many observers of the German cultural setting have observed that workplace relationships appear to be bounded by formal categories and rules (Borneman, 1992; Hall, 1990). A second observation is that affective expression in workplace relations is somewhat muted, or at least slow to develop, compared to that in other countries (Lewin, 1948). Both of these features might reflect that interactions are guided by an impersonal bureaucratic standard. In a system based on such a norm, an ego decides how to act toward a given alter according to the alter's formal status, not according to what the alter, as a specific individual, offers the ego (as in the market system) or according to the filial relation established between the ego and the alter (as in the familial system).

Given this characterization of German workplace relations as guided by a legal-bureaucratic norm, on what dimensions of social values or relations should German employees stand out? First, compared to the previous two systems, there is less reason to expect endorsement of the value of economic individualism or achievement through competition. Second, a central prediction of this system is a low level of expressive collectivism or empathetic involvement with the work group. Related to this second value prediction, there are straightforward predictions about properties of workplace relations. More specifically, informal relations should follow the lines of formally required interaction, as opposed to interaction that spans formal categories and ranks and that might result in other systems for reasons of opportunism, filial loyalty, or loyalty to old friends. Informal relations also should be characterized by lower affective intensity than in other systems.

Spanish Work Relationships: Affiliative Orientation

Anthropologists who have described work relations in the context of Spanish culture have pointed to strong norms of warm sociability toward the peer friendship group (Murphy, 1983). Similarly, as we have reviewed, psychological studies of social behavior have observed an expectation of warm and friendly behavior among coworkers (Triandis et al., 1984). It is instructive to consider how the implications of an affiliative norm differ from those of the legal-bureaucratic norm. In both systems, actions toward others depends on *who the other is* rather than *what the other does,* that is, on characteristics rather than performances. Yet, it is a different type of characteristic that matters. The German norm turns on characteristics of the alter that are defined by the formal organization (e.g., rank), whereas the Spanish norm turns on characteristics that are defined in relation to the ego (e.g., centrality in one's group of friends). The consequence is that whereas for German employees it is appropriate to adjust their friendship networks as their job titles change, for Spanish employees it is not normative to change their patterns of interaction after transfers or promotions.

Now, let us review the distinctive features of workplace social values and relations in the Spanish system of interaction based on an affiliative norm. With regard to subjective values, Spanish employees should stand out as high in expressive collectivism (affective involvement with coworkers) as well as high in economic collectivism (sharing resources with coworkers). With regard to features of social relations, the Spanish workplace should be characterized by relations high in affective intensity and in longevity. The duration of relations should be longer than in other systems because the relations are not delimited by instrumental purposes (as in the North American and Chinese systems) or by formal job categories (as in the German system).

A CONTROLLED CROSS-NATIONAL COMPARISON

The predictions that we have derived about North American, Chinese, German, and Spanish relations were tested in a survey of employees in an MNC, the Citibank consumer bank. Two policies of this firm make it particularly appropriate as a site to test our hypotheses. First, employees are hired from the locality in which the bank is situated. This policy of "embeddedness" allows for local norms of interaction to arise within the workplace even though the bank is a North American corporation. Second, there is a "global" strategy of standardizing organizational structure and products across countries. The formal organization chart and job categories, the physical layout of the bank branches, and the financial services provided and sold are similar across the retail operations in the different countries that we sampled. This policy of maximizing cross-country variation in the human composition of the organization while minimizing cross-country variation in the formal structure and practical content of work virtually creates a natural experiment for investigating the effects of cultural norms on workplace interaction.[8]

To test our hypotheses about the four countries, we gathered data from retail bank employees in North America, Hong Kong, Germany, and Spain. Within each country, we selected several areas for greatest equivalence on ecological variables such as city size and density. Within a selected region, all employees above the level of part-time tellers and below the level of area directors were sampled. Employees answered a survey that presented questions tapping social values and social relations. The survey was presented in the official language(s) of each country. Very high response rates were obtained. For full details about sampling, procedures, and materials, see Morris et al. (1997). In what follows, we review the measures of values and relations used to test our descriptive proposals about differences in the normative systems that arise in work settings in different countries.

Measures of social values drew primarily on the items developed with university student samples by Triandis and Gelfand (1998) to capture economic and expressive aspects of individualism and collectivism, although scale items were winnowed and altered to fit our research setting. Other items were adapted from other previous instruments or were generated based on suggestions by cultural informants to capture other dimensions of social values relevant to our hypotheses such as filial loyalty and deference to superordinates. For each dimension of interest, a scale could be formed from several items that clustered together in each of the four countries.

Measures of relational features were based on those in previous studies of employee relations (Podolny & Baron, 1997); however, the measures were refined and extended based on input from Chinese, Spanish, and German researchers to avoid disproportionate emphasis on issues salient in the United States. The survey asked employees to list (using code names) individuals with whom they interact during the work day. Specifically, respondents named the others with whom they share personal friendships, the others with whom they exchange task advice, and the others on whose "buy in" or power they depend. Our focus is on the first type of relation given that it is most open to volition and least determined by the structure of the organization. Respondents were asked questions about their relations to the alters, about attributes of the alters, and about the relations perceived among the alters. For each respondent, we calculated purely formal relational features such as the size and density of the friendship network. We also calculated the extent to which friendship ties overlapped the advice exchange network, the extent to which they overlapped the power-dependence network, and the extent to which they followed the vertical and horizontal lines of the formal organization. Finally, we calculated the average affectivity and longevity of each respondent's workplace friendships.

EVIDENCE FOR DISTINCT
SOCIOCULTURAL SYSTEMS

In this chapter, our goal is not to comprehensively review the results of our study but rather to highlight selected results relevant to our current argument that incorporating relational concepts enriches research on culture and organizational behavior. A first point is simply that the goal of incorporating relational contructs brings us to a fruitful level of analysis—normative systems that are constituted by a combination of subjective values and relation patterns. As we have argued, this level of analysis is particularly helpful in that it distinguishes different types of cultural collectivism that have been conflated in simpler frameworks. We illustrate this by stepping through the subjective and relational variables in our study and describing how the data fit predictions of our account and of previous accounts of cultural collectivism.

Subjective Value Measures

Let us begin by looking for evidence for our distinctions in employees' subjective values. Figure 3.1 shows the extent to which employees in the four countries endorsed *economic individualism* or a belief in achievement through social competition (e.g., measured by level of agreement with statements such as "Competition is the law of nature" and "Winning is everything"). As expected, employees in the North American setting adhered to this value more than did employees in the other three settings. The difference was not reliable in relation to Chinese employees; this is not unexpected given that Chinese norms favor competition in general but not within the in-group. Figure 3.1 also shows a specific *within-group competition* scale constructed from items referring specifically to competition within the circle of one's coworkers (e.g., "Without competition between colleagues, it is not possible to have a good company"). Here, as expected, employees in the North American setting were significantly higher than those in the Chinese setting as well as those in the German and Spanish settings. Overall, the results in Figure 3.1 establish the familiar point that Americans are extreme in endorsing competition, and the results also clarify that some types of competition are highly endorsed in Chinese culture as well.

Figure 3.2 reports several scales tapping different forms of collectivism or social solidarity. The first scale tapped solidarity and sentiment toward one's supervisor in the form of *filial loyalty* (e.g., "A good manager is more like a parent than a friend," "If my supervisor had a rivalry with another manager, it would be inappropriate for me to become friends with that manager"). As expected, Chinese employees endorsed this value dimension far more than did employees in the other three settings. Here, our analysis draws attention to a subjective value in Chinese collectivism that differs markedly from German and Spanish collectivism.

Also shown in Figure 3.2 are two dimensions that concern solidarity with the peer group of coworkers. These are two scales based on dimensions distinguished by Triandis and Gelfand (1998), which we label *expressive collectivism* (e.g., "The well-being of my coworkers is very important to me," "I feel good when I cooperate with others") and *economic collectivism* (e.g., "I like to share things and share advice with my 'neighbors' at work," "A group of coworkers should stick together, even if sacrifices are required"). Expressive collectivism was predicted to be relatively high in Spain, and our findings support this prediction. High levels of economic collectivism were expected in all three collectivist settings for different reasons. Economic collectivism was predicted in the Chinese setting as part of the syndrome of group-level achievement striving, in the German setting as part of the obligation felt to the fellow members of one's formal unit, and in the Spanish setting as a byproduct of one's intense affective connections to coworkers. These predictions received mixed support. As can be seen in Figure 3.2, Chinese and Spanish employees were significantly higher than Americans on economic collectivism; however, Germans were lowest of all, an unexpected result.

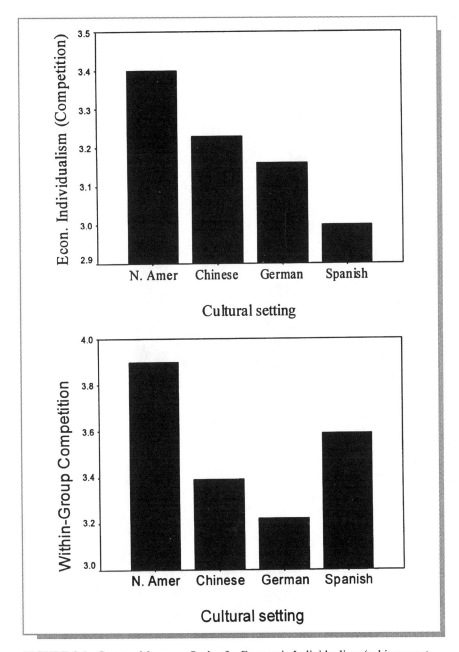

FIGURE 3.1. Country Means on Scales for Economic Individualism (achievement through competition) and Within-Group Competition

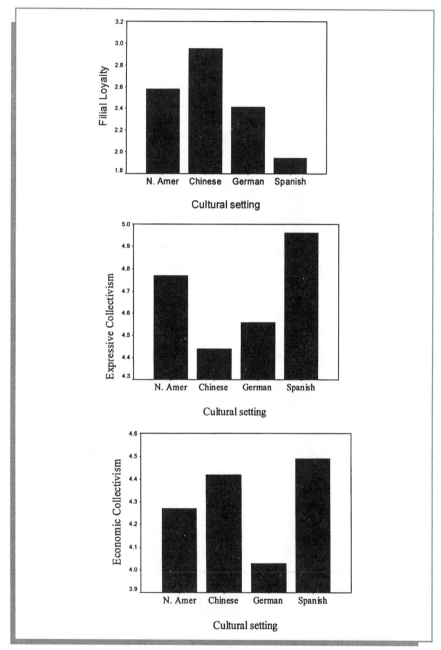

FIGURE 3.2. Country Means on Scales for Filial Loyalty to Superordinates, Expressive Collectivism (affective involvement with the in-group), and Economic Collectivism (belief in sharing with/sacrificing for the in-group)

Let us summarize how well our proposal stands after reviewing the evidence from subjective value scales. Although not fitting the data perfectly, our predictions fit better than those from the unidimensional individualism-collectivism framework (i.e., North American culture on the individualist pole, Germany and Spain near the center, and Chinese culture on the collectivist pole; Hofstede's [1980] construct). The clearest indication is that, looking across the different value measures, American and Chinese employees in our data are fairly similar to each other. This comports with the Parsonian notion that American and Chinese cultures are similar in important ways; they are not the antipodean opposites that sometimes have been depicted in research within the individualism-collectivism rubric. Where the evidence from subjective value variables falls short is in supporting our predictions about the German cultural setting. We predicted that German employees would be characterized by economic collectivism (sharing resources with the in-group) but not expressive collectivism (affective involvement). Counter to our predictions, German employees were very low in endorsing sacrifice for the in-group. It might be that their formal rule orientation means that they share resources with the in-group only to the extent that their jobs require and, hence, do not subjectively construe this as sharing but merely as proper rule following. On the other hand, it might be that our characterization of interpersonal norms in the German setting is out of date or inapplicable to the banking industry. If we had only subjective value measures, then we would not know. Fortunately, our characterization also can be tested with relational measures.

Relational Measures

In reviewing the profiles for each country on relational measures, we begin with the pure formal relational features and then move to features that involve form and content. As Figure 3.3 illustrates, there were no reliable differences across the four settings in the average *size* and *density* of friendship networks. In other words, there is no support for the notion that the differences between cultural settings can be reduced to pure social structure, that is, to the geometry of relations that surround individuals in different cultural settings.

Moving on to the relational features that involve form and content, we first assessed measures of the multiplexity or the overlap of differing relational contents. In particular, we assessed the proportion of the *advice-exchange* network with whom each respondent also shared friendships. Second, we assessed the proportion of the *power-dependence* network with whom the respondent shared friendships. As can be seen in Figure 3.4, these two measures show the same basic profile across the four settings. As expected, North American employees had less multiplex networks than did employees in the other three countries.

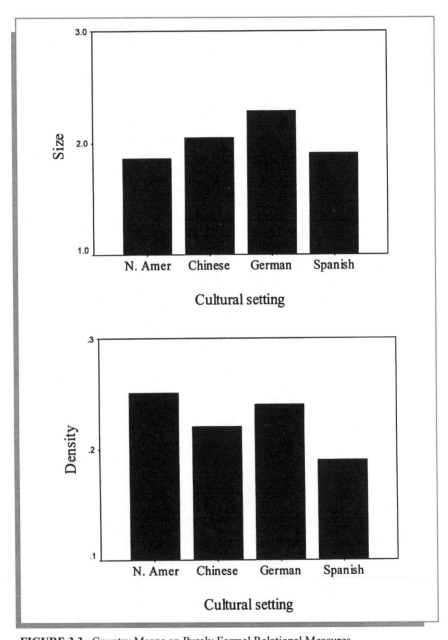

FIGURE 3.3. Country Means on Purely Formal Relational Measures

NOTE: Size of network is the number of people listed as personal friends at work. Density is the mean proportion of other friends to whom friends are connected. These were the only variables on which no country differences were reliable.

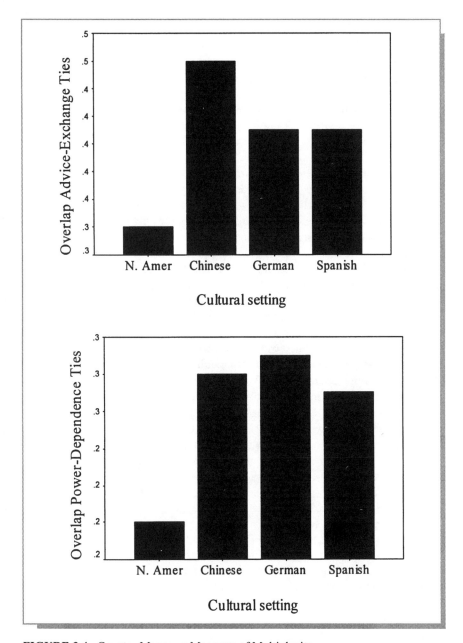

FIGURE 3.4. Country Means on Measures of Multiplexity

NOTE: These scores are the proportions of others in a respondent's advice-exchange ties and power-dependence ties for which the others also were listed as friends.

Whereas the aforementioned multiplexity measures capture the alignment of friendships with other types or contents of informal relations, we also derived predictions about the extent to which friendships follow the lines of the formal structure of the organization. A first measure, the average rank of friends relative to the respondent (–1 = *lower*, 0 = *same*, 1 = *higher*) was expected to reveal a more upward orientation among Chinese employees (because they seek filial ties with powerful coworkers). As can be seen in Figure 3.5, Chinese respondents did in fact have the most upward orientation, although they were not significantly higher than Spanish employees. The next measure was the proportion of *same-unit coworkers befriended,* which was predicted to be highest among German employees (because their friendships are bounded by formal categories). German employees did tend to count as friends a higher proportion of their work units than did North American and Chinese employees but not Spanish employees (middle panel of Figure 3.5). A final measure of the extent to which informal friendship followed the lines of formally prescribed interaction was a measure of how closely a respondent's interaction frequency corresponded with the officially required level. As predicted from the notion that German friendship relations follow the lines of the formal organization, we observed that German employees showed the least *interaction beyond that officially required* (bottom panel of Figure 3.5). On this last measure, the sharp contrast between German and Spanish employees is noteworthy; the affiliative norm in the Spanish setting results in nearly twice the level of nonrequired interactions with friends than does the legal-bureaucratic norm in the Chinese setting. Overall, the proposal that interpersonal relations follow the lines of formal categories and rules finds consistent support in the three measures. Compared to employees in other countries, German employees are oriented toward same-rank coworkers, had befriended a high proportion of the others within their units, and interacted with those others about as much as was officially required by their jobs.

Finally, we measured the average *affective closeness* and *duration* of the workplace friendships in the four settings. For these features, we had predicted that Spanish employees would stand out because of an affiliative norm that makes friendship an end in itself. As expected, we observed that Spanish employees had friendships that were significantly higher in affective closeness and in duration than were friendships of employees in the other three cultural settings (Figure 3.6). Importantly, these two variables did not have identical profiles. Consistent with Lewin's (1948) arguments, relative to German employees, North Americans had friendships that were affectively closer but not more enduring.

Overall, results from our measures of relational constructs greatly help in understanding the differences among the norms of workplace interaction in these four cultural settings. Interestingly, the purely formal features—size and density—did not vary. It might be that the intuitively appealing thesis that collec-

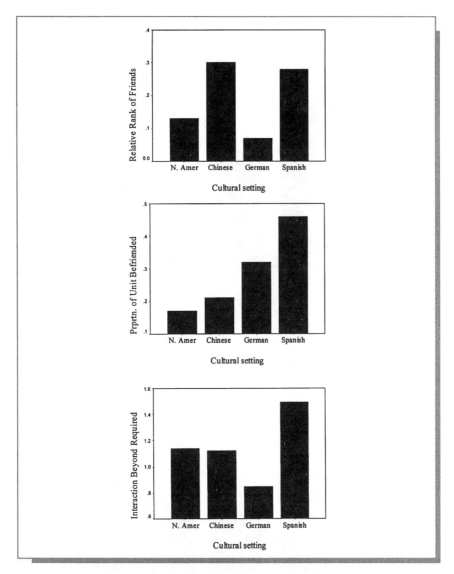

FIGURE 3.5. Country Means on Measures of the Alignment of Friendship Ties With the Formal Structure

NOTE: The measure depicted in the top panel averages a rating of the relative rank of alters (this is zero if the average friend is at the respondent's own rank and is positive if the average friend is at a higher rank). The measure depicted in the middle panel is the proportion of same-unit coworkers who are listed as friends. The measure depicted in the bottom panel is derived from the difference between a rating of level of interaction with an alter and a rating of the level officially required with that alter.

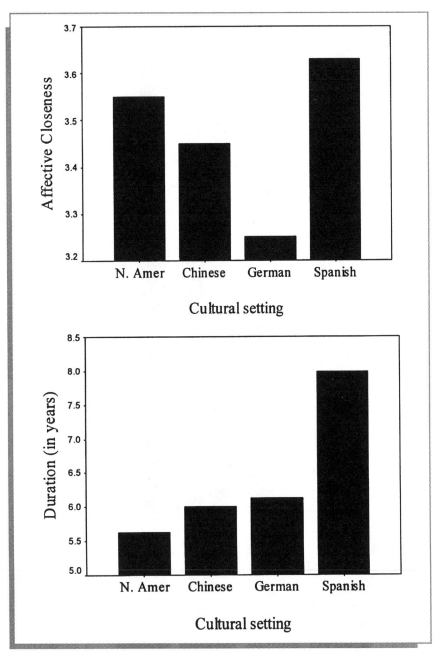

FIGURE 3.6. Country Means on Measures of Affective Closeness (1 = only as close as needed to work together, 5 = one of my closest personal friends) and Duration (in years)

tivism is associated with density (Fischer & Shavit, 1995) is true of friendships outside of the workplace, but the basic quantity and shape of informal interaction in this work setting is fairly constrained by the structure of the bank branches. Where cultural norms did shape interaction was in how friendships were oriented in relation to other types of informal ties (i.e., multiplexity), how friendships were oriented in relation to the formal structure, and the affective intensity of work friendships. What makes the relational evidence for distinct cultural norms impressive is that these different relation patterns had to be established against a common set of constraints—the physical layout of branches, the formal structure of command and control, and the job design. In a sense, these relational measures demonstrate what Giddens (1984) labeled as "structuration"—the creation and eventual crystallization of a structured system of interaction by individuals carrying norms and associated habits of interaction.

HOW VALUES AND RELATIONS INFLUENCE BEHAVIOR

Thus far, we have provided evidence for our descriptive proposals of four socio-cultural systems. However, we also want to briefly illustrate how these proposals generate predictions about outcomes that follow, that is, about individual behaviors that are important to the functioning of organizations. We limit our discussion to one outcome variable, but we use this to illustrate our view of the distinct roles that subjective values and relationship structures play in influencing individual behavior.

The outcome that we focus on in this discussion is the obligation that an employee feels to help others at work. The organizational literature on obligation contains a basic divide between theorists who maintain that employees are primarily obligated in *vertical* relations to those in power and those who emphasize an obligation in *horizontal* relations to peers. The emphasis on vertical relations is evident in Weber's (1947) description of bureaucratic organizations in post-World War I Germany, where obligation to the leader was based on the perceived legitimacy of the hierarchical system. This view concerning the direction of obligation persists in leading American theories of administration, although more emphasis is placed both on the instrumental rationality of obligation to those in power (Simon, 1945; Thompson, 1967) and on a social exchange process (Blau, 1955). A contrary tradition has argued that in many organizational contexts, the primary obligations lie in horizontal relations to peers rather than in vertical relations to authorities. Roethlisberger and Dickson (1939) observed that workers in a bank wiring room felt strong bonds of obligation to cohesive peer groups. The insight that the social rewards of horizontal relations provide an important source of work motivation and job satisfaction sparked the human relations school of management theory (e.g., Dalton, 1959).

Despite the large volume of research concerning obligation in vertical and horizontal relations, surprisingly little work has sought to establish the boundary conditions determining whether an employee's primary obligation will occur in vertical relations to those who provide power and opportunity or in horizontal relations to coworkers who provide friendship and socioemotional support. The major theoretical position on this question is Merton's (1969) argument that a focus on horizontal relations develops when an employee's original focus on vertical relations has been discouraged by frustrated mobility aspirations (Kanter, 1977). We have argued (Morris et al., 1997, 1998b) that such a description might be accurate for a dynamic that occurs within the North American normative context but not in all cultural contexts. In other words, whereas previous theorists have taken it as given that the default direction of employee obligation is toward those in power rather than toward peers, we suggest that this depends on the culturally bound system of norms.

The vertical orientation is consistent with the market norm in the North American setting, as well as with the familial norm in the Chinese setting, because social energies are directed toward the end of achievement. Moreover, the German legal-bureaucratic system, with its emphasis on formal status, also should lead to a vertical orientation of obligation. A different prediction, however, follows from the Spanish affiliative norm. Ethnographies of Spanish workplaces stress that honor obliges fulfilling obligations to the friendship clique but not necessarily requests from those in power (Gilmore, 1982, 1987). To illustrate, a recent ethnography of a blue-collar work group in Spain described a system in which it was normative to treat managerial requests with suspicion yet deplorable either to withhold a favor requested from within the peer group or to comply cheerlessly (Murphy, 1983). The significance of honor, loyalty, and friendship in determining obligation is echoed in descriptions of white-collar corporate settings (Alvarez & Cantos, 1994).[9]

In the four-country study that we have described, a measure of obligation to each alter was taken in a vignette tailored to the retail banking context that assessed the likelihood that the respondent would volunteer to help that alter. This variable allowed us to calculate the average level of obligation to the power network and the average level to the friendship network. Because our concern is comparative, we focused on the differential obligation to friends. Consistent with expectations, Spanish employees had a much greater differential obligation to friends than did employees in the other three settings (Morris et al., 1997). To check our understanding of this pattern of outcomes, we tested for evidence of mediating and moderating variables.

An influential strategy of analysis in the subjectivist tradition of cultural research is to test whether measures of cultural values mediate (or come between) nationality, on the one hand, and an outcome behavior, on the other. In the work of Leung and Bond (1984) on in-group favoritism or the work of Earley (1989) on social loafing, an important feature of the results were correlations between collectivism scores and the respective outcome variables.[10] Although dispositionally held general values and attitudes may not be the proximal causes of behavior, they should have a tighter association than more distil variables (e.g., country) that have a remote causal connection to most outcome behaviors of interest. We conducted a mediation analysis in our data and found that the country effect on obligation orientation is mediated by subjective values. That is, when our measures of individualism and collectivism are entered into a regression model simultaneously with the country dummy variables, they remain significant predictors, whereas the dummy variable for Spain no longer predicts differential obligation to the friendship network. A similar finding has emerged from another recent study of country differences in obligation (Cialdini, Wosinska, Barrett, Butner, & Gornik-Durose, 1998); hence, the dependent variable of obligation can be added to the list of behavioral tendencies that are influenced by individualist versus collectivist orientations.

Although the subjectivist tradition has succeeded in identifying values as mediators of country differences, the subjectivist approach has not been strong in identifying moderating variables. Even the most widely known studies of social and organizational behavior across cultures that take into account moderating factors (e.g., Earley, 1989; Leung & Bond, 1984) typically have been conducted in laboratory paradigms that bear only an abstract resemblance to the actual contexts of organizations. Within these laboratory paradigms, slight variations in procedures often have meant a failure to replicate patterns of cultural difference (Leung, 1997). One way in which to analyze this problem is to assert that the subjectivist tradition has not had very good tools for analyzing the moderating variables that really matter—the social contexts that condition the activation of subjective rules, ultimately resulting in culturally varying patterns of action in organizations.

The potential for fine-grained measurement of the social contexts that moderate individual action might be where relational variables make their largest contribution. Relational variables offer a way in which to measure the relevant social contexts that surround a particular action decision. Differences between normative systems should be sharper when the relevant moderating conditions are identified. Consider Employee A who is asked for a favor by a friend and whose friends are interlinked in a dense clique. Now, consider Employee B who is also asked for a favor by a friend but whose friends do not know each other. How will this difference in density of their networks affect the intensity obligation felt? Does this, in turn, vary as a function of the surrounding normative system?

Following from our analysis of why Spanish employees are differentially obligated to the friendship network, we reasoned that in the Spanish context,

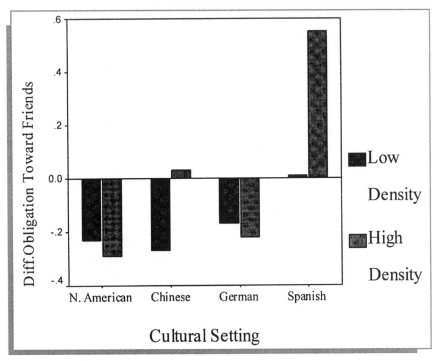

FIGURE 3.7. Differential Obligation to Friendship Network as a Function of
Cultural Setting and the Density Level of the Respondent's Network
NOTE: This figure illustrates an interaction effect in which high density of the friendship
network created a greater differential obligation to the friendship network in the Spanish
setting but not in the other cultural settings.

where doing a favor for a friend is a matter of honor, dense networks should
increase the pressure of obligation to friends. By contrast, if American employees are obligated to friends primarily as a function of how the friends help their
own advancement, then Americans conversely may feel less obligated in a dense
network than in a network that is less dense (in Burt's [1992] terms, a non-
redundant network). As can be seen in Figure 3.7, this predicted interaction pattern was observed. High friendship density makes Spanish employees more
oriented to the friendship network, whereas Americans move nonsignificantly
in the opposite direction. When this interaction effect is entered into a regression
model with the main effect of country, the interaction remains significant but
the main effect does not. Hence, the interaction underlies the main effect. This
example illustrates that measures of relational structure pick up situational variables that make a great deal of difference in behavioral responses. Understanding
these situations allows a way in which to better contextualize findings about
cultural differences.

CONCLUSION

This chapter has presented selected findings from a research program investigating the proposal that cultural differences in organizational behavior can be understood in terms of normative systems of interpersonal interaction, that is, systems constituted by subjective values and by relational structures. Although this level of analysis is less parsimonious than a purely subjectivist or purely structuralist approach, it offers a more comprehensive understanding of how culture influences individual behavior. Whereas the subjectivist and structuralist approaches have been regarded as rivals, we argue that neither suffices alone. Moreover, the two approaches complement each other. Subjective measures pick up the individual traits and cognitive structures that serve as mechanisms in the influences of macro-level variables such as country. Relational measures identify micro-level social contexts that condition these influences (for a similar use of subjective and relational variables in predicting financial risk taking, see Hsee & Weber, 1999; in predicting justice perceptions, see Morris & Leung, 2000).

A final benefit of this sort of cross-cultural study is that it reveals cultural assumptions that are implicit in formal academic theories of organizational behavior. We have argued that the assumption of Merton and others about the default direction of obligation should be understood as culturally bound. More generally, there might be many assumptions in organizational theory (OT) that are valid in the cultures where these theories were developed but not elsewhere. Consider Weber's observations of the "modern" bureaucratic form in post-World War I German hospitals, where "all purely personal . . . emotional elements" are eliminated in the interactions among employees (quoted in Gerth & Mills, 1958, pp. 215-216). Given our findings concerning affectivity, one must wonder whether this description, so pivotal in the intellectual history of OT, would have arisen if Weber had made his observations in a Spanish hospital rather than in a German hospital.

NOTES

1. We use the term *structuralism* the way in which it is used by sociologists (e.g., Mayhew), not the way in which it is used by cognitive anthropologists (e.g., Levi-Strauss). That is, we refer to the view that action is caused by social structures, not the view that thinking is shaped by cognitive structures.

2. This is not to deny that these same individuals adhere to differentiated subcultures and have other cultural alliances and identities that are fragmented and context dependent rather than unified and context general (Martin, 1992).

3. Triandis and colleagues referred to these dimensions as *vertical* and *horizontal* aspects. This terminology would be confusing in the current context, so we substitute the more concrete descriptors *economic* and *expressive,* respectively.

4. Our discussion focuses on analyses of egocentric networks in which the unique network surrounding each individual is the unit of analysis because this method is mostly amenable to cross-cultural comparisons. Another approach to network analysis is to study all relations that exist within a group of people. One issue with this method is the boundary problem of choosing which group to study. Given that the in-group/out-group boundary might differ across cultures, this seems to particularly complicate analyses of collectivism. Another issue with this method is that a near perfect response rate is required. Some of the methods that researchers use when there are missing data probably are differentially valid across cultures. For example, one technique is to symmetrize relations, that is, to infer that A has a particular relation to B and that B has the same relation to A (Scott, 1991). Although the assumption underlying this technique might approach accuracy in egalitarian societies, it is highly problematic in hierarchical societies that foster asymmetric relations such as the exchange of filial loyalty for paternal protection (Ho, 1976, 1998).

5. Much of this research is rooted less in network analysis than in the more processual approach to relationships taken by researchers in communications and psychology (for a review, see Duck, West, & Acitelli, 1997).

6. Descriptive shortcoming might be excused by the fact that Parsons was primarily attempting a contribution to meta-theory; his writings consist chiefly of a priori arguments concerning dilemmas between particular social values that limit the possible combinations of values that could function in homeostasis as a social system. Yet, even scholars who have appreciated his descriptive proposals about particular value systems have balked at his insistence on the grander system of systems that encompasses these proposals, which posits inexorable dilemmas and trade-offs by the dozen that would seem to arbitrarily limit the possible forms of social systems and, hence, the possible directions of social and cultural diversity.

7. Although Parsons' model often is portrayed as a dimensional analysis, he argued very clearly that these dilemmas are not to be interpreted as independent dimensions. Certain patterns of answers to these dilemmas arise as cultural forms, but not all combinations are possible, and a culture's answer to one dilemma cannot be understood in isolation from its answer to the other dilemma. For example, interwoven with patterns of answers to these first two dilemmas are answers to the dilemma of affectivity—whether to express and act on affective reactions to others or to control one's affective reactions. Parsons discussed three other axes, or what he called "pattern variables," but he integrated these other axes into his discussion of the four-category typology that arises from the intersection of these two dominant axes.

8. The "experiment" provides a conservative test of the hypotheses, of course, because cultural differences are diluted by the Citibank organizational culture. If a pattern of predicted cultural differences can be observed in the contrast between employees of Citibank Hong Kong and Citibank Spain, then we would expect the same differences to be much sharper in the contrast between two completely local firms.

9. Although we know of no previous comparative studies of networks and obligations in the workplace, results from studies of networks and social support also are somewhat consistent with our argument concerning the primacy of obligation to the friendship network in Latin contexts. Hollinger and Haller (1990) found that in the Latin country in their data (Italy), expectations with regard to friends' obligations were not conditional on

the kins' proximity. This differed from the pattern in other countries, where the obligation of friends was inversely related to the proximity of kin.

10. These correlations tend to be weak, but this is reasonable to expect given that the social attitudes are measured at such a high level of generality. The specific action rules that determine a given decision about, for example, allocation of resources or effort are much narrower than cultural value dimensions.

REFERENCES

Alvarez, J. L., & Cantos, C. M. (1994). From escapism to resented conformity: Market economies and modern organizations in Spanish literature. In B. Czarniawska-Joerges & P. G. de Monthoux (Eds.), *Good novels, better management: Reading organizational realities*. Chur, Switzerland: Harwood.

Baker, W. (1993). *Networking smart: How to build relationships for personal and organizational success*. New York: McGraw-Hill.

Bellah, R. N., Madsen, R., Sullivan, W. M., Swidler, A., & Tipton, S. M. (1985). *Habits of the heart: Individualism and commitment in American life*. Berkeley: University of California Press.

Benedict, R. (1934). Continuities and discontinuities in cultural conditioning. *Psychiatry, 1*, 161-167.

Blau, P. M. (1955). *The dynamics of bureaucracy: A study of interpersonal relationships in two government agencies*. Chicago: University of Chicago Press.

Bond, M. H., & Hwang, K. K. (1986). The social psychology of Chinese people. In M. H. Bond (Ed.), *The psychology of the Chinese people* (pp. 213-266). Hong Kong: Oxford University Press.

Borneman, J. (1992). *Belonging in the two Berlins: Kin, state, nation*. Cambridge, UK: Cambridge University Press.

Brint, S. (1992). Hidden meanings: Cultural content and context in Harrison White's structural sociology. *Sociological Theory, 10*, 194-208.

Burt, R. (1992). *Structural holes: The social structure of competition*. Cambridge, MA: Harvard University Press.

Cantril, H. (1965). *The pattern of human concerns*. New Brunswick, NJ: Rutgers University Press.

Cialdini, R. B., Wosinska, W., Barrett, D. W., Butner, J., & Gornik-Durose, M. (1998). *Compliance with a request in two cultures: The differential influence of social proof and commitment/consistency on collectivists and individualists*. Unpublished manuscript, Arizona State University, Department of Psychology.

Dalton, M. (1959). *Men who manage*. New York: John Wiley.

de Toqueville, A. (1945). *Democracy in America*. New York: Vintage Books. (Originally published in 1848)

Diaz-Guerrero, R. (1967). *Psychology of the Mexican*. Austin: University of Texas Press.

Doi, L. T. (1962). Amae: A key concept for understanding Japanese personality structure. In R. J. Smith & R. K. Beardsley (Eds.), *Japanese culture: Its development and characteristics*. Chicago: Aldine.

Dore, R. (1983). Goodwill and the spirit of market capitalism. *British Journal of Sociology, 34,* 459-482.

Duck, S., West, L., & Acitelli, L. (1997). Sewing the field: The tapestry of relationships in life and research. In S. W. Duck (Ed.), *Handbook of personal relationships* (2nd ed., pp. 1-23). Chichester, UK: Wiley.

Durkheim, E. (1933). *The division of labor in society.* New York: Free Press. (Originally published in 1893)

Durkheim, E. (1951). *Suicide.* New York: Free Press. (Originally published in 1897)

Earley, P. C. (1989). Social loafing and collectivism: A comparison of the United States and the People's Republic of China. *Administrative Science Quarterly, 34,* 565-581.

Earley, P. C. (1994). Self or group? Cultural effects of training on self-efficacy and performance. *Administrative Science Quarterly, 39,* 89-117.

Emerson, R. M. (1962). Power-dependence relations. *American Sociological Review, 27,* 31-40.

Emirbayer, M., & Goodwin, J. (1994). Network analysis, culture, and the problem of agency. *American Journal of Sociology, 99,* 1411-1454.

Erez, M., & Earley, P. C. (1993). *Culture, self-identity, and work.* New York: Oxford University Press.

Fischer, C. S., & Shavit, Y. (1995). National differences in network density: Israel and the United States. *Social Networks, 17,* 129-145.

Fiske, A. P. (1991). *Structures of social life: The four elementary forms of human relations.* New York: Free Press.

Fiske, A. P., Kitayama, S., Markus, H. R., & Nisbett, R. E. (1998). The cultural matrix of social psychology. In D. T. Gilbert, S. T. Fiske, & G. Lindzey (Eds.), *Handbook of social psychology* (4th ed.). Mahwah, NJ: Lawrence Erlbaum.

Garfinkel, H. (1967). *Studies in ethnomethodology.* Englewood Cliffs, NJ: Prentice Hall.

Geertz. C. (1976). From the native's point of view: On the nature of anthropological understanding. In K. Basso & H. Selby (Eds.), *Meaning in anthropology* (pp. 221-237). Albuquerque: University of New Mexico Press.

Gerth, H., & Mills, C. W. (1958). *From Max Weber: Essays in sociology.* New York: Oxford University Press.

Giddens, A. (1984). *The constitution of society.* Oxford, UK: Polity.

Gilmore, D. D. (1982). Anthropology of the Mediterranean area. *Annual Reviews in Anthropology, 11,* 170-205.

Gilmore, D. D. (1987). Honor, honesty, shame: Male status in contemporary Andalusia. In D. D. Gilmore (Ed.), *Honor and shame and the unity of the Mediterranean.* Washington, DC: American Anthropological Association.

Gluckman, M. (1967). *The judicial process among the Barotse of northern Rhodesia.* Manchester, UK: Manchester University Press.

Gorer, G. (1943). Themes in Japanese culture. *New York Academy of Sciences, 5,* 106-124.

Gross, J. L., & Raynor, S. (1985). *Measuring culture.* New York: Columbia University Press.

Gudykunst, W. B. (1983). *International communication theory.* Beverly Hills, CA: Sage.

Hall, E. T. (1990). *Understanding cultural differences.* Yarmouth, ME: Intercultural Press.

Ho, D. Y. F. (1976). On the concept of face. *American Journal of Sociology, 81,* 867-884.

Ho, D. Y. F. (1998). Interpersonal relationships and relationship dominance: An analysis based on methodological relationism. *Asian Journal of Social Psychology, 1,* 1-16.

Ho, D. Y. F., & Chiu, C. Y. (1994). Component ideas of individualism, collectivism, and social organization: An application in the study of Chinese culture. In M. Kim, H. C. Triandis, C. Kagitcibasi, S. C. Choi, & G. Yoon (Eds.), *Individualism and collectivism: Theory, method, and application.* Thousand Oaks, CA: Sage.

Hofstede, G. (1980). *Culture's consequences: International differences in work-related values.* Beverly Hills, CA: Sage.

Hofstede, G. (1991). *Culture and organizations.* Newbury Park, CA: Sage.

Hollinger, F., & Haller, M. (1990). Kinship and social networks in modern societies: A cross-cultural comparison among seven nations. *European Sociological Review, 6,* 103-124.

Hsee, C., & Weber, E. U. (1999). Cross-national differences in risk preference and lay predictions. *Journal of Behavioral Decision Making, 12,* 165-179.

Hsu, F. L. K. (1953). *Americans and Chinese: Two ways of life.* New York: Abelard-Schuman.

Hsu, F. L. K. (1985). The self in cross-cultural perspective. In A. J. Marsella, G. De Vos, & F. L. K. Hsu (Eds.), *Culture and self* (pp. 24-55). New York: Tavistock.

Ibarra, H. (1997). Paving an alternative route: Gender differences in managerial networks. *Social Psychology Quarterly, 60,* 91-102.

Inkeles, A. (1960). Industrial man: The relation of status to experience, perception, and value. *American Journal of Sociology, 66,* 1-31.

Inkeles, A. (1978). National differences in individual modernity. *Comparative Studies in Sociology, 1,* 47-72.

Inkeles, A., & Levinson, D. (1954). National character: The study of modal personality and social systems. In G. Lindzey (Ed.), *Handbook of social psychology* (pp. 975-1020). Reading, MA: Addison-Wesley.

Kanter, R. M. (1977). *Men and women of the corporation.* New York: Basic Books.

Kapferer, B. (1969). Norms and the manipulation of work rules. In J. C. Mitchell (Ed.), *Social networks in urban situations: Analyses of personal relationships in Central African towns.* Manchester, UK: University of Manchester Press.

Kardiner, A. (1939). *The individual and his society.* New York: Columbia University Press.

Kashima, Y., Yamaguchi, S., Kim, U., Choi, S-C., Gelfand, M., & Yuki, M. (1995). Culture, gender, and self: A perspective from individualism-collectivism research. *Journal of Personality and Social Psychology, 69,* 935-937.

Keesing, R. M. (1974). Theories of culture. *Annual Review of Anthropology, 3,* 73-97.

King, A. Y. C. (1991). Kuan-hsi and network building: A sociological interpretation. *Daedalus, 120,* 63-84.

Leung, K. (1987). Some determinants of reactions to procedural models for conflict resolution: A cross-national study. *Journal of Personality and Social Psychology, 5,* 898-908.

Leung, K. (1997). Negotiation and reward allocations across cultures. In P. C. Earley & Y. M. Erez (Eds.), *New perspectives on international industrial/organizational psychology* (pp. 640-675). San Francisco: Jossey-Bass.

Leung, K., & Bond, M. H. (1984). The impact of cultural collectivism on reward allocation. *Journal of Personality and Social Psychology, 47,* 793-804.

Lewin, K. (1948). Social-psychological differences between the United States and Germany. In G. W. Lewin (Ed.), *Resolving social conflicts.* London: Souvenir.

Lincoln, J. R. (1982). Intra- (and inter-) organizational networks. *Research in the Sociology of Organizations, 1,* 1-38.

Lindsley, S. L., & Braithwaite, C. A. (1996). You should "wear a mask": Facework norms in cultural and intercultural conflict in maquiladoras. *International Journal of Intercultural Relations, 20,* 199-225.

Lonner, W. J., & Adamopoulos, J. (1997). Culture as antecedent to behavior. In J. W. Berry, Y. H. Poortinga, & J. Pandey (Eds.), *Handbook of cross-cultural psychology,* Vol. 1: *Theory and method* (pp. 43-83). Boston: Allyn & Bacon.

Lukes, S. (1967). Alienation and anomie. In P. Laslett & W. Runciman (Eds.), *Philosophy, politics, and society* (3rd ed., pp. 134-156). Oxford, UK: Basil Blackwell.

Lukes, S. (1973). Types of individualism. In P. P. Wiener (Ed.), *Dictionary of the history of ideas: Studies of selected pivotal ideas* (Vol. 2, pp. 594-604). New York: Scribner.

Martin, J. (1992). *Culture in organizations: Three perspectives.* New York: Oxford University Press.

Marx, K. (1972). Economic and philosophical manuscripts of 1844. In R. C. Tucker (Ed.), *The Marx-Engel reader* (pp. 53-103). New York: Norton. (Originally published in 1844)

Mayhew, B. (1980). Structuralism versus individualism: Shadowboxing in the dark. *Social Forces, 59,* 586-596.

Mayhew, B. H., & Levinger, R. L. (1976). Size and the density of interaction in human aggregates. *American Journal of Sociology, 82,* 86-110.

Mead, M. (1935). *Sex and temperament in three primitive societies.* New York: William Morrow.

Merton, R. K. (1969). *Social theory and social structure.* New York: Free Press.

Morris, M. W., & Leung, K. (2000). Justice for all? Progress in research on cultural variation in the psychology of distributive and procedural justice. *Applied Psychology: An International Review, 49,* 100-132.

Morris, M. W., & Peng, K. (1994). Culture and cause: American and Chinese attributions for social and physical events. *Journal of Personality and Social Psychology, 67,* 949-971.

Morris, M. W., Podolny, J. M., & Ariel, S. (1997, November). *The ties that bind in different cultures: A cross-national comparison of the determinants of employee obligations to coworkers.* Paper presented at the Citibank Behavioral Research Council Conference, New York.

Morris, M. W., Podolny, J. M., & Ariel, S. (1998b). *Culture and normative systems of informal interaction at work: A study of North American, Chinese, German, and*

Spanish operations of a multinational consumer bank. Unpublished manuscript, Stanford University, Graduate School of Business.

Morris, M. W., Podolny, J. M., & Ariel, S. (1998c). *Culture and the orientation of obligation among employees in an international financial institution.* Unpublished manuscript, Stanford University, Graduate School of Business.

Murphy, M. (1983). Coming of age in Seville. *Journal of Anthropological Research, 39,* 376-392.

Nakane, C. 1970. *Japanese society.* Berkeley: University of California Press.

Nakao, K. (1987). Analyzing sociometric preferences: An example of Japanese and U.S. business groups. *Journal of Social Behavior and Personality, 2,* 523-534.

Osgood, C. E. (1964). Semantic differential technique in the comparative study of cultures. *American Anthropologist, 66,* 171-200.

Parsons, T. (1951). *The social system.* New York: Free Press.

Pascale, R. T., & Athos, A. G. (1981). *The art of Japanese management.* New York: Simon & Schuster.

Podolny, J. M., & Baron, J. N. (1997). Resources and relationships: Social networks and mobility in the workplace. *American Sociological Review, 62,* 673-693.

Pye, L. (1982). *Chinese commercial negotiation style.* Cambridge, MA: Oelgeschlager, Gunn, & Hain.

Redding, G., & Wong, G. Y. Y. (1986). The psychology of Chinese organizational behavior. In M. H. Bond (Ed.), *The psychology of the Chinese people* (pp. 213-266). Hong Kong: Oxford University Press.

Roethlisberger, F. J., & Dickson, W. (1939). *Management and the worker.* Cambridge, MA: Harvard University Press.

Rohlen, T. (1974). *For harmony and strength: Japanese white-collar organization in anthropological perspective.* Berkeley: University of California Press.

Ronen, S. (1986). *Comparative management and multinational management.* New York: John Wiley.

Ronen, S., & Shenkar, O. (1985). Clustering countries on attitudinal dimensions: A review and synthesis, *Academy of Management Review, 10,* 435-454.

Ross, L. D., & Nisbett, R. E. (1991). *The person and the situation: Perspectives of social psychology.* New York: McGraw-Hill.

Sanchez-Burks, J., Nisbett, R. E., & Ybarra, O. (1998). *Relational schemas, cultural styles, and prejudice against outgroups.* Unpublished manuscript, University of Michigan, Department of Psychology.

Schwartz, S. H. (1994). Beyond individualism/collectivism: New cultural dimensions of values. In U. Kim, H. C. Triandis, & C. Kagitcibasi (Eds.), *Individualism and collectivism: Theory, methods, and application* (pp. 85-119). Thousand Oaks, CA: Sage.

Scott, J. (1991). *Social network analysis: A handbook.* Newbury Park, CA: Sage.

Simon, H. (1945). *Administrative behavior: A study of decision making processes in administrative organization.* New York: Macmillan.

Singelis, T. M., Triandis, H. C., Bhawuk, D., & Gelfand, M. J. (1995). Horizontal and vertical dimensions of individualism and collectivism: A theoretical and measurement refinement. *Cross-Cultural Research, 29,* 240-275.

Swidler, A. (1986). Culture in action: Symbols and strategies. *American Sociological Review, 51,* 273-286.

Thompson, J. (1967). *Organizations in action: Social science bases of administrative theory.* New York: McGraw-Hill.

Tonnies, F. (1957). *Community and society.* New Brunswick, NJ: Transaction Books. (Originally published in 1887)

Triandis, H. C. (1967). Interpersonal relationships in international organizations. *Journal of Organizational Behavior and Human Performance, 2,* 26-55.

Triandis, H. C. (1972). *The analysis of subjective culture.* New York: John Wiley.

Triandis, H. C. (1995). *Individualism and collectivism.* Boulder, CO: Westview.

Triandis, H. C., & Gelfand, M. J. (1998). Converging measurement of horizontal and vertical individualism and collectivism. *Journal of Personality and Social Psychology, 74,* 118-128.

Triandis, H. C., Leung, K., Villareal, M., & Clark, F. L. (1985). Allocentric vs. idiocentric tendencies: Convergent and discriminant validation. *Journal of Research in Personality, 19,* 395-415.

Triandis, H. C., Marin, G., Lisansky, J., & Betancourt, H. (1984). Simpatia as a cultural script of Hispanics. *Journal of Personality and Social Psychology, 47,* 1363-1375.

Triandis, H. C., McCusker,, C., & Hui, C. H. (1990). Multimethod probes of individualism and collectivism. *Journal of Personality and Social Psychology, 59,* 1006-1020.

Weber, M. (1947). *The theory of social and economic organization.* New York: Oxford University Press.

Weber, M. (1963). *The sociology of religion.* Boston: Beacon. (Originally published in 1922)

Wertsh, J. V., del Rio, P., & Alvarez, A. (1995). *Sociocultural studies of mind.* Cambridge, UK: Cambridge University Press.

Wheeler, L., Reis, H. T., & Bond, M. H. (1989). Collectivism-individualism in everyday life: The Middle Kingdom and the melting pot. *Journal of Personality and Social Psychology, 57,* 79-86.

White, H. C., Boorman, S. A., & Breiger, R. L. (1976). Social structure from multiple networks. *American Journal of Sociology, 81.*

Wrong, D. H. (1961). The oversocialized conception of man in modern sociology. *American Sociological Review, 42,* 32-56.

chapter 4

The Cultural Metaphor

A Grounded Method for Analyzing National Cultures

MARTIN J. GANNON
PINO G. AUDIA

There are several ways in which to study national cultures including reviewing a nation's literature and art, ethnography, and cross-cultural surveys either of values such as individualism and assertiveness or of cultural orientations toward phenomena such as time and space. This chapter describes a new grounded method, the *cultural metaphor,* for analyzing national cultures. A cultural metaphor is a unique or very distinctive institution, phenomenon, or activity of a nation's culture that most or all of its citizens consider to be very important and with which they identify closely (e.g., the Swedish *stuga* or unadorned summer house). Typically, three to six characteristics of the cultural metaphor are employed to describe the culture of a nation. A *grounded* cultural metaphor serves as a supplement to, and sometimes as an alternative to, the dimensional approach, which forces comparisons between national cultures but does not provide a thick description, thus providing breadth but not depth of understanding. In this sense, we believe that the dimensional approach is extremely useful but incomplete. Essentially, we feel that a visitor to another culture needs a general frame of reference that can serve as an initial guide or map if he or she is to see the culture from the perspective of insiders, and cultural metaphors constitute such guides. They also are mnemonic devices that are relatively easy to remember and use.

For many years, metaphors were viewed simply as literary devices. However, a more broadened study of metaphors suggests that our conceptual system is largely metaphorical. Lakoff and Johnson (1980) were leaders in this broader approach, and they summarized their thesis quite boldly: "If we are right in suggesting that our conceptual system is largely metaphorical, then the way we think, what we experience, and what we do every day is very much a matter of metaphor" (p. 1). An equally fresh perspective was provided by Ortony (1975), who aptly titled his seminal article "Why Metaphors Are Necessary and Not Just Nice."

Some cultural anthropologists have employed metaphors as conceptual rather than literary devices quite effectively. Following the lead of earlier anthropologists, Hall (1959) defined culture as communication, but in a specific manner, and he likened culture to music in that if one knows the musical score or the method of communication in a culture, it is easy to understand the culture (see also Hall & Hall, 1990). In fact, Hall's influential work on low-context versus high-context communication was built around metaphors rather than scientific hypotheses deduced from a theory, as the titles of some of his books indicate—*The Hidden Dimension* (Hall, 1966), or his focus on space, and *The Dance of Life* (Hall, 1983), or his focus on time.

However, it was Geertz (1973) who authored the pioneering study of using metaphors as conceptual systems. Through a set of improbable but fascinating situational factors, he studied 500 Balinese cockfights both ethnographically and statistically, and he demonstrated convincingly that the Balinese cockfight represents the hidden culture of Bali, particularly the male culture. (For other anthropological perspectives on using the metaphor as a conceptual device, see Fernandez, 1991.)

We designed cultural metaphors specifically to describe the culture of one nation rather than one group within a nation or across two or more nations. At times, it has taken us several years to identify a cultural metaphor for even one nation, but we believe that doing so is important, if not critical. If citizens of a nation do not possess at least one institution, phenomenon, or activity with which most of them can identify, it might well be that no national culture exists, in which case the bonds holding individuals and groups together probably are very weak.

In this chapter, we first describe the grounded theory method and then show how it was tailored to discover, develop, and statistically test for the significance of cultural metaphors. We then compare our grounded method, which is an emic or culture-specific approach to studying each national culture, to cross-cultural surveys of many nations that focus on either values such as individualism and assertiveness or cultural orientations toward phenomena such as time and space. Such surveys are designed to be culture general or etic in the sense that the resulting dimensions are employed to analyze many nations. Finally, we describe some applications of cultural metaphors.

THE GROUNDED THEORY METHOD

Grounded theory, which more accurately should be termed the grounded theory method, was developed by Glaser and Strauss and was elaborated in a series of four books (Glaser, 1978; Glaser & Strauss, 1967; Strauss, 1987; Strauss & Corbin, 1990). Many of the issues that they raised are not germane to the present discussion, at least in part because they were addressed to sociologists and related researchers with decidedly different points of view from that expressed by Glaser and Strauss. Over time, however, some of their basic ideas have become part of the research rubric. Here, we describe those that relate directly to the discovery, development, and testing of cultural metaphors.

Glaser, Strauss, and their associates contrasted grounded theory with logico-deductive theory, which primarily emphasizes the testing of hypotheses derived from a theory. Frequently, this logico-deductive theory itself is derived from another prominent theory or theoretical perspective, and so the hypotheses tested eventually result in only minor changes in the theoretical perspective; that is, the system is partially or largely closed to new viewpoints and ideas. Glaser and Strauss (1967) provided several insightful analyses of such testing. For example, Blauner's (1964) *Alienation and Freedom* is largely based on Marx's theory of alienation and is a refinement of it in that Blauner described four major types of alienation but did not entertain opposing hypotheses or viewpoints. As Glaser and Strauss (1967) remarked in their summary of Blauner's approach, "In short: Verify (and qualify) this great body of received theory—with every expectation of its relative accuracy. Fortunate indeed are we for our perceptive ancestors!" (p. 125).

Glaser and Strauss emphasized the importance of discovery and development of theory. Grounded theory is the discovery of theory from data. A more formal definition was provided by Strauss and Corbin (1990):

> A grounded theory is one that is inductively derived from the study of the phenomenon it represents. That is, it is discovered, developed, and provisionally verified through systematic data collection and analysis of data pertaining to that phenomenon. Therefore, data collection, analysis, and theory stand in reciprocal relationship with each other. One does not begin with a theory [and] then prove it. Rather, one begins with an area of study, and what is relevant to that area is allowed to emerge. (p. 23)

These writers took pains to emphasize that they were not opposed to the logico-deductive framework, for eventually a grounded theory must meet the canons of science and be tested empirically. However, they argued against an overreliance on prominent theoretical perspectives that limit the vision of the researcher. Thus, they accepted the importance of formal theory in which hypotheses are formally derived, but they also believed that this formal theory should be *substantive* in the sense that it is grounded in some way to the phenomena that it is trying to explain. As Glaser and Strauss (1967) stated, "Thus, one canon for judging the usefulness of a theory is how it was generated—and we suggest that it is likely to be a better theory to the degree that it has been inductively developed from social research" (p. 5).

In addition, Glaser and Strauss advocated that the theory should be readily understandable by researchers and laypeople alike. Moreover, they argued strongly that triangulation—using a variety of methods including historical data, qualitative data provided through means such as interviews and panel discussions, and quantitative data of a statistical nature—should be employed to gather data and confirm the conclusions put forth by the researcher (see also Denzin, 1978). If there are conflicts, then additional data from a variety of sources should be collected until the conflicts are resolved.

Glaser and Strauss termed grounded theory "the constant comparative method of analysis." The researcher should continue to collect data until repetition of responses and information occurs and no new information is being obtained. Glaser and Strauss termed this phenomenon "saturation." They distinguished sharply between statistical sampling (in which the samples selected are predetermined) and theoretical sampling (which is used with the grounded theory method). Theoretical sampling ceases when saturation is reached. Thus, there is an element of subjectivity when theoretical sampling is employed, but typically saturation is easily recognizable by researchers engaged in this form of discovery.

These writers have described at length the manner in which they believe a specific grounded theory should be tested. Although we generally agree with this approach, the study of national cultures requires some modifications, particularly in the testing of the concepts, simply because of the size of the endeavor. We now turn to a description of cultural metaphors and the manner in which they were grounded in the sense of being discovered, developed, and tested for accuracy.

GROUNDED CULTURAL METAPHORS

The impetus for this work began when the first author, Martin Gannon, was teaching and living in Thailand. Although he had prepared thoroughly for this sojourn by reading several books on Thai culture and history and was well acquainted with the research of cross-cultural psychologists such as Hofstede and Rokeach, he was mystified by the Thai behavior, much of which did not align with the reading he had completed. For example, Hofstede (1980), in his classic study of 53 nations, categorized Thailand as highly collectivistic, but much of the Thai behavior is individualistic. Eventually, like a few other sojourners with whom he had come into contact who happened to be fortunate enough to have read Fieg's (1976) classic description of Thai culture (revised by Fieg & Mortlock, 1989), Gannon discovered that a simple image of a rubber band held loosely but tightened periodically characterized Thai behavior. This image is especially useful when compared to American behavior, which can be portrayed as a rubber band held tightly except for short periods of loosening. Keeping this image in mind facilitated personal interactions, not only in Gannon's case but also in those of other foreigners he met who had undergone this same experience, even to the extent of stumbling onto Fieg's work and immediately perceiving its relevance to understanding Thais.

This experience led Gannon to the realization that foreigners can use cross-cultural dimensions such as individualism and power distance, but only to scratch the surface of a national culture. He thought that one way in which to reduce the distance between the stranger and the native was to identify a critical institution, phenomenon, or activity that is culture specific and with which people in that nation identify. Such an activity or institution seemed to be the missing link in the dimensional approach. The crucial step in linking the activity or institution to the culture of a nation was to identify a set of characteristics of the metaphor that incorporate values, attitudes, behaviors, and assumptions. Importantly, the iterative process, which leads to the development of a cultural metaphor, is difficult to plan and emerges in large measure spontaneously, as the example of the Italian opera (discussed shortly) illustrates. That is, the iterative process varies with the nation under study, and the means by which its cultural metaphor and underlying characteristics are identified and described are tailored to each situation. However, the stages of this process can be described in terms of grounded theory for anyone interested in developing cultural metaphors.

Gannon then established an experimental M.B.A./doctoral seminar at the University of Maryland focusing on national cross-cultural behavior. Students were encouraged to study one nation in-depth through interviewing individuals and groups from that nation. Given the large number of foreigners in the Washington, D.C., area, it was possible to conduct such interviews. The students also reviewed the cross-cultural and travel literature specifically targeted on that nation and collected data on a variety of measures including economic growth and population growth.

In all of their readings and interviews, the students, many of whom had lived in the chosen nation for several years, examined the following areas to provide a uniform method: religion; early socialization and family structure; small group behavior; public behavior; leisure pursuits and interests; total lifestyle including work, leisure, and home as well as the time allocated to each; aural space or the degree to which members of a society react negatively to high noise levels; roles and status of different members of the nation and its culture; holidays and ceremonies; greeting behavior; humor; language including both oral and written

forms of communication; sports as a reflection of cultural values; political structure of the nation's culture; the educational system of the nation; traditions and
the degree to which the established order is emphasized; history of the society,
but only as it reflects cultural mind-sets or the manner in which its members
think, feel, and act rather than a detailed history; food and eating behavior; social
class structure; rate of technological and cultural change; organization of and
perspective on work such as the society's commitment to the work ethic and
superior-subordinate relationships; the well-known cross-cultural frameworks
developed by Hofstede (1980) and Hall (Hall & Hall, 1990); and any other categories they considered important.

Discovering the cultural metaphor of even one nation was a very tedious process, particularly during the early stages of the study. Once experience had been
gained and a paper effectively describing one nation in terms of a metaphor had
been written, it became easier to identify cultural metaphors that would work
effectively. It also became easier to know when a particular metaphor was not
appropriate for a particular nation.

Still, during the first semester of this course, not 1 of the 18 students was able
to identify a cultural metaphor, even though an iterative process—the constant
comparative method advocated by Glaser and Strauss—was employed. Students
interviewed subjects individually and in groups, presented preliminary ideas to
the class, read voraciously, reinterviewed subjects, and so forth. At the end of the
semester, Gannon employed the cultural metaphor of the opera to describe Italian
culture in a paper developed from two class papers on Italy because the descriptions they provided suggested such a cultural metaphor when the disparate
insights were organized logically into three to six characteristics. He then asked
Stefania Amodio, a professor of Italian, to critically analyze the paper. She consulted with a professor of Italian opera and then indicated that the metaphor was
accurate but that the categories were incomplete. Eventually, these categories
became pageantry and spectacle, voice, exteriority, and the interaction between
soloists and chorus. To demonstrate the power and effectiveness of cultural metaphor, we ask the readers of this chapter to define these operatic dimensions at
this point in terms of their relationship to Italian culture. Later in the chapter, we
define voice and exteriority to highlight some of the differences between etic and
emic approaches.

As noted previously, it should be emphasized that the students, although
starting at the same place and in the same seminar, tended to use different
approaches at times, in accordance with the concept of triangulation. Sometimes
"brainwriting" (a well-known technique for enhancing creativity) was employed,
sometimes group interviews were stressed over individual interviews, sometimes
foreign students were subjects and other times diplomats were subjects, and so
forth. In addition, once a cultural metaphor was identified—in some cases, even
this process consumed 4 or 5 years—it frequently was refined over several

semesters as another student used previous papers on a nation to structure his or her own paper.

Furthermore, it was difficult to identify three to six categories or characteristics of each metaphor, but eventually we were able to do so. Although we employed only three to six characteristics to keep the metaphor manageable, other characteristics certainly could be added. Moreover, we feel that alternative cultural metaphors for each nation are possible, but we emphasize that in many cases we found it difficult to identify even one.

Once a metaphor and a set of characteristics of the metaphor were identified, the next step was to validate them empirically. To accomplish this objective, we gathered a team of researchers to undertake a six-nation questionnaire study, two nations at a time (Gannon & Associates, 1997). Thus, three questionnaires were employed in a study of college students: those for Italy and Germany, Taiwan and the United States, and England and India. Specifically, to test the Italian metaphor and its characteristics, we gave Italian and German students (sample sizes of 141 and 65, respectively) a questionnaire containing items describing the metaphors hypothesized for the two countries and the characteristics of the two metaphors. Our reasoning was that if the characteristics of a metaphor were robust enough, then they would emerge when the items of a particular metaphor were combined with the items of a metaphor of a different country. Factor analyses supported two of the hypothesized characteristics of the Italian metaphor (expressive voice and love of pageantry), did not support the robustness of two of the hypothesized characteristics (exteriority and spectacle), and identified one emergent characteristic (importance of family). Moreover, t tests showed that Italians were significantly higher than the Germans on expressive voice, love of pageantry, and importance of the family and that Italians identified themselves with opera as a cultural metaphor for their country more than did the Germans. Although this was only a first step toward empirical verification, it showed that the metaphor approach represents a new inductive approach to derive cultural dimensions. Two of the characteristics of the metaphor passed empirical tests, whereas two others were not confirmed. Moreover, similar to previous survey research (Hofstede, 1980), a dimension emerged from the factor analyses.

Retrospectively, it seems clear that Gannon's approach to develop a cultural metaphor is consistent with the method proposed by Glaser and Strauss to develop grounded theory. Gannon, rather than deriving a hypothetical description of a nation's culture using an existing theoretical framework(s), discovered and developed a description of a nation's culture through systematic data collection and analysis of data pertaining to that phenomenon. Triangulation was employed in that several different types of data sources were used including cross-cultural survey data, interviews with different types of respondents, historical analysis, and objective measures such as rates of economic growth over time. Data were collected, sometimes over several years, until saturation occurred. Rather than statistical sampling, Gannon employed theoretical sampling, that is, using the inductive process and continuing to collect data until the point of saturation. In brief, the grounded cultural metaphor method includes the following stages: (a) immersion in the history, traditions, and society of the nation (triangulation); (b) search for a critical institution, phenomenon, or activity with which people in that nation identify (saturation); (c) search for dimensions or characteristics that link that activity or institution to unstated assumptions, values, and attitudes (saturation); and (d) validation of each metaphor and its characteristics (statistical sampling).

As these descriptions suggest, developing a grounded cultural metaphor for a nation requires both thick description and statistical testing. However, such national metaphors must be able to describe an extremely large number of activities in a parsimonious manner and must make conceptual sense as opposed to literary sense. The focus is on the conceptual system.

Next, we compare the grounded cultural metaphor method to other approaches used to study national cultures.

CROSS-CULTURAL DIMENSIONS
APPLICABLE TO MANY NATIONS

The most influential method for studying national cultures in which the culture rather than the individual is the unit of analysis is the questionnaire survey either of values such as individualism and assertiveness or of cultural orientations to phenomena such as time and space, and there are several competing frameworks in this area. This method seeks to be etic or culture general in the sense that the items selected reflect values found in all cultures to a lesser or greater extent. As indicated previously, the cultural metaphor is emic or specific to one culture. However, a cultural metaphor can overlap with the cultural metaphors of other nations. If the comprehensive questionnaire survey involving such metaphors and many nations as described previously is completed successfully, then this clearly emic approach has the potential of being both etic and emic.

Currently, there are four well-known studies that have attempted to profile the cultures of nations through the use of a comprehensive survey. Smith and Schwartz (1996) described three of these surveys/studies in-depth, namely those developed by Hofstede (1980), Schwartz (1994), and Trompenaars (1993), and the fourth was completed recently by Maznevski and DiStefano (1997). All four possess particular strengths. It is not our purpose to describe each of them fully, as this has been accomplished very effectively elsewhere (e.g., Smith & Schwartz, 1996). Rather, we seek to contrast and compare the most influential and best known of these four frameworks with the grounded cultural metaphorical method, namely Hofstede's (1980) pioneering study of 50 nations and 3 territories categorized as nations. We focus on the degree to which his framework is

+ logico-deductive and/or substantive;

+ understandable both to researchers and to laypersons, particularly practicing managers and business students;

+ scientifically sensible;

+ closed to new perspectives and viewpoints;

+ helpful to other researchers seeking scales to measure national cultures, which are then related to other variables such as national rates of innovation and economic development; and

+ helpful in management education and training.

Hofstede's (1980) study of 53 nations and their respective values represented a watershed in the history of such studies. It is based on only 22 questionnaire items included in a larger IBM survey involving 117,000 of its employees, supervisors, and managers during the years 1967 to 1973. Hofstede carefully reviewed the social scientific literature developed by Europeans and Americans in the area of values during at least the past 100 years. Through theory and interitem correlations, he posited the existence of two dimensions of national cultures: power distance and masculinity (later termed aggressiveness). He also constructed two additional dimensions through a factor analysis of 14 items: individualism-collectivism and uncertainty avoidance (or desire for certainty). Furthermore, Hofstede tested for reliability by correlating his measures with previous measures of national cultures such as those developed by McClelland (1975) and Rokeach (1973).

Hofstede's (1980) study can be considered exploratory. It is partly logico-deductive in nature in that two scales (power distance and masculinity) were derived from theory and partly inductive in that two scales (individualism and uncertainty avoidance) were derived from factor analysis. He was heavily influenced by concepts developed by earlier theorists, for example, Tonnies'(1887/1963) distinction between Gemeinschaft and Gesellschaft as well as Durkheim's (1892/1960) similar distinction between the collective conscience and the individual conscience. Hofstede's dimensions are mirrored in concepts found in earlier formulations; for example, McClelland's (1975) power motivation is similar to power distance. Triangulation, or studying a situation or issue through multiple methods, was not part of the method employed by Hofstede. Thus, Hofstede's study does not meet the criterion of grounded theory.

Furthermore, Hofstede's framework is easily understandable both by researchers and laypersons, and it is one of the first cross-cultural frameworks whose terms have become part of the accepted management vocabulary. This framework also is scientifically sensible, as Hofstede was very careful in his methodology, even though there have been innumerable discussions about the 22 items selected, the statistical procedures, and so forth. What is most persuasive is that at least two other studies using radically different methodologies completed during the 1980s basically confirmed the validity of the original framework (Confucius Connection, 1987; Hoppe, 1990). Peterson and Smith (1997) pointed out that this framework is superior to others in the sense of replication.

However, Hofstede's framework does seem at least partially closed to new perspectives and viewpoints. It is true that an additional dimension, the degree to which a national culture emphasizes the deferral of present gratification to achieve long-term goals, was added during the 1980s (Confucius Connection, 1987). Still, some of the most persistent issues remain problematic, for example, the degree to which a national culture is collectivistic. Triandis (1995) demonstrated very effectively that there are at least two types of individualism (vertical and horizontal) and two types of collectivism (vertical and horizontal) (see also Triandis & Gelfand, 1998). Admittedly, Schwartz, whose work begins with Hofstede's framework, has advanced the discussion of types of collectivism and individualism significantly, but the basic Hofstede framework that has become so popular is difficult to enlarge or extend.

Still, Hofstede's framework of cross-cultural dimensions of values has been particularly helpful to other researchers who have employed his scales and related them to phenomena such as innovation, entrepreneurship, economic growth, and even airline accidents per capita per nation (Hoppe, 1993; Kedia & Bhagat, 1988; Schneider & DeMeyer, 1991). They also have proved to be helpful in the area of management education and training and are regularly taught within this milieu.

Comparison With Cultural Metaphors

We now can compare the cultural metaphors, which are grounded rather than logico-deductive in nature, to Hofstede's (1980) cross-cultural survey in terms of the criteria discussed heretofore so as to highlight differences and complementarities. First, metaphors are readily understandable to both researchers and laypersons because they are anchored to easily recognized phenomena. Preliminary evidence, cited previously, suggests that they are scientifically sensible, but much work needs to be completed in this area. Also, they represent the only framework that has the potential to be both etic and emic—emic in the sense that each metaphor mirrors a national culture and etic in the sense that a comprehensive survey of several nations might well lead to the construction of dimensions reflective of all nations in the survey, only some nations, or only one nation.

Furthermore, the cultural metaphor method is open to new perspectives and viewpoints, and new metaphors for a particular nation are welcome if they increase emic understanding. At the current time, this framework is not helpful to other researchers seeking scales to measure national cultures that they then relate to other phenomena simply because a comprehensive survey similar to the one described here has not been undertaken. Finally, cultural metaphors are very helpful in management education and training.

To return to the emic Italian concepts of voice and exteriority, we can point out that the Italian language has far more vowels than consonants and, hence, has a musical cadence to it. Some experts consider the Italian language to be among the most musical, if not the most musical, in the world. Thus, when Italians are talking, they are engaging in a form of singing, and from this perspective it is easy to understand why the opera was created in Italy. Exteriority refers to a deeply held belief among most Italians that the individual cannot keep thoughts and emotions to himself or herself; thoughts must be expressed, first in the family and then outside of it in the piazza or square, which is a staple of Italian opera. Even today, large Italian cities are structured to have many piazzas, although the numbers of spacious parks found in other nations are comparatively small. At the same time, Italy has far more bars and restaurants per capita than do comparable European nations—257 inhabitants per cafe/restaurant in Italy versus 451 in Britain, 795 in France, 558 in Germany, and 778 in Spain (Richard, 1995). A recent Italian doctoral dissertation emphasized the importance of exteriority but changing cultural circumstances by suggesting that the large piazza is more descriptive of southern Italian culture, whereas bars (and the adjoining small parks) are more descriptive of northern Italian culture (Venezia, 1997).

The etic or culture-general framework does not directly analyze such emic or culture-specific issues. However, it is an empirical question as to whether voice and exteriority apply to all nations, to only some nations, or to only Italy. The proposed survey of cultural metaphors using only one questionnaire in several nations will be a first step toward resolving such issues. Finally, it should be mentioned that cultural metaphors are far broader in their focus than are etic frameworks, which presuppose that knowledge of values and cultural orientations is sufficient to understand national cultures. Such a presupposition is questionable and narrow in focus because it leaves out of consideration many cultural issues that are captured by an emic approach.

EVOLUTION OF SPECIFIC CULTURAL METAPHORS

We have described only one metaphor, the Italian opera, in-depth. To give the readers a better sense of cultural metaphors, we provide brief descriptions of the evolutions of some of them.

As indicated previously, the metaphors evolved through the use of an M.B.A./ doctoral seminar. Two students independently were struggling to develop a metaphor for England, but neither was successful. One of them, an American who had studied in England for about 10 years, had difficulties in expressing the major differences between Americans and the English, but she felt quite strongly that the forms of individualism in the two nations were markedly different. She argued that in America everyone seems to be like an individual atom, whereas in England there appears to be an invisible glue uniting people. An English woman, who was married to an American, identified this invisible glue as similar to the mortar of a traditional British home, thus leading to the development of this cultural metaphor with its related characteristics of laying the foundations of the house, building it, and living in it.

Another paper was written by a Swedish American woman who had spent her childhood in a closely knit Swedish community in Minnesota. Although she had visited Sweden for only 1 week in her lifetime, her descriptions were extremely apt and engaging. However, she could not identify a particular cultural metaphor. In the subsequent semester, a Turkish student taking this seminar happened to be discussing the Swedish paper with her Swedish roommate, a doctoral student at the University of Maryland, who responded enthusiastically to the description and agreed with it after reading the paper. However, this doctoral student suggested the Swedish stuga or the unadorned Swedish summer house as the appropriate metaphor with its attendant characteristics of the love of untrammeled nature and tradition, individualism through self-development, and equality.

As we have suggested, there might be overlap between some nations, and indeed seemingly the same metaphor can be interpreted differently in two or more nations, for example, the Portuguese bullfight and the Spanish bullfight (Gannon & Associates, 1994, 2001). Also, it is quite possible that migration might be accompanied by a particular group in different nations sharing the same metaphor, which seems to be the case of the ethnic Chinese. Originally, we focused on the Chinese living in China, but eventually we wrote about the 57 million ethnic Chinese living outside of China. At least some of our observations also are valid for those living in China.

Our initial interviews with the Chinese were discouraging. Several Chinese students wrote papers on this topic but with limited success, and they were unable to identify an appropriate metaphor. In the interviews, the most pervasive image offered was that the Chinese are like actors; they behave in different ways in response to the situation; in particular, the distinction between familial and nonfamilial behavior is quite important. However, as we said at the time, many people behave one way at home and another way in public regardless of their culture; it is typical human behavior.

Finally, group interviews with several Chinese students helped to identify the Chinese family altar as clearly reflective of Chinese culture, particularly among the 57 million expatriate Chinese living in various nations. Such altars are commonplace, and they may include pictures of descendants, Buddha images, and even representations of spirit gods. Family members pray before the altar and leave food for their descendants, many of whom might have died hundreds or thousands of years earlier. They even converse with these descendants and ask for their advice.

The first dimension or characteristic is roundness or the physical presence of the altar as representative of the family as a well-integrated social unit, and this includes members both living and dead and extending over hundreds or even thousands of years. Roundness stands for the continuity and structural completeness of the family; it symbolizes the family as the basic, distinct, and enduring feature of Chinese culture. Harmony within the family is the second characteristic. The third characteristic, fluidity, represents the capacity of the family to change while maintaining solid traditions.

APPLICATIONS OF CULTURAL METAPHORS

It frequently seems as if the etic national cultural frameworks are in competition with one another. For example, if one accepts the Hofstede framework, then the Trompenaars framework appears less attractive. (This is not the case with the Hofstede and Schwartz frameworks, as Schwartz built on the work by Hofstede.)

However, this Darwinian struggle for supremacy does not necessarily have to be the case. It is possible to combine and integrate two or more frameworks and apply them to management education and training. Gannon (1998) recently described a training program combining three frameworks: Hofstede's framework, Hall's high-context framework, and cultural metaphors. Essentially, Gannon presented Hofstede's framework, emphasized its many advantages, and asked what is wrong with it. He then described six cultural metaphors and asked small groups to apply one of them to the development of a marketing and advertising plan designed to attract tourists to the United States. Later, he described a revision of Hall's context dimension and requested that the trainees apply all three frameworks to an analysis of the cross-cultural interactions found in Part 2 of the video series, *Going International* (Griggs Production, 1983).

There is no reason that such integration cannot proceed in a relatively rapid fashion. For example, cross-cultural role-plays could be devised and analyzed through the use of all of the frameworks described in this chapter. Minimal work has been accomplished in this area. Furthermore, thus far most management training and development has emphasized the existence of cross-cultural differences, but only minor attempts have been made to link this understanding to the classic business functions of accounting, marketing, finance, and so forth.

It is not our purpose to describe every application of cultural metaphors; Gannon currently is completing a book in this area (Gannon, 2001). However, some applications are obvious, for example, asking individuals or groups to come up with a cultural metaphor for a specific nation and then explaining the one that already has been constructed in Gannon and Associates (1994). Gannon and Associates also have developed two paragraphs for each of the six nations without mentioning their names. One paragraph explicitly mentions the cultural metaphor, and the other does not. These paragraphs were derived from their 1994 book. Trainees are asked to identify the nations being described by the paragraphs.

A related approach is to list the eight types of individualism and four types of collectivism identified by Gannon and Associates (1994) for 17 nations. Trainees or students then are asked to relate the type of individualism or collectivism to the 17 nations. They also are asked to discuss this specific type of individualism or collectivism in terms of the two generic types both of individualism and of collectivism discussed previously (Triandis & Gelfand, 1998).

Similarly, some of the percentage responses by nation reported by Trompenaars (1993) can be highlighted and then discussed within the context of the specific cultural metaphors that might shed some light on why citizens from these nations provide such modal responses.

It also is possible to identify standard business school cross-cultural cases, such as establishing a subsidiary in another nation, and to apply some or all of the frameworks to them. For example, one well-known exercise in the business strategy area is to use the description of the battle plans of the French and Germans in World War I and the resulting battle that occurred and to then ask trainees or students what the French strategy was and how it differed from the German strategy (Mintzberg & Quinn, 1993). The cultural metaphors for these two nations, French wine and the German symphony, and their respective dimensions could be used to structure this discussion, as could the ranking of these two nations along various dimensions by the etic researchers described in this chapter.

It is our belief that there are many applications of cross-cultural frameworks, particularly if they are viewed as supplementary rather than exclusionary. All of these frameworks discussed in this chapter, including cultural metaphors, possess not only weaknesses but also strengths. We believe that renewed efforts should be made to integrate them in the area of applications rather than to emphasize only one or two frameworks.

In summary, cultural metaphors represent a grounded perspective on national cultures. They provide culture-specific or emic understanding and can be employed simultaneously with etic frameworks. However, much work needs to be done. The grounded theory method must be employed to refine existing cultural metaphors and to develop new ones for additional nations. Also, a comprehensive survey of several nations focusing on the overlap among cultural metaphors needs to be completed. Nevertheless, we believe that cultural metaphors already have proved themselves to be very useful for highlighting differences; creating understanding among students and management trainees; and moving the discussion of culture beyond that of values, cultural orientations, and the superiority of one approach or framework over others.

REFERENCES

Blauner, R. (1964). *Alienation and freedom.* Chicago: University of Chicago Press.

Confucius Connection. (1987). Chinese values and the search for culture-free dimensions of culture. *Journal of Cross-Cultural Psychology, 18,* 143-164.

Denzin, N. (1978). *The research act.* New York: McGraw-Hill.

Durkheim, E. (1960). *The division of labor in society.* Glencoe, IL: Free Press. (Originally published in 1892)

Fernandez, J. W. (Ed.). (1991). *Beyond metaphor.* Stanford, CA: Stanford University Press.

Fieg, J. (1976). *A common core: Thais and Americans.* Yarmouth, ME: Intercultural Press.

Fieg, J., & Mortlock, E. (1989). *A common core: Thais and Americans* (rev. ed.). Yarmouth, ME: Intercultural Press.

Gannon, M. (1998, June-July). *Integrating cross-cultural dimensions, context, and cultural metaphors in management education and training.* Paper presented at the international meeting of the Western Academy of Management, Istanbul, Turkey.

Gannon, M. (2001). *Working across cultures: Applications and exercises.* Thousand Oaks, CA: Sage.

Gannon, M., & Associates. (1994). *Understanding global cultures.* Thousand Oaks, CA: Sage.

Gannon, M., & Associates. (1997, August). *Cultural metaphors as frames of reference for nations: A six-country study.* Paper presented at the annual meeting of the Academy of Management, Boston.

Gannon, M., & Associates. (2001). *Understanding global cultures* (rev. ed.). Thousand Oaks, CA: Sage.

Geertz, C. (1973). *The interpretation of culture.* New York: Basic Books.

Glaser, B. (1978). *Theoretical sensitivity.* Mill Valley, CA: Sociology Press.

Glaser, B., & Strauss, A. (1967). *The discovery of grounded theory.* Chicago: Aldine.

Griggs Production. (1983). *Going international,* Part 2: *Managing the overseas assignment* [video]. San Francisco: Author.

Hall, E. (1959). *The silent language.* New York: Doubleday.

Hall, E. (1966). *The hidden dimension.* New York: Doubleday.

Hall, E. (1983). *The dance of life.* New York: Anchor/Doubleday.

Hall, E. T., & Hall, M. R. (1990). *Understanding cultural differences.* Yarmouth, ME: Intercultural Press.

Hofstede, G. (1980). *Culture's consequences.* Beverly Hills, CA: Sage.

Hoppe, M. (1990). *A comparative study of country elites.* Unpublished doctoral dissertation, University of North Carolina at Chapel Hill.

Hoppe, M. (1993). The effects of national culture on the theory and practice of managing R&D professionals abroad. *R&D Management, 23,* 313-325.

Kedia, B., & Bhagat, R. (1988). Cultural constraints on transfer of technology across nations: Implications for research in international and comparative management. *Academy of Management Review, 13,* 559-597.

Lakoff, G., & Johnson, M. (1980). *Metaphors we live by.* Chicago: University of Chicago Press.

Maznevski, M., & DiStefano, J. (1997). *The cultural orientations framework and international management research.* Working paper, University of Virginia.

McClelland, D. (1975). *Power.* New York: Irvington.

Mintzberg, H., & Quinn, J. (1993). *The strategy process: Contexts and cases.* Englewood Cliffs, NJ: Prentice Hall.

Ortony, A. (1975). Why metaphors are necessary and not just nice. *Educational Theory, 25*(1), 45-53.

Peterson, M., & Smith, P. (1997). Does national culture or ambient temperature explain cross-national differences in role stress? No sweat! *Academy of Management Journal, 40,* 930-946.

Richard, C. (1995). *The new Italians.* New York: Penguin.

Rokeach, M. (1973). *The nature of human values.* New York: Free Press.

Schneider, S., & DeMeyer, A. (1991). Interpreting and responding to strategic issues: The impact of national culture. *Strategic Management Journal, 12,* 307-320.

Schwartz, S. (1994). Beyond individualism/collectivism: New cultural dimensions of values. In U. Kim, H. Triandis, C. Kagitcibasi, S. Choi, & G. Yoon (Eds.), *Individualism and collectivism* (pp. 85-122). Thousand Oaks, CA: Sage.

Smith, P., & Schwartz, S. (1996). Values. In J. Berry, M. Segall, & C. Kagitcibasi (Eds.), *Handbook of cross-cultural psychology,* Vol. 3: *Social behavior and applications* (2nd ed., pp. 77-118). Boston: Allyn & Bacon.

Strauss, A. (1987). *Qualitative analysis for social scientists.* New York: Cambridge University Press.

Strauss, A., & Corbin, J. (1990). *Basics of qualitative research.* Newbury Park, CA: Sage.

Tonnies, F. (1963). *Community and society.* New York: Harper & Row. (Originally published in 1887)

Triandis, H. (1995). *Individualism and collectivism.* Boulder, CO: Westview.

Triandis, H., & Gelfand, M. (1998). Converging measurement of horizontal and vertical individualism and collectivism. *Journal of Personality and Social Psychology, 74,* 118-128.

Trompenaars, F. (1993). *Riding the waves of culture.* Burr Ridge, IL: Irwin.

Venezia, E. (1997). *Cross-cultural management: Un solo management nella differenziata realta Italiana?* Doctoral dissertation, Bocconi University, Milan, Italy.

chapter 5

Strategic Human Resource Management in International Joint Ventures

J. MICHAEL GERINGER
COLETTE A. FRAYNE

Fundamental environmental and organizational changes, including trends toward internationalization of markets and competition as well as the increasing cost and complexity of technological developments, have caused many companies to incorporate joint ventures and other forms of alliances as key elements of their international strategies (Harrigan, 1988; Yoshino & Rangan, 1995). Joint ventures involve two or more separate organizations (the partners), each of which actively participates in the decision-making activities of the jointly owned entity. A joint venture is considered to be an international joint venture (IJV) when at least one partner organization has headquarters outside the venture's country of operation (Geringer & Frayne, 1990).

Although the frequency and strategic importance of IJVs have increased dramatically since the early 1980s (Geringer & Woodcock, 1989; Lynch, 1993), many IJVs have failed to achieve their performance objectives due to the unique challenges associated with managing these interorganizational ventures (Geringer & Hebert, 1991; Geringer & Woodcock, 1995; Harrigan, 1986; Yoshino & Rangan, 1995). The challenge results from the presence of two or more partner organizations that often are competitors as well as collaborators

(Geringer, 1991; Hamel, 1990). Partners often simultaneously have convergent or complementary *and* divergent or even opposing alliance motivations, goals, and operating policies as well as disparate national and organizational cultures (Buckley & Casson, 1988; Frayne & Geringer, 1990; Geringer & Woodcock, 1995; Laurent, 1986; Lynch, 1993). As a result, a large proportion of IJV failures have been attributed not to financial or technical problems but rather to "cultural" or "human resource" factors such as conflicts in management styles, cultures, and operational practices (Devlin & Bleackley, 1988; Ganitsky & Watzke, 1990; Geringer & Frayne, 1990, 1997; Shenkar & Zeira, 1987). Indeed, these factors help to explain why many IJVs begin to experience operational problems even after years of relatively stable performance.

Human resource management (HRM) is concerned with the practices and policies through which organizations attract, recruit, motivate, reward, and develop their employees as well as ways in which the employment relationship can be terminated. All organizations, of necessity, perform these activities at some point during their life spans, although there might be substantial differences among organizations in the degree to which such activities are integrated, formalized, and strategic. Due to the unique nature of IJVs and the associated tensions, HRM is a particularly difficult, complex, and multifaceted undertaking in these ventures. Yet, despite the challenging context and the critical role of HRM in IJVs' operations and performance, HRM issues have received relatively limited attention in the academic and practitioner literatures on IJVs (Bleeke & Ernst, 1991; Cyr, 1995; Frayne & Geringer, 1994; Geringer & Frayne, 1990, 1997; Shenkar & Zeira, 1987). The objective of this chapter is twofold: (a) to identify key variables associated with the management of human resources within IJVs and (b) to propose a conceptual framework of IJVs and the strategic role of HRM in the design and implementation of IJVs.

The next section of the chapter provides an overview of HRM and its role in IJVs. A conceptual framework is then developed, identifying key variables associated with IJV formation and the role and nature of HRM systems and practices in new and ongoing IJVs. Considerations regarding the role of, and challenges for, human resource professionals in IJVs are then addressed, followed by implications of the framework for research and practice pertaining to IJVs.

HRM IN IJVs

HRM has been recognized as an important variable influencing the overall competencies and the potential for competitive advantage of organizations (Pfeffer, 1994), thereby promoting acceptance of a strategic role of HRM (Doz & Prahalad, 1986; Rosenzweig & Nohria, 1994; Schuler, Dowling, & DeCieri,

1993). In this respect, strategic HRM includes responsibilities that extend beyond the traditional operational roles of staffing, training and development, performance appraisal, and compensation and benefits. Strategic HRM also includes the design of HRM systems and their linkages with other elements of an organization, responsibility for the development and transfer of distinctive competencies, and related issues and activities (Schuler et al., 1993).

Although there has been a substantial recent literature on strategic aspects of HRM, particularly in multinational corporations, limited attention has been devoted to issues of HRM within the context of IJVs. Given the embryonic stage of this latter research, it is not surprising that much of the work thus far has tended to be descriptive, to address a restricted range of HRM practices, and to be based on samples of limited scope or generalizability (Parkhe, 1993). Given this apparent gap, it appears that a framework needs to be developed that identifies HRM practices within IJVs and determinants of these practices (Geringer, 1998, p. 134). This chapter attempts to address that need by proposing a conceptual framework of the strategic management of human resources in IJVs.

A CONCEPTUAL FRAMEWORK
OF HRM IN IJVs

Before focusing specifically on HRM practices, we first identify key variables that might function as determinants of HRM practices in IJVs. The conceptual framework proposed in this chapter identifies several factors that appear to have important relationships with the HRM practices that would be implemented within an IJV. The following subsection identifies and discusses several of these factors and their relationship with HRM practices before the discussion turns specifically to the HRM practices themselves.

Achieving Shared Vision: Strategic and Environmental Determinants of HRM Practices in IJVs

A number of scholars have examined the determinants of HR strategies in general and, to a limited extent, of those in IJVs in particular. A review of this literature suggests that the two most influential and frequently discussed factors determining HRM strategies are the business strategy of the partner organization(s) and the environmental context confronting the partners and the IJV (Dyer, 1984; Fombrun, 1982; Geringer & Frayne, 1990). The relationship of IJV strategy with business- and corporate-level strategy, and with environmental context, has been addressed extensively by numerous authors (Geringer & Hebert, 1989;

Harrigan, 1986; Porter, 1986; Yoshino & Rangan, 1995). To conserve space, this issue is not reviewed here.

The critical issue with respect to the current chapter is the need for the partners to identify a common, or at least a compatible, vision of the proposed alliance. A shared vision among the respective partners' organizations should take into account, and be consistent with, the respective strategic and environmental pressures that confront the partners' organizations. This suggests the need for identifying IJV goals and strategy that are consistent with the respective business and corporate strategies and objectives of each partner firm. This vision also should be consistent with the environmental context in which the partners and the IJV will operate including the industry (or industries) in which they compete and the respective home and host countries in which they operate.

The strategic challenge of achieving a shared vision includes the task of identifying a compatible partner organization (Geringer, 1988, 1991) that will facilitate the development—and maintenance over time—of a fit among the partners' respective strategic requirements and the environmental context of the IJV.

Translating Vision Into Organizational Requirements

To operationalize their shared vision and achieve their respective strategic objectives, the partners' organizations must establish an appropriate structure for the IJV and for relations between the partners and the IJV (Geringer & Frayne, 1990, 1997; Geringer & Hebert, 1989). Despite recognition of the need for a smooth relationship, there often is tension between the IJV and the partners' organizations. For example, managers confront pressures arising from the need for local responsiveness at the IJV level and global integration at the level of the partners' organizations (Bartlett, 1986; Doz & Prahalad, 1984). Demands for local responsiveness might develop due to factors such as differences in customer needs, local culture, market structures, distribution channels, pressure from the host government, and limited dependence on the partners' organizations for managerial, technological, marketing, or other resources. Pressure for integration of the IJV with the activities of a partner organization might emanate from the existence of multinational customers, global competitors, and related factors. These pressures can influence a host of decisions such as the degree of centralization of decision making, organizational culture and management style, and the integration mechanisms that are employed (Davidson, 1984; Gates & Egelhoff, 1986; Prahalad & Bettis, 1986; Prahalad & Doz, 1981). Tensions between the partners' organizations and the IJV as a result of integration and responsiveness pressures, therefore, have fundamental implications for the structure and operation of the IJV including the design and implementation of HRM strategies and practices.

The Role of HRM Systems in IJVs

After a decision is made to engage in an IJV, the partners' organizations must design and implement appropriate HRM systems for the venture. The partners must identify the critical tasks that must be completed to attain their strategic objectives as well as the employee positions in the IJV and in the partners' organizations that must be created, staffed, and managed to satisfactorily accomplish these tasks. The partners also must assess their individual and collective ability, based on expertise and systems, to create and encourage employee behaviors that are consistent with the tasks inherent in the IJV's and the organizations' strategies. Individual HRM practices should be consistent with the environmental context, strategic objectives, and organizational requirements of the IJV. These HRM practices also must complement and be consistent with each other to maximize effectiveness of the overall system. Each practice should be evaluated within the context of the partners' and the IJV's strategic objectives and of the other practices comprising the IJV's HRM system.

Implications for Performance

To build, maintain, and develop their corporate identities and competitiveness, organizations must strive to find consistent ways in which to manage their personnel on a worldwide basis. Yet, to be effective locally, organizations also must adapt their practices to the norms and customs of the different societies and operational contexts in which they operate. Whereas the global pressures of a partner organization's business might call for standardization, diversity in the cultural environments among the partners or the IJV might—simultaneously and paradoxically—promote differentiation. In this respect, the performance of the IJV and of the partners' organizations, and thus their ability to achieve their respective strategic objectives, might be influenced by the ability to achieve and maintain a correspondence among the components of the conceptual framework presented here. The framework presented also suggests the strong and direct relationship that is predicted between the HRM systems in the IJV and the resulting performance of the IJV and for the partners' organizations. The next section of this chapter attempts to explain this relationship in greater detail by identifying and discussing critical components of HRM systems in IJVs.

COMPONENTS OF HRM SYSTEMS IN IJVs

Effective management of human resources represents perhaps the most important task in operating a successful IJV. Although good organizational structure and design might be prerequisites for successful venture operations, it is people who implement the venture's strategy. Thus, for partner organizations to design and implement IJV operations more effectively, recognition of the use and importance of HRM systems and practices is essential. This section identifies seven components of an IJV's strategic HRM system: planning, staffing, performance appraisal, training and development, compensation and reward, career development, and competence development and transfer. Figure 5.1 presents these seven components and their role within our overall framework for HRM within IJVs. In what follows, each of these components is discussed along with its relevance for IJV design and management.

Human Resource Planning

Competence and appropriate strategy are necessary, but not sufficient, conditions for high performance by organizations. An organization also requires people, structures, and systems to translate capability into action. Strategic human resource planning requires the organization to anticipate the type and amount of human resources that will be needed at key points during the implementation of the IJV and to compare these requirements against forecasts of human resource availability. Although many authors talk about a single standard of HRM embracing all employees, in most firms one must distinguish the relatively sophisticated and expensive techniques used in the recruitment, reward, and development of managers from the less sophisticated and often uneven standards applied to lower grade, higher turnover employee categories.

Research in the fields of strategic management and HRM has emphasized the importance of achieving a "fit" between an IJV's HRM systems and its strategic and operating contexts. Indeed, the fit between strategy and human resource practices has been argued to be one of the most important determinants of an organization's success (Kerr & Slocum, 1987; Pfeffer, 1994). This is due to the fundamental requirement that firms support any strategic decision, short or long term, with the appropriate level and quality of management talent and other human resources (Kerr, 1985). HRM practices represent an essential integrating mechanism through which the efforts of individuals are directed toward the organization's strategic objectives (Frayne & Geringer, 1990). They help to define the values and norms that are expected to guide the behavior of an organization's employees and also help to determine the types of employees that an organization attracts, retains, and promotes (Jensen & Murphy, 1990).

To the extent that an organization's HRM practices are consistent with and support the attainment of the organization's strategic objectives, the interests of the organization will be promoted. From this perspective, to efficiently and effectively direct the efforts of the organization's members and to promote attainment of strategic objectives, HRM systems should be consistent with the demands of the external environment (e.g., industrial, cross-national, cross-cultural),

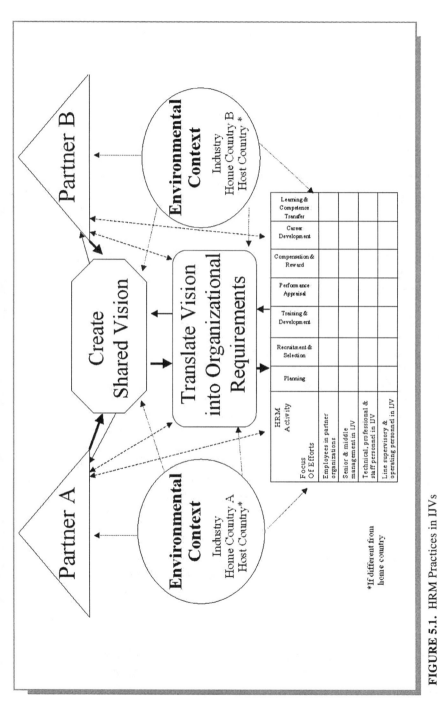

FIGURE 5.1. HRM Practices in IJVs

NOTE: HRM = human resource management; IJV = international joint venture.

between the IJV and its partners' organizations (e.g., the IJV's role within the partners' international webs of activities and its dependence on the partners' organizations for resources), and within the IJV's specific operational context (e.g., internal fit) (Geringer & Frayne, 1990; Hannon, Huang, & Jaw, 1995; Milliman, Von Glinow, & Nathan, 1991; Shenkar & Zeira, 1987). The complexity of an IJV's activities has important implications for the type of controls that the venture will require and, therefore, for the type and effectiveness of human resource policies that can be implemented (Geringer & Hebert, 1989; Ouchi, 1977).

    The achievement of effective integration of strategy and human resources in IJVs represents a difficult challenge. The presence of geographic distance, different time zones, divergent national and corporate cultures, language differences, and the like is the bane of most organizations whose operations transcend national borders. The control of key resources by a partner organization, or by a subsidiary or a local institution, might provide it with bargaining power that can be used to alter the nature and fit among the components of the HRM system (Martinez & Ricks, 1989; Prahalad & Doz, 1981; Schuler et al., 1993). The extent of these difficulties tends to be magnified with IJVs due to the existence of multiple partner organizations. Indeed, a fundamental problem underlying many of the difficulties encountered by IJVs is the tendency for partner organizations to evidence divergent strategic profiles and to embody different, or at least non-identical, motives for participating in these ventures. These differences often manifest themselves through efforts to implement IJV strategies and policies that might not be consistent with the attainment of their partners' objectives for the venture.

    In light of the internal and external tensions within an IJV and across organizational boundaries, including with the partners' organizations, human resource planning for IJVs confronts a particular challenge to achieving balance between (a) partners' desire for consistency in the way in which employees are managed and (b) pressures to adapt to the business practices and mores of the country or region in which the IJV will operate (Hofstede, 1980; Martinez & Jarillo, 1991). Although interdependencies of the IJV with the parent firms are critical factors influencing HRM strategies (Baliga & Jaeger, 1984), relationships between partner firms and an IJV are not static (Frayne & Geringer, 1990; Prahalad & Doz, 1987). As an IJV evolves, the venture often develops technological, marketing, and managerial capabilities, as well as relational networks within its institutional environment, that might impact the partners' ability to unilaterally and effectively manipulate these competencies and resources and to influence the IJV's (and parents') strategy (Hannon et al., 1995; Meyer & Scott, 1983; Zucker, 1988). The complexity of these relational networks and resource dependencies must be recognized and anticipated while initially planning HRM systems for an IJV, and it must be monitored and managed throughout the postimplementation phases of the IJV's life cycle.

Staffing

A fundamental staffing decision for the partners' organizations is whether there will be employees of the IJV itself versus merely employees of the partners' organizations or outside entities. In addition, IJV staffing decisions are concerned with issues such as recruitment, selection, internal promotion versus the use of outside staffing, the use of expatriates, and socialization. Staffing has been recognized as a key success factor for an IJV's operations including its influence on the venture's operating policies, organizational values and norms, and IJV control (Geringer & Frayne, 1990; Geringer & Hebert, 1989; Lasserre & Schutte, 1995; Lynch, 1993; Shenkar & Zeira, 1987).

In recruiting and selecting IJV personnel, several authors have suggested the importance of matching characteristics of managers with the nature and challenges of the specific business being pursued (Gerstein & Reisman, 1983; Olian & Rynes, 1984; Schuler & Jackson, 1987; Szilagyi & Schweiger, 1984). The importance of linking the nature of the business to staffing practices, especially of middle and upper levels of management, has been based on the different behaviors demanded of personnel who are involved in different strategic and operational contexts. The implication is that not all individuals are appropriately qualified to excel across all contexts and that recruitment and selection of appropriate personnel are strategically important staffing decisions. The unique and demanding nature of positions such as the venture's general manager suggests that this caveat is particularly salient for the case of IJVs (Frayne & Geringer, 1992, 1994; Geringer & Frayne, 1993).

Whereas much has been written on the importance of matching top managers with the nature of a business, less attention has been given to the other employees in an organization. Yet, it seems reasonable to assume that the rest of a workforce also might need to be selected and managed differently depending on the business context. Each of the venture's personnel must have the technical, organizational, and interpersonal skills necessary to ensure the successful operation of the IJV and to satisfy the partners' objectives. Personnel also must have the capacity for understanding, and functioning effectively within, an organizational form that involves the variety of national and corporate cultures that characterize IJVs. In addressing staffing issues, therefore, consideration must be given to recruitment and selection of appropriately qualified personnel for a variety of short- and longer term positions associated with the IJV. This includes employees in the partners' organizations (e.g., key strategic, technical, and operational contacts between the partners and the IJV); senior and middle managers comprising the IJV's management team; technical, professional, and staff personnel in the IJV; and line supervisors and operating personnel in the IJV.

Within an IJV context, a critical staffing issue is where to recruit employees. Partner organizations may rely on their own internal labor markets (e.g., transferring employees from one or another of the partners' respective operations, whether from the headquarters or other operations), on external labor markets (e.g., hiring new employees from among host country or third country nationals), or (more commonly) on recruiting from a mix of internal and external labor markets. The staffing issue must be addressed in terms of the initial start-up phase of the venture as well as over time, in conjunction with the evolution of the IJV and its workforce over the venture's life cycle.

A corresponding consideration associated with staffing is the issue of divided loyalties and conflicting interests of personnel. For example, employees transferred from a partner organization (to which the employees expect to return after the assignments are completed) can have a profound effect on HRM and other decisions in an IJV. Expatriates are more likely to place the partner's interests above those of the IJV or another partner (Martinez & Ricks, 1989). Consideration also might need to be given to the families of expatriate employees given that this issue has been repeatedly recognized as an important influence on the recruitment and subsequent performance of expatriate personnel and the venture as a whole. Locally sourced personnel also might experience conflict between allegiance to the IJV or the host nation (or perhaps to a locally based partner organization) and allegiance to a foreign-based partner organization and its objectives for the venture. Conflicting loyalties might be complicated by differences arising along professional, hierarchical, and cultural dimensions. These differences might affect relationships among personnel in the partners, the IJV, and other institutions, and they might influence the activities and performance of the overall venture.

Performance Appraisal

Performance appraisal is a formal structured system of measuring and evaluating an employee's job-related behaviors and outcomes. Performance appraisal systems can provide managers with information regarding the strengths and weaknesses, as well as the likelihood for future success, of managers and other employees involved in executing an IJV's strategy and meeting objectives. Performance appraisal also can assist in identifying who is responsible for completing specific IJV-related tasks and how well they are performing them. Numerous studies have documented the pressures and causes for failure, particularly in international and IJV assignments (e.g., Frayne & Geringer, 1992, 1994; Tung, 1984). An appraisal system that addresses these critical areas is more likely to effectively match personnel to appropriate situations and reduce continued performance problems or undesired turnover.

Performance appraisals serve many specific purposes in an IJV including management and staff development, performance improvement, and compensation. Performance appraisals can provide a framework for future employee development by identifying and preparing individuals for increased responsibilities in the venture. In addition, appraising employee performance can encourage continued successful performance on interpersonal, task-related, or other dimensions and can help to identify and overcome individual weaknesses to make IJV employees more effective and productive. It also allows partner firms to monitor progress toward attainment of critical IJV objectives. Finally, performance appraisals can help in determining appropriate pay or other rewards for performance and the provision of equitable salary and bonus incentives based on merits and results. Although it might not be appropriate to use the same evaluation procedures for strategic alliances as for wholly owned activities, the infrequency with which IJVs occur in most firms often works against such adaptations. Indeed, many partner organizations have failed to successfully use performance appraisals as a means of enhancing IJV performance (Frayne & Geringer, 1993; Janger, 1980).

Partner companies can influence IJV performance by establishing and reinforcing expectations for the venture's operations through the purpose, method, and frequency of performance appraisal that is employed. Emphasis should be placed on assessing performance vis-à-vis the individual's key tasks and assignments as well as on nonroutine tasks that are critical to the IJV's success (Howard, 1987). The performance criteria that should be used will depend on the specific circumstances of the IJV. It is common for partners to have different objectives for establishing an IJV and, therefore, to want to apply different evaluation criteria. Yet, different does not necessarily mean incompatible, and it might be possible to transform these various objectives into a set of consistent criteria on which the IJV general manager's or other employees' performance appraisals may be based.

In designing and implementing a performance appraisal system for an IJV, a number of critical issues should be considered. First, it is necessary to determine the type of performance appraisal to conduct as well as how often and for what purpose the employees are being evaluated. Once the purpose of the appraisal is established, it is necessary to address performance criteria and standards to be achieved, career planning issues, and alternatives for training or retraining. Systems for determining equitable compensation and rewards should be devised that are linked to the outcomes of the performance appraisals. Personnel who will be involved in completing the appraisals must be selected and trained in the appropriate appraisal procedure.

To maintain the effectiveness of a performance appraisal system, it must take into account problem areas beyond the control of the venture employee being evaluated. It also might be prudent to periodically review the objectives of the IJV and the partners' organizations and to reassess the political, economic, competitive, and business conditions that confront the venture. As changes in operating conditions arise (e.g., when the venture progresses from an input to an output orientation [Anderson, 1990]), it might be necessary to respond to these changes through modifications in the performance appraisal system and criteria. In addition, the appraisal process must be adjusted according to the categories of employees in the alliance. Consideration must be given to cultural appropriateness of the methods and techniques used.

Training and Development

Employee training and development includes any attempt to improve current or future employee performance by increasing, through learning, an employee's ability to perform, usually by changing the employee's attitudes or by increasing his or her skill level and knowledge. Training programs generally should be tailored to the individual through the appraisal process. As deficiencies are identified, the employee may be placed in a special training program. When implemented correctly, training and development can remove performance deficiencies, thereby improving the employee's ability to perform better and allowing the organization to be more effective. In fact, these programs offer such great potential in promoting IJV performance that it has been recommended that a formal policy regarding the form and content of training and development be addressed in the venture negotiations and legal agreement (Davidson, 1987). Behaviors learned in these training programs should be reinforced through further performance appraisals and rewards.

Formal in-house training and development programs tend to be less common for smaller partner firms or IJVs (Lasserre & Schutte, 1995), which instead tend to use outside firms for providing some or all of these programs. Yet, whether the training is conducted by a partner organization, by someone in the IJV, or by an outside organization, the content of the training program is the critical concern. Many training programs fail to adequately address the problems that confront the trainees (Black & Mendenhall, 1991; Frayne & Geringer, 1993) and, therefore, do not have the intended effect on the performance of the individual and the IJV.

To be effective, it is critical that training be specific to the trainees' location, customs, and ways of thinking as well as to the actual problems that are being confronted. Therefore, it usually is valuable for the human resource and operating personnel from the IJV, and often from the partners' organizations as well, to participate in identification of the issues that must be addressed and in formulation of a training program that would overcome these problems. It also might be necessary to implement a monitoring system, possibly in conjunction with the IJV's performance evaluation process, to assess the effectiveness of the training program and any modifications that might be necessary over time (Frayne & Geringer, 1993).

Training can serve many functions in an IJV context. These include (a) socialization to the general context through language and cultural training including improved understanding of the partners' cultures, objectives, and business practices; (b) specific contextual and developmental or corrective training focused on job-specific skills, local norms and regulations, the introduction and reinforcement of formal and informal policies and practices of the IJV and methods for enhancing individual and team-based learning and competence transfer abilities; (c) improved interpersonal and team-based performance through training in skills such as coaching, negotiation, conflict resolution, feedback, performance appraisal, and networking within the IJV and with the partners or other institutions; (d) improved self-management capability through training in self-management skills; and (e) developmental activity through teaching employees new skills for a current or, particularly in conjunction with career development efforts, a different job in the IJV or a partner's organization (Frayne & Geringer, 1993). Training programs also may be developed to assist IJV employees in effectively implementing key technologies within the IJV as well as in reducing undesired diffusion of technology to outside firms, thereby helping to enhance or maintain the partners' or IJV's competitive advantage (Geringer & Frayne, 1990).

Compensation and Reward

Compensation and reward systems are much more complex than merely establishing base wage rates. Compensation includes those rewards—monetary and nonmonetary, direct and indirect—that an organization exchanges for the contributions of its employees, both job performance and personal contributions. Rewards are incentives for specific types of behavior, and they should be carefully planned to be consistent with the objectives, short or longer term, of the IJV and the partners' organizations. For partners to effectively use compensation—particularly pay—to increase IJV performance, its importance to the target employees must be known (Frayne & Geringer, 1992; Hofstede, 1980). The purposes that an organization hopes to accomplish through compensation also must be determined. Three primary organizational needs that compensation addresses are the attraction of potential employees to the IJV, the motivation of employees to perform, and the retention of good employees.

In designing an IJV's compensation and reward system, it is essential that the system be balanced in terms of internal equity and external competitiveness to attract and retain qualified and committed personnel. Emphasis on individual-level versus group-level rewards must be considered, contingent on the venture's goals and operating context (e.g., the individualism vs. collectivism orientation characterizing the current or desired cultural context of the IJV) (Hofstede, 1980; Lasserre & Schutte, 1995). The system should be sufficiently flexible that consistency can be maintained across the competitive, organizational, and cultural environments in which the individuals will be working, and the establishment of explicit links between the IJV's or partners' strategic objectives and employee rewards often is useful. As part of an effective compensation and reward system, and to provide the basis for effective performance appraisals, it is essential that the system's objectives and procedures be able to be clearly and consistently communicated to, and understood by, the IJV's personnel. The system also must be affordable in both the short and the long run, be easy to implement, and be responsive to organizational change.

It might be both unnecessary and undesirable to use the same reward system in the IJV as is employed by the partners' organizations. Particularly if an objective is to orient employees' loyalty first and foremost toward attainment of the IJV's objectives, different sets of behavior might be required from venture personnel; therefore, differences in reward systems will be necessary. In addition, because the required behaviors might vary over the course of a venture's life cycle, it also might be necessary to monitor the compensation and reward system over time and to modify it accordingly. The increasing need to bring multinational and multicultural perspectives and practices to the HRM function of employee compensation should be monitored as well.

Career Development

IJV assignments frequently are outside the normal career paths of those appointed to the positions, particularly expatriate personnel. Unless the venture is able to provide long-term opportunities for career development, IJV personnel might risk becoming de facto organizational outcasts with constrained career opportunities within the IJV or the partners' organizations. The result might be a diminished ability to attract and retain competent IJV personnel, particularly within senior management and technical positions. This situation can have important implications for the quality of human resources available to the IJV and for the venture's associated performance.

A critical strategic human resource issue is whether to create one or several career paths for IJV employees. If an organization decides to pursue the development of formal or informal career paths, then a related issue is whether these career paths should be broad or narrow (e.g., whether to promote employee acquisition of skills that might be relevant to a variety of functional areas or to be concentrated within a narrowly applicable specialization) and within the IJV or the partners' organizations. A related challenge is identifying the criteria to use in deciding which employees to retain, promote, and develop.

Another career development issue, particularly for expatriate personnel, involves the duration of the IJV appointment. For example, during the initial establishment of IJVs in high-context relationship-based settings, there often is a critical need for establishing constructive relationships with local personnel and host country institutions. This situation may promote the use of longer term assignments, particularly for key managerial personnel and during the initial stages of an IJV's establishment (Lasserre & Schutte, 1995). Although potentially advantageous for the partners' organizations, extended assignments might have important career development implications for expatriate personnel including their ability to develop and sustain personal and professional networks in the partners' organizations. Employee effectiveness and career success also might require the identification and implementation of an appropriate set of support mechanisms such as pre-assignment training, career advancement protection, mentoring, and repatriation preparation and support to assist expatriates (and their families) who are assigned to longer term postings (Tung, 1986).

Competence Development and Transfer

Distinctive competence is any well-developed ability that enables an organization to perform, directly or indirectly, a value-adding activity better than most of its competitors (Andrews, 1980; Selznick, 1957). A fundamental goal of an organization, particularly one that is competing across national borders, is to create and sustain competencies that are superior to the competition in an area valued by the customers (Porter, 1985, 1986). IJVs are commonly used as strategic tools to promote the development or leveraging of distinctive competencies for competitive advantage (Geringer & Hebert, 1989; Hamel, 1990; Harrigan, 1986). In this respect, HRM represents a fundamental variable in the intra- and interorganizational development and transfer of competencies among the IJV and the partners' organizations or other entities because organizational learning and sustained competence development ultimately are accomplished through and dependent on people, individually or in groups.

Even if a partner organization possesses competence that is relevant and important to the competitiveness of the IJV, the partner also must possess the ability to effectively transfer the competence. Factors such as structure and control systems affect the parent-IJV relationship and can, in turn, enhance or inhibit the ease of transfer (Geringer & Frayne, 1990; Geringer & Woodcock, 1995; Hamel, 1990). Factors at the IJV or host country location, including legal environment and culture, also can influence the ability and effectiveness of competence development and transfer.

Organizational control systems also can affect the decision and ability to transfer competencies between the IJV and the partners' organizations (Geringer & Hebert, 1989; Geringer & Frayne, 1990). For example, output-oriented systems (Egelhoff, 1984) involve greater emphasis on monitoring of the IJV by the partner firms through objective data (e.g., market or financial performance measures, budgets, plans). Culture-oriented control systems (Baliga & Jaeger, 1984) encourage the acquisition and development of companywide understanding of appropriate behavior and goals, and they rely on techniques such as social interaction, personnel transfers, and socialization of employees to direct and control

IJV performance. This also can be achieved by sending partner company personnel to the IJV to exchange and transfer expertise and information and to train and socialize new organizational members (Egelhoff, 1984; Geringer & Frayne, 1990). Although information and expertise may be transferred between partner organizations and the IJV in both types of control systems, the type of expertise transferred can differ. In an output-oriented system, technical skills and personnel are more likely to be transferred (Baliga & Jaeger, 1984), whereas in a culture-oriented system, there might be a tendency to transfer knowledge about the organization's culture (which is perceived as a basis for the organization's competitive advantage).

Host country factors, such as laws and culture, also can affect the development and transfer of competencies between the partners' organizations and the IJV because of constraints they might place on the relevance of the competencies across national contexts. For example, marked differences across nations might restrict the relevance or appropriateness of competencies such as training programs, compensation and reward systems, and management practices (Baliga & Jaeger, 1984; Frayne & Geringer, 1990, 1992; Geringer & Woodcock, 1995; Hofstede, 1980).

As suggested here, an important HRM challenge involves the determination of which approach, such as people or systems, will be most appropriate for achieving strategic goals in terms of the development and transfer of competencies between the partners' organizations and the IJV. The decision to develop or transfer competence should be made as part of the larger decision regarding business strategy, and only when external and internal conditions are appropriate.

THE ROLE OF, AND CHALLENGES FOR, HUMAN RESOURCE PROFESSIONALS IN IJVs

The preceding discussion identified the important strategic role of HRM in the operation of IJVs and the attainment of venture and partner objectives. However, awareness of the importance of HRM is not synonymous with the ability of organizations to transform this function from being a frequently subordinated staff function to being recognized as an essential strategic element. Overcoming traditional perceptions, biases, and relationships, and establishing HRM as a strategic function integrated with and critical to the attainment of organizational objectives, often is a difficult challenge and one that many organizations have been unable to successfully transcend.

A particular organizational challenge for transforming HRM into a strategic function is being able to adequately staff the function. The mix of personality, interests, and skills of individuals competent to serve effectively as strategic human resource managers is relatively scarce. Identifying, developing, and empowering qualified personnel, therefore, becomes an important strategic priority in partner organizations and the IJV.

Although there is a key strategic importance associated with the initial design and implementation of HRM systems, that represents only a starting point. Once an IJV has begun operation, it will be necessary to monitor the HRM systems and their fit with the strategic and operational context of the venture. Many IJVs will fail to deliver the benefits originally envisioned (Anderson, 1990; Geringer & Hebert, 1991). The strategies and objectives of the partners themselves can change over time, and this implies changes in associated HRM practices. The IJV's environmental context also can change over time (e.g., changes in industrial structure or competition, changes in government regulations or level of economic activity in the IJV's primary market). As these changes occur, the chances of any one partner being fully satisfied with the IJV's operations and performance can diminish, and modifications in the IJV or its operations might be necessary to reestablish balance. A poorly performing IJV might be turned around by improving the implementation of the HRM systems or by redesigning the HRM systems to be more effective. The key HRM practices must be consistent with the context in which they are used. These HRM practices also must be consistent with each other to stimulate and reinforce particular needed employee behaviors. Identifying, defining, implementing, and integrating best practices in HRM is a complex and ongoing undertaking. Maintaining a fit between HRM practices and the IJV's context over the course of a venture's life cycle, therefore, represents a continuing challenge for personnel involved in the design and implementation of the venture's HRM systems.

CONCLUSION AND IMPLICATIONS

Organizations are increasingly using IJVs as tools for attaining their strategic objectives. Yet, because IJVs involve two or more partner organizations that share ownership and decision making, it often is difficult to manage IJVs so that partners' objectives are achieved. Because it represents a critical factor influencing IJV operations and performance, strategic management of human resources is experiencing a corresponding increase in attention from managers and scholars. However, understanding of HRM in IJVs appears to have lagged behind the demands of practice, and many organizations have chosen to bypass the IJV option or have entered ventures without adequate preparation. These organizations not only might be missing potentially valuable opportunities, they ultimately might be compromising their competitiveness within entire industries or regions. This concern is particularly salient when it involves participation within highly competitive global or globalizing industries.

Clearly, the successful management of human resources in IJVs represents a challenge to all of the parties involved in the ventures. Furthermore, each IJV is unique in its own way, and correspondingly, each may require an HRM system appropriate to and designed expressly for its specific circumstances. As with every other aspect of management in an IJV, HRM systems are subject to nego-tiation (Janger, 1980). The fact of shared ownership and decision making often serves to significantly complicate the management of IJVs compared to more conventional forms of ownership. Although its potential has been largely ig-nored in prior IJV literature (Geringer & Frayne, 1990; Shenkar & Zeira, 1987), we have argued that strategic management of human resources within the IJV may represent a critical factor for influencing the venture's operations and performance.

In this chapter, we have identified factors related to the design and implemen-tation of strategic HRM systems in IJVs. We have discussed the nature of these factors, particularly partner firms and their strategies, the environmental context of the partners' organizations and the IJV, the shared vision underlying the IJV itself, and organizational requirements. We also have presented a conceptual framework that integrates these factors with the HRM systems implemented within IJVs, and we have identified and discussed seven aspects of these HRM systems that are strategically important to IJV design and implementation, both initially and over the ventures' life cycles.

This chapter provides several theoretical contributions. First, it extends the study of HRM practices into an increasingly critical and relatively unexplored area of interest, namely, the management of IJVs. Second, it presents a concep-tual framework that identifies factors associated with the design and implementa-tion of IJVs and the relationships among these factors, particularly with HRM practices. Third, it addresses seven key practices that are important components of strategic HRM systems in IJVs: planning, staffing, performance appraisal, training and development, compensation and reward, career development, and competence development and transfer.

The conceptual framework presented in this chapter is preliminary in nature. Continued effort is needed for refinement of this framework, possibly involving the inclusion of additional factors or revision of the relationships identified among components. The relationships suggested in this framework also should be subjected to rigorous empirical assessment across a variety of IJV contexts to test and refine the relationships proposed in the framework. Nevertheless, the framework presented here is intended to serve as a basis for promoting research and enhancing the successful application of strategic HRM practices within IJVs.

REFERENCES

Anderson, E. (1990). Two firms, one frontier: On assessing joint venture performance. *Sloan Management Review, 31*(2), 19-30.

Andrews, K. R. (1980). *The concept of corporate strategy.* Burr Ridge, IL: Irwin.

Baliga, B. R., & Jaeger, A. M. (1984). Multinational corporations: Control systems and delegation issues. *Journal of International Business Studies, 15*(2), 25-40.

Bartlett, C. A. (1986). Building and managing the transnational: The new organizational challenge. In M. E. Porter (Ed.), *Competition in global industries* (pp. 367-404). Boston: Harvard Business School Press.

Black, J. S., & Mendenhall, M. (1991). A practical but theory-based framework for selecting cross-cultural training methods. *Human Resource Management, 28,* 511-539.

Bleeke, J., & Ernst, D. (1991). The way to win in cross-border alliances. *Harvard Business Review, 69*(6), 127-135.

Buckley, P., & Casson, M. (1988). A theory of cooperation in international business. In F. Contractor & P. Lorange (Eds.), *Cooperative strategies in international business* (pp. 31-53). Lexington, MA: Lexington Books.

Cyr, D. J. (1995). *The human resource challenge of international joint ventures.* Westport, CT: Quorum.

Davidson, W. H. (1984). Administrative orientation and international performance. *Journal of International Business Studies, 15*(2), 11-23.

Davidson, W. H. (1987). Creating and managing joint ventures in China. *California Management Review, 29*(4), 77-94.

Devlin, G., & Bleackley, M. (1988). Strategic alliances: Guidelines for success. *Long Range Planning, 30*(3), 12-18.

Doz, Y., & Prahalad, C. K. (1984). Patterns of strategic control within MNCs. *Journal of International Business Studies, 15*(2), 55-72.

Doz, Y., & Prahalad, C. K. (1986). From Socrates to expert systems: The limits of calculative rationality. *Technology in Society, 6,* 217-233.

Dyer, L. (1984). Studying human resource strategy: An approach and an agenda. *Industrial Relations, 23,* 156-169.

Egelhoff, W. G. (1984). Patterns of control in U.S., U.K., and European multinational corporations. *Journal of International Business Studies, 15*(2), 73-83.

Fombrun, C. (1982). Environmental trends create new pressures on human resources. *Journal of Business Strategy, 3*(1), 61-69.

Frayne, C. A., & Geringer, J. M. (1990). The strategic use of human resource management techniques as control mechanisms in international joint ventures. In G. R. Ferris & K. M. Rowland (Eds.), *Research in personnel and human resource management* (pp. 53-69). Greenwich, CT: JAI.

Frayne, C. A., & Geringer, J. M. (1992). A training program for general managers of international joint ventures. *Journal of Management Education, 16,* 94-115.

Frayne, C. A., & Geringer, J. M. (1993). Self-management: A training program for joint venture general managers. *Research in Personnel and Human Resource Management,* *11*(Suppl. 3), 301-321.

Frayne, C. A., & Geringer, J. M. (1994). A social cognitive approach to examining joint venture general manager performance. *Group and Organization Management, 19,* 240-262.

Ganitsky, J., & Watzke, G. (1990). Implications of different time perspectives for human resource management in international joint ventures. *Management International Review, 30*(Suppl.), 37-51.

Gates, S. R., & Egelhoff, W. G. (1986). Centralization in headquarters-subsidiary relationships. *Journal of International Business Studies, 17*(2), 71-92.

Geringer, J. M. (1988). *Joint venture partner selection: Strategies for developed countries.* Westport, CT: Quorum.

Geringer, J. M. (1991). Strategic determinants of partner selection criteria in international joint ventures. *Journal of International Business Studies, 22*(1), 41-62.

Geringer, J. M. (1998). Assessing replication and extension: A commentary on Glaister and Buckley—Measures of performance in U.K. international alliances. *Organization Studies, 19*(1), 119-138.

Geringer, J. M., & Frayne, C. A. (1990). Human resource management and international joint venture control: A parent company perspective. *Management International Review, 30,* 103-120.

Geringer, J. M., & Frayne, C. A. (1993). Self-efficacy, outcome expectancy, and performance of international joint venture general managers. *Canadian Journal of Administrative Sciences, 10,* 322-333.

Geringer, J. M., & Frayne, C. A. (1997). Controlling IP in alliances is ideal goal. *Les Nouvelles, 32*(1), 24-29.

Geringer, J. M., & Hebert, L. (1989). Control and performance of international joint ventures. *Journal of International Business Studies, 20*(2), 235-254.

Geringer, J. M., & Hebert, L. (1991). Measuring performance of international joint ventures. *Journal of International Business Studies, 22*(2), 249-263.

Geringer, J. M., & Woodcock, C. P. (1989). Ownership and control of Canadian joint ventures. *Business Quarterly, 54*(1), 97-101.

Geringer, J. M., & Woodcock, C. P. (1995). Agency costs and the structure and performance of international joint ventures. *Group Decision and Negotiation, 4,* 453-467.

Gerstein, M., & Reisman, H. (1983). Strategic selection: Matching executives to business conditions. *Sloan Management Review, 24*(2), 33-49.

Hamel, G. P. (1990). *Competitive collaboration: Learning, power, and dependence in international strategic alliances.* Unpublished doctoral dissertation, University of Michigan.

Hannon, J. M., Huang, I. C., & Jaw, B. S. (1995). International human resource strategy and its determinants: The case of subsidiaries in Taiwan. *Journal of International Business Studies, 26*(3), 531-554.

Harrigan, K. R. (1986). *Managing for joint venture success.* Lexington, MA: Lexington Books.

Harrigan, K. R. (1988). Strategic alliances and partner asymmetries. In F. Contractor & P. Lorange (Eds.), *Cooperative strategies in international business* (pp. 205-226). Lexington, MA: Lexington Books.

Hofstede, G. (1980). *Culture's consequences: International differences in work-related values.* Beverly Hills, CA: Sage.

Howard, C. G. (1987, June). Out of sight—Not out of mind. *Personnel Administrator,* pp. 83-90.

Janger, A. R. (1980). *Organization of international joint ventures.* New York: Conference Board.

Jensen, M. C., & Murphy, K. J. (1990). CEO incentives: It's not how much you pay, but how. *Harvard Business Review, 68*(3), 138-149.

Kerr, J. L. (1985). Diversification strategies and managerial rewards: An empirical study. *Academy of Management Journal, 28,* 155-179.

Kerr, J. L., & Slocum, J. W., Jr. (1987). Managing corporate culture through reward systems. *Academy of Management Executive, 1*(2), 99-108.

Lasserre, P., & Schutte, H. (1995). *Strategies for Asia Pacific.* New York: New York University Press.

Laurent, A. (1986). The cross-cultural puzzle of international human resource management. *Human Resource Management, 25,* 91-102.

Lynch, R. P. (1993). *Business alliances guide: The hidden competitive weapon.* New York: John Wiley.

Martinez, J. I., & Jarillo, J. C. (1991). Coordination demands of international strategies. *Journal of International Business Studies, 22,* 429-444.

Martinez, Z. L., & Ricks, D. A. (1989). Multinational parent companies' influence over human resource decisions of affiliates: U.S. firms in Mexico. *Journal of International Business Studies, 20*(3), 465-487.

Meyer, J. W., & Scott, W. R. (1983). *Organizational environments.* Beverly Hills, CA: Sage.

Milliman, J., Von Glinow, M. A., & Nathan, M. (1991). Organizational life cycles and strategic international human resource management in multinational companies: Implications for congruence theory. *Academy of Management Review, 16,* 318-339.

Olian, J. D., & Rynes, S. L. (1984). Organizational staffing: Integrating practice with strategy. *Industrial Relations, 23,* 170-183.

Ouchi, W. G. (1977). The relationship between organizational structure and organizational control. *Administrative Science Quarterly, 22,* 92-112.

Parkhe, A. (1993). "Messy" research, methodological predispositions, and theory development in international joint ventures. *Academy of Management Review, 18,* 227-268.

Pfeffer, J. (1994). Competitive advantage through people. *California Management Review, 36*(2), 9-28.

Porter, M. E. (1985). *Competitive advantage.* New York: Free Press.

Porter, M. E. (1986). *Competition in global industries.* Boston: Harvard Business School Press.

Prahalad, C. K., & Bettis, R. A. (1986). The dominant logic: A new linkage between diversity and performance. *Strategic Management Journal, 7,* 485-501.

Prahalad, C. K., & Doz, Y. L. (1981). An approach to strategic control in multinationals. *Sloan Management Review, 22*(4), 5-13.

Prahalad, C. K., & Doz, Y. L. (1987). *The multinational mission: Balancing global demands and global vision.* New York: Free Press.

Rosenzweig, P. M., & Nohria, N. (1994). Influences on human resource management practices in multinational corporations. *Journal of International Business Studies, 25*(2), 229-251.

Schuler, R. S., Dowling, P. J., & DeCieri, H. (1993). An integrative framework of strategic international human resource management. *Journal of Management, 19,* 419-459.

Schuler, R. S., & Jackson, S. E. (1987). Linking competitive strategies with human resource management practices. *Academy of Management Executive, 1*(3), 207-219.

Selznick, P. (1957). *Leadership in administration.* New York: Harper & Row.

Shenkar, O., & Zeira, Y. (1987). Human resources management in international joint ventures: Directions for research. *Academy of Management Review, 12,* 546-557.

Szilagyi, A. D., & Schweiger, D. M. (1984). Matching managers to strategies: A review and suggested framework. *Academy of Management Review, 9,* 626-637.

Tung, R. L. (1984). Strategic management of human resources in the multinational enterprise. *Human Resource Management, 23,* 129-143.

Tung, R. L. (1986). Corporate executives and their families in China: The need for cross-cultural understanding in business. *Columbia Journal of World Business, 21*(1), 21-26.

Yoshino, M. Y., & Rangan, U. S. (1995). *Strategic alliances: An entrepreneurial approach to globalization.* Boston: Harvard Business School Press.

Zucker, L. G. (1988). *Institutional patterns and organizations.* Cambridge, MA: Ballinger.

PART II

Meso-Organizational Approaches

Extending Agency Theory With Event Management and Foreign Direct Investment Theories

U.S. Investments in Brazilian Banks

MARK F. PETERSON
CARLOS L. RODRIGUEZ
PETER B. SMITH

When corporations invest across national borders, the investor's usual problems of monitoring and controlling the investment become both more complex and less familiar. Agency theory (Eisenhardt, 1989; Jensen & Meckling, 1976) has become the typical starting point for analyzing how a principal monitors and controls an agent. The principal delegates work. The agent performs work. Agency theory focuses on "determining the most efficient contract governing the principal-agent relationship given assumptions about people (e.g., self-interest, bounded rationality, risk aversion), organizations (e.g., conflict among members), and information (e.g., information is a commodity which can be purchased)" (Eisenhardt, 1989, p. 58). However, are the main components

AUTHORS' NOTE: The authors would like to thank the editors, Peggy Golden, Paul Koku, and Paulo Rocha for their comments on the paper. Special thanks to Bob Londoño whose insights from many years of senior positions as a U.S. banker responsible for Brazilian operations provided details and corrections to an earlier draft.

of agency theory and the usual beliefs underlying suggestions about what makes for efficient contracts universal?

Recent international perspectives on management theory have provided both persuasive rationales (Boyacigiller & Adler, 1991; Erez & Earley, 1993; Hofstede, 1983) and robust empirical evidence (Hofstede, 1980; Schwartz, 1994; Smith & Peterson, 1995; Smith, Dugan, & Trompenaars, 1996) that many of the ways in which we understand organizational life are not universal. Consequently, some tenets of agency theory might need to be modified due to particular characteristics of societies outside the United States, the country where the theory originated. Considerable scholarly effort is going into modifying and extending agency theory to deal with special topics such as managing relationships having atypical power asymmetries (Sharma, 1997) or those in which the agent is not likely to be risk averse (Wiseman & Gomez-Mejia, 1998). Several scholars have sought to overcome limitations in the international application of agency theory, particularly for Japan's context of a more implicit norm-based rather than explicit contract-based business system (Bird & Wiersema, 1996; Hill, 1995).

We draw on the main themes of an international line of research and theory about the ways in which managers make sense of work events (Peterson, 1998; Peterson, Smith, Misumi, & Bond, 1990; Smith & Peterson, 1988; Smith, Peterson, & Misumi, 1994) to suggest two basic directions for progressing further toward a global theory of agency. One is that the issues likely to arise within any single principal-agent relationship are not homogeneous but rather vary with the types of work events and situations with which the agent is confronted. The second is that neither principal nor agent is an entirely autonomous entitity. Each is instead a focal point in a larger system of giving events meaning and taking action. This second point develops a theme that sometimes is included, but at least as often is overlooked, in agency analyses. Rather than stopping by making these two points, we offer a framework providing taxonomies of types of events and sources of meaning. As an example, we apply our proposed analytic framework to the agency problem of a hypothetical American bank manager seeking to influence manager behavior in a recently acquired financial institution in Brazil.

The major non-U.S. agency analyses discuss Japan and focus on reliance on norms versus contracts as a key quality differentiating Japan's business systems from the U.S. system. Our focus on Brazil points to various other types of differences. Some of these fall along generalized dimensions such as typical power relationships, whereas others remind us that analyzing two countries is not comprehended by generalized concepts such as norm- versus contract-based relationships and power relationships.

Our analysis has five main sections. We begin by reviewing agency theory and extending it based on a form of sensemaking theory that we have been calling event management research. The analysis then turns to the banking context of Brazil and research comparing the cultures of Brazil and the United States to suggest how national differences, both in general and in banking, might affect agency relationships between parties from these two countries. The principal's reasons for engaging in foreign direct investment (FDI) in Brazil and the implications for the agency relationship are outlined. We then describe the agent's background and perspective. Although our focus is on agency theory, we conclude with implications not only for improving agency theory but also for improving FDI and event management research.

A SENSEMAKING EXTENSION OF AGENCY THEORY

Agency theory is used to understand the interaction between two parties in a cooperative mixed-motive relationship (Eisenhardt, 1989). The cooperative element of the relationship lies in both parties' recognition that the well-being of each one depends on maintaining the relationship. The mixed-motive element lies in the potential each party has to exploit the relationship to achieve personal goals that are not in the interest of the other party. Agency theorists usually attribute such mixed motives to only one side in the relationship—agents. Agents can misrepresent their abilities so as to be hired (i.e., *adverse selection*) or not put the agreed amount of effort into performing their contractual obligations (i.e., *moral hazard*). As it originally appeared in the management literature, the *agency problem* derives from the separation between ownership and management in the modern corporation. Many dispersed owners (principals) need the expertise of managers (agents) to run their investments, but because monitoring and controlling the managers is difficult and costly, managers become the de facto owners of the corporations. In this situation, the agents/managers might become tempted to make decisions that benefit themselves, in most cases to the detriment of the principals/ owners. Some authors (e.g., Albanese, Dacin, & Harris, 1997) have suggested that agency theory should not emphasize the divergence of interests and the eventual conflicts that can derive from this situation but rather should view principals and agents as simply self-interested. During recent years, agency issues have been recognized in many other types of situations in which one party assigns work to be done by another party (Sharma, 1997; Wiseman & Gomez-Mejia, 1998).

Agency Theory

Agency theory has its origins in the property rights literature (e.g., Alchian & Demsetz, 1972) and in analyses of risk and risk sharing that were introduced into the economics literature during the 1960s and 1970s (Arrow, 1971; Wilson, 1968). It was designed and has been most thoroughly tested in the United States (for reviews, see Hoskisson, Hitt, Turk, & Tyler, 1989; Snider, 1994). It draws from the fundamental microeconomics principle that individuals are utility maximizers where utility is the difference between reward and effort. It has been used extensively in diverse social science and business specialties including accounting (Demski & Feltham, 1978), economics (Schattler & Sung, 1993; Spence & Zeckhauser, 1971), finance (Fama, 1980), marketing (Basu, Lal, Srinivasan, & Staelin, 1985; Bergen, 1992), political science (Mitnick, 1986), organizational theory (Eisenhardt, 1989; Fleisher, 1991), and sociology (Eccles, 1985). In finance, since Jensen and Meckling's (1976) seminal work, agency theory frequently has been applied to shareholders' problem of monitoring and controlling managers (Agrawal & Knoeber, 1996; Barnes, Davidson, & Wright, 1996; Denis, Denis, & Sarin, 1997; Jassmin, Dexter, & Sidhu, 1988; Jensen, 1986; Lippert & Moore, 1995; Lynn & Timme, 1993; Mohd, Perry, & Rimbey, 1995; Noe & Rebello, 1996; Rose, 1992; Shleifer & Vishny, 1997). Our application to the problem that headquarters managers face in controlling overseas facilities is a related type of owner-agent example.

Eisenhardt (1989) distinguished between two major streams of agency theory research. The "positivist" stream focuses on situations in which the principal and agent are likely to conflict and evaluates possible governance mechanisms for controlling the agent's opportunistic and self-serving behavior. The "principal-agent" stream is a mathematical approach that analyzes the most efficient forms of contracts under different levels of outcome uncertainty, risk aversion, and information. Its objective is to provide a basis for selecting the most efficient manner for governing every type of agency relationship such as shareholder-manager, employer-employee, doctor-patient, and buyer-supplier. Differences in the most efficient methods of controlling these relationships are attributed to differences in the cost of obtaining necessary monitoring information. Efficiency depends on the costs of gaining information to monitor behavior versus outcomes. Our analysis here seeks to contribute to the first of these two streams.

In spite of the growing use of agency theory in organization behavior and management studies (Bird & Wiersema, 1996), its limitations are well recognized. Donaldson (1990) criticized its exclusive reliance on the narrow model of a utility-maximizing individual and its theoretical isolation from previous contributions to organizational studies. Perrow (1986) pointed out the bias of agency theory in placing primacy on the interests of the principal and in considering that only agents shirk. Consistent with many current views of the value of regulation in making markets function in a societally acceptable manner, Perrow's view is that exploitation by principals has the same ethical quality as does shirking by the agent. Agency theorists tend to gloss over the possibility that principals abuse their superior position to control resources with the argument that the firm's need to protect its reputation will ensure responsible principal behavior.

Some scholars (e.g., Davis, Schoorman, & Donaldson, 1997; Donaldson & Davis, 1991) have presented alternatives to the *homo economicus* individualist perspective of agency theory. A "stewardship" theory of management would stress situations in which goals of agents would be aligned with those of principals. In these cases, attitudes of mutual trust would promote pro-organizational behavior to the benefit of a larger group of stakeholders. Stewardship theorists consider such situations as being as plausible as situations stimulating opportunistic and self-interested behavior. Agency theorists have addressed some of these critiques by recommending more comprehensive or alternative models of contract to regulate the principal-agent interface (Eisenhardt, 1989) or by suggesting that situations in which interests are aligned are simply a special atypical case of agency relationship (Albanese et al., 1997).

Making Sense and Managing Events

Agency theory began from the domain of economic theory that has benefited from insights provided by other social sciences to understand why organizations exist and how they function (Barney & Hesterly, 1996). The type of theory that we propose using to further develop agency theory is that of making sense, interpreting events, and managing meanings. In this view, principals and agents are negotiating meanings with one another and are doing so in a larger social context. Several lines of theory about making sense have been developing. The best known in organization studies is Weick's (1995) work on sensemaking. Weick's work places priority not so much on observable actions or even the decisions that managers announce as on how organization members collectively understand situations.

A closely related line of international research developing at the same time as Weick's (1995) sensemaking perspective is *event management* research (Maznevski & Peterson, 1997; Peterson, 1998; Peterson et al., 1990; Smith & Peterson, 1988, 1995; Smith, Peterson, & Wang, 1996). This line of study draws attention to several aspects of organization life, as summarized in Figure 6.1. The most central aspect is that managers attend to particular events. Consistent with Weick's (1995) use, an event is defined as "a partially abstracted bit of social reality which serves as a unit of information processing, interpretation, or meaning by a social actor in interaction with other social actors" (Maznevski & Peterson, 1997, p. 64). A second aspect is that managers always are meaning makers and only sometimes are decision makers. Organization life is seen as "a series of initially ambiguous events whose interpretation and implications managers strive to influence" (Smith & Peterson, 1995, p. 4). Organizational scholars are increasingly using events as a unit for analyzing process and seeking to understand the ways in which social actors first separate bits of experience from context and then creatively reconnect them (Peterson, 1998). From childhood, much of our initial cognitive experience is with physical things. Piaget (1928) initiated a well-known field of study for analyzing the developmental process through which we learn about physical objects. The physical habit of thinking is carried

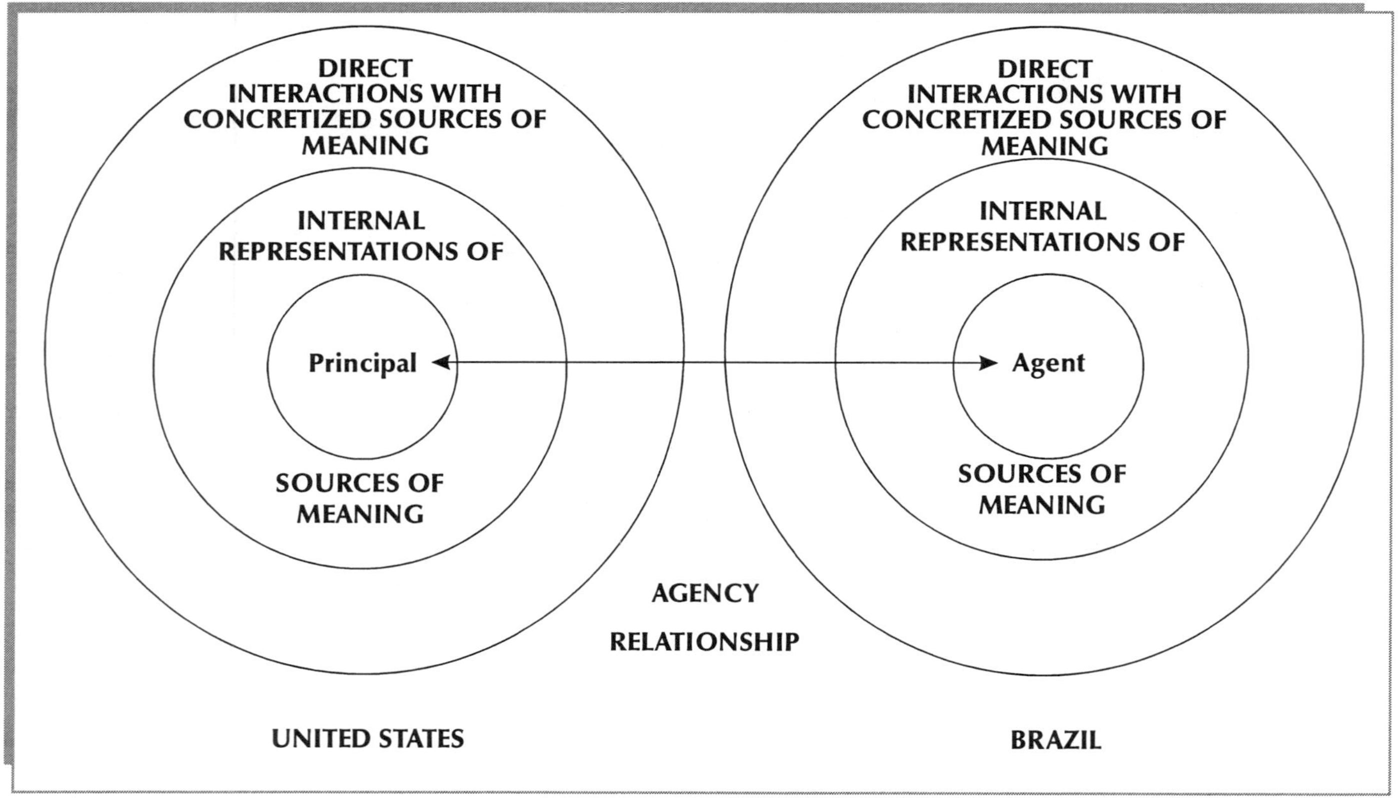

FIGURE 6.1. Meaning Frameworks of Principal and Agent

into our social experience when we concretize the social things—the events—that we notice.

We use the event *management* label to indicate that managers are continuously engaged in a social process of influencing the meanings and implications that events are given. Social interpretation and social influence are interwoven. A third aspect is that whereas events or categories of events sometimes can be meaningfully discussed in themselves as "particles," it often becomes helpful to make explicit how they fit into larger contexts of "waves" or "fields" of events and meanings.

Consistent with our dual interest in things that happen and contexts within which they happen, our empirical event management studies ordinarily include questionnaires (Smith et al., 1994; Smith, Peterson, & Wang, 1996) and often include analyses of larger aspects of industry, nation, or organization context (Peterson, Elliott, Bliese, & Radford, 1996). Event management research connects to various initiatives by organization researchers including those seeking to promote cross-situation learning from qualitative analysis and those seeking to make quantitative contingency research more precise. To do so, we design surveys with "when" questions to ask managers how they tend to respond to different categories of things that happen to them. For example, we would be more inclined to ask a person "How do you feel when you first encounter your boss in the morning?" than to ask "How do you feel about your boss?" We analyze events or categories of events to disaggregate situations into components and to avoid overgeneralizing (Peterson, 1998).

Most of the empirical research and theory development about event management has focused on international themes. Consequently, the problem of universals in the way that events are given meaning as compared to what varies around the world has been a prime concern. One universal element underlying the research is the belief that people in all societies do not make decisions in quite the same way for quite the same reasons. For example, variance in how decisions are made might be associated with cultural factors such as different time orientations and linearity or a tendency toward structured rational analysis as compared to less precise but more pictorial or holistic thinking (Maznevski & Peterson, 1997). In spite of such variation, all humans seek to make sense of a myriad of events by linking them to prior experiences. People organize prior experiences into cognitive structures or schemata (Smith & Peterson, 1988, chap. 4), at least some of which have emotive content. The structure of schemata is affected by cultural factors as well as by experiences idiosyncratic to individuals.

Another universal reflected in our international research is that individuals do not react to events in isolation but rather do so in relation to various sources of meaning. Sources of meaning provide frameworks or structures for understanding events. A taxonomy of sources often found within organizations has been described based on the *role* of the sources relative to any focal individual (e.g., colleague, superior, normative) and the *explicitness* of how these sources are recognized (e.g., explicit, implicit, ad hoc) (Smith & Peterson, 1988, chap. 6). Empirical projects have used examples from and extensions of this taxonomy (Peterson et al., 1996; Smith & Peterson, 1995). An ongoing project distinguishes among *rules, organization norms, national norms, superiors, colleagues, subordinates,* and *one's own experience* (Smith & Peterson, 1995). When an agent responds to the requirements of a principal, the agent does so in relation to sources such as these. Both principal and agent will have internalized these to a sufficient extent to at least partially anticipate their viewpoints. Others require direct interaction.

Passions, Temptations, and Tempters: Linking Event Management to Agency Problems

One implication of event management research for agency theory is that the principal's job does not end by finding a way in which to manage an agent's generalized interest in shirking or acting opportunistically. Both principal and agent draw from multiple sources of meaning to respond to multiple situations. The traditional agency problem focuses on *passions*—those things that parties desire, often reduced to economic self-interest. Our view is that the principal not only needs to understand these passions but also needs to anticipate and continuously manage quite a range of specific *temptations* that appear as particular events and situations the agent faces. A second implication is that the principal needs to be concerned not only with the agent's own internal impulses or preferences for self-interested behavior but also with the effects of *tempters.* Some of these are other parties who the agent might view as competing principals. Some applications of agency theory deal with multiple principals. However, our view is that conceiving all of social life using the language of principal-agent economics is not particularly helpful for capturing the essence of many types of relationships. Other sources of meaning we consider are systems of norms, beliefs, and values. These are even less typically incorporated into agency analyses, and many that are relevant to international affairs may or may not be consistent with an American principal's intuition for what is in the agent's economic self-interest.

Empirical results indicate that organization members make more or less use of different sources of meaning to handle various events and that the sources used most heavily vary among countries (Smith et al., 1994). For agency theory, these results imply that principals not only face the problem of maintaining an overall degree of control over the sources of meaning that the agent uses to inform or support opportunistic responses to events providing shirking opportunities, but principals also need to recognize that the combination of sources on which a person draws is a function of characteristics such as the uncertainty that the event creates for the agent. Also, the sources of meaning from which an agent draws most heavily are likely to vary among countries in ways that correspond to prior research about country cultures (Smith & Peterson, 1995).

In summary, we agree with other scholars who argue that agency relationships are not based exclusively on agents' economic interests and on principals' economic interests in a narrow sense. We extend the developing literature augmenting agency theory to suggest that principals and agents draw meanings from multiple sources. The particular sources used most heavily, and the meanings they suggest for both principal and agent, will be affected by the reasons why the principals and agents have come together in the first place and the types of situations they encounter. The patterns of sources from which principals and agents draw also are likely to vary with each party's cultural background. Large cultural distance between principals and agents will create added challenges. To set the stage for using an event management perspective to improve agency theory, we now turn to a hypothetical example from banking about the relationship between American principals and Brazilian agents. We apply the ideas of passions, temptations, and tempters to uniquenesses in the agency situation created when organizations follow different reasons for FDI. First, however, we need to introduce the banking situation in Brazil.

THE OPENING OF THE
BRAZILIAN FINANCIAL MARKET

Our banking example envisions a situation that only recently has started to occur but that shows evidence of gaining momentum. It is the acquisition of a bank in Brazil by a U.S. bank. There are several reasons to expect that such acquisitions will occur more frequently from this time onward and to provide a guess as to what they will be like when they do.

Even more than world economies in general, financial markets are becoming increasingly integrated. The former Communist bloc imploded during the late 1980s. Developing countries of the Far East have shown high rates of economic growth during most of the past 25 years. The closed models of tariff protection by developed countries and economic development through import substitution followed in developing countries have lost much of their appeal. In countries such as Brazil, an established stream of research shows a strong relationship between outward-oriented economic policies and gross national product (GNP) growth (Lal & Rajapatirana, 1987; Otani & Villanueva, 1990; World Bank, 1995). Particularly in the financial sector, there is a strong rationale for liberalizing financial services (World Trade Organization, 1997). Research shows that practices promoting increased competition in financial services improve not only microeconomic efficiency with lower costs and better resource allocation by individual financial institutions but also macroeconomic management through sounder government policies. These policies also have led to an explosive growth in FDI flows aimed toward developing countries. According to recent figures from the United Nations (1997), FDI inflows into developing countries reached a record of U.S. $349 billion in 1996, 34% above prior-year levels.

Most countries that had followed inward-oriented, highly protectionist economic models during previous decades now are rapidly opening their borders. Brazil is a striking example. Until around 1993, Brazil not only had one of the world's most isolated and protected economies but also had one of the world's highest inflation rates. In the area of foreign trade, for example, imports in 1995 corresponded to only 8% of gross domestic product compared to an average of 25% for the other "upper middle-income" countries in the classification used by the World Bank (1997). As for inflation, the average annual rate was 875.3% during the period from 1985 to 1995, second in the world only to Nicaragua, with 961.6% per annum. The Brazilian financial system was disproportionately large in relation to the country's GNP having reached 14.2% in 1993, the year before an inflation stabilization plan was launched. No foreign commercial banks were allowed to operate in Brazil except those that already were in the country before foreign capital regulations were established during the early 1960s. And even those banks were forbidden to open new branches. As a result, foreign banks held only 9.4% of the total assets of the market in 1996, compared to 22% held by foreign banks in the United States and 21.7% and 21.4% in Argentina and Chile, respectively (World Trade Organization, 1997).

The liberalization process in Brazil was similar to what already had occurred in other countries that underwent rapid reductions in their inflationary processes. The number of commercial banks operating in Brazil declined dramatically. Between 1993 and 1995, the financial sector was reduced to less than half of its size or to approximately 6.5% of GNP (Instituto Brasileiro de Geografia e Estatística, 1997). Mergers between financial institutions undoubtedly were an important factor, but there also were a significant number of bank liquidations. Although Brazil does not have a formal deposit insurance program, the rights of investors were preserved through a special fund that provided assistance to clients of institutions that were liquidated. The costs of this program, however, were high. The process of consolidation still was going on at the time of this writing.

In this new scenario, the Brazilian government started considering, on a case-by-case basis, some exceptions to the restrictions on the acquisition of Brazilian commercial banks by foreign financial institutions. The interest of foreign banks in the local market is increasing. Since December 1996, several significant acquisitions have occurred. Banco Bamerindus, Brazil's then fourth-largest bank, was acquired by Britain's HSBC Group. Spain's Banco Santander acquired Banco Noroeste. Banco Boavista, also among Brazil's largest institutions, was acquired by Portugal's Espirito Santo Group. More recently, Spain's Banco Bilbao-Vizcaya acquired the large Excel-Economico bank, which already was the result of the incorporation of a failed institution into a healthier domestic concern, and the Netherlands' ABN-AMRO purchased a controlling interest in Banco Real. There also have been acquisitions of smaller local institutions, some of which were not having specific financial problems. In such cases, the Central Bank of Brazil is using the special authorizations to stimulate the same movement of concentration and consolidation in the financial markets that is being observed in other countries including the United States. Among the acquirers of some of these smaller Brazilian banks, we find Nationsbank, Mellon Bank, and GE Capital of the United States and Fleming of the United Kingdom ("Foreigners Flock," 1998). The entry in the Brazilian market of American financial institutions, in spite of the smaller size of the acquired operation, signals the initial stages of an important trend that we expect to increase. In the case of acquisitions of troubled financial institutions, one of the conditions for approving an acquisition is that the foreign institution becomes fully responsible for the acquired local operation and that the previous owners totally surrender their controlling stock. This requirement can be quite demanding due to the financial problems the local operation is facing. Although the Central Bank of the Brazilian federal government, rather than the acquiring bank, accepts responsibility for nonperforming loans, both the internal business practices and the reputation of the acquired bank are likely to need rebuilding.

American financial institutions are closely following developments in Brazil. All major investment banks have opened representative offices in that country. In recent auctions of former state-owned banks, U.S. investors were among the bidders. Because the United States traditionally has been Brazil's major foreign partner, holding a 35%-to-40% share of the country's stock of FDI, American institutions are likely to acquire a number of local commercial banks. If they do, then the active, direct local involvement of the acquirers' managements will create more agency relationships between American principals and Brazilian agents. These relationships pose concerns about monitoring and control that we expect to be heightened by the cultural differences between the two countries.

National Culture

Our analysis of the cultural similarities of and differences between Americans and Brazilians is based on the way in which cultural characteristics affect individuals' behavior. Not only does culture have an effect on what one tends to value (Dukerich, Golden, & Jacobson, 1996), it has an even stronger influence on the interpretive schemata and behavioral scripts that individuals use to understand events and respond appropriately (Smith & Peterson, 1988, chap. 4; Thomas, Ravlin, & Wallace, 1996). Schemata and scripts are, in part, a cognitive expression of the values and core beliefs that characterize a culture. Of course, schemata and scripts also reflect the idiosyncrasies of individuals. The same cultural environment will be experienced differently by different individuals (Erez, 1990). Our view is that whereas individuals (e.g., our hypothetical Brazilian bankers) may or may not accept the *values* typical in their culture and industry, it is very difficult for them to not have schemata that provide an *understanding* of their culture and industry. For example, it is conceivable that someone from the United States will not like or agree with the value that *all men are created equal,* but it is harder to conceive of any American not having a more highly developed schema linked to this quote than would most people with non-U.S. cultural heritages.

Triandis (1990) related cultural variables to behavior by positing that the probability of an act is a function of habits and behavioral intentions and that facilitating conditions moderate the way in which people express habits and intentions. Culture affects each construct and relationship in Triandis's model. He also compared culture to a "base rate" around which later accidents of an individual's history would build other influences. Other researchers have suggested that cultural values are *core* values formed during childhood, in contrast to *peripheral* values formed later in life (Lachman, 1983). Several lines of research (Erez & Earley, 1993; Hofstede, 1980, 1983; Thomas et al., 1996) have suggested that individuals from different cultures evaluate situations and potential courses of action according to different behavioral scripts and sets of values. We also expect that core cultural values are learned during early childhood through family socialization, so that culture maintains a very stable deep influence on individual values and behaviors (Hofstede, Neuijen, Ohavy, & Sanders, 1990; Maznevski & Peterson, 1997).

Cultural Characteristics of Brazil and the United States

Are there real, significant cultural differences between Americans and Brazilians? Could these differences become a concern when the sort of mixed-motive interaction that agency theory envisions occurs between people from the two countries? Or, is banking such a powerful determinant of behavior and values that national culture has little relative impact? To attempt answers to such questions, we can draw from international research about cultural differences in values and social relationships. A modest number of studies have compared just the United States and Brazil (Bontempo, Lobel, & Triandis, 1990; Brent, 1988). A few larger scope studies have included these two countries among many others (Bigoness & Blakely, 1996; Chinese Culture Connection, 1987; Peterson et al., 1995; Schwartz, 1994; Smith, Dugan, & Trompenaars, 1996; Smith & Peterson, 1995; Trompenaars, 1994). The most widely cited of these is one by Hofstede (1980, 1983).

TABLE 6.1

The United States and Brazil Along Hofstede's
Dimensions of Cultural Values

	Power Distance	*Uncertainty Avoidance*	*Individualism-Collectivism*	*Masculinity-Femininity*	*Short-Long Term*
United States	38 (low)	43 (low)	1 (highest)	15 (high)	14 of 20 (short term)
Brazil	14 (high)	21-22 (medium/high)	25-26 (medium)	27 (medium)	5 of 20 (long term)
Relative distance (number of positions)	24	21-22	25-26	12	9

Hofstede (1980, 1983) used responses gathered between 1967 and 1972 from participants in 50 countries and 3 regions to characterize typical national values. He uses four value dimensions to describe culture differences (Hofstede, 1994): (a) power distance ("the degree of inequality among people which the population of a country considers as normal" [p. 5]), (b) uncertainty avoidance ("the degree to which people in a country prefer structured over unstructured situations" [p. 5]), (c) individualism versus collectivism ("the degree to which people in a country prefer to act as individuals rather than as members of groups" [p. 6]), and (d) masculinity versus femininity ("the degree to which values such as assertiveness, performance, success, and competition, which in nearly all societies are associated with the role of men, prevail over values like the quality of life, maintaining warm personal relationships, service, care for the weak and solidarity, which in nearly all societies are more associated with the role of women" [p. 6]). Hofstede subsequently collaborated with researchers identifying themselves as the Chinese Culture Connection (1987) and added a fifth dimension—Confucian work dynamism or long-term versus short-term time orientation. This dimension is based on the relative importance of perseverance and thrift and the relative unimportance of stability and tradition, a configuration thought to facilitate a proactive and entrepreneurial culture. Despite critiques about the age and representativeness of the data (Triandis, 1982), Hofstede's results have shown reasonable consistency in 61 studies testing various aspects of their implications (Sondergaard, 1994). The positions of Brazil and the United States on the five dimensions are shown in Table 6.1.

As can be seen in Table 6.1, the country mean scores for the United States and Brazil are distinctly different. One example is in the dimension of individualism versus collectivism, considered by many authors (e.g., Triandis, 1990) to be the most powerful representation of cultural differences among societies. Whereas the United States has the highest individualism score of all countries studied, Brazil is at the exact median of the sample. This is the dimension on which the two countries differ the most from each other. Looking at the dimensions as a set, Brazilian culture tends toward collectivism, aversion to uncertainty, recognition for the normalcy of authority and status differences, and a longer time orientation as compared to U.S. culture.

We have conducted another project designed to take a next step toward understanding how cultural values are reflected in management-related social processes (Smith & Peterson, 1995). This project has included Brazil and the United States among 40 countries surveyed to date. The Brazilian respondents were from the national capital, Brasilia, and from Sao Paulo, Brazil's largest city. The Americans were from various parts of the country but especially the Southwest (for sample details, see Peterson et al., 1995). Participants were middle managers, most of whom were attending either university- or consulting company-based training programs. Respondents were presented with eight widely occurring events such as instances of good and poor performance by subordinates and instances of cooperation problems between departments. Respondents were requested to indicate how much use they believed was made of eight possible sources that could be used to give meaning to and make decisions in such situations. The sources were the respondents' own experience, formal written rules and procedures, unwritten rules of their organizations, subordinates, staff specialists, colleagues at about their same levels, their bosses, and widespread beliefs of their societies at large. Scores based on their answers have been adjusted for demographic differences (e.g., age, occupation, organization ownership) among the participating countries to minimize the sample difference problems that usually arise when conducting cross-national research. The use of any one source also has been standardized relative to the use reported of all other sources to take into account any propensity for people in one country to use the higher end of rating scales than is typical in another country (Smith & Peterson, 1995).

Ranking the countries across each of the sources shows that the average difference between the country scores of Brazil and the United States is 10 positions. In a 40-country sample, this implies that Brazil and the United States would be in different quarters of the set. The most substantial differences are in how much managers report relying on subordinates (8 positions), unwritten rules (9 positions), immediate superiors (24 positions), and staff experts (32 positions). Brazilian managers show less use of subordinates, more use of unwritten organizational rules, less use of immediate superiors, and more use of staff experts when handling events than do U.S. managers. The sense that U.S. managers make more use of subordinates than do Brazilian managers is consistent with our experience in each country and with Hofstede's results. The finding that bosses are not heavily relied on in Brazil is inconsistent with some interpretations of Hofstede's results that show Brazil to be high on power distance. Consistent with Hofstede's (1980) description of counterdependent reactions to high power distance in some societies, subordinates in Brazil might prefer to avoid interaction with their bosses, especially on minor matters. Thus, they would have to find alternative sources of meaning that would possibly represent their bosses' views and desires. Our results would suggest that unwritten rules and staff experts are among these alternative sources in Brazil.

In general, the large cultural distance observed in Hofstede's (1980, 1983) study between Brazilians and Americans also is seen in some of the other studies cited (Bigoness & Blakely, 1996; Chinese Culture Connection, 1987; Trompenaars, 1994). In relation to agency theory, where the relationship between principal and agent is assumed to reflect "efficient organization of information and risk-bearing costs" (Eisenhardt, 1989, p. 59), the characteristics of nationals of the two countries suggest conflicting goals in negotiating and carrying out agreements. The event management results suggest that the Brazilian agent might not be accustomed to using the boss's opinions for handling situations where the American agent would do so. Similarly, delegation from principal to agent might be difficult if the American principal in a superordinate role is accustomed to using input from people in subordinate roles similar to the Brazilian agent, whereas the Brazilian agent expects fewer requests for giving input to a boss.

Measuring Relative Cultural Distance Between Brazil and the United States

Kogut and Singh (1988) proposed a formula to quantify the relative cultural distance between countries (Thomas et al., 1996). The index is based on the difference in culture dimensions among a set of countries, correcting for differences in the variances of each of the culture dimensions. It is calculated as follows:

$$\text{Cultural Distance} = \frac{\Sigma^4 \left[\left(I_{ij} - I_{iu} \right)^2 / V_i \right]}{4},$$

where I_{ij} is the index for the ith cultural dimension of the jth country, I_{iu} is the index for the ith cultural dimension for the uth country, and V_i is the variance for the ith cultural dimension.

Using Hofstede's data, this index is 2.04 for the two countries. As a base for comparison, the cultural distance between the United States and Japan is 2.63 and that between the United States and Canada is 0.25. According to this formula, and in the sample of 53 countries and regions included in Hofstede's (1980, 1983) work, Brazilian and American cultures show considerable differences.

For the agency problem of Americans and Brazilians interacting in banking-related agency situations, this cultural distance is important. In hierarchical intercultural relations in general, Shaw (1990) suggested that difficulties occur between managers and subordinates from different cultures due to basic differences in individuals' schemata. Black and Mendenhall (1990) suggested that culture distance explains the high failure rate of expatriate managers because different interaction skills are required when dealing with foreigners than when dealing with one's own group. The agency situation is a particular example of such interactions. Misunderstandings that arise from cross-cultural interactions result from faulty attributions about the motives and meanings of one another's behaviors because attributions are based on the attributer's own cultural background. Hofstede's (1980, 1983) results lead us to expect that the cognitive structures of individual Americans and Brazilians, affected as they are by national culture, typically will be different in ways that affect their interactions.

Ordinarily, as the Shaw (1990), Black and Mendenhall (1990), and other intercultural articles (e.g., Maznevski & Peterson, 1997) illustrate, the intercultural implications of cultural differences in cognition are not well developed or tested. Similarly, agency analyses tend to generalize broadly. The idea that principals seek profit is taken as self-evidently meaningful. The idea that agents are opportunistic also is a generalized idea. Our sense is that these ideas are not universal. We propose that applying agency theory to intercultural situations facing multinational corporations (MNCs) requires a more careful analysis of the types of interests that both principal and agent really have. In this sense, our perspective differs from the views of authors who have focused on implications of agency theory for improving contractual arrangements. In our perspective, we do not view the agency problem as being a moral anomaly that can be corrected by developing contracts to more completely anticipate potential conflict situations. Instead, agency analyses need to consider the multiple sources of meaning drawn from by both principals and agents and need to manage them through contracts, seeking to establish norms and managing issues as they arise on an ongoing basis. Before returning to the theme of how cultural factors enter into the thoughts and actions of principals and agents, we suggest that theories of FDI provide a more complete understanding of what principals really want than can be readily expressed in a contract.

Reasons for FDI, Corporate Governance Mechanisms, and Principals' Sources of Meaning

Consistent with prior event management projects, we have offered an analysis of the industry and national culture contexts within which our hypothetical agency relationship is to occur. In addition to these "field" contexts, these events need to be understood within a context of "purposes" (Peterson, 1998). When the principal and agent in our example are acting under a contractual agreement that partially regulates their exchanges, they are part of a chain of previous decisions and events that placed both of them in such a situation. One represents the acquirer, and the other represents the target.

The principal has engaged in a decision-making process that has brought the need to hire the agent to run the foreign operation. The principal now is seeking ways in which to see that the agent does not only what is contractually expected of the agent but also what is more generally in the interest of the principal. Transaction cost theory, including agency theory as a special case, argues that it is this limitation on what can be specified and enforced in contracts that creates value in the type of acquisition we are considering here. The contracts most evidently in view are those governing the ownership relationship between the acquired and the acquirer and those specifying the conditions for compensating the agent. The latter type of contract brings all of the stresses typical of compensation agreements given the need to encourage constructive behaviors that are not readily rewarded and to balance the need to reward potentially conflicting criteria such as short-term operating profit with longer term organization building and local area profit versus global industry profit. Controlling for shirking and other types of self-serving behavior by the agent is part of the problem but is a simplification. A principal who believes that for an agent to not specifically follow a contract is shirking might miss the mark. An equally challenging problem is to promote appropriately constructive action by the agent in an uncertain ambiguous world even given the ideal of absolute devotion with no thought of shirking or opportunism.

The agent not only is seeking personal benefit and career success but also is trying to understand the principal's motives. The agent does so to follow not just the formally stated contract but also interests and intents of the principal that are difficult to specify contractually. Both parties are part of a large and complex system in which various other players participate. Being members of two different cultures and two quite different parts of the (now) same organization, each one is most directly faced with a different part of this system. This difference is not only one of purpose but also one of perspective (Peterson, 1998). The parties not only encounter different events but also connect the events they see to different scripts and schemata and draw from different sources to interpret and respond to their experiences.

We expect that the strategic motives behind the decision to acquire a financial institution in such a geographically and culturally distant country are critical to the way in which American principals view events and interact with Brazilian agents. To simplify by stating that the principal's motive for FDI is profit is too incomplete to be useful. The principal's motives are better understood as reflecting a strategy. The strategic rationale of a U.S. bank acquiring its first operation in Brazil is likely to be affected by whether it previously has done correspondent lending to other banks, government lending, corporate lending to MNCs, or corporate lending to Brazilians (R. Londoño, personal communication, April 1998). These prior experiences are likely to influence in complex ways the bank's reason for a new FDI in Brazil. We draw on the theory of FDI and corporate governance to describe the strategies most relevant to our bank acquisition situation. We exclude important FDI explanations such as the market power, product life cycle (Vernon, 1966), and eclectic (Dunning, 1980, 1988) theories as being less directly related to FDI in banking than the ones we discuss. We then suggest how the reason for FDI affects what types of events the principal is most likely to notice, the sources of meaning from which the principal is most likely to draw, and the goals and priorities associated with these sources that are most likely to affect the principal's actions.

There are two major streams of FDI theory (Grosse & Trevino, 1996). These lines of work often are tested as competing hypotheses about why FDI occurs in particular industries or areas. They extend transaction cost economics to explain the boundaries of the firm (Barney & Hesterly, 1996). *Macroeconomic* explanations analyze the reasons behind the flows of investment between countries and consider variables such as product life cycle and trade patterns. *Microeconomic* reasons consider the internal attributes of organizations making investments and the structure of the industries of which they are a part. It is this second group of rationales that is most relevant to the purposes being followed by principals. We treat the microeconomic reasons as alternative rationales that U.S. banking managers may consider when deciding when and how to establish and manage FDI. Cantwell (1991) clustered these microeconomic rationales into two groups that are relevant to banking: market imperfections/internalization and international competition/rivalry. In addition to these two main categories, we note some specifics within them that are especially relevant to agency issues in banking.

Market Imperfections/Internalization

The *market imperfections/internalization* rationale is that the investing company can take advantage of specific strengths in the target market that are unavailable to local firms. Among these might be access to capital at a reduced cost, better management, privileged knowledge about important clients, and more advanced technology. In the case of commercial banking, long-term lending in Brazil is more readily done in dollar-denominated loans through foreign banks rather than local banks (Londoño, personal communication, April 1998). FDI occurs when the best way for the investing company to preserve these competitive advantages is through its own presence in the foreign country by internalizing operations instead of using contractual (e.g., licensing, franchising) or market (e.g., direct exporting, cross-border lending) methods. It is the explanation currently favored by most economists (Hill, 1996). The purest version states that the firm will engage in those projects among available alternatives with the most positive net present value. In banking, this might be termed a "Brazil premium" (Londoño, personal communication, April 1998). A later version (Brennan & Schwartz, 1985; Myers, 1977), the *options* argument, indicates that an initial investment need not have a positive net present value if it "buys" an option to make valuable investments later. Some forms of the options rationale are based on the knowledge acquisition opportunities provided by an initial investment. Such approaches emphasize *organizational learning* (Casson, 1994). Information obtained from diversified, smaller, initial foreign investments allows the firm to build a knowledge base, and investments increase over time with experience. This internationalization strategy is labeled "sequential entry" (Chang, 1995).

Banking regulation/receptivity. Specifically in the banking industry, some authors (e.g., Tschoegl, 1987) suggest a *banking regulation/receptivity* rationale. Most governments, from developed countries and less developed countries (LDCs) alike, establish tighter regulations for entry and operation by foreign banks than those used for locally owned banks. These tighter regulations are related to depositor safety concerns. Host governments do not have the power to influence the financial system requirements of the countries of origin of the institutions applying for entry. Through tighter regulations, governments try to avoid "importing" financial difficulties or bankruptcy by the headquarters institution, contingencies over which they have little control.

Sometimes, however, due to economic conditions such as the liberalization policies noted earlier following from the 1994 *Plano Real,* "windows" open during which foreign banks can gain permission to operate locally. Some foreign banks include only moderately predictable windows in their strategic planning so that they are ready to take the opportunity to enter new markets when windows open in view of future growth possibilities. This approach is a specific form of the options rationale and is especially important for our Brazilian example. In times of turmoil and shrinkage in the financial system (as are now occurring), a government might view foreign banks as safer than local institutions. This regulation/receptivity variation of the learning/options rationale is quite likely for U.S. banks now considering entrance into Brazil.

Follow-the-client. Research about investments by multinational banks in LDCs indicates that a related version of the market imperfections/internalization rationale, the practice of *follow-the-client,* often occurs (Sabi, 1988). According to this rationale, imperfections in host markets give unique value to the knowledge that banks have about their important clients. Unable or unwilling to sell or contract use of this knowledge, banks internalize the servicing capabilities and accompany the foreign expansion of their clients. This is a likely reason for an American bank to invest in Brazil.

International Competition/Industry Rivalry

The second major class of rationales that Cantwell (1991) suggested is *international competition/industry rivalry*. This rationale focuses on strategic considerations that pervade a particular industry sector, specifically in how firms react to significant rivals' perceived or real strategies. A derivative of this hypothesis (Knickerbocker, 1973) is that firms adopt a *follow-the-leader* approach as they imitate their major competitors by following them to new locations overseas. This explanation received empirical support, especially in industries dominated by a small number of large organizations (Caves, 1982). As discussed earlier, only a few American banks—generally the largest American banks—currently operate in Brazil. This imitation rationale is a possible reason behind an American bank's new entry.

Diversification due to opportunism and hubris. We noted earlier that one critique of agency theory has been that principals are not viewed as shirking or acting opportunistically (Barney & Hesterley, 1996; Perrow, 1986). The theory of FDI provides business rationales for principals to engage in FDI. However, the parties we are treating as principals in our present example are managers. They are simultaneously the agents in another set of relationships—those with the ultimate owners, the stockholders. In the agent role that also is occupied by our principals, they face problems discussed in the literature on corporate governance. Financial markets in industrialized countries have developed advanced methods for monitoring headquarters managers in the dual role of principals to overseas FDI and agents of local shareholders. Despite such mechanisms, some motives for FDI amount to a sophisticated form of opportunism by headquarters managers—the bigger the bank, the bigger the paycheck. Theories of FDI have tended to take a rational business point of view and, as a consequence, have deemphasized this rationale. The event management perspective, consistent with sensemaking research and a great deal of social theory derived from "bounded rationality," recognizes that people often are not particularly rational.

Shleifer and Vishny (1997) discussed governance issues that deal "with the ways in which suppliers of finance to corporations assure themselves of getting a return on their investments" (p. 737). Starting with the separation between ownership and control of companies, agency problems between shareholders and headquarters managers are responsible for firms maintaining diversification strategies that *reduce* the value of their stock (Denis et al., 1997). One particularly robust result suggests that *diversification* serves only managers' purposes, bringing the financial markets to penalize firms that engage in such strategies, usually by reducing the value of their stock. Such research posits that personal and career benefits would accrue only for managers. These advantages include the increased power and prestige associated with managing a larger firm, higher pay from compensation packages related to firm size, reduced risk from undiversified portfolios, and the possibility that diversification, especially international diversification, would make the manager more indispensable to the firm.

A derivative of this perspective is what some authors (e.g., Barnes et al., 1996) called the "hubris" hypothesis. In their search for ways in which to become more indispensable to the firm, managers would engage in "empire-building" strategies of acquisition, in many cases overpaying for targets just for the sake of the increased power derived from acquisition. This would be the main factor causing the market to reduce the value of acquirers. The strong support found in recent research for what we call the *diversification/hubris* rationale has not yet been considered in the FDI literature. We believe that such an explanation is another plausible motivation for an American bank to invest in Brazil.

FDI Theories and Banking

Our analysis of the agency relationship in banking began by describing the banking and cultural context within which the relationship was embedded. We introduced the possibility that these fields will affect the way in which events are given meaning, and we did so using a causal language similar to what one might use to describe the types of effects one considers in physical situations. The purposes represented by reasons for FDI show a quite different type of effect, a sort of teleological pull from an anticipated future state. Both types of effects need to be represented (Peterson, 1998).

We have examined purposes for FDI and corporate governance issues that provide alternative reasons why a principal might be interested in acquiring a bank in Brazil. Although these alternative motives ordinarily are used to explain why a principal makes an investment, we believe that they also affect how the principal will manage the investment. Table 6.2 summarizes some of these implications. We next use this table to explain the consequences that the rationale used for FDI is expected to have for the principal's focus of attention when monitoring the FDI, the parties and other sources of meaning that the principal will use most heavily to make sense of what is happening in the FDI, and the criteria that will be paramount in assessing whether it is functioning adequately.

TABLE 6.2

Foreign Direct Investment Motivations: Criteria for Investment,
Focus of Attention of Principal, and Reference Parties

Foreign Direct Investment Perspective	Criteria for Investment	Focus of Attention of Principal	Reference Parties
Follow-the-client	Continue, on a global basis, the relationship with the client established in home country	Important client's needs; local competitors' moves toward the client; smaller emphasis on local results	Client (headquarters and local representatives); local competitors; bank's board of directors
Industry competition/ rivalry	Prevent significant competitors' unchallenged gain of market share	Significant competitors' actions and market shares (global and local); smaller emphasis on local results	Significant competitors (global and local); peers in rival institutions; bank's board of directors
Follow-the-leader	Imitate market leader's moves; industry isomorphism	Market leader's actions; smaller emphasis on local results	Market leader (as an institution) and peers at market leader; peers at other banks
Diversification/ hubris	Increase manager's power, prestige, and compensation for managing a larger and more diversified operation	Short-term financial results of the local operation; future career prospects (external labor market)	Principal's self-serving interests; other banks in home market; peers at own and rival institutions; managers in acquired institution
Learning/options	Sense the local market for decision on future expansion; knowledge acquisition	Environmental conditions in local market; similarities with other potential markets; avoidance of risk; smaller emphasis on local short-term financial results	Other members of the organization involved in knowledge acquisition; bank's board of directors; subordinate managers in host country; local financial authorities

THE AMERICAN BANKER
AS PRINCIPAL

For purposes of our hypothetical example, we select what we expect to be an ordinary arrangement of principal and agent responsibilities. We use the example of a U.S. headquarters placing in charge of Brazil an operational officer who is likely to have either multiple responsibilities in Brazil or responsibilities in other countries as well. We call this individual a regional vice president (RVP). Although the U.S. organization as a whole is a principal at one level, we refer to the individual RVP as the principal for the usual purposes of a dyadically focused agency analysis.

We would expect the RVP to be a powerful employee of the U.S. bank reporting to a senior executive vice president or, most likely, directly to the chief executive officer. The RVP is expected to have substantial information about the strategic FDI reasons for acquiring the Brazilian bank and perhaps had participated in the decision-making process itself. The RVP would know the relative influence of the board of directors compared to that of the bank's top officers and whether the decision was influenced more by business-driven shareholder interest or by manager-driven personal interest.

We make the RVP a woman and do not try to suppose too much about her personal background and education. She certainly will have had prior assignments in international banking and will know the organization practices and culture of the headquarters bank. Although substantial demographic biases in U.S. banking remain, our experiences with the Brazilian banking community, supported by insights from bank managers experienced in both countries, indicate that it is more difficult to anticipate the personal background, education, and career experience of the U.S. principal than to anticipate those of the Brazilian agent. This observation also is consistent with characteristics of Brazilian society suggested by the country's stage of development and by cultural dimensions such as masculinity-femininity (Hofstede, 1980). We can expect, however, that the RVP would have demonstrated previously, in Brazil or in another geographic environment, a keen sense of the functioning of markets different from the United States (Londoño, personal communication, April 1998).

We expect that the RVP typically would have an active role in managing the Brazilian operation. Although a narrower control function involving only receiving reports and checking whether financial results are in line with what was planned would be possible, we expect it to be less common in the new acquisition situation we envision than in other business situations. Due to previous restrictions on the entry of foreign financial institutions in Brazil, most American entrants into the financial markets will be newcomers in the country. In the past, the bank's contact with Brazil is likely to have included substantial cross-border lending, but the way of managing operations in Brazil will introduce extensive learning opportunities. Given the types of banks in Brazil that authorities open to foreign investors, the Brazilian bank also is likely to be sufficiently weak that any FDI rationale would require active management rather than more passive control.

Because the agency relationship associated with managing Brazilian parties is a new one for the bank, the principal is likely to need to rely on personal experience and judgment rather than on established practices, norms, and other experts in the same bank to find ways in which to control and monitor agent behavior. The RVP will be able to confer with other colleagues who might know Brazil well from experiences gained in lending, even if not in managing operations. The principal's role in an agency relationship is affected by market mechanisms that also help to control the agent. Whereas the United States, Germany, Japan, and the United Kingdom have the most fully developed corporate governance mechanisms in the world, such mechanisms are practically nonexistent in emerging markets and LDCs (Shleifer & Vishny, 1997). Agency problems ranging from simple incompetence to pure theft are much more problematic in emerging markets. Established control mechanisms such as influence by large institutional shareholders, use of debt and outside directors, and the market for corporate control (i.e., organizations with poor managers can be acquired by others) provide considerable protection in the United States and other developed countries. Those mechanisms are devised and set by the markets themselves, however, with little involvement from governments except for indirect measures to safeguard depositors' interests and fair trading and to prevent excessive concentration in the industry (Agrawal & Knoeber, 1996). The efficiency of such control mechanisms is more limited in Brazil, due in part to the smaller size and little global integration of the capital markets. Our RVP will need to sort out the problem of the extent to which the Brazilian agent is affected by local market and government controls when considering how to adequately influence the agent's behavior.

How Reasons for FDI Affect the Principal's Interpretations and Actions

We have specified reasons for FDI and described something about the background of a hypothetical principal. In so doing, we have begun to extend the principal side of the agency formula beyond the view predominantly adopted in U.S.-based agency theory research that the principal seeks only to promote profit seeking and to avoid shirking by the agent. Our next step is to apply the ideas of passions, temptations, and tempters introduced earlier to connect our event management variant of sensemaking to an agency analysis of reasons for FDI.

Events in Banking

The events that bankers encounter in their work, from the routine of dealing with deposits or simple loan applications to the strategic interpretation of major regulatory and financial market swings, can range in duration and complexity from discrete particle-like events such as loan applications to longer term characteristics of situations within waves or larger field contexts such as the Brazil situation since the 1994 Plano Real. Events provide the temptations or opportunities for principal and agent toward either cooperation or opportunism.

Passions, Temptations, and Tempters in Banking

Events also can come to be linked to alternative future outcomes or *purposes* of an observer (Peterson, 1998). The viewpoints and purposes of other sources of meaning outside the isolated principal or agent are what we identified earlier as the tempters facing both parties. The strategic reasons for FDI, the principal's role within the headquarters bank, and personal interests influence the principal in three ways. The first is what *criteria* are made most salient by the motivation behind the investment and how these might affect what events the principal views as threats and opportunities. These are the purposes preferred by the principal or agent that may or may not be influenced by those of surrounding parties and norms. They are not simply the cold economics of cooperation and opportunism in agency theory but rather the passions of sensemaking.

The second way is by affecting the principal's *focus* of attention. Focus recognizes that prior experience with a certain type of threat or opportunity increases the chance that events and circumstances consistent with prior experience are noticed. Past experience identifies temptations to do good or to do otherwise. Attention always is selective. In finance, analysts with sufficient experience will notice and give particular consequence to events reminiscent of the Latin American debt crisis of the early 1980s. Newcomers will be oblivious to or coldly cognizant of them. This sort of noticing reflects regularities or wavelike forms in events over time. Reasons for FDI provide a frame or field that influences the events noticed and meanings given. We later detail how different reasons for FDI raise questions such as "Does this situation help me to learn?" and "What is my competitor doing?"

The third way is the *parties* from which the principal draws most heavily to interpret what is happening in the facility in Brazil. The social meaning of events is affected by the unique *perspective* or portion of events noticed by an observer. The roles of these parties, like the purposes of the principal and the events most relevant to the investment, are likely to vary according to the motivation for FDI. We select examples of parties that we expect to particularly influence the principal's attention and interpretations as she works under different FDI motives.

Learning/Options and Banking Regulation/
Receptivity Motivations

The purpose of the Brazilian government in opening a window to allow a foreign bank to acquire a troubled Brazilian bank complements a learning/options motivation. Both the government's and the foreign investor's purposes have a strong long-term component. Because the investment is a late attempt at handling an existing banking problem faced by the government, and because the size of the investment relative to the parent bank's total operations is unlikely to be significant, neither party will be taking a large risk.

Criteria, purposes, and passions. The banking regulation/receptivity rationale for entry makes learning a particularly likely purpose for new entrants into Brazil. If the major motive behind the U.S. bank's investment decision is one of the learning/options type, then one major purpose of the principal will be to deepen local market knowledge from the bank's base in prior cross-border lending experience, and another will be to learn how to manage Brazilian employees within a Brazilian banking operations culture. In both motives, learning will be a key criterion. The U.S. bank expects future business growth. The U.S. headquarters managers have decided that being directly present in Brazil is the best way in which to understand more fully its huge market. Information gained will become part of the knowledge base that U.S. headquarters will draw from to respond to any future windows the Brazilian government opens for investment and will inform decisions to take initiatives in other countries that the bank considers similar to Brazil. The principal will expect the investment to have its most substantial pay-offs when viewed from a longer term perspective. The bank might not need quite the usual returns from this new operation, but it will not accept sizable losses. The RVP's responsibility will be to manage the local operation to maintain this balance and to see that learning objectives are achieved.

Attention, events, and temptations. The purpose of learning will affect what events in Brazil receive most of the principal's attention. The learning purpose encourages the principal to take a broad and relatively unfocused approach to environmental scanning, that is, to broadly "take the pulse" of the market and to notice and reflect on internal management experiences reported by the agent. Our RVP's focus of attention cannot be as narrow on events communicated in financial reports that indicate immediate financial results as it will under other motivations. Neither will the focus be on looking for events that provide opportunities for major commitments with concomitant risks. If the window of opportunity that permitted the acquisition required special authorization from the Brazilian government, then our RVP will scan for events that signal that this authorization could be withdrawn. Among these would be published statements or informal comments from associations of local banks or key bankers and actions by depositors or special interest groups such as nationalist parties that reflect changes in the bank's credibility. Special attention also will be devoted to the agent's reports of internal management issues including the effects of various organization design changes, human resource program changes, and social and interpersonal experiences.

Parties, sources of meaning, and tempters. The purposes for the investment that we focused on in the preceding are mainly of one party—the principal as an individual. Most managers in the United States (the principal's home country), as in most other countries, believe that their own experience is the source they draw from most intensely (Smith & Peterson, 1995). Still, the way in which the principal interprets events will be influenced by the purposes and perspectives of other parties. The acquisition set in motion a learning process for many parties. Our RVP, more than any other organization member, will become the central repository of corporate knowledge about the Brazilian market and Brazilian management practice. However, the mobility typical of American managers, as well as the need for at least a working consensus in American management, requires that this learning be diffused internally. Parties seeking to influence the Brazilian investment will seek to influence what the RVP notices, how she interprets what she notices, and how and to whom she communicates her lessons.

We have found the opinions and views of the immediate superior to be the second most typically reported source of meaning by American managers (Smith & Peterson, 1995). Superiors in our example include both more senior managers and the board of directors. The decision to learn how to manage a facility in a new location will have been actively reviewed by the board representing the bank's shareholders. Major shareholders, interested as they are in higher returns, will be concerned about a move with a learning motive that might delay returns. The risks of investing in Latin American banking became painfully evident during the early 1980s, and subsequent experiences in Mexico and Asia have done little to assuage fears. The senior U.S. bank managers will have been pressed to compare the equity investment to continuing their prior cross-border lending, which allows them to acquire knowledge of Brazil's market but requires less capital and management cost than does an acquisition. Monitoring by the board of directors will be extremely important to our RVP. Unless the board's confidence in management and its consensus in support of the investment decision both are unusually high, our RVP's attention will be directed to events that support the wisdom of the investment. To the extent she succeeds in finding them, she will become a more visible and more valuable employee. As Figure 6.1 indicates, over time, we expect the RVP to internalize the types of interests expressed by the board so that they become part of her intuition when making sense of similar future events.

The Brazilian authorities, another source of meaning, express their interests in several ways that will affect the RVP's interpretations. One way is through formal rules expressed as banking laws and regulations. Our research indicates that American managers tend to draw substantially on formal organizational rules, some of which are internal expressions of national regulations. Brazilian authorities in powerful positions are likely to seek more direct influence as well, influence that an American in Brazil would learn with experience. Government goodwill toward future growth of the American bank's operations would be promoted if the acquisition furthered macroeconomic national goals such as financial stabilization and avoidance of massive layoffs. The RVP will need to respond to these interests that, although not directly opposed to learning purposes, are different from them.

Other parties besides headquarters executives and the Brazilian government also are seeking to influence the RVP's perceptions. The dynamics giving rise to the banking regulation/receptivity window of investment opportunity raise the significance of the Brazilian congress and various political groups. Brazilian banks and banking associations might feel threatened by the presence of a new and powerful player in the market. The Brazilian local manager, whom we discuss in the role of the agent later, will be another important source of meaning. The principal's position is not as a singular entity with an unambiguous purpose toward an agent but rather is a complex one that must respond to a variety of parties.

Follow-the-Client Motivation

Many of the passions, temptations, and tempters surrounding the principal when following a learning/options reason for FDI also apply to other reasons for FDI. These we do not repeat, but we now turn to the uniqueness of our second category of FDI rationales, the follow-the-client rationale.

Criteria, purposes, and passions. A single client or a certain group of clients (e.g., those in a particular industry) might be a sizable part of the bank's business either in its home market or, if it has a large international presence, in its global business. If such key clients start operations in Brazil, then the bank might believe that its direct presence in Brazil is the best way in which to serve the clients by providing local currency financing (Londoño, personal communication, April 1998). This reasoning reflects the market imperfections theory, which suggests that the international scope of a U.S. bank gives it a competitive advantage vis-à-vis local financial institutions in providing service to these clients. In fact, many American companies also are starting operations in Brazil now and might wish to continue working locally with their home bankers. In this case, the principal's attention is turned toward seeing that benefits are provided to the client in Brazil. The principal's success in promoting service to key clients in Brazil can affect the relationship of the client's headquarters with other parties at the bank's headquarters.

Attention, events, and temptations. The attention of the RVP will, in this case, be focused on the important clients of the bank, especially on their needs in the Brazilian market. She also will try to monitor the actions of local competitors, which might be interested in conquering a new and perhaps profitable customer, and even more significantly the actions of global competitors, which might use Brazil for global tactical advantage. As in the learning/options situation, indicators of financial results in Brazil itself might not be very important. The global results that the bank obtains from serving the important client may supersede local considerations.

Parties, sources of meaning, and tempters. A follow-the-client motivation will make the client's local representatives and headquarters the most significant party shaping the meanings that the RVP gives to the financial world of Brazil. The RVP also will be seeking to use viewpoints taken by other banks operating in Brazil, including subsidiaries of other American institutions, that might threaten the advantage the bank has developed with the client. The RVP's superiors, including the board of directors, will in this case be closely monitoring those of her actions likely to affect the client's relationship with the institution as a whole.

Industry Competition and Follow-the-Leader Motivations

Criteria, purposes, and passions. Industry competition and follow-the-leader motivations balance a principal's interests in local financial performance with both the longer term performance most relevant in the learning/options rationale and the global performance most relevant in the follow-the-client motive for FDI. Bank industry competition in Brazil is intensifying. Many global finance industry leaders have, in fact, already entered Brazil. Citibank, Bank of Boston, and Chase, for example, have a significant presence there. Other large international banks, such as the United Kingdom's HSBC, Spain's Santander, and the Netherlands' ABN-AMRO, are part of a wave of acquisitions initiated with the stabilization plan launched in 1994.

Industry competition rationales can be based on a careful and rational analysis of the Brazilian market but also might reflect less thorough analysis. Actions by competitors might genuinely indicate that strategic advantage occurs by accompanying an important competitor into a new market to avoid losing global clients, to take advantage of global opportunities to minimize fund cost or maximize returns from loans, or to maintain position. Alternatively, the tendency toward isomorphism noted in institutional theory (Scott, 1995) as a semirational way in which to live in an uncertain world implies that an alternative motivation might simply be imitating what an important rival is doing. In either case, the principal will be interested both in the local and global pay-offs of the investment in the near term and beyond and in whether competitors are entering or leaving the country.

Attention, events, and temptations. Whereas the learning/options motive focused the RVP's attention on Brazil and the follow-the-client motive focused attention on the client, industry competition focuses the principal's attention on the world of global competition. Making sense of events in Brazil requires that the principal be attuned to what competitors are doing globally. The RVP will be looking for events that indicate the relative support that parties in Brazil are giving to her own bank as compared to globally significant rivals' banks. If major players in the entire global banking community are simply jockeying for initial position in Brazil, then indicators of development of long-term credibility in Brazil might take priority in the RVP's attention over immediate financial results. In this case, the RVP can take the view that if other important industry players have made the decision to enter that market, then the bank *must* be there as well to anticipate an intensification of Brazil's potential for a central future role in global competition.

Parties, sources of meaning, and tempters. The meanings that competitors are giving both to events in Brazil and to global financial events are critical to the RVP under this motivation for FDI. Because competitors generally do not offer proprietary information about their thoughts and intentions, the RVP will need to internalize a type of intuition—a "What are they thinking?" standpoint—when anticipating how competitors are viewing events in Brazil. Competitors' observable actions and sources of informal information provide clues. This sort of internal representation is reflected in the intermediate of the three rings in Figure 6.1, but unlike most situations, it is more difficult to supplement by the direct interaction represented by the outer ring. Whereas the board and senior bank officers will be very interested in the RVP's actions under the two motivations described previously, the interest will be even more intense if the rationale for entry in Brazil is global competition. The bank's global standing, then, might be on the line. Officers in the bank, including our RVP, also can expect rivals to notice what they have done to acquire or maintain the status of a competitor that deserves a higher degree of respect.

Diversification/Hubris Motivation

The finance literature strongly supports the adverse effects of many examples of diversification on shareholders' wealth. In geographic diversification into Brazil, the officers of the U.S. bank, including our RVP, might be mainly interested in the power, prestige, compensation, and indispensability that tend to come to managers of a larger operation. There is another important agency relationship here—between the shareholders as principals and the U.S. directors as agents (including our RVP). The hubris motivation certainly is not going to be explicit. It will be linked to one of the other explicit legitimate reasons for FDI.

Criteria, purposes, and passions. Diversification into Brazil following a hubris motivation implies a primary interest in making the job of the managers easier and compensating it better. Shirking by the RVP here is subtle and perhaps not even conscious. The RVP might be part of a managerial team, at least some members of which genuinely believe that expanding into Brazil will be in the shareholders' interest. Regardless of whether it is or not, it may well fit the personal purposes of the RVP.

Attention, events, and temptations. Because the hubris motive for diversification is not a legitimate one to publicly endorse, much of what our RVP attends to will be directed by whichever other rationale for FDI is the explicit one. Adding an element of hubris, however, is likely to slant what the RVP notices. Attention to risk-taking alternatives for further expansion could be heightened. Situations providing short-term pay-offs that the RVP can personally use as the basis for soliciting a better position with a competitor might be sought even if the long-term consequences appear problematic.

Parties, sources of meaning, and tempters. The sources of meaning of most concern under a hubris rationale are the RVP and the managers. The RVP probably received authorization from her superiors to increase the volume of operations of the bank in Brazil because they also might want the bank to become a major player in that market. Depending on the degree of self-awareness that the main pay-off is to the managers and not to the shareholders, the viewpoint of the board might be recognized as a sort of guilty conscience. Immediate results might assuage the guilty conscience, even if they come at the expense of local credibility and tension with local authorities. At the same time, expansion will increase the RVP's prestige in the eyes of the board as well as the external labor market. The views of her peers in other institutions, therefore, are going to be another important reference for her actions. Finally, the Brazilian agent, the manager of the local operation, will have an important role because the RVP will depend more on the agent to obtain short-term financial results in a market with which she is not yet familiar.

Perrow's (1986) critique of agency theory suggested that the principal also can hide her true motivations when selecting an agent. The RVP might have no intent to maintain a long-term employment relationship with the agent and could be only looking for an agent who will reflect a certain image or bring a portfolio of clients.

THE AGENT:
IT'S A "BRAZIL THING"

The interests of the principal substantially affect what is wanted of the agent and how these wants are best achieved. The interests of the agent have similar implications. The American principal, still trying to make complete sense of what the board and managerial superiors expect in the new arrangement, has a special interest in knowing about the agent so as to minimize the usual agency problems of moral hazard and adverse selection. An American idiom, "It's a ____ thing" (where the blank gets filled in with a demographic characteristic of the speaker), communicates something about the situation. There are some things about the members of a community, such as the agent, that are not readily understood outside that community, as by the principal. Still, we try to give some indications of what our principal can expect including both some cultural generalities from our surveys and some specifics about banking in Brazil.

Who is this person that the RVP, the principal in this agency relationship, is going to contract to run the local operation? To this point, we have left the agent as a type of empty box. To color in the box, we anticipate that the most common situation in the acquisition of a Brazilian financial institution by an American bank will be for the American principals to have the operation be managed locally by a Brazilian. The reasons for FDI are less immediately apparent to this person than to the principal. Instead of focusing on reasons for FDI, expanding the agent side of agency requires us to give an identity to this individual by taking into consideration characteristics not only of the Brazilian financial markets but also of the country's social and educational systems. Considering the expected cultural distance between individuals of the two countries and the different motivations of the players, Eisenhardt (1989) would suggest this to be a typical agency situation in which "contracting problems are difficult" (p. 71). They also resemble, in some respects, the reversal of power that Sharma (1997) described in relationships where the agents are professionals having expertise that the principals are not fully capable of evaluating.

The Agent's Business Experience

The direct experience that one of us has with the banking community in Brazil indicates that we can specify more about the probable agent than we could about the principal. The U.S. bank certainly would want an agent with substantial experience in the local financial markets and with handling management situations, especially someone who has held prior senior executive positions. In addition to the usual factors implying that an MNC should staff with a host country national when acquiring a new operation in an unfamiliar country, the long period of hyperinflation that Brazil had from around 1982 to 1994 makes it especially unlikely that an outsider would understand local banking conditions well enough to manage a facility in Brazil. Inflation rates went down after the 1994 stabilization plan to approximately 5% to 6% per year in 1996 and 1997, but there always are concerns about price stability. The U.S. headquarters is unlikely to have many managers with the experience needed to handle the technical financial aspects of this market and is even less likely to have someone with managerial experience in Brazil who could head the operation there. The acquiring bank could select an existing employee of the acquired local operation as the agent. However, because we are assuming that the Brazilian authorities are permitting acquisition because the local bank is in distress, the U.S. principal is likely to want somebody not associated with the previous controlling group.

Consistent with typical practice for senior positions in other financial organizations in Brazil, the agent will have experience with and expect an outcome-based contract, one that bases manager compensation on local performance. As in the United States, such contracts are very common in Brazil at top levels in financial services organizations. Manager turnover in financial institutions has been high, especially during the inflationary years. Our local manager is likely to have had similar positions in various other organizations. Hiring a former senior officer from one of the other large U.S. banks that operate in Brazil would be a reasonable choice consistent with common practice. Then, language would not be a problem, and the banking experience would be adequate in terms of both the job itself and familiarity with American banking practices. This move could signal the serious intentions of the RVP's organization to other players in the Brazilian market. Another alternative that many foreign financial institutions have adopted is to employ a former officer of the Brazilian central bank.

The Agent's Upbringing

Even in comparison with the United States, there still are very few women in top positions in Brazilian financial institutions. For this reason, we treat this individual as a male. He has to have a good working knowledge of English, having possibly lived in the United States either for his education or in a working assignment. To achieve a significant role in Brazilian financial institutions, the Brazilian agent must have had a high-quality education. He probably has been educated in private schools given that the public primary and secondary school system in Brazil generally is considered to be very deficient. Families that can afford to send their children to private schools do so. In the event our local manager went to college in Brazil, he probably went to a public university because these are considered to be, on average, better than private institutions. Given the finances needed to support such an education and the lack of financial support by universities or the state for people without their own resources, we can expect that this person comes from an upper middle-class family. Brazil, like most other LDCs, does not have a very large middle class. The differences between the richer and the poorer still are extremely significant. Brazil has one of the world's most concentrated income distributions (World Bank, 1996), and consequently, there is little class mobility. Compared to what the American principal will have experienced at home, even recognizing the demographically linked barriers to senior positions in the United States, the range of backgrounds among people qualified to manage the Brazilian operation is quite restricted.

The Agent's Expectations

What is going on in the mind of this agent when he prepares to meet with his new boss? What are his fears and concerns related to the new job, to his perceptions of what is expected of him in the new position, and to the relationship with the American principal in general? We know a little bit about the types of issues that can arise in intercultural supervisory situations, but most such analyses are of relationships between Japanese bosses and Americans and are in manufacturing contexts where direct interaction is more frequent than is the case here (Brannen, 1994; Peterson, Peng, & Smith, 1999). He might not have sufficient understanding of the reason for the FDI, especially to the extent that the reason does not focus only on immediate, local financial results. Although he probably will have had substantial prior relationships with Americans, cultural research indicates the potential for stereotyping. Agency theory points to the agent's interest in personal financial rewards or the career implications of the prestige from working for a foreign organization. The Brazilian manager certainly is going to acquire a higher standing among his peers, possibly offering him better career prospects. Given the support provided by resources from the American institution, the Brazilian manager also is betting that he can turn the distressed institution around. Doing so will increase his standing in Brazil's financial community.

Even when seeking the principal's benefit, the agent will be concerned with factors specific to the Brazilian financial markets. The local financial system is decreasing in size and as a percentage of the country's GNP. The process of liquidations and mergers being orchestrated by the Brazilian financial authorities is, at the time of this writing, still in force. This represents added uncertainty for the agent, uncertainty that compounds the effects of potential misunderstandings with the principal.

Potential Principal-Agent Misunderstandings

Agency theory proposes that control mechanisms are central to the agency relationship. The principal needs to motivate the agent to pursue the financial well-being of the principal. Our discussion of reasons for FDI implies that communication of intent actually is more central. The significance of communicating intent is evident when we consider what directions might be taken by an agent who is highly motivated to pursue the principal's success but unaware of what the principal means by success.

Based on his prior banking experience, the motivated agent might expect that his new employer wants to increase market share in Brazil. In this case, he will propose to aggressively reduce the cost of credit and of other banking services or to increase the interest paid to investors. If the motivation of the principal is to use the operation to carefully learn about the Brazilian market, then the principal will disapprove such plans.

Alternatively, the motivated agent who believes that the American headquarters does not have enough experience in LDCs might suggest increasing its presence in the Brazilian market more gradually by making fewer loans with lower risks. He also could be concerned that an unexpected return of inflation in Brazil would create problems for the U.S. bank. However, if the motivation of the principal is not just shareholder interest but also managerial hubris, then the RVP would demand higher risks and immediate results than the agent might consider to really be in the best interest of the headquarters.

An experienced Brazilian banker who sees that the new parent bank has long experience with a client who operates in Brazil might conclude that seeking local profit through relating to that client is a clear road to success. If the U.S. bank's major motivation is of the follow-the-client type, however, then the principal might decide that the operations with the client in Brazil should yield flat or even slightly negative returns in the local books. This could occur if the client relationship is highly profitable globally but the key sources of the profit come from the relationship in other parts of the world. Explaining this situation effectively to a Brazilian agent who is being rewarded on an outcome-based contract tied to locally generated results is likely to be quite challenging.

Different perceptions provide opportunities for misunderstandings between the two parties in this agency relationship. Effectively managing the agency relationship requires that the agent know that the U.S. bank acquired the Brazilian operation for specific reasons related to global competition in the banking indus-

TABLE 6.3

Agent's Responsibilities and Key Challenges
According to Selected Foreign Direct Investment Motives

Reasons for Entry	Agent Responsibility	Key Agency Challenges
Follow-the-client	Treat the global client of the bank with differential attention	Understanding, on the part of the agent, of the importance of the client for the institution (client might be new for bank in the country)
Industry competition/ rivalry	Engage in proactive actions with the objective of gaining market share over rivals	Agent has to make sense of a competition that might not be directly his or hers; agent might not be willing to make moves that threaten local competitors, where some of his or her friends or relatives might be working
Follow-the-leader	Demonstrate responsible management through conformity	Sources on which the principal is drawing most likely are not available for the agent and are, in general, external to the country
Diversification/hubris	Increase global market share	Agent might have difficulties in understanding the true motives behind the principal's actions
Learning/options	Contribute to corporate knowledge base having potential future value	Agent might not be able to make complete sense of an operation that apparently has no immediate concern for results

try. His own self-interest might lead him to want to focus on new clients or more profitable operations to increase the rewards in his outcome-based contract. The point of most agency arguments is that this is exactly what a good agency relationship should seek to achieve. However, the examples we have noted indicate that it might be a very subordinate thing to achieve. Success in achieving profits and growth without providing the principal with information about competitors' moves and other aspects of the local situation would be shirking. The implications of some such motivations by the principal for the agent are presented in Table 6.3.

The Agent and Multiple Sources of Meaning

Agency theory uses the idea of self-interest in a social psychologically under-developed way. The idea of "self"-interest seems clear but in fact is not. Our extension is consistent with other recent attempts to augment agency theory by suggesting that an agent responds to viewpoints and interests of various other parties besides the principal. These might even include some that the agent does not view as promoting his "self"-interest. In our banking example, these include parties such as potential future employers, federal banking laws, key government officials, and the banking community; business norms such as those about appro-priate use of personal relationships for business purposes and acceptance of informal personal payments; and non-business parties and norms such as family expectations. Our analysis has suggested some elements of the influence that some of these sources might have, but the RVP and agent in our situation will need to deal with other complexities as well.

Considering the high level of mobility in the financial markets, the interests of the agent's future potential employers are an important source of meaning for him. Corporate governance theory posits that the need to keep a reputation vis-à-vis potential employers is one of the major factors that help to align interests of principals and agents. This reputation can be primarily based on results, but it also can be influenced by strong ties with powerful politicians or government authorities such as career officers of the Central Bank.

Another source that some authors (e.g., Amado & Brasil, 1991) have stressed is the federal government. It affects Brazilian business, both because banks are concerned about its regulatory and other actions and because senior bankers con-sidering later government careers will be personally concerned to have good reputations with government officials. The government can be especially influ-ential for a U.S. bank that has entered the Brazilian market on the basis of special government authorization. The Brazilian constitution, approved by the congress as recently as 1988, established general principles for regulating financial markets, but in most cases, such principles have not yet been made into specific laws.

The government can be a particularly salient source in cases where the agent is a former government officer such as a director of the Brazilian Central Bank. These sorts of agents employed by foreign banks have received special attention in the Brazilian media. If this is his background, then our agent might be con-cerned about the political consequences of what the American principal would require of him, consequences that could make it difficult for him to return to a government position. This career interest might make certain riskier, more con-troversial operations aimed at producing short-term results not acceptable to him.

These sources of meaning might have conflicting implications for our agent. Reputation in the Brazilian domestic banking community, reputation in the foreign banking community in Brazil, and reputation in the Brazilian government can be different things. Financial results are likely to be the most important factor in the first two, whereas compliance with local regulations and being a good citizen through, for example, an active role in charity work would matter more in the third. Even success in saving a distressed financial institution, keeping jobs in a labor-intensive industry, and representing foreign capital could influence the agent's reputation differently in various groups. In fact, a factor that might be impressive for a particular constituency could have the opposite effect for another constituency. For example, betting against the local currency could result in large and quick profits for the agent's employer but could create hostility among the financial authorities. These considerations and the agent's career aspirations will affect the sources from which the agent draws most heavily.

Whereas many of these sources are likely to be understood less fully by the U.S. RVP than by the Brazilian agent, one source of meaning provides greater common ground for understanding. The financial services industry is one of the more globalized sectors of the world economy. Powerful forces associated with the growth of international trade and communications provide an incentive for large commercial banks to be present in most major markets. Globalization produces forces toward a convergence of banking practices in structures, then, in two ways. One is through the efficiencies for all parties that are provided by consistency, and the other is through transfer of practices between countries within a single bank.

These commonalties in explicit aspects of financial reporting are quite strong between Brazil and the United States. In the Brazilian financial markets, events happening with the country's major trading partner and investor, the United States, are felt immediately. The interconnection of markets, or cointegration, is becoming a concern in the financial services industry because it mitigates against portfolio diversification. There are signs that the Brazilian and U.S. financial markets are becoming increasingly linked. Interest rates in Brazil have been among the highest in the world. Brazil's monetary authorities set the high interest rates to stabilize the Brazilian real and control inflation. Many Brazilian companies have been forced to look for less expensive capital in other financial markets, mainly the United States, the world's major financial center. The need to meet the requirements of American lenders has produced a convergence between Brazilian accounting standards and American financial practices. The immediate cause is not American government imposition of standards on Brazil but rather the practical need to facilitate communication and presentation of financial information. The similar institutional frameworks in the financial services industry between the two countries provide a common background for the agency relationship.

Some Examples of Banking-Related Events

Agency theory frames a principal's problem in controlling an agent as one of controlling those of the agent's passions or purposes that diverge from those of the principal. We provide two examples in what follows to add that the particular passions or purposes that become salient to an agent vary depending on specifics of the situations, events, and temptations that the agent faces. Agency theory, with its focus on an isolated principal and agent dyad, contributes one type of understanding to these events. An event management perspective that broadens the scope of interpretation to include multiple parties and a wider range of purposes beyond simple economics contributes further understanding.

A Large Commercial Development Project

The first event is an investment project proposed to the bank by a potential client. The project is a large commercial development requiring capital from a syndicate that is to include multiple debt and equity sources as well as our bank. The commitment requested by the developer exceeds what the U.S. principal has indicated to be acceptable. The agent knows about the strict credit policies set by the U.S. headquarters to try to overcome the difficulties of a weak local institution, but he decides to bring the project to his boss, the RVP, anyway. Both parties will recognize that concerns about possible real devaluation will require that the loan be denominated in dollars and that the loan will be either directly held by the U.S. head office or based on a loan from the head office to the Brazilian subsidiary, subsequently lent to the syndicate (Londoño, personal communication, April 1998). Agency theory encourages the RVP, after receiving the request and hearing the arguments of the local manager, to consider possible shirking, that is, that there might be other hidden factors involved in the operation. The local manager might be shirking his responsibilities by not doing a thorough credit analysis of the syndicate applying for the credit. Agency theory would encourage the RVP to consider that the local manager is only interested in personal benefits from the financial effects that the approval of the project will have given a reward system based on credit volume.

Considering the sources of meaning and social context to which an event management analysis directs attention requires that the agent's situation be understood even more broadly. One scenario that would not be unusual in Brazilian banking and that provides a broader view might be as follows. The first contact was an informal encounter at a social gathering hosted by the local manager, our agent. This developer happens to be a politically influential and powerful individual in Brazil. The two friends talk briefly about the project and arrange for technical people from their respective organizations to meet to discuss specifics.

The project presents interesting returns, the financial guarantees are liquid, and many other local banks already have agreed to participate in the syndicate. The size of the project, however, is very large for the bank, which has a limit for commitment to individual clients. The local manager feels that he needs to join the operation, not only because it presents adequate terms but also because of the political power of his friend. The fact that other banks, including direct competitors, already have agreed to the project is another strong motivation. Finally, the development is going to be built in a low-income region in northeastern Brazil and will provide much-needed employment for the local population. Participation will enhance the standing of the bank as a "good citizen" vis-à-vis the Brazilian financial authorities. The agent, now acting on behalf of a foreign organization, finds the citizenship element important given the special way in which it acquired its license to operate in the country. The situation, therefore, has encouraged the agent to consider multiple sources of meaning including the views of an influential network of business and government people, the viewpoints of the community in general, and a sense of societal norms about what projects are good and right for a manager to pursue. The local manager is convinced that the operation is in the principal's best interest and should be approved. The principal might disagree, but for her to take the usual agency view that the suggestion represents shirking probably is misleading. She needs to look beyond what Americans usually would think of as shirking to consider that she must work through with the agent the sources of meaning from which he draws.

The situation we have described is consistent with banking projects in Brazil that we have experienced. An emphasis on agency concerns about shirking could lead here to an inappropriate conclusion given several of the reasons for FDI noted earlier. The project provides opportunities for learning and developing long-term credibility with less risk than might appear on the surface. Effectively taking advantage of the opportunity, however, would require that the principal accept the costs of becoming quite well informed about the agent's situation. Considering the full sources of meaning from which the agent is drawing provides guidance as to what the principal needs to do to become adequately informed.

A Change in Global Capital Markets

As a second example, our principal and agent will need to make sense of events in global capital markets that affect the bank's position in Brazil. Let us give our local operation a reputation for being an aggressive player in the capital markets. It manages a number of investment funds having a significant percentage of their assets invested in the Brazilian stock markets. Most of the investors are foreigners, including institutional clients of the American bank, who were attracted to the higher potential returns of the Brazilian capital markets. The investment instruments are highly leveraged, based on futures and options that can present extremely elevated positive returns. They also show sizable losses when market movements do not go in the expected direction. Just such sizable losses are among the reasons our Brazilian bank became sufficiently troubled that it was acquired by foreigners.

Beginning in late 1997, a large number of loans to organizations throughout Asia were threatened. The sudden perception of severe economic problems in other emerging markets causes turmoil in the world's major stock markets. The perception of Brazil as just another emerging market provokes concern among important international investors. These investors consult the bank in the United States on the best way in which to avoid investment losses. The principal is called by her superiors to present her recommendations.

The American principal knows that the profile of the bank's investors in Brazil tends to be conservative. The first reaction of the investors most likely will be to immediately sell all of their local holdings. The principal firmly believes that the best course of action is to maintain the positions in the Brazilian markets but decides that she needs more information from the Brazilian agent to support her decision. The moment she does that, however, she becomes concerned about what the true motivations behind the agent's view could be. The problems of the United Kingdom's Barings Bank, caused by an overambitious money manager, still are in her mind. Opportunism is something she was taught to be concerned with in her dealings with subordinates. She might be especially concerned about a new subordinate in a culturally distant country about which she does not have full information.

Due diligence requires that she consult the Brazilian agent for his possibly better informed perception of the local response to global financial events. Both might agree that there is no rational reason for concern about the Brazilian financial markets. The Brazilian manager, however, informs her that other local portfolio managers, his peers in local institutions, expect violent swings in the prices of Brazilian stocks. He believes that after a few weeks the market will stabilize, with favorable perspectives, and that the net position after the movements of the indexes will be very positive. The agent is trying to have his own sources of meaning used by the RVP.

CONCLUSION

Our starting point has been agency theory. Our technique of creating characters for our hypothetical principal and agent and taking them through two examples of banking terrains where the events they face include financial monsters will be familiar to those who enjoy fantasy games. We have used this device to develop some theoretical ideas to suggest the value that the theory of FDI, interpreted from a sensemaking perspective, has for improving agency theory. Agency theory, at least in its earlier forms, provides a less detailed and less colorful simulation of life. FDI considerations take the agent into unfamiliar roles.

Challenges for American Bankers Investing in Brazil

Our analysis should have implications for U.S. banks considering acquisitions in Brazil. We expect that the interest of American investors in acquiring Brazilian banks will develop successfully. It certainly would provide the opportunity for empirical research to evaluate the conjectures presented here. We wish both parties well as they seek joint benefits, as each benefits the other party with legitimate interests in their relationship, and as they help to create a functioning, global competitive market in financial services. As they do so, our version of agency theory, now augmented by FDI and sensemaking, points to some challenges for principals and agents to overcome.

In our specific example, the American acquirers of the financial institution in Brazil typically would send at least some American employees to the Brazilian operation. The specific role of the American managers could be mainly a communication role between managers at the U.S. headquarters and the Brazilian operation or a more direct supervisor-subordinate relationship. Anywhere along this continuum, the contribution that expatriates can make to transferring knowledge and organizational culture from parent to subsidiary is a major reason why MNCs will accept the stress and pay the high labor costs typical for such employees. Expatriates are the usual conduits for transferring knowledge between the foreign owner and the local operation, but a number of challenges must be overcome to realize their potential (Peterson et al., 1999). These include a *communication challenge* (related to the problems that subordinates have trying to accurately interpret the supervisor's intentions), an *influence challenge* (how cultural norms affect the legitimacy of a supervisor's influence attempts), a *circumvention challenge* (given that supervisors compete with other sources [e.g., colleagues, norms, formal rules] on which subordinates can draw to govern and legitimate their actions and attitudes), and a *symbolic challenge* (how common stereotypes about the supervisor's nationality affect the meanings that subordinates give to their actions and intentions). All of these factors pose concern to a relationship in which the basic premises already suggest significantly different worldviews.

Specifically in banking, a communication dilemma between principal and agent can arise when the operation in Brazil is considering a loan to what to them is a new multinational client. If this client had only recently started operations in Brazil, then it might not yet have enough local assets to serve as collateral for the loan. Given the stronger norm supporting secured loans in Brazil as against loans based on more general credit considerations in the United States (Londoño, personal communication, April 1998), the agent's technical analyst would recommend for the credit request to be denied. This new client, however, could be a large and traditional client of the U.S. headquarters bank, and the principal would expect this established relationship and the client's general creditworthiness to be taken into account in the agent's analysis. The principal, nevertheless, does not want to override loan review procedures established to protect the financial health of the local subsidiary by preventing it from making bad loans. The agent would then have difficulties interpreting the real intentions of the principal.

An influence challenge can occur if the U.S. bank headquarters learns informally that a loan with insufficient guarantees probably is going to be approved by the agent. Following American norms to delegate and promote individual action, principals might not want to directly challenge the authority of the local agent. A nonconfrontational alternative would be to request that the agent provide a credit analysis revealing the weakness of the loan guarantees. The person assigned to do such a credit analysis, however, usually will be a lower level employee in the local operation, one who would be unlikely to challenge the decisions of a superior in Brazilian banking culture. In this case, where the credit analyst senses different interests between a local superior and the international headquarters, the local cultural norms of high power distance would compete with the principal's influence attempts to promote delegation and individual local responsibility.

A circumvention challenge issue can arise when the local agent proposes hiring a government liaison officer for the bank. U.S. headquarters might not agree with the need for such a position because it is not typical in U.S. banking or think that the agent's preferred candidate for the job does not have the necessary technical qualifications. The agent, however, might need this person to gain access to local governments in which the candidate has well-positioned friends or relatives. Increased access to local authorities can be a symbol of prestige in the country, and the agent will appear as more powerful to his peers in the local financial market. The business aspects of such a decision in this case have been superseded by other influential sources of meaning that are significantly important for the local agent.

Finally, symbolic challenges can be the most common type of issue when the principal and agent are from two different cultures. In our example, Brazilian agents could expect, from usual stereotypes about Americans, the setting of a more informal style in hierarchical relationships in the organization. American principals, however, might have decided differently. Based on information on the importance for Brazilians of more formal superior-subordinate relationships, they could have decided to start the managing of the operation by maintaining more status-conscious attitudes, believing that local agents would be more comfortable with distant initial exchanges. Progressively, a more liberal approach could be adopted as both parties get better acquainted with each other. It can easily be imagined how eventual misunderstandings and frustrations could arise from such situations.

Agency Theory, Risk, and Shirking

Our conclusions about risk and shirking have not always been the ones that would follow from many treatments of agency theory. If FDI is based on a learning/options rationale, then the principal needs to see that the agent behaves conservatively and avoids risks that might produce the greatest local operating profit. Given this FDI motive, for the agent to do otherwise could be to shirk in the hopes of getting a better position with another employer in the industry. If FDI is based on a follow-the-client rationale, then the principal needs to make sure that the agent satisfies key global clients who will reward the bank's home office regardless of implications for local operating performance. In that case, an agent who vigorously seeks to extract high profit from the client is shirking and could jeopardize a relationship that has global implications. This is not the typical link between risk and shirking postulated in agency theory. If FDI is based on a follow-the-leader rationale, then the principal needs to see that the agent seeks both long- and short-term profitability. This is most consistent with traditional agency theory, although several nuances qualify the general principle that seeking profit is an unambiguous criterion. If FDI is based on the logic of managerial hubris, then the agent can shirk responsibility to an immediate principal by expressing loyalty to the principal's principals—the shareholders. The upshot of this analysis is to encourage agency analyses to be thoughtful in clearly specifying what desirable agent behavior means and to be cautious about treating shirking as having a self-evident meaning.

Improving Agency Theory

Agency theory continues to contribute to organization studies. We agree with Eisenhardt (1989) regarding her emphasis on the explanatory power and unique insights that agency theory provides into certain aspects of the way in which organizations function such as individual motivations, information use, and the problems that arise in hierarchical cooperative relationships where the parties have different backgrounds and goals. We also agree with her recommendation that agency theory be coupled with other complementary perspectives, acknowledging that "agency theory represents a partial view of the world that, although it is valid, also ignores a good bit of the complexity of organizations" (p. 71). This is exactly what we have sought to do in this chapter.

The complex part of organizational life that Eisenhardt (1989) mentioned, in our view, fundamentally reflects individual complexity. Our banking services industry example has experienced some convergent forces toward globalization. Still, multiple perspectives appeared when we conceptually investigated the exchanges between Brazilians and Americans in a contextualized agency relationship. Our speculations opened the possibility for enlarging the view of this relationship by going beyond the narrow and unilateral view of an efficiency-motivated principal trying to control the behavior of a self-serving agent. Simply expanding the reasons and criteria for FDI showed that an individual's motivation can be triggered by a number of different and sometimes divergent purposes or passions. We also brought an event management approach to sensemaking theory to indicate that even an individual's focus of attention can be assailed by many temptations. Finally, we suggested that there are many and varied references on which the two parties can draw to interpret events and act. These parties are, in our view, the tempters that bring the multifaceted intricacy of reality to a relationship that appeared to be one of simple interpretation. Principals and agents emerged as only two of the various possible sources of meaning available, always competing with these alternative sources.

Sensemaking and Event Management Theory

The event management perspective we adopt, in line with previous work in sensemaking research (Weick, 1974, 1995), is consistent with a growing trend in management literature that emphasizes the collective aspects of noticing and interpreting organizational events (Isabella, 1990; Rentsch, 1990; Smith & Peterson, 1995). Sensemaking analysis has taken the form of a perspective rather than a theory. The event management approach to sensemaking spells out the perspective by offering a set of variables—purposes (passions), events (temptations), and sources of meaning (tempters). Some analyses have offered taxonomies of events (Peterson, 1998) and sources of meaning (Peterson & Smith, in press; Smith & Peterson, 1988). In our framework, the discussion of events at different levels of aggregation, from more complex issues such as the basic motivations for the investment to individual idiosyncrasies in the interpretation of influence attempts, showed the flexibility of that type of research in handling those differences. This capability was mentioned in previous studies (Peterson, 1998) as having the potential to improve other traditional lines of contingency research. The present chapter provides the first systematic example of how the perspective can be used to help develop a particular theory, in this case agency theory. Similar contributions are possible in numerous other lines of organization studies research.

FDI Theory

Our purpose in discussing the theory of FDI was to help broaden agency theory. In so doing, we also found ways in which to understand the managerial implications of FDI theory. These sometimes are present but usually are not emphasized in the FDI literature. In particular, using our prior work on cultural differences in event management between Brazilians and Americans directed our attention toward opportunism on the part of what for our purposes is a principal, but one who is simultaneously an agent in another relationship. In fact, international analyses of all sorts remind us that we never are the agent of any one other party and never are autonomous principals. We have responsibilities beyond those in any dyadic business relationship.

Using a Sensemaking Theory of Agency

The tentative combination of the three lines of theory we used in this chapter—agency, FDI motives, and sensemaking and event management—was intentionally done in a very specific context to bring life to our conjectures. The acquisition of a Brazilian bank by a U.S. institution is an increasingly likely possibility in view of the recent developments in the financial markets of the two countries. Similar acquisitions are occurring throughout the world. The issues in our example will apply to parties from a variety of other pairs of countries. Our setting also was purposely intercultural, emphasizing the aspects of interaction and integration that currently prevail in international business (Adler & Boyacigiller, 1996). The typical cultural differences between nationals of Brazil and the United States enriched our discussion of the possible ways in which an American principal and a Brazilian agent can interact in their mixed-motive relationship.

International organization studies needs a theory base for dealing with issues of control. Agency theory has provided the starting point that many have found the most attractive for understanding such issues. We recommend several modifications of agency theory. The purpose of agency theory, establishing the most efficient contract for governing the agency relationship, can be preserved. Agency theory's assumptions about people, particularly self-interest, bounded rationality, and risk aversion, are modified. Self-interest is redefined to cover the interests of a variety of parties affecting the agent, potentially including the agent's sense of the principal's own principal. Bounded rationality is reconsidered following advances in cognitive studies, but the core idea that agents are not fully rational remains. Risk aversion becomes less universal a problem than the problem of fully understanding and acting on behalf of the principal's interests. The view that information can be purchased is retained, but with the caveat that the adequacy of what can be purchased to effectively control an agent often is doubtful. These revisions should promote a sensemaking theory of agency.

REFERENCES

Adler, N. J., & Boyacigiller, N. (1996). Global management and the 21st century. In B. J. Punnett & O. Shenkar (Eds.), *Handbook for international management research* (pp. 537-558). Cambridge, MA: Blackwell.

Agrawal, A., & Knoeber, C. R. (1996). Firm performance and mechanisms to control agency problems between managers and shareholders. *Journal of Financial and Quantitative Analysis, 31,* 377-397.

Albanese, R., Dacin, T. M., & Harris, I. C. (1997). Agents as stewards. *Academy of Management Review, 22,* 609-611.

Alchian, A. A., & Demsetz, H. (1972). Production, information costs, and economic organization. *American Economic Review, 62,* 777-795.

Amado, G., & Brasil, H. V. (1991). Organizational behaviors and cultural context: The Brazilian "jeitinho." *International Studies of Management and Organizations, 21*(3), 38-61.

Arrow, K. (1971). *Essays in the theory of risk bearing.* Chicago: Markham.

Barnes, P., Davidson, I., & Wright, M. (1996). The changing nature of corporate control and ownership structure. *Journal of Business Finance & Accounting, 3,* 651-671.

Barney, J. B., & Hesterly, W. (1996). Organizational economics: Understanding the relationship between organizations and economic analysis. In S. R. Clegg, C. Hardy, & W. R. Nord (Eds.), *Handbook of organization studies* (pp. 115-147). Thousand Oaks, CA: Sage.

Basu, A., Lal, R., Srinivasan, V., & Staelin, R. (1985). Salesforce compensation plans: An agency theoretic perspective. *Marketing Science, 4,* 267-291.

Bergen, M. (1992). Agency relationships in marketing: A review of the implications and applications of agency and related theories. *Journal of Marketing, 56*(3), 1-25.

Bigoness, W. J., & Blakely, G. L. (1996). A cross-national study of managerial values. *Journal of International Business Studies, 27,* 739-752.

Bird, A., & Wiersema, M. F. (1996). Underlying assumptions of agency theory. In S. B. Bacharach, P. A. Bamberger, & M. Erez (Eds.), *Research in the sociology of organizations* (Vol. 14, pp. 149-180). Greenwich, CT: JAI.

Black, J. S., & Mendenhall, M. (1990). Cross-cultural training effectiveness: A review and a theoretical framework for future research. *Academy of Management Review, 15,* 113-136.

Bontempo, R., Lobel, S., & Triandis, H. (1990). Compliance and value internalization in Brazil and the U.S.: Effects of allocentrism and anonymity. *Journal of Cross-Cultural Psychology, 21,* 200-213.

Boyacigiller, N., & Adler, N. J. (1991). The parochial dinosaur: The organizational sciences in a global context. *Academy of Management Review, 16,* 262-290.

Brannen, M. Y. (1994). *Your next boss is Japanese: Negotiating cultural change at a western Massachusetts paper plant.* Doctoral dissertation, University of Massachusetts, Amherst.

Brennan, M. J., & Schwartz, E. S. (1985). Evaluating natural resource investments. *Journal of Business, 58,* 135-157.

Brent, S. S. (1988). Civil servant attitudes toward administrative rules and procedures: A comparative analysis of Brazil and the United States. *Review of Public Personnel Administration, 8*(3), 17-39.

Cantwell, J. (1991). A survey of theories of international production. In C. Pitelis & R. Sugden (Eds.), *The nature of the transnational firm* (pp. 16-63). New York: Routledge.

Casson, M. (1994). Internalization as a learning process: A model of corporate growth and geographical diversification. In V. N. Balasubramanyam & D. Sapsford (Eds.), *The economics of international investment* (pp. 14-46). Aldershot, UK: Edward Elgar.

Caves, R. E. (1982). *Multinational enterprise and economic analysis.* Cambridge, UK: Cambridge University Press.

Chang, S. J. (1995). International expansion strategy of Japanese firms: Capability building through sequential entry. *Academy of Management Journal, 38,* 383-407.

Chinese Culture Connection. (1987). Chinese values and the search for culture-free dimensions of culture. *Journal of Cross-Cultural Psychology, 18,* 143-164.

Davis, J. H., Schoorman, D. F., & Donaldson, L. (1997). Toward a stewardship theory of management. *Academy of Management Review, 22,* 20-47.

Demski, J., & Feltham, G. (1978). Economic incentives in budgetary control systems. *Accounting Review, 53,* 336-359.

Denis, D. J., Denis, D. K., & Sarin, A. (1997). Agency problems, equity ownership, and corporate diversification. *Journal of Finance, 52*(1), 135-160.

Donaldson, L. (1990). The ethereal hand: Organizational economics and management theory. *Academy of Management Review, 15,* 369-381.

Donaldson, L., & Davis, J. H. (1991). Stewardship theory or agency theory: CEO governance and shareholder returns. *Australian Journal of Management, 16,* 49-64.

Dukerich, J. M., Golden, B. R., & Jacobson, C. K. (1996). Nested cultures and identities: A comparative study of nation and profession/occupation status effects on resource allocation decisions. In S. B. Bacharach, P. A. Bamberger, & M. Erez (Eds.), *Research in the sociology of organizations* (Vol. 14, pp. 35-89). Greenwich, CT: JAI.

Dunning, J. H. (1980). Toward an eclectic theory of international production: Some empirical tests. *Journal of International Business Studies, 11*(1), 9-31.

Dunning, J. H. (1988). The eclectic paradigm of international production: A restatement and some possible extensions. *Journal of International Business Studies, 19,* 1-31.

Eccles, R. (1985). Transfer pricing as a problem of agency. In J. Pratt & R. Zeckhauser (Eds.), *Principals and agents: The structure of business* (pp. 151-186). Boston: Harvard University Business School Press.

Eisenhardt, K. M. (1989). Agency theory: An assessment and review. *Academy of Management Review, 14,* 57-74.

Erez, M. (1990). Toward a model of cross-cultural industrial and organizational psychology. In H. C. Triandis, M. D. Dunnette, & L. M. Hough (Eds.), *Handbook of industrial and organizational psychology* (Vol. 4, 2nd ed., pp. 559-608). Palo Alto, CA: Consulting Psychologists Press.

Erez, M., & Earley, P. C. (1993). *Culture, self-identity, and work.* New York: Oxford University Press.

Fama, E. (1980). Agency problems and the theory of the firm. *Journal of Political Economy, 88,* 288-307.

Fleisher, C. S. (1991). Using an agency-based approach to analyze collaborative federated interorganizational relationships. *Journal of Applied Behavioral Science, 27,* 116-131.

Foreigners flock to grab a share. (1998, March). *The Banker,* p. 28.

Grosse, R., & Trevino, L. J. (1996). Foreign direct investment in the United States: An analysis by country of origin. *Journal of International Business Studies, 27*(1), 139-155.

Hill, C. W. L. (1995). National institutional structures, transaction cost economizing, and competitive advantage: The case of Japan. *Organization Science, 6,* 119-131.

Hill, C. W. L. (1996). *International business: Competing in the global marketplace.* Burr Ridge, IL: Irwin.

Hofstede, G. (1980). *Culture's consequences: International differences in work-related values.* Beverly Hills, CA: Sage.

Hofstede, G. (1983). National cultures in four dimensions. *International Studies of Management and Organizations, 13,* 46-74.

Hofstede, G. (1994). Management scientists are human. *Management Science, 40,* 4-13.

Hofstede, G., Neuijen, B., Ohavy, D., & Sanders, G. (1990). Measuring organizational cultures: A qualitative and quantitative study across twenty cases. *Administrative Science Quarterly, 35,* 286-316.

Hoskisson, R. E., Hitt, M. S., Turk, T. A., & Tyler, B. B. (1989). Balancing corporate strategy and executive compensation: Agency theory and corporate governance. *Research in Personnel and Human Resources Management, 7,* 25-57.

Instituto Brasileiro de Geografia e Estatística. (1997). *Fundação Instituto Brasileiro de Geografia e Estatística, national accounts—GDP.* (Available: http://www.ibge.gov.br)

Isabella, L. A. (1990). Evolving interpretations as a change unfolds: How managers construe key organizational events. *Academy of Management Journal, 33,* 7-41.

Jassmin, A., Dexter, C., & Sidhu, A. (1988). Agency theory: Implications for financial management. *Managerial Finance, 14,* 4307-4358.

Jensen, M. (1986). Agency costs of free cash flow, corporate finance, and takeovers. *American Economic Review, 76,* 323-329.

Jensen, M., & Meckling, W. (1976). Theory of the firm: Managerial behavior, agency costs, and ownership structure. *Journal of Financial Economics, 3,* 305-360.

Knickerbocker, F. T. (1973). *Oligopolistic reaction and multinational enterprise.* Boston: Harvard Business School Press.

Kogut, B., & Singh, H. (1988). The effect of national culture on the choice of entry mode. *Journal of International Business Studies, 19*(3), 411-432.

Lachman, R. (1983). Modernity change of core and periphery values of factory workers. *Human Relations, 36,* 563-580.

Lal, D., & Rajapatirana, S. (1987, July). Foreign trade regimes and economic growth in developing countries. *World Bank Observer,* pp. 189-217.

Lippert, R., & Moore, W. (1995). Monitoring versus bonding: Shareholder rights and management compensation. *Financial Management, 24*(3), 54-62.

Lynn, P., & Timme, S. (1993). Corporate control and bank efficiency. *Journal of Banking and Finance, 17,* 515-530.

Maznevski, M. L., & Peterson, M. F. (1997). Societal values, social interpretation, and multinational teams. In C. S. Granrose & S. Oskamp (Eds.), *Cross-cultural work groups* (pp. 61-89). Thousand Oaks, CA: Sage.

Mitnick, B. (1986). *The theory of agency and organizational analysis.* Working paper, University of Pittsburgh.

Mohd, M., Perry, L., & Rimbey, J. (1995). An investigation of the dynamic relationship between agency theory and dividend policy. *Financial Review, 30,* 367-385.

Myers, S. (1977). Determinants of corporate borrowing. *Journal of Financial Economics, 5,* 147-175.

Noe, T. H., & Rebello, M. J. (1996). Asymmetric information, managerial opportunism, financing, and payout policies. *Journal of Finance, 51,* 637-660.

Otani, I., & Villanueva, D. (1990). Long-term growth in developing countries and its determinants: An empirical analysis. *World Development, 18,* 769-783.

Perrow, C. (1986). *Complex organizations: A critical essay.* New York: McGraw-Hill.

Peterson, M. F. (1998). Embedded organizational events: Units of process in organization science. *Organization Science, 9,* 16-33.

Peterson, M. F., Elliott, J. R., Bliese, P. D., & Radford, M. H. B. (1996). Profile analysis of the sources of meaning reported by U.S. and Japanese local government managers. In S. B. Bacharach, P. A. Bamberger, & M. Erez (Eds.), *Research in the sociology of organizations* (Vol. 14, pp. 91-147). Greenwich, CT: JAI.

Peterson, M. F., Peng, T. K., & Smith, P. B. (1999). Using expatriate supervisors: A longitudinal, intercultural study of leadership style, attitudes, and performance. In J. Liker, M. Fruin, & P. Adler (Eds.), *Remade in America: Transplanting and transforming Japanese production systems* (pp. 294-327). New York: Oxford University Press.

Peterson, M. F., & Smith, P. B. (in press). Meanings, organizations, and culture: Using sources of meaning to make sense of organizational events. In N. Ashkanasy, C. Wilderom, & M. F. Peterson (Eds.), *Handbook of organizational culture and climate.* Thousand Oaks, CA: Sage.

Peterson, M. F., Smith, P. B., Akande, A., Ayestraran, S., Bochner, S., Callan, V., Cho, N. G., Jesuino, J. C., Amorim, M. D., Francois, P. H., Hofmann, K., Koopman, P. L., Leung, K., Lim, T. K., Mortazavi, S., Munene, J., Radford, M., Ropo, A., Savage, G., Setiadi, B., Sinha, T. N., Sorenson, R., & Viedge, C. (1995). Role conflict, ambiguity, and overload: A 21-nation study. *Academy of Management Journal, 38,* 429-452.

Peterson, M. F., Smith, P. B., Misumi, J., & Bond, M. H. (1990). Personal reliance on alternative event management processes in four countries. *Group and Organization Studies, 15,* 75-91.

Piaget, J. (1928). *Judgment and reasoning in the child.* New York: Harcourt, Brace.

Rentsch, J. R. (1990). Climate and culture: Interaction and quantitative differences in organizational meanings. *Journal of Applied Psychology, 75,* 668-681.

Rose, P. S. (1992). Agency theory and entry barriers in banking. *Financial Review, 27,* 323-353.

Sabi, M. (1988). An application of the theory of foreign direct investment to multinational banking in LDCs. *Journal of International Business Studies, 19*(3), 433-447.

Schattler, H., & Sung, J. (1993). The first-order approach to the continuous-time principal-agent problem with exponential utility. *Journal of Economic Theory, 61,* 331-372.

Schwartz, S. H. (1994). Cultural dimensions of values: Theoretical advances and empirical tests in 20 countries. In U. Kim, H. C. Triandis, & G. Yoon (Eds.), *Advances in experimental social psychology* (Vol. 25, pp. 1-65). Thousand Oaks, CA: Sage.

Scott, W. R. (1995). *Institutions and organizations.* Thousand Oaks, CA: Sage.

Sharma, A. (1997). Professional as agent: Knowledge asymmetry in agency exchange. *Academy of Management Review, 22,* 758-798.

Shaw, J. B. (1990). A cognitive categorization model for the study of intercultural management. *Academy of Management Review, 15,* 626-645.

Shleifer, A., & Vishny, R. W. (1997). A survey of corporate governance. *Journal of Finance, 52,* 737-783.

Smith, P. B., Dugan, S., & Trompenaars, F. (1996). National culture and the values of organizational employees: A dimensional analysis across 43 nations. *Journal of Cross-Cultural Psychology, 27,* 231-264.

Smith, P. B., & Peterson, M. F. (1988). *Leadership, organizations, and culture: An event management perspective.* London: Sage.

Smith, P. B., & Peterson, M. F. (1995, August). *Beyond value comparisons: Sources used to give meaning to management work events in 29 countries.* Paper presented at the annual meeting of the Academy of Management, Vancouver, British Columbia.

Smith, P. B., Peterson, M. F., & Misumi, J. (1994). Event management and team effectiveness in Japan, Britain, and the U.S.A. *Journal of Occupational and Organizational Psychology, 67,* 33-43.

Smith, P. B., Peterson, M. F., & Wang, Z. M. (1996). The manager as a mediator of alternative meanings: A pilot study from China, the U.S.A., and U.K. *Journal of International Business Studies, 27,* 115-137.

Snider, H. K. (1994). CEO pay and firm performance: Theory vs. practice. *Financial Markets, Institutions and Instruments, 3,* 60-75.

Sondergaard, M. (1994). Research note: Hofstede's consequences: A study of reviews, citations, and replications. *Organization Studies, 15,* 447-456.

Spence, A. M., & Zeckhauser, R. (1971). Insurance, information, and individual action. *American Economic Review, 61,* 380-387.

Thomas, D. C., Ravlin, E. C., & Wallace, A. W. (1996). Effect of cultural diversity in work groups. In S. B. Bacharach, P. A. Bamberger, & M. Erez (Eds.), *Research in the sociology of organizations* (Vol. 14, pp. 1-33). Greenwich, CT: JAI.

Triandis, H. C. (1982). Review of culture's consequences: International differences in work-related values. *Human Organization, 41,* 86-90.

Triandis, H. C. (1990). Cross-cultural, industrial, and organizational psychology. In H. C. Triandis, M. D. Dunnette, & L. M. Hough (Eds.), *Handbook of industrial and organizational psychology* (Vol. 4, 2nd ed., pp. 103-172). Palo Alto, CA: Consulting Psychologists Press.

Trompenaars, F. (1994). *Riding the waves of culture: Understanding diversity in global business.* Burr Ridge, IL: Irwin.

Tschoegl, A. E. (1987). International retail banking as a strategy: An assessment. *Journal of International Business Studies, 18*(2), 67-88.

United Nations. (1997). *World investment report.* New York: Author.

Vernon, R. (1966). International investments and international trade in the product life cycle. *Quarterly Journal of Economics, 80,* 190-207.

Weick, K. (1974). Middle range theories of social systems. *Behavioral Science, 19,* 357-367.

Weick, K. (1995). *Sensemaking in organizations.* Thousand Oaks, CA: Sage.

Wilson, R. (1968). On the theory of syndicates. *Econometrica, 36,* 119-132.

Wiseman, R. M., & Gomez-Mejia, L. R. (1998). A behavioral agency model of managerial risk taking. *Academy of Management Review, 23,* 133-153.

World Bank. (1995). *World development report 1995: Workers in an integrating world.* New York: Oxford University Press.

World Bank. (1996). *World development report 1996: From plan to market.* New York: Oxford University Press.

World Bank. (1997). *World development report 1997: The state in a changing world.* New York: Oxford University Press.

World Trade Organization. (1997). *Opening markets in financial services and the role of the GATS.* Geneva: Author.

chapter 7

Strategic Social Partnerships for Change

A Framework for Building Sustainable Growth in Developing Countries

CATHY A. ENZ
CRIST INMAN
MELENIE J. LANKAU

> Becoming world class means joining the world class. Success in the global economy derives not just from meeting high standards for competition in world contests but also from strong relationships—networks that link to global markets and networks that build collective local strength.
> —R. M. Kanter, *World Class,* p. 325

One of the hallmarks of an increasingly global world is the opportunity for wider access to consumers, capital, and information from around the world. To capture global customers, companies and countries must build relationships that enhance access to knowledge, information, capital, and other resources needed to grow and compete effectively. As the importance of international relationships among varied groups of private investors, providers of services, and governments increases, the ability of developing countries to compete often is determined by the quality of their relationships with strategic partners.

The strategies devised and implemented for economic development have important outcomes for the citizenry of emerging economies (Andrews, 1980).

To become competitive (i.e., to increase wealth) in the global economy, developing countries must shed their natural inclination toward protectionism and
embrace both foreign partners and rivals without losing their social and cultural
identities. The private and public sectors in developing countries need to build
relationships with companies and countries that can provide them with innovative new ideas and knowledge, operational skills to meet global customers' high
standards, and easy access to capital from around the world. Determining which
of many possible ways in which to build relationships is not an easy or straightforward issue. Clearly, selection of a type of partnership is a choice with long-
term consequences for a developing country. The form of partnering can either
enhance or hamper sustainable development. Thus, the choice of how to think
about strategic partnerships is as important as the choice of the specific partners
with which one does business.

New frameworks are needed to understand the variety of different relationships that can be established and sustained in strategic multinational partnerships
with developing countries. In this chapter, we explore a framework that considers the relationship between the business operating orientation of the multinational corporation (MNC) and the economic development orientation of the
developing country. From this framework, we present four different models for
building strategic partnerships and illustrate the types of business relations that
emerge under each. In the latter portion of this chapter, we illustrate the four
models for development in the country of Costa Rica because Central American
countries are in the midst of inventing their own systems for future development.
The approach that they take will shape economic growth, national transformation, and the long-term use of human capital. The chapter also concentrates on
tourism services because tourism historically has been a major force in advanc-
ing economic growth for developing countries. Developing countries in many
parts of the world are aware that they need to be more active and innovative
in building their economies, and the use of tourism services is the most cost-
effective and easily available means for many to begin the process.

THE EVOLUTION OF
STRATEGIC PARTNERSHIPS

Forming and building business relationships often has been likened to marriage
and family, with all of its unique complexities. The analogy of marriage and family is particularly useful because it evokes the importance of trust, loyalty, and
respect. It further highlights the role of emotion, values, and shared responsibilities. In forming business partnerships, two substantially different orientations
can be evoked. Depending on the orientation adopted by partners, the relation-

ship will focus on control and maximizing individual interests (what we call a self-interest orientation) or collaboration and maximizing community interests (what we call a social contract) (Donaldson, 1982). Different forms of strategic partnership are suitable for different situations and environmental conditions.

Since the industrial revolution, the dominant design for partnerships around the world has been based on the economic theory and justifications of self-interest and wealth maximization. This view is deeply rooted in the foundation of American enterprise theory and has been a guiding light for the industrial world for the past 200 years (Friedman, 1962). Parties enter into contracts with the expressed purpose of economic benefit to the key players. These transactional contracts often are limited in duration and possess well-specified performance terms (Rousseau, 1995). In this orientation, expansion into developing countries is a means to the end of enhanced shareholder wealth through growth in which the shareholders are a select and limited few partners. The agreements with strategic partners are equity focused and legal. In a self-interest orientation to partnership, foreign investors have one driving responsibility, both morally and legally, and that is to maximize the value of shares to those who have invested capital in the corporation or who are engaged in contracts that enhance the wealth of shareholders (Reich, 1998). In short, the parties to the contracts make promises to each other, and their commitments are to ensure their own wealth. Repeated mutually beneficial exchanges that appeal to their common interests will, over time, engender trust and sustain their business contracts (Creed & Miles, 1996; Kramer & Tyler, 1996).

Differences in management styles, cultural mores, business practices, and even language barriers have repeatedly threatened or destroyed relationships based on traditional profit-maximizing assumptions. Shane (1994), for example, found that the perceived trustworthiness of the international partners influenced the type of governing mechanism that a firm put in place when beginning to globalize. Others have found that negotiation styles and management beliefs across different cultures have made strategic alliances and global strategies challenging (Adler, Brahm, & Graham, 1992; De Forest, 1994).

Market forces and increased access to knowledge and capital have governments, local investors, and citizens in developing countries more sensitive to the potentially negative long-term economic, environmental, and cultural effects of their current partnerships with corporations. International tourism is considered vital to providing needed foreign exchange earnings and capital to the economies of developing countries. However, the anticipated gains in economic benefits in many instances were offset by the numerous sociocultural and environmental changes that altered and often harmed the people and resources of a country (Oppermann & Chon, 1997). These self-interest-focused contracts, although beneficial to the business partners, violated the social contract, defined by Rousseau (1995) as collective beliefs regarding appropriate behavior in a society.

As developing countries seek new ways of creating their futures, the opportunity for radically different forms of relationships emerge. Global competition also has begun to force MNCs to contemplate dramatic changes in their relationships with customers, employees, investors, and other stakeholders. As organizations and developing countries evolve and adapt to changes in business, the nature and forms of their strategic partnering also may evolve.

Sustainable Economic and Environmental Development

Organizations influence societies in developing countries in numerous ways. A well-documented pattern of social consequences emerges when developing countries begin to "modernize." Deep changes take place in the social structure and value systems of countries. To generate much-needed foreign revenues, service sector businesses often are the most easily available entry points to reaching global customers and modernizing. Tourism, for example, is an industry that many developing countries select as their primary vehicle for economic development. In so doing, these countries open their cultures to the rest of the world. With this opening comes often unexpected, and sometimes undesired, consequences. Statistically, the vast majority of tourists come from countries in the Northern Hemisphere. Most developing nations embracing tourism as a form of economic development are in the Southern Hemisphere. Hence, differences in the value and perception of time between cultures in the two hemispheres are profound. Although theoretically fascinating, these differences are problematic when developing service standards among tourism service providers.

To satisfy the exacting demands of tourists from developed economies, service providers and training authorities engage in wide-reaching attempts to alter the fundamental ways in which their working populations think and behave. On the surface, increasing the speed of service sounds like a relatively simple task— merely a matter of incentives—but in practice it often requires deep remodeling of sociocultural values. Incentives themselves are not without wide-reaching ramifications. For example, the introduction of tipping in many countries is linked to a loss of the native hospitality that prevailed prior to the development of these tourism practices.

In addition to the influences on the less visible and less tangible facets of a society, tourism development has an obvious influence on the way in which countries appear. Architectural patterns adapt to global standards. Many developing tourism economies offer tourism investment incentives that lead to rapid proliferation of hotel and attraction infrastructure, replacing indigenous homes and communities with buildings and activities suited for foreigners. These standardized architectural forms might leave countries and regions visually indistinguishable from one another.

Although tourism seems to have a cheapening effect on many aspects of local values and arts, it need not lead to a loss of meaning for local people. The Amish of Pennsylvania are cited as an example of sustained quilting tradition in the face of modernity (Boynton, 1986). Numerous authors have examined the effects of tourism as a means of modernizing people's values, resulting in the degeneration of customs and traditions into a mere "tourist show." Greenwood (1989), in a study of the *Alarde* (a ritual of the people of northern Spain), argued that by commoditizing the ritual, it no longer was viewed as significant by the towns-people. By contrast, the effects of tourism in Bali have shown that tourism strengthened Balinese arts, crafts, and tradition by providing profits (Noronha, 1979). In this instance, the economic interactions between Balinese and tourists bound the two parties together, but the Balinese were actively involved in how their traditions would be used in the exchange (Harrison, 1992).

For many countries, foreign investments by large MNCs brought new problems and failed to solve the need for industrialization. In Costa Rica, for example, the country's post-1960 business climate was divided between small-scale local industry and export-oriented, large foreign-owned corporations. In other countries in Latin America such as Guatemala and Chile, large corporations actively promoted interventions against egalitarian democratic governments (Sheahan, 1987). As these examples show, partnerships with individuals, government, and businesses in developing countries influence the structure of social relationships within those countries (Hall, 1991). In particular, the United States has had a dramatic impact on the development of Central America. In recent years, many developing countries have become fearful that their natural resources and people have been exploited by outsiders, causing both environmental and cultural harm without the anticipated economic benefits.

There also has been increasing international public and governmental recognition of the urgency of environmental issues resulting from the rise of industrial development on a global scale. Concerns by the international public, mostly in developing countries, about overpopulation and environmental degradation are creating pressures on organizations to modify current practices toward growth and expansion and to incorporate a more environmentally oriented strategic objective called sustainable development (Shrivastava, 1995). Lewellan (1995) defined the concept of sustainable development as

> a complex concept that implies the integration of three systems: the biological, the economic, and the social. The goals of the biological system are genetic diversity, productivity, and the resilience to thrive under changing conditions. The economic system ideally strives toward increased production of goods and services, the satisfaction of basic needs, the reduction of poverty, and increased equity. Social system goals might include cultural diversity, social justice, popular participation in politics, and increased gender equity. (p. 207)

Sustainable development requires global corporations to alter the way in which they conduct business to establish new and fundamentally different relationships with more explicit societal obligations and shared commitments to address social and environmental problems. The expectation that global businesses preserve the long-term viability of the planet through protective, community-enhancing agreements with governments and local citizens might have the effect of shifting the terms of partnerships. Whereas the international public is concerned with preservation and protection of natural resources, local citizens worry about poverty, unemployment, education, and their economic futures. The melding of these concerns requires a different approach to long-term, sustainable economic and environmental development.

Social Contracts and the New Partnership

Social contracts are the mutual expectations, promises, and obligations that members of society hold for their relationships with businesses, governments, and each other (Kochan, 1997; Rousseau, 1995). A social contract orientation is deeply rooted in culture and argues for partnerships that move the focus of business interests from the individual employee and employer or business partner relationships to include others. The common social interests of a full range of parties including citizens, public agencies, complementary local businesses, and governments, if considered thoughtfully, could have profound positive consequences for the economic and environmental development of a newly industrialized region. The partnerships are win-win arrangements in which all actors have responsibility for the development of the total community. The social contract orientation seeks to produce a long-term benefit for the entire citizenry, regardless of whether citizens are directly employed by a particular MNC or a local business. When a community and its foreign businesses recognize that they have common interests and build cooperative relations, trust will become the byproduct. As the work of Powell (1996) suggests, trust is neither chosen nor embedded; rather, it is learned and reinforced and, hence, is a product of ongoing interaction and discussion.

A social contract perspective suggests that individuals and organizations have an ultimate responsibility for society (Donaldson, 1982; Mahoney, Huff, & Huff, 1994). In this view, social consciousness fuels relationships linking the good for any party to the good for all in the community. Maximizing individual interests is an orientation in marked contrast to maximizing collective benefits.

A social contract approach is similar to the moral model offered by Etzioni (1988) in which it is argued that individuals choose both their means and ends and that these are based on their values and emotions. Etzioni noted, "People do not seek to maximize their pleasure but [rather] to balance the services of two major purposes—to advance their well-being and to act morally" (p. 83).

Researchers provide support for the idea that moral beliefs, altruism, and the institutionalization of normative practices are significantly more powerful in predicting behavior than are self-interest motives (Latane & Darley, 1970; Tolbert & Zucker, 1983). Hence, a social contract versus self-interest approach to economic development highlights the importance of caring for and about the needs and interests among all players in a community to ensure trust and commitment and that all obtain benefits.

A social contract approach rests on fulfilling the responsibilities of being a part of the context (Etzioni, 1993). It has as its base moral criteria such as the elimination of poverty, direct care for the poor, creation of employment opportunities, and widespread education of the citizenry. At its foundation is the idea that the genuine good for any individual in society rests with the good of all (Bowie, 1991). Because no contract exists in a vacuum, implicit social contracts influence how all forms of contracting are interpreted. Development and the solution to serious economic problems are beyond the capability of individual businesses to manage alone. To attempt to do so is to potentially lose competitive advantage. However, an effort to establish social contracts and obligations more explicitly as an operating orientation for all strategic partnerships could result in more sustainable and profitable contributions to the communities in which MNCs do business.

As more global business relationships emerge, a social contract orientation redefines the boundaries of care. Perhaps because of the shift to global identity, it becomes a greater leverage point for competitive advantage when global companies commit to and fulfill obligations that ultimately benefit the local community and all of its stakeholders, even when they are not attached to or affiliated with the organization. At the present time, both self-interest and social contract orientations exist concurrently, although forces in the environment are pushing companies and countries toward a change in orientation.

Anticipating Changes

Much of the literature on change argues that periodically there is a need for discontinuous versus incremental change, resulting in the emergence of a new and fundamentally different era (Tushman & O'Reilly, 1997). We currently are in the period of discontinuous change shown in Figure 7.1 where the forms of strategic partnership are shifting due to increased concerns that MNCs should assume a broader social responsibility in their economic transactions (Shrivastava, 1995).

Using the familiar S-curve, Figure 7.1 illustrates the gradual evolution of a contract-focused self-interest orientation based on traditional economic theory. According to the S-curve, the cycle of benefit from this type of strategic partnership ultimately reaches a plateau where little incremental advantage is achieved

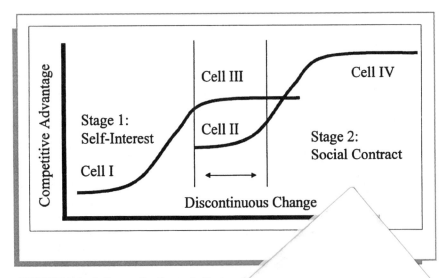

FIGURE 7.1. S-Curves for Strategic Partners'

from this approach. We may consider this end of th   of an era,
as the self-interest orientation no longer is the pre.   international
relationship building.

As Figure 7.1 suggests, during a period of disco. .uity, the previous
approach loses its advantage, necessitating a radically different approach. Social
contracts are a new form of strategic partnership, based on cooperative community obligations, and can emerge as a powerful tool for socioeconomic development in an information-driven world.

We suggest that the most likely model for success in small developing countries is to consider developing social contracts and further that the traditional
self-interest orientation might be losing its benefit for economic development. If
one pursues a social contract or a self-interest approach, then these views will
shape in different and noticeable ways the practical execution on economic
development. The approach taken will alter human capital and its long-term
development as well as the sustainability of natural resources.

Unexplored and assumed, the self-interest orientation will produce inescap-
able long-term outcomes. The operating success of businesses in developing
countries will manifest itself in how management practice takes shape and how
human resources are developed. To embrace one approach and its assumptions is
to not embrace the other approach; this is why the shift requires radical change.
Although different players might be working with different approaches, the net

effect is that one will dominate because of governmental policy. Competitive, legal, economic, and cultural outcomes of each approach also will shape the viability of moving from one model to another.

Developing countries are at different levels of self-sustaining growth and economic development, making a radical shift to a social contract framework more or less likely in the short term. Some countries (e.g., Costa Rica) have been politically stable for decades and have high literacy rates, whereas other countries (e.g., Nicaragua) have long functioned under unstable military dictatorships in which the wealthy citizens have lived in exile in other countries. It is expected that nations will have varying degrees of growth and investment from inside versus outside the country and, as a result, will be constrained in the forms of partnership that they can design and use most effectively. This would suggest that although we predict an evolution to more social contract relationships, the possibility of other intermediary forms of relationships do exist and will continue to exist for countries driven by outside versus inside sources of capital, knowledge, and skills. In addition, some industries, such as technology and tourism, might move more quickly to social partnership than will agricultural and manufacturing-based industries. Given the business operating orientation of MNCs (self-interest vs. social contract) and the development orientation of developing countries (inside pull vs. outside push), we would expect different models of partnership. To explore this more fully, we pose the question: What models or options for sustainable competitive development exist in emerging markets? In the next section, we provide four different models of partnership.

MODELS FOR BUILDING CROSS-CULTURAL STRATEGIC PARTNERSHIPS

Four different models for strategic partnership emerge from examining the interface between business operating orientation and the economic development orientation of a developing nation. Figure 7.2 shows the different types of strategic partnerships that can exist between companies and countries. We have labeled the four cells of our matrix according to the types of relationships that exist, as follows: Contractual Exchange (Cell I), Limited Social Covenant (Cell II), Joint Partnership (Cell III), and Integrated Social Covenant (Cell IV). Each cell in the matrix is discussed in turn.

Contractual Exchange: Cell I

MNCs that operate from a self-interest and outsider push orientation enter into traditional contracts that are short term and based on strategic initiatives to

Business Operating Orientation

		Self-Interest	Social Contract
Economic Development Orientation	Outside Push	**CONTRACTUAL EXCHANGE** **Cell I** Little infrastructure in country Few players in country Country is dependent Company has power Country is short term Company is short term	**LIMITED SOCIAL COVENANT** **Cell II** Caretaker approach by company Paternalistic/provide direct help Less infrastructure Fragmented relationships Company is short term/present Company is long term/future
	Inside Pull	**JOINT PARTNERSHIP** **Cell III** More infrastructure in country More players (due to development of middle class) New agreements/local owners more flexible Country is long term/short term Country has power/can be more selective in choosing partners Cooperation in meeting respective goals	**INTEGRATED SOCIAL COVENANT** **Cell IV** Most infrastructure in country Company takes local and global perspective Self-help model Company and country both are future oriented and long term Holistic Coordination of goals

FIGURE 7.2. Strategic Partnerships Between Foreign Companies and Developing Countries

expand the corporate market, reduce costs, and maximize shareholder value. The developing country is characterized by an economic system that is largely dependent on foreign investment for growth and development of infrastructure. Because the means to economic growth for the country are focused outward and originate from external sources, a clear power differential exists, and the terms, forms, and benefits of the relationship are dictated by the MNCs.

The political and social systems in a country under a Cell I model are influenced and managed by an elite class of business and governmental players whose motivation also is driven by self-interest. The interactions of the few powerful MNCs and the country create a context in which partnerships are based on contractual exchanges. This exchange is asymmetric because many developing countries cannot bring knowledge, skills, capital, or technology to the bargaining table but can offer governmental tax incentives, land, and inexpensive labor in exchange for developmental expertise, capital, and jobs. The gains for the country, however, are experienced or received not by the whole society but rather by the few business players who have the capacity in terms of land ownership, wealth, and influence to enter into these exchange relationships. In countries such as Costa Rica where there are many small land holders, the exchange might be less asymmetric, and the potential for personal gains for the citizenry might be greater.

This type of partnership is similar conceptually to the ideas of Williamson's (1975) transaction cost analysis and is applicable to both developed and developing countries. This form of partnering fosters an economic quid pro quo orientation in which there is little consideration of collective long-term benefits for the host community. Foreign investors are searching for short-term returns and are hesitant to build the infrastructure required to develop for the long term. Quick and standardized development projects are advocated to achieve synergies and rapid returns on investment. To secure capital and enhance the ease of working with foreigners, local investors and governments must demonstrate affiliation with the investing MNCs, altering their own social identities. To meet the economic ends they seek, local owners and country leaders support the values and strategies of the organizations despite the short-term orientation, lack of attention to the preservation of the country's natural resources, and minimal investment in skill development for the country's people.

Figure 7.3 summarizes each of the models on a variety of features—time orientation, cultural identification, learning relationship, management focus, and human resource strategy. This list of features is meant to be illustrative and incorporates the perspectives of both developing countries and global organizations. The categories examined in the figure are not exhaustive but are important and frequently cited factors. In addition, this figure does not attempt to differentiate among various forms of multinational structure and operation, although those differences in organizational form would likely influence the nature of the social partnerships.

As the Figure 7.3 suggests, in a Cell I model of relationships, the short-term home country focus of organizations might be evident in the extensive use of expatriate managers and a minimal investment in the training and development of local citizens. Economic efficiencies ultimately reinforce societal inequalities, and learning is acquired from outside and imposed on the people within the country. The developing country identifies with the global firms and seeks to acquire the needed expertise to advance its own economic wealth.

Feature	Model I	Model II	Model III	Model IV
Time orientation				
Developing country	Short term	Short term	Building long term	Long term/short term
Global organization	Short term	Building long term	Short term	Long term/short term
Cultural identification				
Developing country	Foreign host	Foreign host	Local	Local/global
Global organization	Home country	Home country	Home country	Local/global
Learning relationship	Acquire (transformation)	Correct	Adapt (internal)	Innovate
Management focus	Expatriates/ standardized	Expatriates	Unique	Both unique and adaptive
	Fix disabilities/work With limits	Unique (prescribed)	Evolving	
Human resource strategy	Low investment	High investment	Low investment	High investment
	High control Minimize training	High control Not managers	Low control Highest worker alienation	Low control Mentoring
	Survival focus	Worker compliance		Teaching/listening

FIGURE 7.3. Features of Different Strategic Social Partnerships

Limited Social Covenant:
Cell II

In Cell 2, the conditions and characteristics of the developing country are the same as in Cell I, but the operating orientation of the MNCs is vastly different. Owners and managers of these organizations are aware of the implications of the host community's dependence on their organizations and are more sensitized to the impact that productive corporations can have on local communities. These organizations operate with the assumption that strategies to optimize short-term gains undermine longer term benefits for the community and, most important, for the organizations as well. These companies hope to create long-term sustainable development for themselves through the process of contributing to the whole community. There is mutual consideration of what is best for the corporations and what is best for the national economy, culture, and people of the developing country.

Developing countries rely on global organizations for capital, technology, skills training, and development of infrastructure. However, these MNCs must manage the fragmented self-interest efforts of local business owners, investors, and government officials, and this may constrain the type of relationships that can emerge between multinational organizations and developing countries. Due to the imbalance of resources, MNCs with a sense of social responsibility are more likely to enter a developing country with a caretaking paternalistic orientation. The inability or unwillingness of the country's influential leaders and key organizations (business and political) to contribute to the social partnership, or the inability of the MNCs to create and sustain the network of relationships necessary for an integrated social partnership, creates a limited and potentially fragile social covenant.

Under these circumstances, the corporations provide direct help to the developing country. This limited social covenant will reinforce the country's outward dependence on externally driven growth. Much of the MNCs' efforts to contribute to the knowledge, skills, technology, and economic conditions of the community will not be sustainable in the long term and only serves the needs of the corporation and the few who are willing to take advantage of this paternalism in the short term.

As noted in Figure 7.3, these limited social covenants have promise for building the future. Organizations that bring new learning opportunities and technology to correct existing inadequacies ultimately help to reduce the need for external capital and to improve employment opportunities. Companies that believe in the obligation to the local community still might identify with their home countries but also invest in building the skills and education of the local population. Because these companies are few in number, the effective reach of their efforts is heavily limited. In addition, managerial philosophies and human resource practices are likely to be prescribed by the global organization rather than created and established with the consideration of the local citizens' values and needs.

Joint Partnership: Cell III

In Cell III, the means for economic growth shifts to expanding the use of internal resources rather than relying on external sources of investment. Over time, the developing country experiences economic gains from Cell I and Cell II types of relationships, resulting in the development of a better level of infrastructure and an increased number of in-country or in-region investors interested in entering into partnerships. Access to information and capital makes these firms less dependent on large outsiders. These investors become more sophisticated in their relationships with foreign companies, producing more balanced and mutually favorable contracts. Hence, the cross-cultural strategic partnership can be characterized as a joint partnership. Increased competition provides these in-country investors with more potential partners and better terms. Deal structures are easier to put in place, and the easy access to capital markets provides countries with more bargaining power. Regional capital becomes more available, and a larger variety of contracts with an expanding number of businesses are evident. In short, the enclave-style (isolated pockets of development such as banana export) are replaced by more equally distributed locally led business development.

Companies become more willing and driven to venture outside of their traditional markets to do business in unfamiliar locations. The country relies less on a few large companies and becomes involved in more mutually beneficial contracts in which it takes on larger equity participation and lessens its dependence on First World standards and operating approaches. Within-country organizations and investors can be more selective in choosing their partners and the terms of those partnerships. MNCs, however, still are operating at a first-stage self-interest approach to partnership. Cooperation in the joint partnerships will be limited by the extent to which the MNCs are able to achieve their goals, which are essentially focused on the organizations' capital investors and stockholders and not on the host community.

Although this type of strategic partnership is more balanced in terms of equity and contribution on the part of businesses within the developing country, the commitment required to build and maintain a network of interorganizational linkages over the long term will not be provided by the MNCs. This creates a difficult challenge for the developing country—creating these networks and supporting them primarily through internal systems and resources. This challenge requires a level of infrastructure, economy, political stability, integration, and coordination of systems that takes time, money, and leadership that the developing country might be lacking.

A Cell III model is a transition model in uneasy harmony because it can slip into a locally protected domestic market or move back to a Cell I multinational-dominated system. As shown in Figure 7.3, local businesses are adapting and learning new business skills, and governmental policy can potentially restrict or limit the success of small players through regulation. Human resource strategies also are evolving, and the framework of enlightened self-interest might yield even more oppressive and exploitative practices than would be the case under foreign-led development because urban and racial bias evident in several countries in Latin America would influence the use of human resources (Sheahan, 1987).

Integrated Social Covenant: Cell IV

A Cell IV, social covenant model of strategic partnerships exists when foreign companies and host countries work together for the local social good and long-term sustainable development of a region, city, country, or group of countries. Under these partnerships, the foreign companies and host country share a commitment to local prosperity and build long-term, integrated sets of business relationships. The ultimate goal is for strategic partnerships to aid the common interests. This approach is not selfless for the companies but rather an essential way in which to ensure long-term strategic competitive advantage and short-term business success.

The Cell IV model of relationships requires redefining the boundaries of care such that organizations must be partners in the local context to transact business. Global businesses are required to identify with the host country and consider themselves as local citizens. The social covenant approach realizes that the actions of one firm or group of firms have implications for the whole and that the terms of the relationship must be driven by a cooperative, collective, community, and inclusive operating orientation. Conducting business in isolation with a few privileged owners and investors within a country is an unacceptable practice in this model of relationships. In addition, the common interests are the focus of all businesses, not just a few (as we saw in the Cell II model). The internal organizational practices and strategic actions are considered to have implications for many actors including governments, employees, investors, managers, and communities. Hence, consideration of the effects of strategic and operational practices of each business on the whole is a necessary part of doing business for all. The objective is to work in collaborative efforts to benefit the entire society and its citizenry, not just customers, investors, managers, and employees.

A social covenant view is one that blends economic investment of individual businesses with social consciousness. The companies' and country's goals are oriented toward the future and are not exclusive but rather inclusive of the parties' contracts and relationships with their respective environments. There is an understanding of the whole, and the partnership is characterized by coordination rather than cooperation. Coordination differs from cooperation in that it involves a process of concerted decision making or action in which the parties participate in planned and integrated change with one another rather than pursue separate goals with a general orientation toward some common issue or outcome (Hall, 1991). A Cell IV approach to strategic social partnerships represents the best opportunity for a developing country and an MNC to work collaboratively to transform both of their abilities to compete in a global world.

Managers cannot rely on the ways of the past when partnerships move into an integrated social covenant. Practices and approaches must be created or invented with the local circumstances and the limits and potential of the citizens factored in. The view of low-skilled employees as deficient must be replaced with a mindset that respects the skill levels that currently exist. It is appropriate for managers to devise a gradual process of development while simultaneously appreciating the current talents and skills of workers. As shown in Figure 7.3, the investment in human capital is very high, and the roles of mentor and teacher are dominant. Efforts to harmonize the more discriminating demands of global customers with the capabilities and education of the population require a development plan that brings together universities and colleges with businesses and governments in cooperative supportive relationships.

The Model in Action

We now turn to an examination of Costa Rica, which has for the past 20 years established itself as a global ecotourism destination. By examining this small Central American country, we can see in action the dynamics of working from and with several different models of strategic partnership. Costa Rica is interesting precisely because it is not a typical case among developing nations and because it provides a working model for what might be a more attractive development path. Although several countries in the Pacific Rim region have been held up as models, rapidly transforming themselves from developing, to newly industrialized, to "tiger" economies, these examples have not been applicable in many developing nations that have explicit democratic and egalitarian social mandates.

Costa Rican social and political traditions would not allow economic development that either stifled or disregarded the institutions of democracy at the national political level, or the institutions of social and economic equity at the company level, for the sake of economic development. Although there is much debate among social scientists about the nature of the relationship between democracy and economic development, the fact is that many developing nations have embraced democratic institutions as an ideal, so the challenge is to find models of economic development appropriate to the context of this ideal. There are numerous countries around the world that provide discrete examples of the various types and phases of partnerships we have proposed here. We have chosen Costa Rica because it already has achieved significant shifts in its economic development, is further along the S-curve of change, and may speak to the larger development of Mexico, Central America, and Latin America.

Tourism and complementary industries are chosen because these are the types of businesses that have migrated to the top of the economic development pyramid in Costa Rica. The choice of industries examined was less important than the choice of the nation that provided examples of various forms of social partnership. We do not expect that the type of industry is determinant of or determined by the phase or cell of development. Rather, as an artifact of history, the banana companies happened to be the first foreign partners (Cell I), followed by maquiladoras (Cell II), whereas now both tourism and technology-based manufacturing are key industries in later phases (Cell III and Cell IV) of development in Costa Rica. Because the economic activities discussed in the next section are so different in each cell, we believe that the focus on service industries in our model is generalizable to other industries and engines of economic growth.

SOCIAL PARTNERSHIP OPTIONS IN COSTA RICA

Contractual Exchanges in Costa Rica (Cell I)

The history of Central American economic development is dominated by Cell I-type foreign investment. Beginning during the 1850s, foreign companies made deals with local governments and businesspersons, particularly on the Caribbean side of the isthmus, to acquire enormous tracts of land at very low prices for the cultivation of banana plantations. There were only a few companies, predominantly from the United States, but their vast landholdings and political influence grew strong enough that the countries in which they operated became known as "banana republics."[1] This name grew out of a combination of factors. The companies became affiliated with and benefactors of local political parties, and they used these affiliations to ensure that strategic national decisions always were made with the banana companies' interests foremost in mind (Sheahan, 1987).

When decisions made at the national level were in conflict with the interests of the banana companies, various mechanisms were used to reverse them. Simplest was the use of both economic and social threats; the companies would shut down their operations, and their workers would be laid off, so not only would the countries lose the foreign revenues (modest as they were after the companies extracted their rents), but they would have to deal with pending social upheaval. More complex, but invoked numerous times, was the threat of military intervention from the U.S. military. Most countries in Central America were occupied at one time or another by the U.S. Marine Corps, instilling the obedience that came to be associated with banana republics.

This situation has changed considerably during recent years such that the banana companies can be said to have much more limited control over the governments of host countries. Yet, the instability and institutional weakness that their historical political actions created were inextricably linked to the attractiveness of Marxism as a liberating philosophy and, in turn, to the social, economic, and military chaos that unfolded during the second half of the 20th century in each of the countries except Costa Rica.

At its worst, Cell I development can lead to disaster on multiple fronts. Now that peace and relative stability have returned to the region for the first time in many decades, the multifaceted disasters of the banana republics have given way to more focused problems. In particular, although the banana companies still are rent seekers, their economic privilege is not questioned as much as is their environmentally destructive growing practices. These include the use of pesticides and fertilizers that are banned in the United States because of toxicity levels. Many of these pesticides and fertilizers are sold to Central American farmers by companies based in the United States that are prohibited from selling them in the United States but are allowed to produce them at home and sell them in foreign countries. The paradox is that they are used in the cultivation of produce that is then exported for consumption in the United States and Europe.

These practices also include the use of large plastic bags to cover every bunch of maturing fruit during the growing season. At harvest time, these millions of bags (a distinctive electric blue color) are removed from the fruit trees and discarded unsystematically. Some of these bags make their way to landfills, others are burned during the dry season, and the rest float around the countryside, making the Caribbean coast of the isthmus look as though the local population does not have enough pride to keep itself tidy. Because that same region is fertile for tourism development, the environmentally unsound practices of the banana plantations work at direct odds with the most significant economic alternative the locals have, which is to work in tourism-related jobs. There have been recent efforts to change some of these practices, and these are discussed in the Cell III subsection later.

The banana republic legacy has not completely been wiped away during the recent return to peace and stability. Not only are the banana companies alive and well (in terms of their own economic interests), but they have been joined by a group of new industries that function almost identically. One category of such industries represents the cutting edge of the Cell I form of foreign direct investment in developing economies—the maquiladora (or maquila for short).

Maquilas are local production subsidiaries of foreign companies. They set up shop in Central American countries primarily because they are given tax incentives from the host countries and often from their home countries as well (especially those based in the United States).

With tax-free status in the host country and tax benefits back home, the inexpensive labor of the host country typically is an added benefit. Because this inexpensive labor typically is unskilled, the types of jobs that are sent with these maquilas are relatively low value-added jobs—parts assembly, sewing, and the like. On top of these benefits to the foreign companies, lax labor laws often permit the type of sweatshop conditions and child labor abuses that these companies could not get away with at home. Maquilas have been faulted not only for these rent-seeking activities but also for not leaving much value in the host country. Apart from the meager wages they pay, maquilas leave very little behind, repatriating revenues and profits to their home countries. Often, their production facilities are built for them as an incentive to bring their productive capital to the host country, but this productive capital is easily moved when more attractive offers appear elsewhere.

Another variation of the Cell I form of investment is found in the tourism sector in the form of large resort development companies that are given lucrative incentives to build in a host country. One difference between this sector and the maquilas is that a resort, once built, cannot be repatriated (except for managers, furniture, and equipment). But although foreign resort companies are putting up more capital that cannot be repatriated (thus, higher risk), this is balanced by several factors. The companies, like maquilas, are given tax incentives and often attractive financing conditions as well. More important, they occasionally are given environmental privileges not granted to others.

In coastal areas of Costa Rica, for example, there is a famous case of a mega-resort project that was courted by the government and allowed to build its enormous infrastructure at the water's edge, even though the country's strict environmental laws clearly prohibited this. Only after strong public outcry was the project shut down. In another case, a world-renowned foreign resort company was allowed to replace hundreds of acres of ecologically critical mangrove forests with landfill and non-native palm trees that were believed to be more attractive to tourists.

Besides such questionable environmental practices, several of the large resort projects in Central America operate like maquilas in the sense that they pay low wages, provide little training, and repatriate the lion's share of their dollar-based revenues back to their home countries (in this case, Spain is the home country more often than the United States). Strategically, these firms are selling a mass tourism product that give customers a standardized and consistent worldwide product rather than a uniquely Costa Rican experience. Alternatives to these Cell I practices are evident in the Cell II orientation.

Limited Social Covenants
in Costa Rica (Cell II)

In more recent history, large MNCs from around the world have been investing heavily in Central America, hoping that as peace and stability matured, market opportunities would follow. Pharmaceutical, electronics, consumer and industrial goods, and other types of companies from North America, Europe, and Asia have made capital investments in Central America even without the tax incentives enjoyed by maquilas (which are created only for the purpose of exportation of their production). Besides these large MNCs, other investors from abroad come to the region and make significant investments in local businesses, bringing with them capital, technology, and managerial expertise.

These investments assume that in the long run, the companies will enjoy a first-movers' advantage with excess returns because they have entered the economies of the region on the ground floor, prior to the competition. In the short run, the outlays for training and expatriate managers are excessive compared to the cost of operating in their home countries. But if the host economies develop, then the return on these investments eventually could become extremely profitable.

One company that represents a Cell II form of development is Intel, with its recent investment in Costa Rica. Worth a reported $200 million, the facility that Intel began operating in San Jose in 1998 had roughly doubled the value of exports of the entire country by the end of its first year of operation. What is more, all of the expatriate managers who were brought from the United States to oversee construction and initial management of the facility were expected to replace themselves with Costa Ricans within the first year or so of operation. Although Intel does not have any Costa Rican capital investment in the project, it is doing more than setting up a local production facility run by its own cadre from the home office.

Intel is building on the investments made by the Costa Rican government in education over the past several decades (because there is no standing army, the funds that many of the neighboring countries spend on military concerns are instead invested in education and environmental protection in Costa Rica), so in a sense, there is a partnership. The government offers a well-educated populace (the literacy rate of Costa Rica is said to be higher than that of the United States), and Intel, acting in its own economic interest as well as that of the country, takes those people and trains them to compete in the new era of global technology-based economic competition.

Another example from Costa Rica is the Aerial Tram. This is the most visited private tourist attraction in Costa Rica (second only to the National Parks system in total visitors), designed to allow visitors to travel by cable car through the canopy of the rain forest. The infrastructure was built using sound ecological practices including the use of helicopters to drop in pylons for the cable system so as not to disturb the jungle floor or any trees. Although the capital for the creation and development of this company is predominantly foreign and the company is explicitly profit oriented, its vision is to serve as a model for environmental protection by showing alternative methods to profiting from the rain forest without cutting down its trees.

The management and staff of the Aerial Tram are nearly all locals who have been trained by the entrepreneurs who founded the venture. In this sense, the company has become a source of economic development for the local community as much as for its own interest. Beyond its normal business operations, which are essentially designed to provide an enjoyable educational experience, the company also engages in not-for-profit educational activities. Free of charge, it regularly hosts students from the public school system of the country, teaching them about the importance of protecting the rain forest. Rather than merely maximizing short-term revenues, this company has made social and economic investments for the long run.

Joint Partnerships in
Costa Rica (Cell III)

The hotel industry in Costa Rica illustrates this Cell III type of development. Costa Rica began developing a global reputation as a tourist destination during the 1980s, particularly after the president won the Nobel Peace Prize. Prior to this period, the hotel industry was relatively small, but as demand grew, many Costa Ricans decided to enter the hotel business. Most of the new hotels were owned and managed by inexperienced investors who learned the business by trial and error. Some of the new hotels were operated by multinational chains that operated in Costa Rica using staff and management from their global operations. Eventually, some local investors asked foreign hotel operators to join them in entering the market as joint partners. The most notable of these was the case of the recently built Marriott Hotel.

The concept to build the Marriott Hotel in Costa Rica came from a group of local successful entrepreneurs (from outside the hotel industry) who wanted to diversify their holdings. Because of Marriott's world-class reputation as a hotel operator, these entrepreneurs asked the company to take a stake in their venture and offered the company a contract to manage the hotel. Although the Marriott company's stake is relatively small, it is large enough to show its commitment to the market. Moreover, the company is being asked to sell its industry expertise to a group of successful local businesspeople. Marriott's stake is largely symbolic, but the inside pull from local investors is significant.

In addition to managing the hotel, Marriott uses what might be the largest training and development budget of any hotel in the region to develop its staff. This model has worked so well in Costa Rica that this model has since been replicated in other countries in the region including Guatemala, El Salvador, and Panama—each with majority local shareholders, a minority stake by Marriott, and a strong training and development component. The hotel industry shows signs of a Cell III form of development precisely because local investors have taken the lead and have brought in multinational partners only for those management tasks that the entrepreneurs cannot effectively handle on their own.

Integrated Social Covenants in Costa Rica (Cell IV)

The world trend toward environmental conservation and ecological issues has helped to establish ecotourism as a substantial component of the tourism industry within Costa Rica. The biological diversity and political stability of Costa Rica succeeded in attracting entities such as the Organization for Tropical Studies (which gathers 55 universities of international renown), the Tropical Agronomic Center for Research and Education, and the Inter-American Institute of Cooperation for Agriculture. For many years, these institutions have done first-class research in the country and have spread the name of Costa Rica among academicians, environmental groups, and the global public interested in environmental preservation as a very special country by reason of its biodiversity and commitment to conserving the environment. Also, Costa Rica has created an exemplary national park system with relatively easy access and a large percentage of national territory (nearly one quarter). These factors contribute to the positioning of the country as a very attractive destination for those tourists who, for professional or personal reasons, are interested in environmental or naturalist issues.

Because the majority of Costa Rica's visitors engage in activities related to natural attractions, this raises the stakes of the partnership between the public and private sectors and between tourism interests and preservation interests. Mass tourism to the country through the usual multinational contractual relationships so prevalent in other developing countries, and clearly within a Cell I framework, creates a dilemma for the country. Which model or approach should Costa Rica employ? Can the country do both at the same time and not confuse global customers and partners alike? Answers to these questions depend on whether a Cell I approach (mass tourism) is consistent with the principles and image that Costa Rica has worked so hard to develop.

The economic benefits that ecotourism has created have led some local entrepreneurs to capitalize on the image that the pioneers (Cell II) created without necessarily adhering to the conservationist/environmentalist principles. Some tour operators and hotel owners misuse the term *ecotourism* to attract a growing population of travelers who are concerned with the environment. The incentive to operate from a Cell III position and "free ride" on the Cell II social contract is great given that most travelers are inclined to pay more for the "privilege" of experiencing a well-preserved natural environment. This has raised difficult questions. Some of the pioneers claim that these new free-riding entrepreneurs are diluting the value and integrity of the equity created by the pioneers. However, these recent entrepreneurs ultimately might help the pioneers to achieve their goals and move toward Cell IV.

Given a limited national budget for tourism promotion, the private sector promotions of Costa Rica (greatly increased by these newer free-riding tour wholesalers/operators, hotels, etc.) as a "natural" destination undoubtedly have led to greater visibility and increased visitation. These visitors spend money visiting protected areas, which in turn ensures their continued protection.

To accomplish the sustainability of the eco-destination requires a new approach to partnership. A social covenant approach provides an option for balancing the environmental, social, and economic agendas. Accomplishing this cooperation might depend on getting more of Costa Rica's citizenry, including those with no direct financial stake in the industry, to understand both the importance of the industry to the country's economy and the relation between sustainable environmental practices and their own behavior. Careful planning and the development of innovative relationships that share the benefit of tourism development are worthy challenges for the leaders of this developing country.

The first step in facilitating any strategic partnership, and particularly building Cell IV forms of social covenants, is to recognize the varied elements of the economic activities that make up the tourism cluster in Costa Rica. Figure 7.4 shows a diagram of the main tourism cluster in Costa Rica, namely, that revolving around tourists particularly inclined to nature-related activities.

At the cluster center are the motivations to visit the country, of which the most relevant are those having a direct relationship to nature. In a circle around motivations are industry sectors with a direct interface with tourists. These are the lodging, transportation, food and beverage, attractions, and promotion sectors. On the peripheral circle are support and related sectors. These are defined as sectors important to the service ultimately received by tourists, although not having a direct interaction with them but rather supporting and supplying the sectors directly related to visitors.

In a Cell I model of contractual relationships, various businesses in the cluster could work independently and for the interests of the one or two financial players involved in the contract. In a Cell II model, caretaker organizations might be established to preserve and protect the environment or might be established as socially conscientious businesses that preserve the forests while building eco-friendly operations. A Cell III model might be represented in the existence of more local lodging, attraction, training, promotion, food and beverage, transportation, and other service businesses and associations working for individual economic gains but in joint venture arrangements or strategic alliances that provide for bundling of services to the global ecotourist customer. A series of local hotels

206

Figure 4. Tourism Cluster in Costa Rica

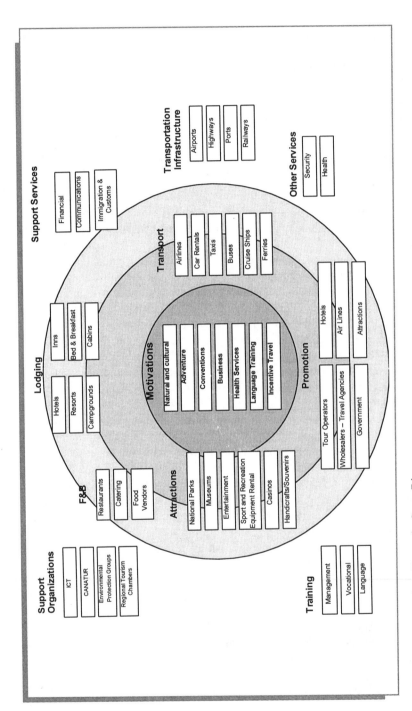

FIGURE 7.4. Tourism Cluster in Costa Rica

NOTE: ICT = Instituto Costarricense de Turismo (Costa Rica Tourism Institute); CANATUR = Camara Nacional de Turismo (National Tourism Chamber); F&B = Food and Beverage.

could contract with local car rental, bus, and taxi services to transport guests to national parks. In a Cell IV model, the various individual entities would work in collaboration with local community members to accomplish the objectives of greater economic benefits to the community members, creating more jobs, and building infrastructure and support services. In Costa Rica, this Cell IV approach would reduce demand for pastures because the citizens no longer would need the agricultural lands for survival, thus curbing deforestation.

We argue that the development and enhancement of the tourism clusters provide benefits to all businesses. By working together to protect the environment, companies share information and contribute to the success of other businesses. An example of this is clearly reflected in Barra Honda National Park, where visitors find services that usually are nonexistent in these zones—a typical food restaurant, lodging, camping facilities within a natural dry forest, a deer nursery, a handicraft shop, a parking area, and local guides. All of these services are the responsibility of a Pro-Development Association, made up of community members, and are offered on the park periphery to leave the natural reserve untouched. In addition, they are voluntarily involved in controlling fires within the park and reforesting with pochote (*Bombacopsis quinatum*) trees. Finally, they provide training in diverse topics such as food handling, English, fire control, and soil conversation.

IMPLICATIONS FOR FUTURE RESEARCH

The framework for social partnerships and the importance of an integrated social covenant approach suggested in this chapter create various avenues for future researchers to examine at the macro, meso, and micro levels. At the macro level, research is needed to examine differences across industries (e.g., manufacturing, telecommunications, agriculture, tourism, financial services) in their design of cooperative partnerships and how these various industries progress toward a Cell IV form of relationship. Future studies could identify the structural barriers within different industries and different developing countries to the establishment of social contracts. Specifically, research examining the characteristics that allow industries and companies to be more agile in their responses to the demands of a rapidly changing environment and sensitive to the unique needs within each partnership would help to define effective paths toward building social contracts. Studies determining which elements in an economic development plan are critical to building social contracts and the minimum requirements necessary in developing countries with regard to infrastructure, political stability, democratization, socioeconomic composition, and the like clearly are needed. Do the dynamics of social contracts differ by region of the world such that Asian, European, African, and American approaches differ? Case studies examining other Central American countries would contribute to further understanding of the conditions needed for change in the region and the likelihood that these countries can move toward social contract forms of global relationships for long-term sustainable development. Even within the United States, the possibility of building social contracts between Native American Indian nations and the federal government might be a promising area for future study.

At the meso level, longitudinal research is needed examining a company's staging and execution of an integrated social covenant form of strategic social partnership. Detailed analyses of how a company goes about the internal changes needed to incorporate this different managerial philosophy and of the interactions with various entities in the developing country will contribute to the understanding of how to design and sustain these cooperative partnerships. The structure of the MNC also can play a role in determining its ability and success in forming new social partnerships. It is possible that agile, matrixed, or networked internal operating systems will enhance the ability of an MNC to form numerous social partnerships. Will the global networks of the federal design presented by Handy (1992) or other forms of innovative organizational design influence the ease and effectiveness of social partnership? Studies also could examine within-country experiments in which global organizations that are operating with Cell I, Cell II, and Cell III forms of partnership are willing to explore building a different model of partnership in an enclave in the country so that comparisons can be drawn among the different approaches. We see naturally occurring experiments extremely promising in the hospitality industry because so much development is under way in Central America that is done in isolated enclaves within countries. It would be interesting to see whether there are specific instances in which the models of Cell I, Cell II, and Cell III are more desirable and productive than the orientation suggested in Cell IV.

At the micro level, research is warranted on the relationships between the four different forms of partnership and the job attitudes of local employees, expatriate managers, and host country managers. The influence of the different forms of partnership on customer loyalty, purchase decisions, and customer satisfaction also would be a fruitful line of inquiry. In addition, studies that examine the managerial skills necessary to operate successfully in an integrated social covenant form of relationship with local communities in developing countries are needed. The ability to speak the local language; knowledge of local culture, history, values, and skill levels of the residents; skill in negotiating, understanding of self-knowledge, understanding of differences, and understanding of appropriate managerial styles and techniques in different work environments (Earley & Erez, 1997) can be crucial competencies for managers working in a social contract in developing countries. The role of training and models for building life and work skills for employees in rapidly evolving economies also would add value to our understanding of cooperative models. The integration and conflicts among personal, work, organizational, and country values would be an exciting stream of research that could be developed by examining employees employed for organizations using the various models described in this chapter.

CONCLUSION

The major premise of this chapter is that sustainable competitive advantage will come from a new way of thinking about partnerships and a different orientation toward relationships with competitors, investors, employees, and the local governments and citizens. It will become increasingly difficult to do business without collaborating and cooperating with the broader community. The future for Central America in particular is not banana republics but rather new industry-based clusters. Two drivers of this new era are the economic gains to be accrued from interdependence and the genuine good for the society. These two benefits support and enhance each other. Flexible human resource strategies and practices will fuel and sustain the shared economic gains. However, as our illustration of ecotourism in Costa Rica suggests, a movement toward the new social contract is fragile and vulnerable. Inertia and resistance to change are formidable barriers. Nevertheless, the more businesses and countries work to create these social partnerships, the more they will become viable and enduring.

NOTE

1. Referring to a country as a "banana republic" is a highly charged phrase, and we use it as such to illustrate the dramatic implications of a country that has managed to escape the confines of such a pejorative descriptor.

REFERENCES

Adler, N. J., Brahm, R., & Graham, J. L. (1992). Strategy implementation: A comparison of face-to-face negotiations in the People's Republic of China and the United States. *Strategic Management Journal, 13,* 449-466.

Andrews, K. R. (1980). *The concept of corporate strategy.* Homewood, IL: Irwin.

Bowie, N. E. (1991). The firm as moral community. In R. M. Coughlin (Ed.), *Morality, rationality, and efficiency: New perspectives on socio-economics* (pp. 169-193). Armonk, NY: M. E. Sharpe.

Boynton, L. L. (1986). The effects of tourism on Amish quilting design. *Annals of Tourism Research, 13,* 451-465.

Creed, W. E., & Miles, R. E. (1996). Trust in organizations: A conceptual framework linking organizational forms, managerial philosophies, and the opportunity costs of controls. In R. Kramer, & T. Tyler (Eds.), *Trust in organizations: Frontiers of theory and research.* Thousand Oaks, CA: Sage.

De Forest, M. E. (1994). Thinking of a plant in Mexico? *Academy of Management Executive, 8,* 33-40.

Donaldson, T. (1982). *Corporations and morality.* Englewood Cliffs, NJ: Prentice Hall.

Earley, P. C., & Erez, M. (1997). *The transplanted executive.* New York: Oxford University Press.

Etzioni, A. (1988). *Capital corruption: The new attack on American democracy.* New Brunswick, NJ: Transaction Books.

Etzioni, E. (1993). *The spirit of community.* New York: Crown.

Friedman, M. (1962). *Capitalism and freedom.* Chicago: University of Chicago Press.

Greenwood, D. (1989). Culture by the pound: An anthropological perspective on tourism as cultural commoditization. In V. L. Smith (Ed.), *Hosts and guests: The anthropology of tourism* (pp. 171-185). Philadelphia: University of Pennsylvania Press.

Hall, R. H. (1991). *Organizations, structures, processes, and outcomes.* Englewood Cliffs, NJ: Prentice Hall.

Handy, C. (1992). Balancing corporate power: A new Federalist paper. *Harvard Business Review, 70*(6), 59-72.

Harrison, D. (1992). Tourism to less developed countries: The social consequences. In D. Harrison (Ed.), *Tourism and the less developed countries* (pp. 19-34). London: Belhaven.

Kanter, R. M. (1995). *World class: Thriving locally in the global economy.* New York: Touchstone.

Kochan, T. (1997, October). *Beyond myopia: Human resources and the changing social contract.* Paper presented at the conference, "Research and Theory in Strategic Human Resource Management: An Agenda for the 21st Century," Cornell University, School of Industrial and Labor Relations, Center for Advanced Human Resources Studies.

Kramer, R., & Tyler, T. (1996). *Trust in organizations: Frontiers of theory and research.* Thousand Oaks, CA: Sage.

Latane, B., & Darley, J. (1970). *Unresponsive bystander: Why doesn't he help?* New York: Appleton.

Lewellan, T. C. (1995). *Dependency and development: An introduction to the Third World.* Westport, CT: Bergin & Garvey.

Mahoney, J. T., Huff, A. S., & Huff, J. O. (1994). Toward a new social contract theory in organizational science. *Journal of Management Inquiry, 3,* 153-168.

Noronha, R. (1979). Paradise revisited: Tourism in Bali. In E. de Kadt (Ed.), *Tourism: Passport to development?* (pp. 177-204). Oxford, UK: Oxford University Press.

Oppermann, M., & Chon, K-S. (1997). *Tourism in developing countries.* London: International Thomson Business Press.

Powell, W. (1996). Trust-based forms of governance. In R. Kramer & T. Tyler (Eds.), *Trust in organizations: Frontiers of theory and research.* Thousand Oaks, CA: Sage.

Reich, R. B. (1998). The new meaning of corporate social responsibility. *California Management Review, 40*(2), 8-17.

Rousseau, D. (1995). *Psychological contracts in organizations: Understanding written and unwritten agreements.* Thousands Oaks, CA: Sage.

Shane, S. (1994). The effect of national culture on the choice between licensing and direct foreign investment. *Strategic Management Journal, 15,* 387-394.

Sheahan, J. (1987). *Patterns of development in Latin America.* Princeton, NJ: Princeton University Press.

Shrivastava, P. (1995). The role of corporations in achieving ecological sustainability. *Academy of Management Review, 20,* 936-961.

Tolbert, P., & Zucker, L. (1983). Institutional sources of change in the formal structure of organizations: The diffusion of civil service reform, 1880-1935. *Administrative Science Quarterly, 28,* 22-39.

Tushman, M. L., & O'Reilly, C. A. (1997). *Winning through innovation.* Boston: Harvard Business School Press.

Williamson, O. (1975). *Markets and hierarchies: Analysis and antitrust implications.* New York: Free Press.

PART III

Macro-Organizational Approaches

chapter **8**

Examining Interfirm Trust and Relationships in a Cross-National Setting

JEFFREY H. DYER

$\mathbf{D}$uring the past 20 years, there has been tremendous growth in international management research as the globalization of industries has made understanding foreign nations, firms, and markets imperative for business executives around the globe. Many of the early international management research studies have been descriptive and comparative with a focus on "how they do things over there" (Earley & Singh, 1995). Furthermore, due to the decidedly practical focus of much of this research, a common criticism of international research is that it lacks rigor and does not enhance our knowledge of fundamental theory. However, cross-national research offers an opportunity to create a better understanding of the theoretical limitations of existing management theories, many of which have been generated within a U.S. context. But for international management research to make contributions to fundamental theory development,

AUTHOR'S NOTE: The research presented in this chapter is based on a model of the determinants of trust developed in another article (with Wujin Chu) for the *Journal of International Business Studies* (in press). I especially thank Wujin Chu for his assistance in the data collection and analysis. I also express my gratitude to the Sloan Foundation and the International Motor Vehicle Program at the Massachusetts Institute of Technology for funding this research.

it is important for international research to be undertaken with extreme care and rigor.

This chapter has two objectives. The first is to present some cross-national research on the determinants of supplier trust in a sample of supplier-automaker relationships in the United States, Japan, and Korea. I define trust and derive a model of its determinants drawing on (a) a sociological/embeddedness perspective, (b) a process-based perspective, and (c) an economic (hostage-based) perspective. The second objective is to use this cross-national study as the basis to discuss some of the strengths and weaknesses of international research on interfirm relationships. In particular, I identify numerous advantages that a multination research design offers over a single nation study. I also discuss issues that the international researcher might want to consider if he or she is planning to conduct a multination study on interfirm relationships.[1]

THE DETERMINANTS OF INTERFIRM TRUST: A CROSS-NATIONAL STUDY

A central issue in the literature on strategic alliances and interfirm cooperation is how firms create trust and control opportunism, particularly when the transactors have made investments in transaction-specific assets.[1] Under these conditions, trust has been described as an important antecedent to interorganizational cooperation and economic efficiency (Sako, 1991; Smith, Carroll, & Ashford, 1995). In fact, recent research suggests that trust in supplier-buyer relations might be an important source of competitive advantage because it (a) *lowers transaction costs* (Barney & Hansen, 1994; Dyer, 1996a; Sako, 1991; Zaheer, McEvily, & Perrone, 1998), (b) *facilitates investments in transaction/relation-specific assets* that enhance productivity (Asanuma, 1989; Dyer, 1996c; Lorenz, 1988), and (c) *leads to superior information sharing* (Aoki, 1988; Clark & Fujimoto, 1991; Fruin, 1992; Nishiguchi, 1994). Moreover, some scholars claim that national economic efficiency is highly correlated with the existence of a high-trust institutional environment (Casson, 1990; Fukuyama, 1995; Hill, 1995; North, 1990). For example, Fukuyama (1995) argued that the economic success of a nation, "as well as its ability to compete, is conditioned by . . . the level of trust inherent in the society" (p. 7). The findings from these and other studies have increased attention to the important role of trust in economic exchanges.

A natural response to these studies has been to exhort companies to build trust with their trading partners ("Japan, USA," 1986; "Learning From Japan," 1992) and to call for increased research on the role of trust in coordinating economic activity (Smith et al., 1995). However, despite considerable academic and managerial interest in trust between trading partners, to date there has been little empirical research on the determinants of interorganizational trust (e.g., between supplier and buyer). In this research study, I examine the determinants or antecedents of supplier trust in a buyer in a sample of supplier-automaker relationships in the United States, Japan, and Korea. I define trust and derive a model of its determinants drawing on (a) a sociological/embeddedness perspective, (b) a process-based perspective, and (c) an economic (hostage-based) perspective. In so doing, I address the following key question: *What variables influence the development of supplier trust in supplier-buyer relationships, and which perspective best explains the production of trust in these different countries?*

THEORETICAL FRAMEWORK AND HYPOTHESES

Defining Trust

Among organizational scholars, trust has received attention as a mechanism of organizational control and more specifically as an alternative to price, contracts, and authority (Bradach & Eccles, 1989; Ouchi, 1980; Powell, 1990). The literature on interorganizational relations offers two general definitions of trust: confidence or predictability in one's expectations about another's behavior and confidence in another's goodwill (Ring & Van de Ven, 1992; Zaheer et al., 1998). I draw on the previous literature in defining trust as *one party's confidence that the other party in the exchange relationship will not exploit its vulnerabilities* (Barney & Hansen, 1994; Dore, 1983; Ring & Van de Ven, 1992; Sabel, 1993; Sako, 1991). This confidence (trust) would be expected to emerge in situations where the "trustworthy" party in the exchange relationship (a) is known to reliably make good faith efforts to behave in accordance with prior commitments, (b) makes adjustments (e.g., as market conditions change) in ways perceived as "fair" by the exchange partner, and (c) does not take excessive advantage of the exchange partner even when the opportunity is available. Thus, my definition characterizes interfirm trust as a construct based on three components: reliability, fairness, and goodwill. My definition of trust is similar to the "goodwill trust" description given by Sako (1991) and the trust definitions offered by numerous scholars (Barney & Hansen, 1994; Ring & Van de Ven, 1992; Sabel, 1993). Thus, trust, as defined here, is not based on contracts or third-party sanctions but rather is based on noncontractual mechanisms.

Conceptually, organizations are not able to trust each other; trust has its basis in individuals. Trust can be placed by one individual in another individual or in a group of individuals such as a partner organization. However, individuals in an organization may share an orientation toward individuals within another organization. From this perspective, "interorganizational trust describes the extent to which there is a collectively held trust orientation by organizational members toward the partner firm" (Zaheer et al., 1998, p. 143).

In this study, I consider trust (this collective orientation) by an automotive supplier in its automaker customer. A supplier's trust in its automaker customer is of particular importance in the auto industry due to supplier investments in customer-specific assets and market uncertainty that places suppliers in a vulnerable position.

The Determinants of Trust

A firm might trust trading partners to refuse to break confidences and exploit vulnerabilities for a variety of reasons. Previous research suggests that trust in interorganizational settings is likely to be produced through (a) social relationships and embedded ties or *relationship-based trust* (Dore, 1983; Granovetter, 1985; Gulati, 1995; Powell, 1990; Uzzi, 1997), (b) institutionalized processes or routines for fairly and reliably dealing with a partner organization or *process-based trust* (Zaheer & Venkatraman, 1995; Zaheer et al., 1998; Zucker, 1986), or (c) an alignment of economic incentives through hostages or *economic hostage-based trust* (Klein, 1980; Williamson, 1983, 1993). In this section, I explore each of these perspectives in greater detail and derive hypotheses.

Social/Embeddedness Perspective

According to the sociological perspective, trust emerges through social interactions between exchange partners (Granovetter, 1985; Light, 1972; Powell, 1990; Uzzi, 1997). Granovetter (1985) stated, "The embeddedness argument stresses the role of concrete personal relations and structures (or 'networks') of such relations in generating trust and discouraging malfeasance" (p. 490). He further argued, "Social relations, rather than institutional arrangements or generalized morality, are mainly responsible for the production of trust in economic life" (p. 491). If a transaction is embedded within a broader reciprocal social relationship, then transactors can rely on social sanctions to protect their interests. Various types of social sanctions may control opportunism—withdrawal of love, respect, and prestige and/or (worst of all) banishment from the social community (Ellickson, 1991; Light, 1972; Smith, 1983). Thus, individuals who take unfair advantage of a trading partner might find any of a number of sanctions imposed by other members of the social network.[2] In summary, the social perspective (Dore, 1983; Granovetter, 1985; Powell, 1990; Uzzi, 1997) suggests that trust will emerge due to social interactions between exchange partners. As the duration and intensity of interactions between transactors increase, bonds of attraction would be expected to develop and social sanctions would be expected to be more efficacious.

Length of relationship. Various scholars have suggested that trust takes time to develop and can only be built slowly over time (Arrow, 1974; Sako, 1991). Embedded ties rely on the formation of dense and stable relationships between individuals, and it takes time for exchange partners to develop the "concrete personal relations" necessary to "generate trust and discourage malfeasance" (Granovetter, 1985, p. 492; see also Larson, 1992). Related to this view is the notion that social knowledge, or knowledge gained through long-term interactions, may be the basis for trust by allowing economic actors to understand and predict others' patterns of behavior (Sohn, 1994; Tolbert, 1988). For example, Sohn (1994) found that in-depth social and cultural knowledge facilitates coordination of transactions by making a potential partner's behavior both understandable and predictable. Moreover, as social knowledge between transactors increases, information asymmetries decrease, thereby reducing behavioral uncertainty. Higher levels of trust are believed to develop when information asymmetries are low and there is less behavioral uncertainty.

Finally, when transactors engage in long-term exchange relationships, they develop a history together. Most individuals are less likely to take advantage of those with whom they have had long and stable past interactions (e.g., family members, friends) because these parties can impose social sanctions on the offending individuals. Through long-term interaction, a "social memory" is created and transactors can achieve "serial equity" (equity/reciprocity over a longer period of time) rather than requiring immediate or "spot equity" (Ouchi, 1984). Thus, higher levels of trust would be expected to emerge in exchange relationships where the transactors have a long history of interacting.

> *Hypothesis 1:* The longer the duration since the first supplier-buyer transaction, the higher the supplier's trust in the buyer.

Intensity of relationship (face-to-face communication). Various studies have found that face-to-face interactions are likely to lead to the development of positive feelings of attraction (Argyle, 1991; Lorenz, 1988). Furthermore, cooperation and trust between individuals has been found to emerge in laboratory settings when individuals can see and talk to each other and engage in social interaction (Argyle, 1991). Face-to-face communication has been described as having a high knowledge-carrying capacity because it presents immediate feedback opportunities and makes use of both visual and audio channels of communication (Daft & Lengel, 1986). Thus, it is considered useful for developing trust because it offers more cues for interpreting a trading partner's behavior and motivations. Moreover, face-to-face contact is viewed as an effective means of developing personal ties, thereby increasing the efficacy of social sanctions. Accordingly, face-to-face communication would be expected to increase supplier-buyer trust by (a) facilitating the development of personal ties, thereby increasing the efficacy of social sanctions, and (b) providing superior information to assist trans-actors in detecting trading partners that are the untrustworthy "type." Thus, as the frequency of face-to-face contact between transactors increases, trust would be expected to increase as well.

> *Hypothesis 2:* The greater the face-to-face interaction between the supplier and buyer, the higher the level of supplier trust in the buyer.

Process-Based Perspective

The process-based perspective differs from the relationship-based perspective in that the trust orientation that individuals in one firm maintain toward a trading partner is based not on personal relationships but rather on a set of institutional-ized processes and routines employed at the partner organization. These would necessarily be interorganizational processes for interacting that suggest that in-dividuals within the trading partner will behave in a trustworthy manner. Zaheer et al. (1998) referred to this as "an institutionalized pattern of dealings" and spec-ulated that "the institutionalized practices and routines for dealing with a partner organization transcend the influence of the individual boundary spanner" (p. 32). Thus, the process-based perspective recognizes that interorganizational trust may be built on impersonal structures, processes, and routines that create a stable context for exchange. Individuals might come and go at the two organizations, but the trust orientation will not be affected because trust is not based on individ-ual relationships.

One might logically ask what processes would likely influence supplier trust in a supplier-buyer relationship. Interviews with automotive suppliers suggested that the buyer's processes or *routines for selecting suppliers* and the buyer's *pro-cesses for responding to supplier problems* (e.g., the extent to which the buyer provides assistance to help the supplier fix problems and improve its operations) were processes that influenced the production of trust.

Supplier selection processes and continuity of relationship. The processes that buyers use to select suppliers for business on an upcoming car model are likely to influence supplier trust. In some instances, buyers might use a competitive bidding process whereby incumbents are not given any advantage in ensuing rounds, regardless of past performance. This is an arms-length competitive bid-ding process typically used by U.S. companies such as General Motors. In other instances, buyers might select suppliers based on their track records for perfor-mance and give incumbents the first opportunity to get new business. This is a selection process that favors incumbents and often is said to typify Japanese supplier-buyer relationships (although recent data suggest that U.S. firms, nota-bly Chrysler, are increasingly using this approach [Dyer, 1996b]). Consequently, in addition to length of relationship, *continuity* in the supplier-buyer relationship can contribute to the development of interorganizational trust. It is possible for trading partners to have had a long-term relationship (i.e., many years have passed since the initial transaction) even though the relationship might not have been continuous. For example, some U.S. suppliers reported that although they began selling parts to a particular automaker 50 years ago, there have been occasions when they have lost the component business to competitors. In other instances, the suppliers continue to rewin the contract year after year due to selection processes that favor the incumbent.[3] Thus, there is a high degree of continuity in the relationship due to the nature of the buyer's supplier selection routines.

Supplier trust is expected to emerge under conditions of continuous repeated exchange (Gulati, 1995) due to buyer purchasing routines that are predictable and consistent and that do not switch (perhaps opportunistically) business to competitors (Butler, 1991; Heide & Miner, 1992). Repeated exchange is particularly important to the development of supplier trust in situations where suppliers have invested in relation-specific assets. Under these conditions, a buyer's willingness to stay with the same supplier is likely to be interpreted by the supplier as a signal of commitment and trustworthiness. By contrast, frequent competitive switching of suppliers would be expected to be associated with low trust because, as Casson (1990) argued, the buyer "will use price comparisons to back up threats to switch trade away unless it gets a better deal" (p. 113). Thus, supplier trust would be expected to be higher when the buyer has a history of continuous repeated exchange with the supplier.

> *Hypothesis 3:* Supplier trust is higher when the buyer has a track record of continuous repeated exchange with the supplier (i.e., the supplier's history of rewinning the contract at the model change is high).

Buyer assistance-giving routines. Zucker (1986) argued that "firms make investments in process-based trust by creating positive 'reputations' " (p. 61). She further argued that one method (process) for building a reputation for trustworthiness is the offering of assistance or gifts to exchange partners. The importance of gift exchange in creating trust and reciprocity in exchange relationships has long been argued by a distinguished line of anthropologists and sociologists (Gouldner, 1960; Malinowski, 1932; Mauss, 1967). Gouldner (1960) suggested that a norm of reciprocity begins with a starting mechanism that may take the form of a gift or other acts of assistance. These actions are particularly likely to result in high levels of trust if they are viewed as routine behavior. For example, in the automotive industry, Toyota and Nissan have long maintained a division of internal "consultants" who are responsible for helping suppliers solve various technical and managerial problems on a regular basis.

According to the suppliers interviewed, the buyer's processes for providing regular assistance to suppliers (in many cases helping suppliers fix operational problems) were likely to influence the degree of trust in the buyer. The rationale behind the trust-creating value of assistance-giving routines is that an exchange partner's offer of "free" assistance serves as a signal of goodwill and commitment because it suggests that the giving party is genuinely concerned with the well-being of the receiving party. Also, the assistance may be viewed as a signal that the giving party does not have opportunistic intent (i.e., is the honest "type") and feels benevolently toward the receiving party. Benevolence is the perception of a positive orientation of the trustee toward the trustor and has been hypothesized to be positively associated with trust (Larzelere & Huston, 1980; Mayer, Davis, & Schoorman, 1995). When a buyer routinely offers free assistance to a supplier (i.e., if assistance is not fully costed), the supplier is likely to interpret such actions as a manifestation of commitment by the buyer and perhaps the basis for trust (Sako, 1991).

Hypothesis 4: The greater the assistance provided by the buyer to the supplier, the greater the supplier's trust in the buyer.

Economic (Hostage-Based) Perspective

Transactors also might behave in a trustworthy manner due to "credible commitments" that they have made with a trading partner (Klein, 1980; Williamson, 1983). Williamson (1993) referred to this as "calculative trust." For example, trading partners might make financial or investment arrangements (e.g., stock swaps, equity participation) that are purposefully designed to align their economic fortunes. These arrangements often are referred to as credible commitments or an exchange of hostages. There is a relatively large literature suggesting that stock ownership, in particular, aligns transactors' incentives and can get them to behave in a more trustworthy fashion (Bolton, Malmrose, & Ouchi, 1994; Dyer & Ouchi, 1993; Gerlach, 1992; Pisano, 1989). Some might argue that this does not really produce trust, as I have defined it, because trust involves goodwill and the complete suspension of "calculation." Indeed, with calculative trust, exchange partners behave in trustworthy behavior because they have created conditions that make it in their economic interest to do so. However, stock ownership can produce trustworthy behavior that, over time, results in higher levels of trust of the noncalculative sort. In many instances, the stock tie acts as a symbol of the relationship, thereby encouraging individuals to develop a trust orientation toward the partner organization (Gerlach, 1992). Shared equity may create conditions for informal trust to develop.[4] Thus, partial equity ownership can build trust both by aligning the trading partners' incentives and by creating conditions for informal trust to develop.

Hypothesis 5: The greater the buyer's ownership of supplier stock, the higher the level of supplier trust in the buyer.

RESEARCH METHODS

Research Setting

I chose to study supplier-automaker relations in Japan, Korea, and the United States for a number of reasons. First, the automotive industry is a large and important industry in each country and, as mentioned previously, is an industry where trust is likely to be important. Studying supplier-buyer relationships in the same industry across different institutional environments allows for some control of extraneous variation. Second, studying supplier trust in a cross-national setting allows us to test the extent to which the findings are robust across national settings. Japan was chosen because it has been described as a high-trust environment where interfirm trust is a key factor that facilitates exchange and creates competitive advantages for Japanese firms (Casson, 1990; Dore, 1983; Hill, 1995; Sako, 1991). By contrast, the United States often has been characterized as a low-trust environment relative to Japan (Dore, 1983; Casson, 1990; Shane, 1994), although recently Fukuyama (1995) questioned that view, suggesting that the United States actually is a high-trust environment (at least compared to other, economically less developed countries). The present study data allow us to examine whether levels of trust are reported as the same or different, and whether the determinants of trust are the same or different, in both the United States and Japan. Finally, Korea was added because Korea's culture is similar to Japan's, yet its management practices have been influenced by U.S. firms (Dubinsky, Kotabe, Lim, & Michaels, 1994; Hamilton & Biggart, 1988). This is particularly true in the auto industry, where long-standing partner relationships have been formed between Daewoo and General Motors (General Motors owned 50% of Daewoo until 1994) and between Kia and Ford. I was interested in seeing whether or not interfirm trust levels were similar to Japan's (perhaps due to cultural similarities) or more similar to the U.S.'s (perhaps due to similar management practices). In summary, by examining supplier-buyer relationships in three countries, it can be determined which factors influence supplier trust across all countries as well as which are country specific.

Sample and Data Collection

The sample consisted of three U.S. (General Motors, Ford, Chrysler), two Japanese (Toyota, Nissan), and three Korean (Hyundai, Daewoo, Kia) automakers and a sample of their suppliers. The authors visited each company's purchasing department and asked the department manager to select a representative sample of suppliers that included both partners (i.e., *keiretsu/chaebol* suppliers) and nonpartner (i.e., independent) suppliers. A total of 30 purchasing managers at the eight automakers' purchasing departments were interviewed to obtain feedback on the appropriateness, completeness, and clarity of the questionnaire as well as to gain a better understanding of the issues arising in automaker-supplier relations.

Sales and engineering vice presidents at 70 suppliers (30 U.S., 20 Japanese, 20 Korean) also were interviewed, during which the survey was developed and pretested. The survey was translated into Japanese and Korean by a team of 2 Korean and 3 Japanese Ph.D. and M.B.A. students, some of whom had worked in the automotive industry. To ensure an accurate translation, the Japanese survey was back-translated by a Japanese M.B.A. student (a Nissan employee), and the Korean survey was back-translated by a colleague at Seoul National University. The interviews with supplier executives helped us to gain a better understanding of the industry and the nature of the supplier-automaker relationship. To minimize key informant bias and follow the general recommendation to use the most knowledgeable informant (Kumar, Stern, & Anderson, 1993), the purchasing manager at each automaker was asked to identify the supplier executive who was most responsible for managing the day-to-day relationship. This person typically was the supplier's sales vice president, sales account manager, or (in some cases) president. The final survey then was sent to the key supplier informant identified by the automaker.

One might question whether a single informant has sufficient knowledge and ability to assess the trust orientation of individuals at multiple levels between his or her supplier organization and the automaker. Although responses from multiple informants would have been preferred (with a cost of a smaller sample), I believe that the informants were well positioned to make this assessment for the following reasons. First, key informants had been employed at their respective organizations for an average of 16 years and, therefore, had long histories of working with the automakers. These individuals had primary responsibility for managing the day-to-day relationship with the customers and were well aware of the variety of interactions between their employees and their customers' employees. Furthermore, in approximately 15 of the in-person interviews with suppliers, the key informants brought to the interviews 23 other top supplier executives (e.g., vice president of engineering, key sales representatives) who previously had filled out the questionnaire separately from the key informants. During the interviews, the group of supplier executives would look at each other's answers and come to a consensus on the "group" answer (I was not able to see their individual responses). The degree of similarity in their responses was remarkable; rarely did the responses vary more than 1 point on a 7-point Likert scale. In the few cases where there was some discussion, the key informant typically brought more information to the discussion than did the other members. Consequently, I believe that the key informant responses reliably represent the responses that would have been received if multiple individuals at the suppliers had been surveyed.

Usable responses were obtained from 135 U.S. (66% response rate), 101 Japanese (68% response rate), and 217 Korean (55% response rate) suppliers. The data collection was done between 1992 and 1994. The U.S. and Japanese data were collected in 1992, reflecting data for 1991, and the Korean data were collected in 1994, reflecting data for 1993. I do not believe that this will bias the results given that the analysis focuses on rather stable measures (i.e., length of relationship, stock ownership, trust) that Korean suppliers indicated had not changed in any significant ways since 1992.

Operational Measures

Recall that the survey was administered to the suppliers. Therefore, the measures reflect the perceptions of suppliers regarding the supplier-automaker relationship. However, during the interviews with the purchasing managers of the automakers, it was discovered that both the supplier and automaker perceptions regarding the relationship were very similar in specific cases that were discussed. There were no instances in which the perceptions of suppliers and automakers were dramatically different. The anecdotal findings are similar to those of Anderson and Narus (1990), who found that suppliers' and buyers' perceptions of levels of trust were quite consistent.

Trust. Consistent with previous studies, trust was operationalized using multiple scale items designed to measure the extent to which the supplier trusted the automaker not to behave opportunistically (Anderson & Narus, 1990; Heide & John, 1988; Zaheer & Venkatraman, 1995). This measure (*TRUST*) was operationalized as the sum of the following submeasures:

1. The extent to which the supplier trusts the manufacturer to treat the supplier fairly

2. The extent to which the automaker has a reputation for trustworthiness (following through on promises and commitments) in the general supplier community

3. If given the chance, the extent to which the supplier perceives that the automaker will take unfair advantage of the supplier (reverse scored)

My trust construct includes key elements of my definition of trust including fairness, reliability, and goodwill (a willingness to forgo opportunistic behavior even when the chance is available). Each scale item was measured on a 7-point Likert scale (1 = *not at all*, 7 = *to a very great extent*). The Chronbach's alpha for this construct was .84, indicating high reliability.

Length of the relationship. This measure (*LENGTH*) was operationalized as the number of years since the supplier first began selling products to the automaker. This measure represents the length of the business relationship with the assumption that the longer the business relationship, the longer the opportunity for individuals at the supplier and buyer to develop "concrete personal relations" through social interaction.

Face-to-face communication. This measure (*FACE*) is operationalized as the annual "person-days" that the supplier-automaker spent in face-to-face contact during the past year. The measure includes face-to-face contact between supplier sales and engineering personnel and automaker purchasing and engineering personnel. Days of contact was calculated by having the key informant identify the number of salespeople that worked directly with the particular automaker. Then, he or she indicated the average number of days per week that the typical salesperson would spend having a face-to-face meeting with automaker personnel. Key informants provided the same information for engineers. Thus, the measure consists of face-to-face communication that occurs between sales and purchasing employees as well as between engineers from the two respective organizations. I acknowledge that this is a measure of interfirm communication, not social communication between individuals at the supplier and automaker in a social setting. However, I would argue that this communication takes place between individuals and that concrete personal relationships between individuals develop largely as a result of these communications. Social interaction outside of work is likely to be highly correlated with face-to-face interaction in a work setting. As one supplier executive noted, "When you work closely with somebody, you get to know them. You're more likely to strike up a friendship and get together for a beer outside of work." In summary, the assumption behind this measure is that as the number of days of face-to-face contact increases, personal relationships are more likely to develop that in turn should result in higher levels of trust.

Continuity of the relationship. Continuity of relationship (*CONTINUITY*) was operationalized as the percentage of time the supplier's business had been renewed when there was a model change. In the automotive industry, the model change is a natural time for buyers to reevaluate suppliers and make changes if deemed appropriate. Suppliers who have histories of rewinning the business at the model change would be expected to have greater continuity in their relationships with the automakers when compared to suppliers with low rewin percentages. This is reflective of the supplier selection processes used by the buyers. Buyers that employ competitive bidding routines will likely have suppliers that experience lower rewin percentages and, therefore, lower continuity in the relationships.

Automaker assistance to the supplier. The interviews with suppliers and automakers prompted us to classify assistance (*ASSISTANCE*) into three types: assistance with the supplier's product quality, assistance with cost-cutting efforts, and assistance with inventory management. The degree of assistance offered by the automaker to the supplier was measured through three items:

1. The extent to which the automaker provides assistance to help the supplier improve product quality

2. The extent to which the automaker provides assistance to help the supplier reduce manufacturing costs

3. The extent to which the automaker provides assistance to help the supplier improve inventory management/delivery

A 7-point Likert scale was used to indicate the degree to which the supplier felt that these three types of assistance were provided by the automaker on a regular basis. The total amount of assistance was the sum of the three respective submeasures. The Chronbach's alpha for the buyer assistance construct was .79.

Stock ownership. The percentage of supplier stock owned by the automaker (*STOCK*) was used as the measure of an economic-based hostage. Because suppliers typically are more at risk than automakers, suppliers are the ones that require a credible commitment, which may come in the form of stock ownership by the automaker.

The Model/Data Analysis

The model that was estimated is shown in Table 8.1. This model was estimated for the pooled sample as well as by country. The following linear ordinary least squares (OLS) regression model was run to test the hypotheses:

$$\text{Model: } TRUST = a + b_1 \ LENGTH + b_2 \ FACE + b_3 \ CONTINUITY \\ + b_4 \ ASSISTANCE + b_5 \ STOCK.$$

A linear regression model was used because there was no reason to assume a nonlinear relationship among the variables. The use of a linear model later was justified by an examination of the residual distribution, which was homo-skedastic and indicated no problems with serial correlation. The data also were analyzed using a Tobit model due to concerns that the dependent variable (which in this case is bounded between 3 and 21) might violate the basic assumptions of OLS and, therefore, that OLS might be a biased estimator (Greene, 1998; Maddala, 1983). However, results were found to be unchanged, so only the results from the OLS regression analysis are reported.

Finally, a regression model that included country dummy variables (reported in the Appendix) was run. Previous research suggests that trust between trading partners not only will vary with the attributes of the transaction but also might vary due to differences in societal culture, politics, networks, and business norms in the institutional environment in which the transactions are embedded (Granovetter, 1985; Hill, 1995). Indeed, although the embeddedness measures attempt to capture variables specific to the bilateral buyer-supplier relationship, another way of measuring embeddedness more broadly is to include a dummy variable for each country to take into account community or society norms that might affect both individual and organizational behavior. Consequently, a regression with the country dummies was run to see whether there are country effects on trust beyond the variables in my model.

I acknowledge that the direction of causality between trust and the independent variables LENGTH and FACE is open to debate. For example, one can argue that high trust leads to long-term continuous relationships and face-to-face contact rather than vice versa. This is a common problem with empirical studies on trust. I have offered theoretical arguments that explain why these particular independent variables might lead to high trust. However, some degree of reciprocal causality would be expected with these variables—in effect, a circle of mutual causality in which the independent variables both influence and are influenced by trust.

RESULTS

The simple descriptive statistics shown in Table 8.1 indicate that supplier trust is significantly higher in Japan than in Korea or the United States, both of which have similar levels of supplier trust. The length of the supplier-automaker relationship was highest in Japan (41.4 years), followed by the United States (32.6 years) and Korea (12.4 years). This result would be expected given the long history of the automobile industry in Japan and the United States compared to that in Korea, where the industry is less than 30 years old. The data also indicate that there is more face-to-face communication between suppliers and automakers in Japan than in the United States or Korea. I conjecture that face-to-face contact

TABLE 8.1

Descriptive Statistics: Pooled Sample and by Country

Variable	Pooled (n = 453)	United States (n = 135)	Japan (n = 101)	Korea (n = 217)	Significant Difference
Trust	14.11	13.63	16.37	13.35	***
Length	21.61	32.56	41.40	12.44	***
Face	2042.56	1245.01	4989.54	1413.41	***
Continuity	0.78	0.71	0.91	0.77	***
Assistance	9.83	7.39	10.15	10.51	***
Stock	0.04	0.00	0.11	0.03	***

NOTE: The final column indicates whether the country means are significantly different from each other (F test), with three asterisks (***) indicating that country samples are significantly different at $p = .01$.

among Japanese automotive transactors might be facilitated by the physical proximity of suppliers and automakers in Japan.[5] These descriptive data suggest that Japanese supplier-automaker relationships are characterized by embedded ties to a much greater extent than are U.S. or Korean supplier-automaker relationships.

Similar country variance is found in the process-based independent variables. There is much greater continuity in the supplier-automaker relationship in Japan than in the United States or Korea. Japanese suppliers rewin the contract more than 91% of the time (with very little variance) at a model change, whereas U.S. and Korean suppliers rewin the contract 71% and 77% of the time, respectively (with much greater variance). These findings are consistent with previous studies suggesting that Japanese automakers do not switch suppliers nearly as often as do U.S. automakers (Dyer & Ouchi, 1993; Helper, 1991). Automaker assistance to suppliers is highest in Korea and Japan, with U.S. automakers offering significantly less assistance to suppliers. The high degree of automaker assistance in the Korean sample might reflect a lack of technological capability on the part of Korean automobile suppliers, which still need large amounts of assistance from the automakers to meet the automakers' minimum quality standards. The degree of assistance in Japan is high despite the strong capability of Japanese suppliers. In the United States, the degree of assistance still is rather low, presumably because U.S. automakers and their suppliers traditionally have maintained arms-length relationships and automakers have not developed assistance-giving pro-

TABLE 8.2

Correlation Matrix

Variable	1	2	3	4	5	6
1. Trust	1.000					
2. Length	.27	1.000				
3. Face	.14	.19	1.000			
4. Continuity	.40	.15	.05	1.000		
5. Assistance	.30	−.10	.11	.16	1.000	
6. Stock	.01	.07	.16	.01	.03	1.000

cesses.[6] Finally, Japanese automakers are most likely to hold minority stock ownership positions in suppliers. Korean automakers rarely hold stock in suppliers, and U.S. automakers do not own any supplier stock.

Table 8.2 presents the pooled sample correlation matrix for the dependent and independent variables. There was concern that there might be interaction effects (multicollinearity problems) among the independent variables, that is, that simultaneously embedded ties would be seen to develop in situations where there were particular processes in place for selecting and assisting suppliers and where there were economic ties (e.g., stock ownership) between firms. However, the pooled sample correlation matrix (Table 8.2) shows reasonably high correlations between *LENGTH* and *TRUST,* between *CONTINUITY* and *TRUST,* and between *ASSISTANCE* and *TRUST* but *not* particularly high correlations among the independent variables. An examination of Table 8.2 indicates that there are no substantial multicollinearity problems; all of the 10 pairwise correlations between the independent variables are less than .33, with only one correlation being greater than .30. Although there might be strong interactive effects among these three perspectives, there need not *necessarily* be strong interactive effects. Embedded ties can exist between two firms without economic ties, and particular processes can be in place to select and assist suppliers without necessarily requiring that embedded ties develop between the two firms. Although there is some correlation in the expected direction among the independent variables, the low correlations suggest that it is possible to separate these perspectives and their effects.

The regression results for the pooled sample and for each country are presented in Table 8.3. The results show that my model was reasonably effective at

TABLE 8.3

Results: Pooled Sample and by Country

Variable	Expected Sign	Pooled Sample	United States	Japan	Korea
Hypothesis 1:	+	.24***	−.02	.25***	−.10
Length × Trust		(.04)	(.08)	(.10)	(.06)
Hypothesis 2:	+	.05	−.09	.08	−.02
Face × Trust		(.04)	(.08)	(.10)	(.06)
Hypothesis 3:	+	.32***	.53***	.05	.21***
Continuity × Trust		(.04)	(.08)	(.10)	(.06)
Hypothesis 4:	+	.27***	.04	.34***	.35***
Assistance × Trust		(.04)	(.08)	(.10)	(.06)
Hypothesis 5:	+	−.02	.04	−.02	−.07
Stock × Trust		(.04)	(.07)	(.10)	(.06)

NOTE: Standard errors are in parentheses.
$R^2 = .268$; Adjusted $R^2 = .259$
**Significant at $p = .05$, ***Significant at $p = .01$.

predicting supplier trust, as demonstrated by an adjusted R^2 of .259, which was significant at the $p < .001$ level. Although my model did a reasonably good job of predicting supplier trust, clearly there must be other important variables that are not accounted for in my model. However, because the formation of a trusting relationship is such a nebulous and complex phenomenon, a formal modeling effort is bound to explain only part of the variance in trust.

Three of the five variables in my model were found to have a significant positive effect ($p < .001$ level) on supplier trust in the pooled sample including one embeddedness variable (length of relationship) and both process variables (continuity of relationship, automaker assistance to the supplier). The relationship between stock ownership and trust was positive in the pooled sample but only because of high stock ownership in Japan, a high-trust subsample. In fact, I was surprised to find that there was a negative relationship between stock ownership and trust in both Japan and Korea. Total face-to-face communication was not useful as a predictor of supplier trust.

In summary, from Table 8.3, the following conclusions could be made:

1. Length of the supplier-automaker relationship had a significant positive effect on supplier trust in the pooled sample, but the relationship held true only in Japan. Therefore, Hypothesis 1 is supported in the pooled sample and Japanese subsample.

2. Face-to-face communication did not have an effect on trust in the pooled sample or within any of the individual countries. Therefore, no support was found for Hypothesis 2, which proposed a positive relationship between face-to-face contact and trust.[7]

3. Continuity in the supplier-automaker relationship (i.e., history of rewinning the contract) had a significant positive effect on supplier trust in the pooled sample and in the United States and Korea. Thus, Hypothesis 3 is supported.

4. Automaker assistance to the supplier is positively associated with supplier trust in the automaker in the pooled sample as well as in Japan and Korea. This relationship did not hold in the United States, where automakers historically have not offered much assistance. Thus, Hypothesis 4 is supported.

5. Stock ownership did not have a significant relationship with trust in the pooled sample or within any of the individual countries. Thus, no support was found for Hypothesis 5.

The separate regression analysis that included country dummies (to test the embeddedness hypothesis more broadly) suggests that there are country-specific effects not captured by my model (see Appendix). The findings indicate that country factors are significant, particularly in explaining significantly higher trust levels in Japan. However, even after taking into account country effects, the process variables still are significant. Thus, it seems reasonable to conclude that both embedded ties and process factors are critical for explaining levels of interfirm trust in the cross-national sample.

DISCUSSION

As reported in Table 8.1, significant differences were found in levels of supplier trust by country. Significant country effects also were found, suggesting that the institutional/country environment plays an important role in influencing interfirm trust. The differences in levels of trust across countries raises an important issue, notably how important the institutional environment is in fostering interfirm trust.

To test whether or not trusting supplier relations can be purposefully created across national boundaries, a sample of U.S. suppliers that worked with both U.S. automakers and Japanese "transplants" in the United States were surveyed.[8] By surveying U.S. suppliers selling the same components to both U.S. and Japanese automakers within the United States, cultural and component (technical) differences that might influence interfirm trust can be controlled. The sample consisted of only U.S. suppliers with at least 3 years of experience and 5% of total sales to Japanese automakers. This was done to exclude U.S. suppliers without significant experience working with Japanese automakers. These 20 suppliers were randomly selected from the U.S. supplier sample.[9] These suppliers then were interviewed and surveyed regarding their relationships with both U.S. and Japanese automakers.

Table 8.4 provides a summary of the sample means (for the sample of U.S. suppliers selling to both Japanese and U.S. automakers) for a number of the independent and dependent (trust) variables used in this study. The results indicate that *Japanese automakers have developed significantly higher levels of trust with U.S. suppliers than have U.S. automakers.*[10] These data suggest that trust *can* be developed relatively quickly and perhaps consciously and intentionally.[11]

The question of how Japanese automakers were able to quickly develop trusting relationships with U.S. suppliers is an important one. An examination of these results in light of the hypotheses provides further insights into the determinants of supplier trust. First, I should note that stock ownership was not a factor in these relationships, so stock ownership can be ruled out as a determinant of trust in these relationships. Second, U.S. suppliers' relationships with Japanese automakers were only of short duration (6 years vs. 22 years with U.S. automakers). Clearly, a long-term relationship is not a prerequisite for high trust. With regard to face-to-face contact, the sample engaged in 1,475 person-days of face-to-face contact with Japanese automakers versus 1,657 person-days with U.S. automakers. On an absolute basis, there are no significant differences.[12] Furthermore, these exchanges are conducted in the United States, an institutional environment that was not found to produce high trust in ways similar to the Japanese institutional environment. These findings suggest that high supplier trust can exist without embedded ties and without the support of community or societywide norms.

Given the short-term nature of the relationships, there was not enough history to accurately assess the rewin rates of U.S. suppliers with Japanese automakers. However, in five cases where suppliers were faced with a model change, suppliers reported rewinning the business in each case. Moreover, the interviews with U.S. suppliers revealed that they believed that they would rewin their business with Japanese customers because (a) Japanese automakers had told them that

TABLE 8.4

Survey of U.S. Suppliers Selling to Both U.S. and Japanese Automakers

Relationship Characteristic	U.S. Supplier/ U.S. Automaker (n = 20)	U.S. Supplier/ Japanese Automaker (n = 20)	T-Value
TRUST			
The extent to which the supplier trusts the automaker to treat supplier fairly[a]	4.1	5.7[b]	2.5
If given the chance, automaker might try to take unfair advantage of supplier[a]	4.0	1.7[b]	3.3
The extent to which the automaker has a reputation for trustworthiness[a]	4.0	5.6[b]	2.4
LENGTH			
Length of relationship	22 years	6 years[b]	6.4
CONTINUITY			
Percentage of time the supplier rewins the business at a model change	.77	1.00[c]	
FACE			
Annual person-days of face-to-face contact	1,654	1,475	0.19
ASSISTANCE			
Extent of cost reduction assistance[a]	1.7	4.1[b]	5.5
Extent of quality improvement assistance[a]	2.5	4.5[b]	4.2
Extent of delivery/inventory management assistance[a]	1.5	2.9[b]	2.5

a. Answers are on a 7-point Likert scale (1 = *not at all*, 4 = *to some extent*, 7 = *to a very great extent*).
b. Tests of group differences are one-tailed *t* tests assuming unequal variances ($p < .01$ level).
c. In each of five cases where the model changed, suppliers rewon the business for the next model.

they would rewin the business if they performed well and (b) Japanese automakers had a reputation for not switching suppliers at the model change. Thus, suppliers had the expectation of a high degree of continuity in the relationships.

The variable that seemed to be particularly critical to the Japanese automakers' ability to develop trusting relationships with U.S. suppliers was offering assistance. U.S. suppliers indicated that, compared to U.S. automakers, they received more assistance from Japanese automakers in reducing costs, increasing quality, and improving delivery. Some U.S. suppliers indicated that they received more help from some Japanese automakers than they believed they deserved given their short-term relationships. They were surprised at the willingness of these Japanese automakers to send consultants, free of charge, to help them improve. As Tom Luyster, vice president of planning for Summit Polymers (a supplier of plastic interior parts), stated,

> I couldn't believe it, but Toyota sent approximately 34 consultants every day for a period of 34 months as we attempted to implement Toyota Production System concepts in a new plant. They gave us a valuable gift [the Toyota Production System]. Naturally, we feel indebted toward Toyota and view them as a special customer. They sincerely want to help us improve. (personal interview, November 19, 1996)

This type of helping behavior on the part of Japanese automakers seemed to be the catalyst for creating, in Gouldner's (1960) terminology, "a norm of reciprocal obligation."

The observation that U.S. suppliers trusted Japanese automakers due to processes rather than relationships is supported by the comments of a U.S. supplier executive:

> It's not that I don't trust the person sitting across from me at General Motors. I may trust him completely. In fact, I may feel more comfortable with him than [with] his Japanese counterpart at Toyota. But what I don't trust is that he will be sitting there a year from now. At U.S. automakers, the people and the rules of the game are constantly changing. Toyota's processes for working with suppliers are fair, predictable, and stable. (personal interview, September 11, 1992)

The point is that the supplier's trust in Toyota is *not* based on "concrete social relations" that are "embedded within a social structure" as proposed by embedded ties theory (Granovetter, 1985). The trust orientation of the supplier toward the automaker is based on the routines/processes, not on the individuals.

In summary, the ability of Japanese automakers to build high levels of trust with suppliers in the United States suggests that the institutional environment might be less important than firm-level practices in influencing trust. These findings suggest that supplier trust might be based largely on *trustworthy behavior that is institutionalized within the buying firms' processes and routines.*

I should note, however, that these findings come from a sample of very large companies (suppliers of roughly $400 million in sales, automakers with at least $5 billion in sales). Some previous studies, such as those by Larson (1992) and Uzzi (1997), have found support for the embeddedness (relationship-based) perspective in the United States. However, these studies were of much smaller firms (the average firm in Uzzi's study had less than 50 employees), so personal ties might be expected to be much more important. I do not mean to suggest that individuals are unimportant in the creation of interorganizational trust. Indeed, suppliers are much more likely to believe that the interorganizational routines are credible signals of commitment when they have confidence in the stability of intraorganizational routines. But I would argue that embedded ties will likely be *less* instrumental in building trust-based relationships between large organizations, in cross-border alliances or partnerships, and in organizations or institutional environments where there is a high degree of labor mobility (e.g., the United States). Under these conditions, it is less likely that trust will emerge from prior social ties or an existing social structure, so it might be necessary for trust to be based on processes rather than on individuals.

Implications for International Research on Interfirm Relationships

Using this study as a reference, I would like to briefly point out some advantages to using a multination research design. However, before doing so, it is important to note that the research design used in this study is not without its limitations. In particular, this research relies on key informants in each country that must be counted on to interpret the survey questions in a similar fashion and to give answers that are representative of their organizations. But this limitation differs from a single-nation study only in the language differences and translation difficulties that might create greater differences in the interpretation of the questions by respondents in different nations. Another weakness of this study is that it involved only three countries and did not sample from any countries in Europe in particular. If I had been able to get similar results in one or two more countries from other regions of the world, then the results would be even more compelling. However, even with these weaknesses, the multination research design offers numerous potential advantages over a single-nation study. Examples include the following:

1. By researching companies (e.g., dyads/networks) in different nations, it is possible to increase the study's sample size (population), thereby making it easier to use a broader range of statistical methods, many of which require large samples.

2. By testing hypotheses with samples in different institutional environments, the researcher is better able to test the robustness of the research results and the generalizability of theory, notably whether or not hypotheses are generalizable across institutional environments.

3. By identifying institutional (i.e., country) environments in which a particular theory or hypothesis does not hold, the researcher has an opportunity to offer modifications to existing theory or to identify the conditions that must be met for a theory to hold (which is, in effect, a further elaboration of the theory).

These last two advantages are critical because they are advantages associated with fundamental theory development. If a theory is empirically supported in the United States but is not empirically supported in Japan, Brazil, or Poland, then there is a weakness in the theory and there is an opportunity to contribute to fundamental theory development. Because an international setting offers much greater variance in the context and conditions under which the theory is tested, it is more likely to expose weaknesses in the theory.

Although there are a number of potential advantages to a multination research design, multinational studies are expensive and difficult to conduct. Consequently, the researcher should be aware of a number of issues when considering a multination research design as the appropriate research method.

Issues to Consider in Multination Studies on Interfirm Relationships

My experience in conducting cross-national studies suggests that the researcher can increase the likelihood of success with a multiresearch design when he or she is aware of the following issues with regard to sample selection, data collection, and data analysis.

Sample Selection

First, select from a range of countries, some that might offer extreme cases and some that might be more representative of a "typical" country. This often involves testing theory in countries from different regions of the world. This allows the researcher to compare outliers and provide a conservative test of theory, that is, the idea that *if the theory holds here (e.g., in a particular institutional environment), then it will hold anywhere.* In my study of interfirm trust, a supe-

rior research design would have included data from a European country and perhaps an emerging market. If my findings had held in these other environments as
well, it would have made my results and conclusions even more compelling. If
the results were different, it would have offered an opportunity to examine the
limitations and weaknesses of the theoretical ideas being tested.

Second, select companies from different countries that compete in the same
industries to control for extraneous variation and to allow for the development of
context-specific measures. I do not mean to suggest that large cross-sectional
studies are never appropriate. However, controlling for industries often is very
important due to the high degree of variation across industries (Winter, 1988)
and the fact that a cross section of leading industries typically looks quite different from country to country (Porter, 1990).

Third, if possible, include in the pooled sample a subsample that allows for a
cross-national comparison while controlling for the institutional environment.
In my study of interfirm trust, I believe that the results are more compelling (in
particular, the evidence that interfirm trust often is based on processes) because
of the data and analysis of the sample of U.S. suppliers selling to both U.S. and
Japanese automakers in the United States. However, the results would have been
even more compelling if I had been able to get a larger cross-national subsample
in the United States and if I had been able to analyze similar subsamples in Japan
and Korea.

Data Collection

In addition to having a survey back-translated, it is prudent to pretest surveys
in all nations with both a "local language" version and an English version. Continue pretesting the local language version of the survey until at least three inter-
viewees can bring a completed survey to the interview and, after going over the
survey item by item, there are no items that are confusing to the respondent or
that do not match with the answer the respondent would have given on the English version. (This presumes some language capability on the part of the respondent; however, in the business environment of the 21st century, a high level of
proficiency in English will be the norm among higher level executives at non-
U.S. firms.) This process effectively results in the survey being previewed and
translated by multiple individuals in the target country. Of particular importance
is the fact that these individuals have the background, culture, and experience
that is representative of the typical respondent.

Data Analysis

Naturally, it makes sense to test hypotheses both in the pooled sample and
within individual country subsamples. This approach will allow the researcher to

identify those relationships among variables (data) that are robust across country environments. In cases where a hypothesis is accepted in one country but not in another country, it affords the opportunity to explore the reasons why the theory does not hold in a particular institutional context. In some cases, it is prudent to test hypotheses while including country dummies to capture country effects. This will allow for greater insight with regard to which hypotheses are truly generalizable across countries and which hold only within particular institutional environments.

CONCLUSION

This chapter presented the research findings from a cross-national study of the determinants of trust in supplier-buyer relationships in the United States, Japan, and Korea. The findings indicate support for the process-based perspective in all countries; embeddedness was important as a determinant of trust in Japan, and the economic hostage-based variable (stock ownership) was not important in any country. More specifically, high supplier trust was found to emerge when (a) automakers have developed supplier selection routines that favor incumbents and that maintain a continuing (repeated) exchange relationship with suppliers and (b) automakers have developed assistance-giving routines to help suppliers solve problems and improve. Although there were some differences across institutional environments, notably higher trust in Japan, the findings are quite robust across the institutional environments. Indeed, in a sample of U.S. suppliers selling to both U.S. and Japanese automakers in the United States, Japanese automakers had developed higher levels of trust with U.S. suppliers than had U.S. automakers. The ability of Japanese automakers to build high levels of trust with suppliers in the United States suggests that the institutional environment might be less important than firm-level practices in the production of interorganizational trust.

This research study also has served as the basis for discussing the advantages and pitfalls of multination research designs. In particular, I argued that a multination research design offers numerous potential advantages over a single-nation study with regard to fundamental theory development. Given the high variance in institutional environments, multination studies offer the opportunity to test how robust the empirical support is for particular theories. When theories do not hold in all countries, the researcher has the opportunity to explore the limitations of existing theories and to contribute to fundamental theory development. Thus, if done carefully, international management research has great potential as a vehicle for future theory development in the management field.

APPENDIX

Regression Model With Country Dummy Variables					
Variable	B	SE B	Beta	T	Significance T
KOREADUM	−0.899513	0.340554	−0.127436	−2.64	.0085
JAPANDUM	1.836328	0.384716	0.233771	4.77	.0000
LENGTH	0.010631	0.011062	0.047251	0.961	.3371
FACE	2.79645E-06	3.4719E-05	0.003296	0.081	.9358
CONTINUITY	5.929032	0.776013	0.305843	7.640	.0000
ASSISTANCE	0.237839	0.036938	0.260372	6.439	.0000
STOCK	−1.418360	1.082204	−0.052231	−1.311	.1907
Constant	6.805090	0.728539		9.341	.0000

NOTE: Multiple $R = .573$
$R^2 = .328$
Adjusted $R^2 = .317$
Standard error = 2.705

NOTES

1. Investments in transaction-specific assets have been found to enhance interfirm coordination and maximize joint performance (Dyer, 1996c).

2. This assumes that exchange partners are part of the same social network.

3. In the language of game theory, contract renewal may serve as a signal to the supplier that the automaker is playing a long-run "cooperative equilibrium." The logic for how repeated games result in more cooperative behavior is well documented in the game theory literature (Axelrod, 1984; Fudenberg & Maskin, 1986).

4. Of course, it also is possible for stock ownership to be inversely correlated with trust. To the extent that stock ownership serves as a credible signal of long-term commitment, it may promote goodwill trust. However, stock ownership also may be viewed as a substitute for goodwill trust. I assume a positive relationship between stock ownership and trust because in every case in the sample, the buyer had owned the supplier's stock for at least 10 years, thereby providing enough time for informal trust to develop.

5. In the sample, the average distances between supplier plants and automaker plants were 82 miles in Japan, 129 miles in Korea, and 477 miles in the United States.

6. The interviews with suppliers confirmed this presumption. As one supplier executive observed, "If you have a problem, you'd better fix it yourself because [U.S. automakers] sure won't help. They just say, 'If you can't fix the problem, we'll find another supplier who can'."

7. The face-to-face contact measure did not take into account personnel turnover. Two sets of exchange partners could engage in the same number of days of face-to-face contact, but the quality of those days of contact could be different if one set of trading partners experienced personnel turnover and the other did not. Social interactions and face-to-face contact would be expected to be more effective at establishing trust when turnover is low. It also is possible that the embeddedness measures, which measure interfirm communication and length of relationship rather than personal social communication, were not effective at capturing social interaction outside of a work setting.

8. Korean automakers were excluded because they did not have plants in the United States.

9. There was no particular reason for choosing 20 relationships other than that there was not a large number of suppliers that had significant experience working with both U.S. and Japanese automakers.

10. These findings are consistent with those of a market research firm, Planning Perspectives, which conducted a survey of 700 U.S. suppliers for Chrysler and Ford in 1992. This large-sample survey found that U.S. suppliers had significantly higher trust in Toyota and Honda than they did in the U.S. automakers.

11. There is some debate about whether or not trust can be purposefully created in exchange relationships. Sabel (1993) presented the argument as follows: "The burden of experience and reflection is that trust can be found but never created. . . . Trust is a byproduct of events which, to the extent they are planned at all, did not have the creation of trust as their goal. Seen this way, trust is one of those states, like drowsiness . . . , which cannot be produced directly by willing them and hence at first blush are inaccessible to individual or collective acts of volition" (p. 1134). The present findings suggest that it might be possible to consciously and purposefully engage in behaviors (e.g., employ particular processes) that create trust in exchange relationships.

12. However, after adjusting for the volume of transactions (sales) between the supplier and the automaker, it is found that U.S. suppliers engage in 50% more face-to-face contact (per dollar of sales) with Japanese automakers.

REFERENCES

Anderson, J. C., & Narus, J. A. (1990). A model of distributor firm and manufacturer firm working partnerships. *Journal of Marketing, 54,* 42-58.
Aoki, M. (1988). *Information, incentives, and bargaining in the Japanese economy.* New York: Cambridge University Press.
Argyle, M. (1991). *Cooperation: The basis of sociability.* New York: Routledge.
Arrow, K. J. (1974). *The limits of organization.* New York: Norton.
Asanuma, B. (1989). Manufacturer-supplier relationships in Japan and the concept of relation-specific skill. *Journal of the Japanese and International Economies, 3,* 1-30.

Axelrod, R. (1984). *The evolution of cooperation.* New York: Basic Books.

Barney, J. B., & Hansen, M. H. (1994). Trustworthiness as a source of competitive advantage. *Strategic Management Journal, 15,* 175-190.

Bolton, M. K., Malmrose, R., & Ouchi, W. G. (1994). The organization of innovation in the United States and Japan: Neoclassical and relational contracting. *Journal of Management Studies, 31,* 653-679.

Bradach, J. L., & Eccles, R. (1989). Markets versus hierarchies: From ideal types to plural forms. *Annual Review of Sociology, 15,* 97-118.

Butler, J. K. (1991). Toward understanding and measuring conditions of trust: Evolution of a conditions of trust inventory. *Journal of Management, 17,* 643-663.

Casson, M. (1990). *Enterprise and competitiveness: A systems view of international business.* Oxford, UK: Clarendon.

Clark, K. B., & Fujimoto, T. (1991). *Product development performance.* Boston: Harvard Business School Press.

Daft, R., & Lengel, R. (1986). Organizational information requirements, media richness, and structural design. *Management Science, 32,* 554-571.

Dore, R. (1983). Goodwill and the spirit of market capitalism. *British Journal of Sociology, 34,* 459-482.

Dubinsky, A., Kotabe, M., Lim, C. U., & Michaels, R. E. (1994). Differences in motivational perceptions among U.S., Japanese, and Korean sales personnel. *Journal of Business Research, 30,* 175-185.

Dyer, J. H. (1996a). Does governance matter? Keiretsu alliances and asset specificity as sources of Japanese competitive advantage. *Organization Science, 7,* 649-666.

Dyer, J. H. (1996b). How Chrysler created an American keiretsu. *Harvard Business Review, 74*(4), 42-56.

Dyer, J. H. (1996c). Specialized supplier networks as a source of competitive advantage: Evidence from the auto industry. *Strategic Management Journal, 17,* 271-292.

Dyer, J. H., & Ouchi, W. G. (1993). Japanese style business partnerships: Giving companies a competitive edge. *Sloan Management Review, 35*(1), 51-63.

Earley, P. C., & Singh, H. (1995). International and intercultural management research: What's next? *Academy of Management Journal, 38,* 347-340.

Ellickson, R. C. (1991). *Order without law.* Cambridge, MA: Harvard University Press.

Fruin, W. M. (1992). *The Japanese enterprise system.* New York: Oxford University Press.

Fudenberg, D., & Maskin, E. (1986). The folk theorem in repeated games with discounting or with incomplete information. *Econometrica, 54,* 533-556.

Fukuyama, F. (1995). *Trust: The social virtues and the creation of prosperity.* New York: Free Press.

Gerlach, M. L. (1992). *Alliance capitalism.* Berkeley: University of California Press.

Gouldner, A. W. (1960). The norm of reciprocity: A preliminary statement. *American Sociological Review, 25,* 161-178.

Granovetter, M. (1985). Economic action and social structure: The problem of embeddedness. *American Journal of Sociology, 91,* 481-510.

Greene, W. H. (1998). *Econometric analysis* (3rd ed.). Englewood Cliffs, NJ: Prentice Hall.

Gulati, R. (1995). Familiarity breeds trust? The implications of repeated ties for contractual choice in alliances. *Academy of Management Journal, 38,* 85-112.

Hamilton, G. G., & Biggart, N. W. (1988). Market, culture, and authority: A comparative analysis of management and organization in the Far East. *American Journal of Sociology, 94*(Suppl.), S52-S94.

Heide, J. B., & John, G. (1988). The role of dependence balancing in safeguarding transaction specific assets in conventional channels. *Journal of Marketing, 52,* 20-35.

Heide, J. B., & Miner, A. (1992). The shadow of the future: Effects of anticipated interaction and frequency of contact on buyer-seller cooperation. *Academy of Management Journal, 35,* 265-291.

Helper, S. (1991, Summer). How much has really changed between U.S. automakers and their suppliers? *Sloan Management Review,* pp. 15-28.

Hill, C. W. L. (1995). National institutional structures, transaction cost economizing, and competitive advantage: The case of Japan. *Organization Science, 6,* 119-131.

Japan, USA: Special report. (1986, July 14). *Business Week,* pp. 45-55.

Klein, B. (1980). Transaction cost determinants of "unfair" contractual arrangements. *American Economic Review, 70,* 356-362.

Kumar, N., Stern, L. W., & Anderson, J. C. (1993). Conducting interorganizational research using key informants. *Academy of Management Journal, 36,* 1633-1651.

Larson, A. (1992). Network dyads in entrepreneurial settings: A study of the governance of exchange relationships. *Administrative Science Quarterly, 37,* 76-104.

Larzelere, R., & Huston, T. (1980). The Dyadic Trust Scale: Toward understanding interpersonal trust in close relationships. *Journal of Marriage and the Family, 42,* 595-604.

Learning from Japan. (1992, January 27). *Business Week,* pp. 52-60.

Light, E. (1972). *Ethnic enterprise in America.* San Francisco: California University Press.

Lorenz, E. H. (1988). Neither friends nor strangers: Informal networks of subcontracting in French industry. In D. Gambetta (Ed.), *Trust: Making and breaking cooperative relations* (pp. 194-210). New York: Blackwell.

Maddala, G. S. (1983). *Limited dependent and qualitative variables in econometrics.* New York: Cambridge University Press.

Malinowski, B. (1932). *Argonauts of the Western Pacific.* London: Routledge and Kegan Paul.

Mauss, M. (1967). *The gift: Forms and functions of exchange in archaic societies.* New York: Norton.

Mayer, R. C., Davis, J. H., Schoorman, F. D. (1995). An integrative model of organizational trust. *Academy of Management Review, 20,* 709-734.

Nishiguchi, T. (1994). *Strategic industrial sourcing.* New York: Oxford University Press.

North, D. C. (1990). *Institutions, institutional change, and economic performance.* Cambridge, UK: Cambridge University Press.

Ouchi, W. G. (1980). Markets, bureaucracies, and clans. *Administrative Science Quarterly, 25,* 124-141.

Ouchi, W. G. (1984). *The M-form society.* New York: Avon Books.

Parkhe, A. (1993). Strategic alliance structuring: A game theoretic and transaction cost examination of interfirm cooperation. *Academy of Management Journal, 36,* 794-829.

Pisano, G. P. (1989). Using equity participation to support exchange. *Journal of Law, Economics, and Organization, 1,* 109-126.

Porter, M. E. (1990). *The competitive advantage of nations.* New York: Free Press.

Powell, W. W. (1990). Neither market nor hierarchy: Network forms of organization. In B. Staw & L. Cummings (Eds.), *Research in organizational behavior* (Vol. 12, pp. 295-336). Greenwich, CT: JAI.

Ring, P. S., & Van de Ven, A. H. (1992). Structuring cooperative relationships between organizations. *Strategic Management Journal, 13,* 483-498.

Sabel, C. (1993). Studied trust: Building new form of cooperation in a volatile economy. *Human Relations, 46,* 1133-1170.

Sako, M. (1991). The role of "trust" in Japanese buyer-supplier relationships. *Ricerche Economiche, 45,,* 449-474.

Shane, S. (1994). The effect of national culture on the choice between licensing and direct foreign investment. *Strategic Management Journal, 15,* 627-642.

Smith, K. G., Carroll, S. J., & Ashford, S. J. (1995). Intra- and interorganizational cooperation: Toward a research agenda. *Academy of Management Journal, 38,* 7-23.

Smith, R. J. (1983). *Japanese society: Tradition, self, and the social order.* Cambridge, UK: Cambridge University Press.

Sohn, J. H. D. (1994). Social knowledge as a control system: A proposition and evidence from the Japanese FDI behavior. *Journal of International Business Studies, 25*(2), 295-324.

Tolbert, P. (1988). Institutional sources of organizational culture in major law firms. In L. Zucker (Ed.), *Institutional patterns and organizations.* Cambridge, MA: Ballinger.

Uzzi, B. (1997). Social structure and competition in interfirm networks: The paradox of embeddedness. *Administrative Science Quarterly, 42,* 35-67.

Williamson, O. E. (1983). Credible commitments: Using hostages to support exchange. *American Economic Review, 73,* 519-535.

Williamson, O. E. (1993). Calculativeness, trust, and economic organization. *Journal of Law & Economics, 36,* 453-486.

Winter, S. (1988). Knowledge and competence as strategic assets. In D. Teece (Ed.), *The competitive challenge: Strategies for industrial innovation and renewal.* Cambridge, MA: Ballinger.

Zaheer, A., McEvily, B., & Perrone, V. (1998). Does trust matter? Exploring the effects of interorganizational and interpersonal trust on performance. *Organization Science, 9*(2), 141-159.

Zaheer, A., & Venkatraman, N. (1995). Relational governance as an interorganizational strategy: An empirical test of the role of trust in economic exchange. *Strategic Management Journal, 16,* 373-392.

Zucker, L. G. (1986). Production of trust: Institutional sources of economic structure, 1840-1920. In B. M. Staw & L. Cummings (Eds.), *Research in organizational behavior* (pp. 53-111). Greenwich, CT: JAI.

chapter **9**

Replication of Keiretsu in the United States

Transfer of Interorganizational Network Through Direct Investment

SEA JIN CHANG

The complex web of corporate network in Japan termed *keiretsu* is now a well-known economic organization to Westerners. In the United States, the keiretsu has been conceived as a symbol of closeness of the Japanese business and economy and, therefore, as a target of the Structural Impediment Initiative of U.S.-Japan trade negotiations. The keiretsu is associated with exclusive and preferential dealing among its own members and is seen as a barrier to foreign companies in penetrating Japanese markets.

On the other hand, others view the keiretsu as a type of alliance structure. Strategic alliances are a very popular form of interfirm cooperation and competition these days, not only in high-technology areas but also in many other conventional businesses. According to these views, the keiretsu structure represents an efficient economic organization given the economic, social, and cultural environments in Japan. Aoki (1984, 1988) proposed that the keiretsu might be the most efficient economic organization that minimizes transactions cost in the long run by positioning in between market and hierarchy. From this perspective, the keiretsu might be at the forefront of a global movement toward complex forms of cooperation and alliances, although the keiretsu bears its unique Japanese cultural and historical heritage (Gerlach, 1992; Piore & Sabel, 1984).

Since the late 1970s, Japanese companies have pursued rapid internationalization by aggressive foreign direct investment (FDI). There are many anecdotes suggesting that Japanese firms can successfully transfer their management systems and economic organizations to foreign countries. Krafcik (1986) described the successful transfer of Japanese management systems in the NUMMI joint venture. Florida and Kenney (1991) examined the transfer of Japanese management systems to the automobile transplants in the United States. If the keiretsu represents an efficient economic organization as explained by Aoki (1984, 1988) and Gerlach (1992), then such an interorganizational network should be replicated in foreign countries by direct investment of keiretsu-affiliated firms. Figure 9.1 shows the increasing pattern of direct investment by keiretsu-affiliated firms during the period from 1976 to 1989. Martin, Mitchell, and Swaminathan (1995) demonstrated how such direct investment by keiretsu-affiliated firms is in fact replicating and extending the keiretsu relationship within the United States.

This chapter examines the extent and determinants of the transfer of the keiretsu structure into the United States by FDI. The study empirically models the direct investment behavior of all keiretsu-affiliated public firms in Japan during the period from 1976 to 1989. The results suggest that firms' investment activities are affected by the ownership control of the keiretsu and the financial capabilities of individual firms. These results are stronger in the case of horizontally connected keiretsus. Vertically connected keiretsus seem not to depend so much on ownership control and financial capabilities as on the buyer-supplier relationship.

MOTIVATIONS FOR FDI

Although the central focus of this chapter is on examining the effects of keiretsu on member firms' overseas investment behavior, we also should consider conventional explanations for FDI. There has been a vast amount of research in explaining motivations for FDI. Hymer (1960) suggested, after observing high correlations across industries between investing overseas and entry barriers into those industries, that a monopolistic advantage encouraged firms to invest overseas. This intuition was reinterpreted by Caves (1971), who identified the sources of monopoly power with rent-yielding intangible assets such as technology or marketing skills (i.e., the knowledge base of a firm). Many empirical studies have confirmed the positive correlation between outward investment activities and intangible assets measured by research and development (R&D) and

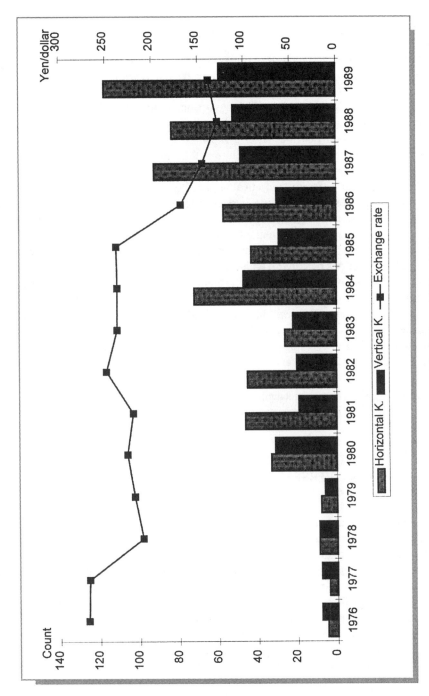

FIGURE 9.1. Trend of Keiretsus' Direct Investment in the United States, 1976 to 1989

advertising intensities (Chang, 1995; Kogut & Chang, 1991, 1996; McClain, 1983; Pugel, 1985).

Another important stream of research in FDI sees the multinational corporation (MNC) as an efficient transfer agent of resources (Buckley & Casson, 1976; Hennart, 1982; MaGee, 1977; Rugman, 1981). An MNC minimizes transactions cost not only by internalizing technology or marketing know-how but also by internalizing raw materials and intermediate goods (Hennart, 1982). Hennart and Park (1994) showed that the larger a Japanese firm's R&D expenditures, the greater the probability it will manufacture in the United States.

Although the transactions cost theory and the monopolistic advantage theory explain FDI from different theoretical angles, both theories often use the same variables (e.g., R&D, advertising intensity) to measure their theoretical constructs. The existence of technology or marketing know-how, measured by R&D or advertising intensity, is the intangible resource that generates the monopolistic advantages and at the same time creates the need to internalize those assets due to the high transactions cost involved in such information-intensive assets.

It is expected that FDI of keiretsu-affiliated firms can be explained by these conventional theories. Kimura and Pugel (1995) found that the existence of intangible assets is a significant indicator for FDI activities of keiretsu-affiliated Japanese firms. In a similar way, I hypothesize that keiretsu-affiliated firms with strong intangible assets (e.g., technology or marketing skills) generally are more likely to enter foreign markets.

Hypothesis 1: The more intangible resources of a keiretsu-affiliated firm, the more likely it is to invest in overseas markets.

EFFECTS OF KEIRETSU SYSTEM ON OVERSEAS INVESTMENT

The keiretsu probably is the most distinctive feature of the Japanese industrial organization. Major Japanese corporations are affiliated with such a complex web of corporate network through financial and personnel ties. As of 1989, there were 1,687 public firms listed on the Tokyo Stock Exchange. According to *Industrial Groupings in Japan,* published by Dodwell Marketing Associates (1992), 713 of the 1,687 listed firms (35%) were associated with either 8 bank-centered, horizontally connected keiretsus or 31 vertically connected keiretsus. The keiretsu listing of the Dodwell directory is only a conservative measure of the extent of the keiretsu structure in Japan given that the boundary of keiretsu used by the directory is not so encompassing.[1]

The modern keiretsu finds its roots in the prewar *zaibatsu*. The 3 major zaibatsus—Mitsubishi, Mitsui, and Sumitomo—were types of conglomerates. Family-owned holding companies owned the majority of stocks of affiliated companies. According to Imai (1987), Mitsui had 294 companies under control, Mitsubishi controlled 241 companies, and Sumitomo controlled 166 companies. These conglomerate-like zaibatsu were dissolved and holding companies were officially banned by the U.S. occupation forces in 1947.[2]

The postwar keiretsus were reconstructed out of voluntary actions of members of the prewar zaibatsus. The Japanese government implicitly encouraged the rebuilding of keiretsus to protect domestic markets and industries from foreign investment by interlocking ownership and close buyer-supplier relationships (Hadley, 1970). Keiretsus also directed scarce capital to strategic industries according to industrial policy. Furthermore, during the postwar rapid economic growth period, independent industrial companies voluntarily formed their own keiretsus with commercial banks and large industrial companies as nuclei. The most important difference between the prewar zaibatsu and the postwar keiretsu lies in the degree of control. In the prewar zaibatsu, the holding company organization ensured tight and direct control from headquarters to the operating companies. In the postwar keiretsu, the exercise of control became more indirect. There are considerable mutual stock holdings on a long-term basis. Large commercial banks at the nucleus extend loans on somewhat favorable terms, and general trading companies help importing and exporting businesses. There are substantial personal ties of executive officers within keiretsus. The "association of presidents" coordinates decision making among member corporations.

There are largely two types of keiretsu in Japan. One is the horizontally connected intermarket keiretsu, centered around major banks along with insurance companies, general trading companies, and large manufacturing firms. According to the Dodwell directory, as of 1989, there were 8 such horizontally connected groups: Mitsubishi, Mitsui, Sumitomo, Fuyo, DKB, Sanwa, Tokai, and Industrial Bank of Japan. The first 3 groups—Mitsubishi, Mitsui, and Sumitomo—are the postwar reconstructions of prewar zaibatsu. The other 5 horizontally connected business groups, formed after the war, center around major banks.

The other type is the vertically connected keiretsu, centered around big manufacturing firms. In 1989, the Dodwell directory reported 31 major vertically connected keiretsus that were centered around large manufacturing firms. For example, Toyota Motors, Hitachi, and Matsushita Electric Company are connected with their own suppliers, subcontractors, and distributors. Many firms in the sample of listed firms have grown out of suppliers of such big manufacturing firms and still are associated with the vertically connected keiretsus. There often are cases where firms are active members of horizontally connected keiretsus while simultaneously forming vertically connected keiretsus with their suppliers. For example, NEC is affiliated with the Sumitomo group, but it also leads its own vertically connected keiretsu.

Such an extensive keiretsu structure might have evolved as the most efficient economic organization given the economic environment of Japan. During the period of rapid industrialization, the keiretsu structure enabled firms to cooperate with other firms in new business ventures, foreign expansion, and development of efficient supply-buyer relationships. The keiretsu system also depends on mutual trust and long-term business relations; therefore, it avoids the problems coming from short-term profit maximization. Aoki (1984, 1988) noted that the coordination within the keiretsu can create informational and transactional efficiency in planning and monitoring across the boundaries of member firms based on the sharing of ex post on-site information (i.e., learned results). Thus, the Japanese system is superior to the conventional hierarchical mode because the information value created by learning and horizontal coordination at the operating level can more than compensate for the possible loss of efficiency due to the sacrifice of operating specialization. In other words, the keiretsu economizes on information and control through regularized communication and exchange while at the same time avoiding the perils of overreliance on hierarchy by keeping contractual arrangements implicit and modes of monitoring and intervention informal and flexible (Hennart, 1993; Williamson, 1975).

During the late 1970s, Japanese firms rapidly became multinational by aggressively pursuing FDI. During this process of internationalization, the keiretsu itself played a very important role and could replicate itself in foreign countries through direct investment by member companies. The rationale for this replication of these firms' close business relations in the United States is simply that the keiretsu is an efficient economic organization for Japanese companies, as pointed out by Aoki (1984, 1988). Because the business relationship within the keiretsu was developed on the basis of mutual trust and cooperation, Japanese firms tend to conduct business with other member companies even in the United States. The president of Mitsubishi Semiconductor described it as follows: "When we came to the U.S., we asked other Mitsubishi companies to support us. . . . If we had to develop everything from scratch or ask other [outside] companies we are not familiar with, it would be more difficult" ("Mighty Mitsubishi," 1990, p. 102). Another Mitsubishi executive stated, "You can trust them. We do not have to exchange business cards" (p. 103).

Effects of Ownership Controls

This study examines the effects of keiretsu membership on overseas investment decisions. In particular, I am interested in the effects of keiretsu ownership on individual member firms' investment decisions. Firms associated with keiretsus are connected by cross-shareholding. The higher the shareholding of a firm by other firms in the same keiretsu, the higher the control that the keiretsu can exercise on that firm. When Firm A in a keiretsu needs capital or assistance in setting up plants in the United States, the keiretsu as a whole can influence a member company, Firm B, to cooperate with Firm A by jointly financing the investment project or by having Firm B set up its own affiliate in the United States to supply parts or provide needed technical or marketing support. Such influential power will differ in the degree of ownership control by the keiretsu. Therefore, it may be hypothesized that the higher the ownership by the keiretsu, the more likely the keiretsu-affiliated firms invest in the United States.

Hypothesis 2: The higher the degree of financial control of keiretsu-affiliated firms, the more likely they invest in the United States.

Financial Resources to Support Member Firms

Hypothesis 2 examines the effects of keiretsu ownership on an individual firm's investment decision. Hypothesis 3 looks at the investment decision from a firm's financial ability to support other keiretsu members. Firms in a keiretsu are supposed to support other firms that require assistance. For example, when Mitsubishi Heavy Industries wanted to start forklift production in Texas, it asked Mitsubishi Corporation, a general trading company, to take a 30% stake in the project and to handle sales activities ("Mighty Mitsubishi," 1990, p. 102). In another case, Mitsubishi Mining jointly acquired a cement factory with 4 other Mitsubishi companies. Mitsubishi Bank and Mitsubishi Trust often financed their member companies' acquisitions in the United States. Today, Mitsubishi Bank is a main bank for all affiliated companies in Japan, and Mitsubishi Bank North America also serves as a main bank for all U.S. affiliates. The U.S. affiliate of Mitsubishi Electric buys most of its semiconductor equipment from other member companies.

These examples of anecdotal evidence based on the Mitsubishi keiretsu are consistent with recent empirical findings of Lincoln, Gerlach, and Ahmadjian (1996) on the profitability of keiretsu-related firms. According to their study, highly profitable (and thus financially strong) firms are supposed to help other firms in the same keiretsu that need assistance. When member firms need assistance in capital and expertise in international venturing, profitable firms often jump in and assist those firms by jointly investing in the projects. As in Sumitomo's turnaround of Mazda, member firms increase their equity investments in the troubled firms while directors are dispatched from the main banks and major investing companies. Lincoln and colleagues explored the possible "redistribution effects" and found evidence that unprofitable firms benefit from keiretsu affiliation and recover faster than do independent firms, whereas previously profitable firms perform less well than do independent firms. Furthermore, the magnitude of such redistribution effects was found to be proportionate to the internal cohesion of the group as indexed by reciprocal shareholding.

It is expected that the ability to cooperate in the keiretsu's strategic decision making and to help other member firms in overseas investment depends on the firm's financial strengths. Only firms that can afford to invest in the United States can cooperate in the keiretsu's long-term expansion in this country. Therefore, I hypothesize that the more profitable a firm after controlling other factors such as intangible assets, international experience, firm size, exchange rate, and industry factors, the more likely it is to invest in the United States.

> *Hypothesis 3:* Firms that have financial abilities to help other firms in the keiretsu are more likely to incur FDI.

Intrafirm Business Transactions

When Toyota set up manufacturing plants in the United States, many suppliers of Toyota set up their own transplants in the United States to continue to supply automobile parts to its assembler. Likewise, the keiretsu-affiliated firms are interrelated by sales of their products to each other. This aspect of the keiretsu is especially distinctive to vertically connected keiretsus in the automobile and electronic industries where affiliated companies are suppliers of parts and raw materials to the large manufacturing company at its core. Martin et al. (1995) shows how the buyer-supplier relationships of Japanese automobile transplants in the United States are recreated and extended.

Even in horizontally connected keiretsus, an affiliate company prefers to do business with firms in the same keiretsu. Table 9.1 shows intra-keiretsu business transactions in the 6 major horizontally connected keiretsus. One can see that those 6 major horizontally connected keiretsus differ from each other in terms of degree of their internal business transactions. In general, 3 prewar-zaibatsu— Mitsubishi, Mitsui, and Sumitomo—have higher levels of intra-keiretsu business transactions than do the other 3 postwar bank-centered keiretsus. Especially, the proportions of intra-keiretsu transactions through *sogo shosha* (the general trading company) are much higher in the case of prewar-zaibatsu firms. Manufacturing firms associated with the Mitsubishi and Daiichi Kangyo keiretsus have higher levels of business transactions with other member manufacturing firms in the same keiretsu. When a customer builds a plant in the United States, the supplying firms are asked to continue supplying parts to U.S. operations as well.

TABLE 9.1
Intra-Keiretsu Business Transactions of Manufacturing Firms
in the Six Major Horizontally Connected Keiretsu

	Mitsubishi	Mitsui	Sumitomo	Fuyo	Sanwa	Daiichi Kangyo
Intra-keiretsu business transactions with sogo shosha	21.39	17.81	37.37	11.16	4.77	6.93
Intra-keiretsu business transactions with other manufacturing firms	4.18	1.03	0.74	1.49	1.53	4.94
Total	25.57	18.84	38.11	12.65	6.30	11.87

SOURCE: Japanese Fair Trade Commission, *Nihon no Roku Dai Kigyo Shodan* (Japan's six major business groups: Organizations and behaviors), 1992.
NOTE: Intra-keiretsu business transactions with other manufacturing firms = manufacturing firms' sales to other manufacturing firms in the same keiretsu / total sales of all member firms in manufacturing in a keiretsu. Intra-keiretsu business transactions with sogo shosha (general trading company) = manufacturing firms' sales to sogo shosha in the same keiretsu / total sales of all member firms in manufacturing in a keiretsu.

Therefore, I expect that firms that have high transaction volumes with other firms in the same keiretsu are more likely to follow their customers to invest in the United States.

Hypothesis 4: Firms of high transaction volume with other firms in the same keiretsu are more likely to invest.

RESEARCH DESIGN

Sample

There is no official list of keiretsu membership. The scope of membership used by researchers differs according to the criteria they use. This study uses the information in *Industrial Groupings in Japan* (Dodwell Marketing Associates, 1992). The directory lists affiliated companies of the 8 horizontally connected keiretsus and 31 major vertically connected keiretsus. Among the 8 horizontally connected keiretsus, we lack information on intra-keiretsu business transactions for Tokai and Industrial Bank of Japan, as in Table 9.1. Therefore, I defined 6 major horizontally connected keiretsus—Mitsubishi, Mitsui, Sumitomo, Fuyo, Sanwa, and Daiichi Kangyo—and 31 vertically connected keiretsus as the sample and then collected information on affiliated companies. To reduce the difficulty in getting firms' financial data, I restricted the sample firms to "listed" companies on the Tokyo Stock Exchange. As of 1989, there were 1,687 firms listed on the Tokyo Stock Exchange. Among those 1,687 firms, 713 were identified as members of either horizontally or vertically connected keiretsus from the Dodwell directory. More specifically, 6 horizontally connected keiretsus had 588 listed firms, and 31 major vertically connected keiretsus included 200 listed firms. Fully 75 firms had memberships in both horizontally connected and vertically connected keiretsus. I defined the 713 keiretsu-affiliated firms as the sample firms for this study.

I then collected investment activities and financial information for those 713 sample firms. Financial information on the sales, assets, R&D and advertising expenditures, and export ratio were acquired from the Nikkei NEEDS electronic database for the period from 1976 to 1989. The database provides basic financial information on all listed firms in Japan. The raw data on the Japanese entries into the United States during this time period were collected by the International Trade Administration at the Department of Commerce. The Japanese entry data for the period from 1974 to 1983 were published in the *Foreign Direct Investment in the United States: Complete Transactions, 1974-83.* The data for the period from 1984 to 1989 were collected from the annual publication of the Department of Commerce under the same title. It provides information on the date and four-digit SIC code for each entry event. Direct investment is defined as setting up a foreign subsidiary by establishing a new operation, by creating a joint venture, or by acquiring an incumbent firm. An investment that expands an existing operation or increases an equity holding of a previous investment also is identified as a foreign investment.

Among all 713 keiretsu-affiliated firms, 432 firms experienced a total of 927 occurrences of direct investment in the United States during the study time period. The other 281 keiretsu-affiliated firms, which also are listed companies, did not record any direct investments in the United States. There were many incidents in which firms made several direct investments. Such longitudinal data at the firm level provide a good setting in which to examine the effects of keiretsus on the individual firms over the 14-year time period. Because there was little investment by Japanese firms before the mid-1970s, the study time period of 1976 to 1989 starts at the initial stage of significant direct investment. In a repeated hazard model, each observation is defined as a distinctive time spell until a direct investment occurs. In a repeated hazard model, a foreign entry may take place in each sample firm at each time during the study time period. There is more than 1 incidence of entry for some firms during the study time period, whereas there is no entry for other firms. For a firm making several direct investments, the interval (or spell) until the next investment constitutes an observation. The time spell from the last investment, or from 1976 for firms with no investments to the right censoring time (1989, the end of the study time period), also constitutes an observation. For example, suppose that Company A has engaged in 3 incidents of direct investment in 1979, 1983, and 1987. These 3 cases of direct investment generate 4 observations in the sample; the first observation is the time spell from 1976 to 1979 (measured to be 3 years), the second is 4 years, the third is 4 years, and the fourth censored observation of Company A is the time spell from 1987 to 1989 (2 years). Even when a firm did not make any direct investment in a line of business during 1976 and 1989, the time spell between 1976 and 1989 (13 years) also is added to the sample as an observation. Using this methodology, the total valid cases of distinctive time spell amount to 1,640 (927 cases of actual entries and 713 observations due to censoring).[3]

Variable Measurement

There are three sets of variables used in this study: firm factors, keiretsu relationship, and industry and macroeconomic controls.

Firm Factors

Following the monopolistic advantage theory and the transactions cost theory, a firm that has intangible assets, reflected in R&D and advertising intensity, would be expected to be more likely to invest in the United States. Export ratio is measured by the export sales deflated by total sales. Export ratio reflects each firm's international business activity served by the export mode before switching to the direct investment mode. It also reflects the international experience on the part of the investing firm as hypothesized by Terpstra and Yu (1988) and Yu (1990). I include the log transformation of total assets to control for the firm size. As found by Kimura (1989) for Japanese semiconductor firms, it is probable that larger companies will be more likely to engage in overseas investment activity. All financial information is from the NEEDS database.

R&D intensity: ratio of the firm's R&D expenditure to total sales (average for 1976-1989)

Advertising intensity: ratio of the firm's advertising expenditure to total sales (average for 1976-1989)

Export ratio: ratio of foreign sales to total sales (average for 1976-1989)

Firm size: log of total assets (average for 1976-1989)

Hypothesis 3 expects that profitable firms are more likely to incur FDI because they have financial capabilities to assist other member firms' international expansion. I measure profitability as the return on assets. I collected financial information from the Nikkei NEEDS database.

Profitability: return on assets (average for 1976-1989)

Keiretsu Relationship

Hypothesis 2 expects that firms under tighter ownership control from keiretsus are more likely to invest in the United States. The Dodwell directory provides the data on keiretsus' overall influential power to individual firms on a 4-point scale. The scale is based on the ratio of a keiretsu's shareholding to the total shares held by the top 10 shareholders. For example, the directory assigns a company the scale of 1 if the ratio of the keiretsu's shareholding to the total shares held by the top 10 shareholders of the company is less than 30%. The scale of 2 is used when the ratio is between 30% and 49%. The scale of 3 is used for companies when the ratio is 50% or higher. The scale of 4 is used for nucleus keiretsu companies.

> *Keiretsu's ownership control:* ratio of a keiretsu's shareholding to the total shares held by the top 10 shareholders

Hypothesis 4 predicts that firms that have large business transactions are more likely to invest in the United States following their customers. Such intra-keiretsu business transactions are more evident in vertically connected keiretsus, especially in the automobile, machinery, and electronics industries. It is very difficult to gather intra-keiretsu business transaction data. Table 9.1 shows the intra-keiretsu business transactions data for the 6 major horizontally connected keiretsus from the Japanese Fair Trade Commission (FTC). The Japanese FTC does not reveal individual firm-level intra-keiretsu business transaction data, nor does it reveal any data for vertically connected keiretsus. Therefore, I test Hypothesis 4 only for horizontally connected keiretsus with the Japanese FTC data shown in Table 9.1. I use two variables for intra-keiretsu business transactions for horizontally connected keiretsus. The first variable measures the proportion of intra-keiretsu transactions with the general trading company (sogo shosha), and the second variable measures the same with other manufacturing companies in the same keiretsu.

> *Intra-keiretsu transactions with trading firms:* the ratio of member firms' sales to the general trading company divided by total sales of all member firms in the same keiretsu

Intra-keiretsu transactions with nontrading firms: the ratio of member firms' sales to other manufacturing firms in the same keiretsu divided by total sales of all member firms in the same keiretsu

Industry and Macroeconomic Controls

Because the sample firms are from a variety of industries, it is necessary to control for industry-specific factors. Industries differ from each other in terms of the degree of using subcontractors and a supplier network and the existence of quota or other types of export restraints. Although I do not have detailed firm-level intra-keiretsu transaction data on vertically connected keiretsus, the relative importance of intra-keiretsu business transactions can be inferred by looking at industry dummy variables. The FDI activities should be higher in assembly-type industries where keiretsus are formed with many specialized component-supplying firms. Industry-specific characteristics are controlled by including dummy variables for broadly defined industries. I define industry affiliation with 10 groups using the broad definition of industry classification scheme in the Nikkei NEEDS database. More specifically, I incorporate 9 dummy variables representing automobile, electronics, chemical and pharmaceuticals, machinery, transportation equipment, steels and materials, foods and textiles, other manufacturing industries, and distribution. Agricultural, construction, and services industries serve as a reference group for these 9 industries.

The effects of exchange rates on direct investment are measured by nominal yen/dollar rates. Actual yearly exchange rates (yen/dollar) are from the *International Financial Statistics Yearbook* (International Monetary Fund, 1991).

Model

In this study, a model of Japanese direct investment by a partial likelihood hazard specification is estimated using repeated measures (Cox & Oakes, 1984). The dependent variable in the hazard model is a hazard rate that denotes a likelihood of a firm to invest in the United States during each time period. Cox and Oakes's (1984) proportional hazard model estimates the influence of explanatory variables (or covariates) on the hazard of direct investment without specifying a parametric form for the precise time of investment. Instead, it rank-orders direct investments in terms of their temporal sequence.

More specifically, this model presumes that hazard rates can be represented as log-linear functions of the covariates. If $h[t; Z, X(t)]$ is the hazard function for an individual with time-invariant covariates vector Z and time-varying covariates $X(t)$, then the proportional hazard model specifies this hazard as the likelihood that the observed direct investment event should have taken place, conditional on the hazards of all firms at risk. This formulation leads to the following specification of the likelihood for the *i*th firm:

$$L_i(t) = h_o(t)\exp[\mu_i Z_i + \beta_r X(t)] / h_o(t)\{\Sigma_{j \in R_t} \exp[\mu_j Z_j + \beta_r X(t)]\}, \qquad (1)$$

where $h_o(t)$ is the baseline hazard rate at time t, j is an index for firms at risk at time t (with R_t being the risk set), Z_i are independent variables for individual firm i that are constant over time, $X_i(t)$ are the time-varying covariates for firm i, and μ and β are coefficients to be estimated. Exchange rate is the only time-varying covariate used in this study; variations in the other variables over time are of small magnitude. With this formulation, the model calculates the ratio of the hazards as the conditional probability of an investment given all other firms in the same risk set.

This model implicitly contains two assumptions. First, it assumes the multiplicative relationship between the underlying hazard rates and the log-linear function of the covariates (the proportionality assumption). Second, it assumes that the effect of the covariates on the hazard function is log-linear. These two assumptions enable the model to leave the baseline hazard unspecified. Because the proportional hazard model does not specify the baseline hazard, there is no bias incurred by misspecifying the stochastic process of the underlying hazard rate. This generality is achieved by assuming further that the baseline hazard rate is the same for all firms in the risk set. From this assumption, $h_0(t)$ cancels out. The likelihood function can be rewritten as

$$L_i(t) = \exp[\mu_i Z_i + \beta_r X(t)] / \Sigma_{j \in R_t} \exp[\mu_j Z_j + \beta_r X(t)]. \qquad (2)$$

The rewritten likelihood function is equivalent to allowing only the conditional probabilities to contribute to the statistical inferences. Multiplying these probabilities together for each of the distinct time spells gives the partial likelihood function to be maximized. No information on the precise time of entry is required, providing a partial (rather than full) maximum likelihood estimate. Thus, partial likelihood estimation involves an efficiency loss because the exact investment time is not considered. Nevertheless, the estimates are consistent and asymptotically normally distributed. The t values can be interpreted as asymptotically close to the full maximum likelihood estimates. (For more detailed information on the assumptions of the model, see Cox and Oakes, 1984.)

There is both left and right censoring in the data for the period from 1976 to 1989. Because there were few Japanese investments in the United States before 1976, left censoring does not pose a serious problem; there is no correction in the specification. Right censoring, caused by truncating the observation period at 1989, is handled by conventional adjustments. Censored observations enter the risk set at each time period under observation but do not contribute to the numerator of the likelihood function. However, in a repeated hazard framework, the risk set remains the same, with alterations entering only through changes in exchange rates.

RESULTS

Table 9.2 presents the results for the repeated hazard model from the entire set of independent time spells until direct investment into the United States takes place for each keiretsu-affiliated firm. Models 1 and 2 in Table 9.2 use both horizontally connected and vertically connected keiretsu firms in the sample.[4] Models 3 and 4 use only horizontally connected keiretsu firms. Models 5 and 6 use only vertically connected keiretsu firms. I include industry dummy variables to control for industry-specific factors in even-numbered models. Among the 1,640 (927 cases of actual entries and 713 observations due to censoring) valid spells, some observations were lost due to missing information in some of the variables, especially in firm-level R&D and advertising spending. No systematic bias is found due to deleting observations with missing information. The actual numbers of observations used in regressions are 1,096, 750, and 346 for Models 1 and 2, Models 3 and 4, and Models 5 and 6, respectively. Models are significant (chi-square for covariates significant at $p < .001$).

In Models 1 and 2 in Table 9.2, the R&D and advertising intensity variables are included to capture intangible assets that lead to FDI. R&D intensity is only weakly positive, replicating the well-established results. The advertising intensity does not turn out to be significant. Export ratio, which captures a firm's international experience, is not significant. Firm size turns out to be strongly significant, suggesting that larger firms tend to invest overseas. The exchange rate variable is strongly significant, suggesting that sharp yen appreciation plays a very important role in shifting production overseas. Hypothesis 2 predicts that firms under tight ownership control from keiretsus are more likely to incur investment in the United States. The keiretsu's influential power turns out to be significantly positive, confirming my conjecture. Hypothesis 3 examines whether firms with strong financial capabilities (measured by profitability) incur more investment. The results show that highly profitable firms are in fact more likely to invest, supporting the redistribution effect hypothesis by Lincoln et al. (1996).[5]

Model 2 in Table 9.2 shows the same regression as Model 1 with nine industry dummy variables. The reference industries (with all nine dummy variables equal to zero) are mainly domestic industries such as agriculture, construction, and services. In Model 2, all dummy variables turn out to be significantly positive. It might be interesting to look at the size and significance levels of industry dummy

TABLE 9.2
Hazard Modeling of Foreign Direct Investment Decisions of Keiretsu-Affiliated Firms

Variable	All Keiretsu Firms (n = 1,096)		Firms in Horizontal Keiretsu (n = 750)		Firms in Vertical Keiretsu (n = 346)	
	(1)	(2)	(3)	(4)	(5)	(6)
Firm-level variables						
Research and development intensity	4.58 (1.88)*	1.85 (0.67)	4.60 (1.53)	0.66 (0.19)	7.06 (1.47)	5.94 (1.12)
Advertising intensity	4.99 (1.01)	3.70 (0.69)	-1.25 (-0.20)	-4.85 (-0.75)	32.42 (2.26)**	37.59 (1.89)*
Export ratio	0.21 (0.76)	-0.24 (-0.74)	0.11 (0.27)	-0.64 (-1.27)	0.57 (0.98)	0.23 (0.32)
Firm size	0.48 (12.52)***	0.56 (12.56)***	0.51 (10.87)***	0.62 (11.09)***	0.51 (4.80)***	0.54 (4.92)***
Profitability	8.53 (2.63)**	9.08 (2.74)***	14.23 (3.29)***	14.62 (3.37)***	-2.16 (-0.30)	-2.88 (-0.39)
Keiretsu relations						
Ownership control	0.13 (2.56)**	0.11 (2.10)	0.17 (2.95)***	0.12 (1.98)**	-0.13 (-0.19)	0.20 (1.05)
Internal transactions with trading firms			0.01 (1.79)*	0.003 (0.76)		
Internal transactions with nontrading firms			0.05 (1.54)	0.04 (1.08)		

Macroeconomic effects						
Exchange rate	–0.01 (–11.26)***	–0.01 (–10.73)***	–0.01 (–10.43)***	–0.01 (–9.99)***	–0.01 (–4.32)***	–0.01 (–4.13)***
Industry dummies						
Automobiles		1.73 (4.99)***		1.45 (1.85)*		2.00 (3.72)***
Electronics		1.30 (4.42)***		1.61 (4.26)***		0.98 (1.97)**
Chemicals		1.25 (4.16)***		1.44 (3.90)***		n.i.
Machinery		1.39 (4.07)***		1.51 (3.39)***		1.56 (2.71)***
Transportation		0.88 (2.55)***		1.04 (2.34)**		0.72 (1.21)
Steels and materials		1.31 (4.52)***		1.52 (4.17)***		1.00 (1.93)*
Food and textiles		1.07 (3.20)***		1.15 (2.84)***		n.i.
Other manufacturing		1.51 (3.51)***		1.98 (4.02)***		n.i.
Distribution		0.89 (2.58)***		0.86 (2.10)**		n.i.
Chi-squared	571.80***	593.14***	399.23***	418.46***	144.99***	150.85***

NOTE: n.i. = not included due to small number of cases.
*** $p < .01$, ** $p < .05$, * $p < .10$.

variables. The automobile, electronics, and machinery industries have the strongest effects by far in prompting FDI. Such industries are largely noted for assembly-based industries with a significant subcontracting structure. When large assemblers shift their production base to foreign countries, their suppliers tend to follow suit to continue their business relations in foreign countries. This provides only indirect support for Hypothesis 4 because I do not have a direct measure of intra-keiretsu sales of individual firms.

To test Hypothesis 4 in a more direct way, I include two variables measuring intra-keiretsu business transactions in Models 3 and 4 in Table 9.2, based on information in Table 9.1. Only weak support is found for Hypothesis 4. The business transaction with trading companies seems to be significantly (at 10%) related to the likelihood of investing in the United States. Such a weakly significant relation, however, disappears when industry dummy variables are included.

The division of the sample into horizontally and vertically connected keiretsus adds more insights. Models 3 and 4 in Table 9.2, which use only horizontally connected keiretsus, show very similar patterns with the pooled regressions as shown in Models 1 and 2. The keiretsu ownership control and profitability are strongly significant. Interestingly, the same variables that are significant for horizontally connected keiretsus, such as keiretsu ownership control and profitability, are not significant for firms in the vertically connected keiretsus. Firms in horizontally connected keiretsus usually are not in the same industry. So, unless the keiretsu exercises influence with ownership control over those firms that can assist other keiretsu members, they might not voluntarily help other firms. Thus, the keiretsu's influential power, measured by ownership, and the profitability of individual firms should be significant factors in determining individual member firms' investment decisions in horizontally connected keiretsus. However, for firms in vertically connected keiretsus, such keiretsu ownership control and individual firms' profitability might not matter much. Rather, continuation of supply relationships might be a more important factor in explaining their investment activities. The industry dummy variables show that firms in the automobile, machinery, and electronics industries have a higher tendency to invest in the United States. Such industries are well known for an extensive web of supplier-buyer relationships.

DISCUSSION AND CONCLUSION

This study examines the effects of keiretsu control in affiliated firms' FDI behavior. By measuring the keiretsu's influential power and individual firms' ability to contribute to the keiretsu, this study empirically tests hypotheses that keiretsu affiliation in fact affects FDI in the United States. This study models the entry behavior at the firm level with longitudinal data. This empirical methodology enables us to control for individual firms' intangible assets and the sharp appreciation of yen during the study time period.

In summary, firms under tight ownership control by keiretsus are more likely to invest in the United States. Also, firms that are profitable and have financial capabilities to assist other firms in the same keiretsu are more likely to invest in the United States. These effects of ownership control and profitability on direct investment are especially true for horizontally connected keiretsus where affiliated firms are operating in different industries. An interesting difference between horizontally connected and vertically connected keiretsus is that firms affiliated with vertically connected keiretsus are not necessarily conditioned by the ownership control and profitability of individual firms in deciding on direct investment. Their overseas investments seem to be determined more by the need to continue buyer-supplier business relationships overseas. The fact that likelihood of investment by firms associated with vertically connected keiretsus is stronger in the automobile, machinery, and electronics industries implies that keiretsu firms in those industries are motivated by the need to move production overseas to continue supply relationships with their customers.

As shown in Figure 9.1, direct investments by keiretsu-affiliated firms show a continuously increasing pattern. However, the fact that 432 out of 713 keiretsu-affiliated firms had entered the United States through direct investment by 1989 shows that such a transfer of keiretsu organizations still was in progress. The remaining 281 firms could be in domestic industries, or they could transfer their production overseas if the yen appreciated more. Such direct investment by keiretsu-affiliated firms enables keiretsus to recreate themselves within the United States. Overseas affiliates of keiretsu firms conduct business with each other on the basis of their business relations in Japan.

The keiretsu is currently under scrutiny from U.S. trade representatives as a target under structural impediment initiatives. However, if the keiretsu might represent an efficient economic organization that maximizes the coordination and information sharing and learning as specified by Aoki (1984, 1988), then the keiretsu-type interorganizational network structure will be diffused to American companies.[6] Ferguson (1990) suggested that U.S. firms should create a variant of the Japanese keiretsu so that they can compete effectively with Japanese rivals. For example, in the information industry, large established companies such as IBM, Xerox, Motorola, and DEC should create three sets of networks: vertical and cross-functional alliances with start-ups for technological development, vertical and cross-corporate alliances for components production and global marketing, and horizontal alliances for strategic leverage in dealing with the U.S. government and Japanese industry. Ferguson envisioned that such alliances will differ from traditional vertical integration and mergers and acquisition in that they will achieve entrepreneurship, market discipline, and flexibility of the innovative companies. This vision is consistent with a view by Gerlach (1992) in understanding the keiretsu as an alliance structure.

This study has several limitations. Only the recreation of the keiretsu organization into the United States by FDI is examined. This study does not look at whether reconstructed keiretsus in the United States actually operate in the same manner as they do in Japan. In addition, more refined firm-level data on intra-keiretsu business transactions need to be gathered.

An extension of this study is to examine the nature of business relationships among overseas subsidiaries of keiretsu-affiliated firms. It would be interesting to see how overseas affiliates of keiretsus operate differently from their parents in Japan. Martin et al. (1995) showed that suppliers often extend the business relationship beyond their own keiretsus when they expand overseas. It would be an interesting research question to analyze further how much isomorphic relations those overseas affiliates have compared to their parents. Institutional theory suggests that the external environment exerts strong conformatory power on organizations (DiMaggio & Powell, 1983). If U.S. affiliates of keiretsu firms adapt to the local environment, then their relationships with overseas keiretsus will be much more loose than their original keiretsus in Japan (Fujimoto, 1992).

Another important extension can be to examine the keiretsu formation by American firms. Strategic alliances are a very popular form of interorganizational network these days. It would be interesting to examine the business relationship of those alliance networks by American firms and to investigate the similarities and differences between American and Japanese versions of the keiretsu.

NOTES

1. The Dodwell directory is by no means an exhaustive listing of keiretsus. The exact number and listing of keiretsus depend on how one identifies whether a firm is associated with keiretsu or not. The Dodwell directory, however, is one of the most comprehensive listings of keiretsus available at this time.

2. For more detailed information on the prewar zaibatsu and its dissolution, see Hadley (1970).

3. See Chang (1995) and Kogut and Chang (1996) for applications of the repeated hazard modeling technique to the FDI activities of Japanese companies.

4. Of the 713 keiretsu-affiliated firms, 75 are associated with both horizontally connected and vertically connected keiretsus. In the empirical modeling of the keiretsu's investment decision, I treat these 75 firms as 2 different companies, each of which is associated with the respective horizontally connected and vertically connected keiretsus.

5. I tested the possible interaction effects between the keiretsu's ownership control and the firm's profitability but found no significant effects.

6. See Kogut and Parkinson (1993) for diffusion of the M-form innovation to other countries.

REFERENCES

Aoki, M. (1984). Toward an economic model of the Japanese firm. *Journal of Economic Literature, 28*, 1-27.

Aoki, M. (1988). *Information, incentives, and bargaining in the Japanese economy.* Cambridge, UK: Cambridge University Press.

Buckley, P., & Casson, M. (1976). *The future of the multinational enterprise.* London: Macmillan.

Caves, R. (1971). International corporations: The industrial economics of foreign investment. *Economica, 38*, 1-27.

Chang, S. (1995). International expansion strategy of Japanese firms: Capability building through sequential entry. *Academy of Management Journal, 38*, 383-407.

Cox, D. R., & Oakes, D. (1984). *Analysis of survival data* (Monographs on Statistics and Applied Probability). London: Chapman and Hall.

DiMaggio, P., & Powell, W. (1983). The Iron Cage revisited: Institutional isomorphism and collective rationality in organization fields. *American Sociological Review, 48*, 147-160.

Dodwell Marketing Associates. (1992). *Industrial groupings in Japan.* Tokyo: Author.

Ferguson, C. (1990). Computers and the coming of the U.S. keiretsu. *Harvard Business Review, 68*(4), 55-70.

Florida, R., & Kenney, M. (1991). Transplanted organizations: The transfer of Japanese industrial organization to the U.S. *American Sociological Review, 56*, 381-398.

Fujimoto, H. (1992, February). Japan's automobile keiretsu changing for the better. *Tokyo Business Today*, pp. 50-51.

Gerlach, M. (1992). *Alliance capitalism.* Berkeley: University of California Press.

Hadley, E. (1970). *Antitrust in Japan.* Princeton, NJ: Princeton University Press.

Hennart, J. F. (1982). *The theory of the multinational enterprise.* Ann Arbor: University of Michigan Press.

Hennart, J. F. (1993). Explaining the swollen middle: Why most transactions are a mix of market and hierarchy. *Organization Science, 4*, 529-547.

Hennart, J. F., & Park, Y. (1994). Location, governance, and strategic determinants of Japanese manufacturing investment in the United States. *Strategic Management Journal, 15*, 419-436.

Hymer, S. (1960). *The international operations of national firms: A study of direct foreign investment.* Cambridge, MA: MIT Press.

Imai, K. (1987, Winter). The corporate network in Japan. *Japanese Economic Studies, 16*, 1-37.

International Monetary Fund. (1991). *International financial statistics yearbook, 1991.* Geneva: Author.

Kimura, Y. (1989). Firm-specific strategic advantages and foreign direct investment behavior of firms: The case of Japanese semiconductor firms. *Journal of International Business Studies, 20*(2), 296-314.

Kimura, Y., & Pugel, T. (1995). Keiretsu and Japanese direct investment in U.S. manufacturing. *Japan and World Economy, 7*, 481-503.

Kogut, B., & Chang, S. (1991). Technological capabilities and Japanese foreign direct investment in the United States. *Review of Economics and Statistics, 73*, 401-413.

Kogut, B., & Chang, S. (1996). Platform investment and volatile exchange rate. *Review of Economics and Statistics, 78*, 221-231.

Kogut, B., & Parkinson, D. (1993). The diffusion of American organizing principles to Europe. In B. Kogut (Ed.), *Country competitiveness: Technology and organizing of work* (pp. 179-202). New York: Oxford University Press.

Krafcik, J. (1986). *Learning from NUMMI* (MIT International Motor Vehicle Project). Cambridge, MA: Massachusetts Institute of Technology.

Lincoln, J., Gerlach, M., & Ahmadjian, C. (1996, February). Keiretsu network and corporate performance in Japan. *American Journal of Sociology, 61*, 67-88.

MaGee, S. (1977). Information and the multinational corporation: An appropriability theory of foreign direct investment. In J. Bhagwati (Ed.), *The new international economic order* (pp. 57-81). Cambridge, MA: MIT Press.

Martin, X., Mitchell, W., & Swaminathan, A. (1995). Recreating and extending Japanese automobile buyer-supplier links in North America. *Strategic Management Journal, 16*, 589-619.

McClain, D. (1983). Foreign direct investment in the United States: Old currents, "new waves," and the theory of direct foreign investment. In C. Kindleberger & D. Audretsch (Eds.), *The multinational corporations of the 1980s.* Cambridge, MA: MIT Press.

Mighty Mitsubishi is on the move. (1990, September 24). *Business Week*, pp. 98-107.

Piore, M., & Sabel, C. (1984). *The second industrial divide.* New York: Basic Books.

Pugel, T. (1985). *The industry determinants of foreign direct investment into the United States.* New York: New York University, Division of Research, Graduate School of Business Administration.

Rugman, A. (1981). *Inside the multinationals: The economies of internal markets.* London: Croom Helm.

Terpstra, V., & Yu, C. (1988). Determinants of foreign investment of U.S. advertising agencies. *Journal of International Business Studies, 19*(1), 33-46.

Williamson, O. (1975). *Markets and hierarchies.* New York: Free Press.

Yu, C. (1990). The experience effect and foreign direct investment. *Weltwirtschaftliches Archiv, 126*, 560-579.

10

Toward a Model of Accelerating Organizational Change

Evidence From the Globalization Process

THOMAS W. MALNIGHT

Research on the structuring of multinational corporations (MNCs) has increasingly highlighted the need for fundamental organizational change. Whereas MNCs traditionally have been organized around functions, products, or geographic markets, emerging organizational models emphasize internally differentiated structures, characterizing MNCs as composed of dispersed, specialized, and interdependent worldwide operations (Bartlett & Ghoshal, 1989, 1990; Hedlund, 1986, 1994; Perlmutter, 1969; Prahalad & Doz, 1987). Pressures for change reflect both the growing interdependence of competition within and across world markets (Kobrin, 1991; Ohmae, 1985; Porter, 1986) and recognition of an expanding array of often conflicting strategic opportunities associated with operating globally (Ghoshal, 1987; Kogut, 1989). Operating across fragmented environments and facing contradictory pressures and opportunities, MNCs often find that devising a global strategy is easier than designing and implementing an organization to achieve its objectives. However, despite the importance and complexity of projected organizational changes, little of the research on firm globalization has addressed the change process leading to internally differentiated firm structures.

Outside the field of international business (IB), the issue of fundamental organizational change has been an important research focus, often associated with the ability of firms to balance the competing pressures for internal continuity and adaptation. Some researchers suggest that companies must change over time to maintain alignment with their external competitive environments (Chandler, 1962; Lawrence & Lorsch, 1967; Mintzberg, 1979; Porter, 1980; Quinn, 1980). Others stress the need for internal consistency to retain and exploit prior learning and to maintain organizational efficiency (Hannan & Freeman, 1989; March & Simon, 1958; Nelson & Winter, 1982; Selznick, 1957). In responding to these competing pressures, two models of fundamental organizational change have been developed. Punctuated equilibrium models (Gersick, 1991; Miller & Friesen, 1980, 1984; Tushman & Romanelli, 1985) posit long periods of organizational stability followed by short periods of comprehensive change or radical reorientation. Incremental change models (Cyert & March, 1963; Mintzberg, 1979; Quinn, 1980) describe fundamental organizational change as emerging over time from localized independent initiatives.

The research reported here investigated the process of fundamental organizational change in the context of firm globalization. To identify characteristics of the change process, the punctuated equilibrium and incremental change models are used as alternative hypotheses for patterns of internal adjustments over time. Given its focus on only two firms, the study does not attempt a comprehensive test of these models. Rather, the study involves a detailed empirical investigation of patterns of organizational change within two leading pharmaceutical firms as they altered how they operated globally, using the two models in identifying and analyzing important components of the change process.

Changes in the organization of key activities within each firm are examined over time. Focusing on activities reflects a managerial orientation to the study of organizational structures, where activities integrate one or more functions across the value chain (Kogut, 1984; Porter, 1985) and are meaningful in terms of differences in the nature of work performed and the mix of goals or objectives pursued.[1] An activity focus also is in line with organizational theory (OT) research that has emphasized the organization of semi-autonomous subunits within firms (Lawrence & Lorsch, 1967) as well as similar approaches in management accounting (Atkinson, Banker, Kaplan, & Young, 1995; Hansen & Mowen, 1995).[2] The study builds on techniques suggested by Miller and Friesen (1984) to develop an empirical characterization, based on a comprehensive set of organizational variables highlighted in prior IB research, of how each firm structured activities. In analyzing the change process, the research then distinguishes similarities and dissimilarities in activity-level structures over time, identifying patterns of internal organizational changes both to quantify the extent and nature of change and to analyze patterns of adjustments. Overall, the study analyzes patterns of organizational change within two firms across 11 common activities, with longitudinal observations collected across four time periods.

The study identifies important differences in the change process from those projected by either the punctuated equilibrium or incremental models. Specifically, the study observes a process of fundamental change occurring through a limited number of interdependent adjustments over time, a change process initially focused within a few activities and subsequently expanding in its impact across the organization. The extent of change in early phases of the process was limited, but the rate of change increased over time. Hence, the observed process involved sequential and accelerating adjustments within the firms, whereby early, and often informal, changes minimized disruptions and focused and enabled subsequent adjustments.

The following section reviews research on organizational evolution within MNCs and describes the two models of fundamental organizational change as theoretical background for the study. Then, the research issues are defined and the methods used in the study are described. After the findings are reported, their implications are considered in terms of a model of accelerating fundamental organizational change.

ORGANIZATIONAL EVOLUTION WITHIN MNCS

Two largely independent streams of research have examined organizations, one in OT and the other in the field of IB. OT research has investigated a wide range of organizations to identify characteristics that are generalizable across a diverse population, whereas IB research has explored the structuring and management of MNCs, emphasizing characteristics of firms operating across multiple national markets. An important stream of OT research has addressed the interdependence between an organization and various characteristics of its environment (Chandler, 1962; Lawrence & Lorsch, 1967; Meyer & Scott, 1983; Pfeffer & Salancik, 1978; Scott, 1987; Thompson, 1967; Woodward, 1958; Zucker, 1988). IB research, by contrast, has reflected a *developmental* perspective, driven by recognition that many firms gradually expand their worldwide operations. In general, this expansion has been found to initially involve exporting products to leverage domestically based operations, then expand local facilities to protect and further build established export markets, and then become increasingly global in terms of building and leveraging dispersed worldwide operations to enhance firm competitive advantage (Kindleberger, 1969; Vernon, 1979).

This gradual expansion has had direct and important implications for the organizations of MNCs, with various IB studies having identified various firm-specific and environmental factors influencing MNCs' organizations. Specific firm-specific factors have been found to include the extent and nature of the firm's worldwide operations (Stopford & Wells, 1972), its national origin (Franko, 1976; Hedlund, 1981; Negandhi & Baliga, 1981; Yoshino, 1976), its information-processing capability (Egelhoff, 1982), and the mind-set of its senior managers (Perlmutter, 1969). In terms of environmental factors, an important distinction has been made between "global" and "multidomestic" strategies (Bartlett & Ghoshal, 1986, 1989; Porter, 1986; Prahalad & Doz, 1987). Whereas multidomestic strategies are associated with environments marketed by relatively *independent* national markets (with MNCs organized around geographically based structures), global strategies are associated with environments marked by *integrated* or contiguous world markets (with MNCs operating through worldwide product or functional structures).

Toward Emerging MNC Organizational Models

More recent IB research has highlighted growing complexity both in the global competitive environment and in MNCs' strategies, calling for fundamental changes in how MNCs organize globally. With growing *interdependence* across world markets, emerging global strategies reflect the pursuit of an expanding array of often conflicting opportunities (Ghoshal, 1987; Kogut, 1989).[3] MNC organizations operating within an interdependent environment have been found to incorporate internally differentiated structures (Bartlett & Ghoshal, 1989, 1990; Ghoshal & Westney, 1993; Hedlund, 1986, 1994). Various studies having identified patterns of internal structural variations within MNCs across products (Bartlett & Ghoshal, 1989; Malnight, 1996; Prahalad & Doz, 1987), functions (Kogut, 1984; Malnight, 1995; Porter, 1986), and national markets (Bartlett, 1986; Gupta & Govindarajan, 1991; Vernon, 1979).[4] For example, MNC structures have been influenced by variations in the technical requirements of individual functions. One common observed pattern involves centralizing upstream functions to take advantage of economies of scale and rising fixed investment costs while decentralizing downstream functions to afford flexibility to respond to national requirements. Other studies have highlighted internal structural variations across national affiliates, identifying the roles of affiliates such as global or local innovators, integrated players, and implementors (Gupta & Govindarajan, 1991).

Overall, the research projects fundamental change within MNCs both in their motivations for operating globally and in their organizational structures. Rather than emphasizing sales of existing products (a frequent motivation for firms to initially expand globally), MNCs increasingly are operating globally to build firm competitive advantage within and across interdependent markets. Rather than being organized around internally homogeneous structures, MNCs increasingly have internally differentiated structures composed of dispersed and often specialized operations that, through coordination and integration, pursue multiple and often conflicting strategic objectives.[5] However, despite the strategic importance of that evolution and the complexity of resulting organizations, little longitudinal research within firms has examined the movement toward the emerging models. An important task for IB research is to investigate the firm globalization process, in line with a long research tradition highlighting the need to understand process to interpret outcomes (Cyert & March, 1963; Simon, 1976).

MODELS OF FUNDAMENTAL ORGANIZATIONAL CHANGE

Outside the field of IB, the issue of organizational continuity and change has received considerable attention, reflecting recognition of two conflicting yet simultaneous pressures. Research emphasizing the need for change has built on the importance of alignment with a firm's environment, the proposition being that organizations that achieve fit with their environment are more *effective* (Chandler, 1962; Lawrence & Lorsch, 1967). Other research has emphasized the importance of internal organizational alignment and continuity, highlighting the importance of exploiting prior success to increase organizational *efficiency* and reduce uncertainty (March & Simon, 1958; Nelson & Winter, 1982).[6] The simultaneous pressures reflect two competing risks (Hannan & Freeman, 1989). If a firm does not maintain strategies that are effective in its competitive environment, then it risks competitive failure. However, altering current structures and practices poses a risk of change process failure and an associated loss of efficiency due to organizational disruption (Hannan & Freeman, 1984; Singh, House, & Tucker, 1986; Winter, 1994). As a result, organizations have been characterized as facing a dual challenge to *explore* new possibilities and *exploit* old certainties (March, 1991; Schumpeter, 1934). Whereas exploration enables a firm to change by identifying and developing strategic alternatives (Quinn, 1980), exploitation of past learning increases the firm's internal efficiency by constraining how it perceives its environment, what alternatives it considers, and what decisions it makes and actions it takes.

Two models of fundamental organizational change have been developed to explain how firms respond to the conflicting pressures and risks. Punctuated equilibrium models (Gersick, 1991; Miller & Friesen, 1980, 1984; Romanelli & Tushman, 1994; Tushman & Romanelli, 1985) build on the premise that organizations generally are clustered into a limited number of configurations representing stable equilibrium organizational states of interdependent and mutually supportive elements. Pressures to remain within configurations result in firms' desire to maintain environmental fit and internal stability. Punctuated equilibrium models project that long periods of stability or equilibrium are interrupted by relatively short periods of fundamental and multifaceted change, referred to as revolutionary periods, that move an organization to new equilibrium states. Romanelli and Tushman (1994) posited three drivers of those radical reorientations: sustained deterioration of performance, changes in leadership, and sudden and major environmental jolts. Gersick (1991) described how the punctuated equilibrium model has been reflected in research in a wide array of fields and at multiple levels of analysis.[7]

Incremental change models (Cyert & March, 1963; Mintzberg, 1979; Quinn, 1980) characterize organizational adjustments as involving disjointed and piecemeal responses to short-term and localized challenges and opportunities. Incremental change models emphasize the relative independence of individual responses, suggesting that fundamental change is the cumulative result of localized actions. As a result, fundamental change can be observed in the long term without any identifiable source of such change, implying emergent strategies and organizations (Mintzberg, 1979).

The two models posit sequential responses to a single dominant pressure or risk at any point in time. The punctuated equilibrium model represents change in a context where the relative risk of competitive failure, based on posited organizational shocks, dominates pressures for internal stability. After the radical adjustments and the establishment of a new equilibrium, the emphasis again shifts to maximizing internal stability and alignment. Incremental change models, by contrast, represent change in a context where the relative risk of competitive failure is small, leading to localized adjustments within or around current organizational systems.

RESEARCH ISSUES

This research investigated the process of fundamental organizational change associated with the firm globalization process, using the punctuated equilibrium and incremental change models as alternative hypotheses of expected patterns of change. In this research, fundamental change is considered to involve major or radical adjustments across multiple critical elements of the organization, building on approaches found in Haveman (1992) and Thompson (1967), among others. As described earlier, in the context of firm globalization, emerging organizational models project radical changes in where firms locate operations globally as well as in how they structure and manage these worldwide operations (for typical discussions on the nature of projected changes, see Bartlett & Ghoshal, 1989, and Malnight, 1995).

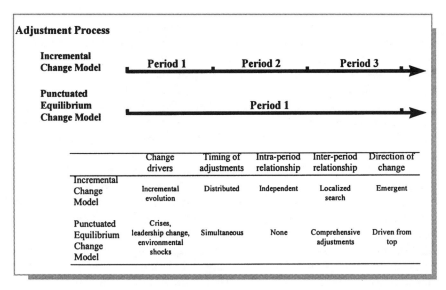

FIGURE 10.1. Incremental and Punctuated Equilibrium Models of Change

The two models of organizational change suggest significantly different characteristics for the adjustment process. The punctuated equilibrium model projects radical and simultaneous internal adjustments across the organization. As the change process involves the introduction of a new equilibrium organizational state within a short time period, the model projects a high degree of interdependence across adjustments made within a time period. Within the model, the direction of change is determined from the top of the organization. The model implicitly suggests little interdependence in adjustments across time given the movement between stable equilibrium states. The incremental change model projects an internal adjustment process characterized by independent initiatives distributed across the organization over time. Given the localized nature of adjustments, interperiod interdependence across changes will be limited. Within the premise of logical incrementalism, however, the model does project path dependence in terms of interdependence over time. The model suggests that the direction of change is emergent from the cumulative sum of localized responses.

Overall, these models suggest important differences in several important components of the change process, as summarized in Figure 10.1. Specifically there are major differences projected in the drivers of change, the timing and rate of adjustments, the nature of interdependence of adjustments within and across time periods, and the direction of the change process.

In investigating the firm globalization process, this research addresses an important issue for OT research on organizational change. Specifically, several assumptions are implicit within the punctuated and incremental change models. Punctuated equilibrium models assume that a known new desired equilibrium state exists, that an organization has all the resources necessary to implement such a model immediately, and that fundamental change occurs only in response to crises or sudden jolts. Incremental models assume that there is a limited need for coordination or integration across initiatives and that new and desired equilibrium states are associated closely enough with the existing organizational model to be achieved through localized initiatives. However, many firms face increasingly dynamic environments that call for the development of new resources and capabilities as well as new and complex approaches to structuring operations. There has been limited comprehensive research on the internal change process in dynamic environments calling for *rapid* and *fundamental* organizational change involving movement toward previously unknown organizational models (for a notable exception, see Haveman, 1992).[8]

Research on firm globalization affords an opportunity to investigate the process of fundamental organizational change within environments outside these assumptions. Specifically, firm globalization has been projected to involve the introduction of complex and previously unknown organizational structures, with pressures for globalization affecting both successful firms and firms facing crises, in response to rapid changes in the global competitive environment. Hence, research on firm globalization also can be used as a further test of the punctuated and incremental models.

METHODS

Research Sites

The research analyzed patterns of organizational change within two leading pharmaceutical firms, Eli Lilly (hereafter Lilly) and Hoffmann LaRoche (hereafter Roche), between 1980 and early 1994, focusing on how they structured and managed their worldwide operations. Lilly and Roche were well suited for research on patterns of fundamental organizational change. In 1980, the structures of the two firms were internally homogeneous and maximally different, with the firms operating globally through vastly different structures. Lilly, founded in 1876 in the United States, had "OUS" (company term for "outside the United States") operations focused on local sales of products developed within its U.S. operation and had strong centralized management of affiliates. Roche, founded in 1896 in Switzerland, had quickly expanded internationally, building research and manufacturing operations in major centers around the world (e.g., Switzerland, United States, United Kingdom, Japan). Until the early 1980s, Roche was organized through a corporate headquarters and local operating companies, with the head of each operating company reporting directly to the chairman and having full authority over largely autonomous local operations. Overall, Lilly and Roche were classic models of centralized (i.e., ethnocentric) and decentralized (i.e., polycentric) MNCs, respectively (Perlmutter, 1969).[9]

During the late 1970s and early 1980s, senior management at both firms increasingly described the need to globalize their operations. By 1994, both firms had moved toward internally differentiated structures, building on a series of initiatives launched throughout the period. Table 10.1 characterizes the emerging structures at the two firms, reflecting fundamental changes in how they structured and managed their worldwide operations. The change processes at Lilly and Roche afford an important opportunity to investigate fundamental change in the absence of organizational shocks. Throughout the study period, both firms remained highly profitable and relative leaders in the industry. Both firms had generally consistent management in place throughout the study period, and both firms also underwent important changes in senior management shortly after the end of the study period. Although a major transformation was under way in the pharmaceutical industry, no single specific and identifiable shock occurred (for a discussion on the globalization of the pharmaceutical industry, see Malnight, 1995). Yet, both firms fundamentally altered their strategies and organizations during the study period. Overall, then, investigation of the change process at Lilly and Roche enabled detailed analysis of the process of fundamental organizational change at two successful firms associated with a single individual initiative (i.e., globalization) and under a single management team.

Activity-Level Analysis

The unit of analysis for the research was the *activity,* building on an approach used in the fields of OT (Lawrence & Lorsch, 1967) and management accounting (Atkinson et al., 1995; Hansen & Mowen, 1995).[10] Applying the activity concept to the study of MNCs involved distinguishing common operations or tasks across the industry value chain (Kogut, 1984; Porter, 1985) that pursue different mixes of goals or objectives and differ in the nature of work performed. Activities can be either individual functions or combinations of functions and are performed by both vertically integrated and specialized firms. For example, drug discovery is performed not only by integrated pharmaceutical firms but also by biotechnology firms, research institutes, and universities.

Activity definition was based on four major pharmaceutical industry processes: drug discovery, regulatory approval, production, and marketing and sales.[11] Within the vertically integrated MNCs in the study, activities within those four major processes drew on common or shared resources located across functions and geographic affiliates. Hence, analysis of structural patterns across

TABLE 10.1

1994 Organizational Structures of Eli Lilly and Hoffmann LaRoche

Company	Major Process	1994 Structure
Eli Lilly	Drug discovery	Structured around global therapeutic area directors, with cross-functional "strategy" and "action" teams conducting actual research studies; discovery operations supported by traditional functional staff units
	Regulatory approval	Centrally managed under compound project teams, operating within common global standards, protocols, and development plans to ensure timely and simultaneous launch of products in major world markets
	Production	Production capacity planning, sourcing strategies, and technical standards controlled by the headquarters functional units, working under a cross-functional manufacturing strategy committee; primary line authority for bulk production facilities managed globally, but line authority for drug formulation and finishing operations managed regionally or nationally
	Marketing and sales	Organization reflected geographic, product, and customer dimensions; headquarters marketing unit established centralized policies for issues with high degrees of interdependence (e.g., pricing); primary line authority rested with regional organizations overseeing activities within national affiliates; company also operated centralized product and customer units to coordinate common strategies across geographic markets

Hoffmann LaRoche		
Drug discovery	Global therapeutic area responsibility allocated across research centers, with local executives in charge of therapeutic areas reporting to local R&D management, to the head of worldwide R&D, and to a senior cross-functional R&D board	
Regulatory approval	Organized around international project teams responsible for individual compounds; international project teams reported to a cross-functional portfolio management board and worked within common international drug development system operating guidelines and policies	
Production	Operations had capacity planning, sourcing strategies, and technical standards coordinated (as opposed to controlled) under a cross-border pharmaceutical technology board; primary line authority for bulk production managed globally, bulk formulation operations managed regionally, and finishing operations managed nationally	
Marketing and sales	Organization sought to coordinate key strategies and product policies under a senior pharmaceutical operations board, but primary line authority remained with the geographically based affiliates; within individual products, international marketing task forces and product teams sought to share information and best practices	

NOTE: R&D = research and development.

activities illustrated how multiple dimensions of a firm's organization were structured. Table 10.2 outlines the 11 activities defined within the pharmaceutical industry.

The research distinguished three activities within drug discovery: the initial discovery of a compound (*DISC*), its development into an initial product (*DPRO*), and the subsequent development of product extensions (*EXT*). Two activities were distinguished for regulatory approval: obtaining initial regulatory approval (*IRA*) and supporting (clinically) local marketing (*LMS*). Three activities were distinguished for production: bulk chemical production (*BC*), bulk formulation production (*BF*), and fill-and-finish activities (F_1). Finally, three activities were distinguished for marketing and sales: development of product- or customer-oriented marketing strategies or programs (*MKTG*) and product sales in major national markets (S_1) and minor markets (S_2).

Organizational Data

Organizational data for the study represented the structures of individual activity-level organizational units within each firm over time, as described in the following table:

	ORGVAR 1	ORGVAR 2	. . .	ORGVAR 19
$ACT_{1,f,t}$	$x_{1,f,t,1}$	$x_{1,f,t,2}$	. . .	$x_{1,f,t,19}$
$ACT_{2,f,t}$	$x_{2,f,t,1}$	$x_{2,f,t,2}$	. . .	$x_{2,f,t,19}$
. . .	. . .	. . .		. . .
$ACT_{a,f,t}$	$x_{a,f,t,1}$	$x_{a,f,t,2}$	. . .	$x_{a,f,t,19}$

where $ACT_{a,f,t}$ is activity a at firm f at time t, $ORGVAR_i$ is the organization variable i, f is the firm (Roche, Lilly), and t is the time of the observation (1980, 1985, 1990, 1994).

Activity structures were characterized through a comprehensive set of organizational variables identified in prior research (see the Appendix). Seven groups of variables were employed, characterizing an activity's resource configuration (i.e., location), orientation (i.e., basis of resource grouping), decision authority, standards and procedures, planning and information systems, culture, and coalition-based (i.e., lateral communication) mechanisms. Further distinctions within variable groups reflected differences in issues addressed and time frames. For example, two variables were used for resource configuration to distinguish between the location of strategic and nonstrategic resources, in line with Bartlett and Ghoshal's (1989) approach. Variables for decision authority and standards

TABLE 10.2
Pharmaceutical Industry Activity Definitions

Unit	Drug Discovery			Regulatory Approval		Production			Marketing and Sales		
	Discover Compounds	Develop Products	Develop Product Extensions	Obtain Initial Regulatory Approval	Support (Clinically) Local Marketing	Produce Bulk Chemicals	Produce Formulation	Produce Final Products	Develop Marketing Programs	Sell Products (First-Tier Markets)	Sell Products (Second-Tier Markets)
	DISC	DPRO	EXT	IRA	LMS	BC	BF	F1	MKTG	S1	S2
Scientifically based	X	X									
Preclinical development	X	X	X	X							
Clinical		X	X	X	X					X	
Manufacturing		X	X	X		X	X	X			
Marketing				X	X				X	X	X
Sales									X	X	X
Regulatory affairs			X						X	X	X

and procedures distinguished strategic, operational, and tactical levels, in line with a distinction made by Lorange, Morton, and Ghoshal (1986). In total, 19 organizational variables were used to provide a detailed characterization of individual activity structures.

The coding of individual variables built on the developmental perspective from IB research on the organizational movement toward globally oriented structures (Kindleberger, 1969; Perlmutter, 1969; Vernon, 1979). Hence, coding of individual variables generally was done on an ordinal scale, with low scores indicating little international involvement (e.g., a strong domestic orientation) and high scores indicating a strong global orientation. Intermediate scores indicated a local (e.g., local market) or regional orientation.

Data Collection, Coding, and Verification

Data were collected in intensive field studies through both semistructured interviews and extensive access to archival documents. The use of data from multiple sources allowed triangulation of findings and subsequent coded data. Interviews lasting about 90 minutes were conducted with more than 125 people at Lilly and with more than 75 people at Roche. Detailed notes were taken, but interviews were not recorded. Interviews at Lilly were conducted in 1989 and 1990, with subsequent interviews in 1993 and 1994, and interviews at Roche were conducted in 1993 and 1994. The president of each company and multiple executives from each function were interviewed, as were staff from multiple geographic affiliates. In addition, multiple interviews were conducted with the senior executives responsible for all major functions.

The researcher coded the organizational data, drawing on interview notes and archival documents. Two exercises verified coding accuracy. For data on Lilly, where extensive case write-ups were prepared, two additional coders were given the variable definitions, coding schemes, and case write-ups; they generated secondary sources for 45% of 1980 and 1994 observations. (The case write-ups were coauthored by the researcher but were extensively reviewed and modified by company officials to ensure accuracy.) The secondary coded values matched exactly those of the researcher for 67% of observations (being ±1 for 89% of observations). At Roche, where case write-ups were not prepared, data for 1980 (which reflected the firm's traditional structure in place for a long period of time) and 1994 were coded by two company executives, both of whom had at least 15 years' experience with the company. Using the activity and variable definitions and coding schemes, they generated secondary sources for 50% of 1980 and 1994 observations. Their coded values matched exactly those of the researcher for 77% of common observations (being ±1 for 97% of common observations).

Data Analysis

Analysis of patterns of organizational adjustments built on techniques suggested by Miller and Friesen (1984). Changes in activity-level structures were analyzed by contrasting the similarity or dissimilarity of activity-level observations over time to quantify the extent and nature of change and to identify patterns of adjustments. Following Miller and Friesen's criteria, similarities and dissimilarities were calculated on the basis of Euclidean distances, defined as

$$d_{ij} = [\Sigma_k(x_{ik} - x_{jk})^2]^{\frac{1}{2}},$$

where d_{ij} is the distance between observations i and j, and x_{ik} is the value for the kth organizational variable for the ith case. Multidimensional scaling (MDS) (for an outline and discussion of the method, see Kruskal & Wish, 1978) was used to analyze the resulting 88 by 88 distance matrix. MDS has the advantage of replacing many ordinal variables with a smaller set of dimensions that have interval metric properties. Hence, MDS was used to reduce the dimensionality of variations while retaining ordinal properties in terms of similarities or dissimilarities across organizational variables. MDS analysis was performed with the STATISTICA (StatSoft, 1995) computer program. Selection of the number of dimensions for analysis followed Kruskal and Wish's (1978) approach of plotting stress values (i.e., eigenvectors in factor analysis) against different numbers of dimensions and selecting where the smooth decrease in stress values levels off to the right.[12] MDS analysis was based on projecting observations in two-dimensional space to identify and analyze patterns of organizational variations within and across the firms. Subsequent analysis interpreted patterns within the MDS scatter diagram, with analysis of organizational change focusing on the movement of individual activities over time.

FINDINGS

This section outlines the results of the analysis of activity-level organizational changes at Lilly and Roche between 1980 and 1994. Figure 10.2 is a two-dimensional MDS scatter diagram of activity-level structures at Lilly and Roche, indicating the observed structures within each firm in 1980 and 1994. The figure supports the distinction between the two firms' traditional organizations, as the ranges of observed structures within both firms in 1980 were tightly concentrated with no overlap across firms. By 1994, the ranges of observed structures had shifted horizontally, with a further significant increase in the dispersion of observed structures and a significant overlap across the firms.

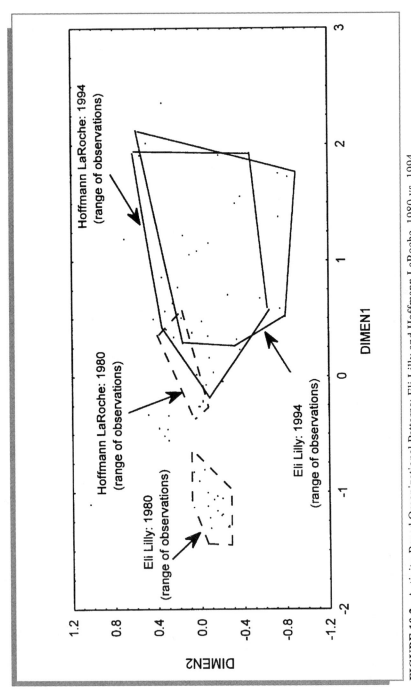

FIGURE 10.2. Activity-Based Organizational Patterns: Eli Lilly and Hoffmann LaRoche, 1980 vs. 1994

NOTE: Figure is a two-dimensional multidimensional scaling scatter diagram.

A measure of the degree of globality, or geographic orientation, of activity-level observations is necessary to analyze patterns of change over time. The horizontal dimension of the MDS scatter diagram is directly correlated with the average (unweighted) coded value across all organizational variables. (Specifically, a regression of the horizontal coordinate from the MDS scatter diagram against the average unweighted value of all 19 organizational variables resulted in an R^2 of .99.) Given that the coding of those variables generally was based on an ordinal scale between domestic and global orientation, with higher values indicating a higher degree of globality, an observation's position along the horizontal dimension represents a measure of the degree of globality of an activity structure.

The extent and timing of adjustments in geographic orientation within each firm are described next. Then, patterns of organizational adjustments within and across activities are analyzed.[13]

Variations in the Extent of Observed Change

To highlight the fundamental nature of change observed at the two firms, changes in globality can be analyzed at two levels: the level of the firm (i.e., average globality across activities) and the level of individual activities. The observed globality levels across activities at each firm during the four observed time periods are plotted in Figure 10.3. They show that all activities at each firm moved to higher levels of global orientation during the study period, but with important differences in the extent of observed change both across firms and within firms across activities. The extent of change observed at Lilly was significantly greater than that observed at Roche, as Lilly's 1980 organization reflected a lower global orientation than that observed at Roche. However, by 1994, both firms had moved to increasingly similar structures in terms of their global orientations across activities.

Important differences also are observed in the extent of change in globality across individual activities. At Lilly, six activities had total change in observed globality higher than the firm average change levels (between 113% and 131% of the firm average) and five activities had total change lower than the firm average (between 60% and 86% of firm average). At Roche, variations in the extent of change across activities were more pronounced. Five activities had total observed change between 116% and 206% of the firm average, and six activities had observed change between 21% and 77% of the firm average. Of the activities with the most pronounced changes, four were common across the two firms: compound discovery, initial regulatory approval, bulk production, and marketing. Similarly, of the activities with the least pronounced changes, four were common across the two firms: local marketing support, final production, sales in major markets, and sales in minor markets.

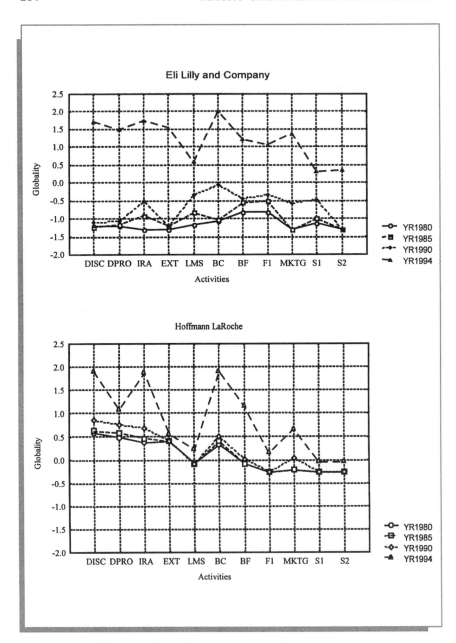

FIGURE 10.3. Activity Globality Levels, 1980 to 1994

NOTE: A total of 88 activity structure observations are plotted, 11 each for Lilly and Roche in 1980, 1985, 1990, and 1994. The ranges of activity observations in 1980 and 1994 indicate patterns of change in structures within the firms.

TABLE 10.3

Euclidean Distances Between Common Activity Structures:
Eli Lilly and Hoffmann LaRoche, 1980 vs. 1994

Activity	1980 Distance	1994 Distance	Distance Change (1980-1994)	Percentage Change From 1980 Distance
Discover compounds (DISC)	7.21	2.83	4.38	61
Develop products (DPRO)	7.07	3.16	3.91	55
Develop product extensions (EXT)	7.00	5.10	1.9	27
Obtain initial regulatory approval (IRA)	6.56	2.00	4.56	70
Support (clinically) local marketing (LMS)	4.47	2.83	1.64	37
Produce bulk chemicals (BC)	5.92	1.41	4.52	76
Produce formulation (BF)	3.61	1.73	1.87	52
Produce final products (F1)	2.65	3.74	−1.10	−42
Develop marketing programs (MKTG)	4.36	3.61	0.75	17
Sell products (first-tier markets) (S1)	3.61	2.24	1.37	38

Comparison of the 1980 and 1994 observations shows growing similarity in observed structures within common activities across firms and growing heterogeneity within firms across activities. In 1980, the structures of the two firms were internally consistent across activities and maximally different across firms. One indication of the growing similarity of common activity structures is based on contrasting changes in the observed distances in the MDS plots in 1980 and 1994. As described earlier, these distances are based on calculating Euclidean distances, reflecting the sum of differences across individual organizational variables comprising each activity's structure. Table 10.3 provides data on observed distances in common activities in 1980 and 1994. In 10 of the 11 activities, there was a decrease in observed distances, suggesting growing similarity within common activities across the firms. There was, however, substantial variation in the extent of convergence across activities, with reductions in observed distances ranging from 17% to 76% of observed 1980 distances. Overall, these findings demonstrate that fundamental change occurred, in line with projections from IB research on the emergence of internally differentiated structures within firms.

Variations in the Patterns of Adjustments Over Time

Earlier, it was described how there were important differences in projections of the characteristics of the process of organizational change in the punctuated equilibrium and incremental change models. In applying these characteristics to observed patterns of change at Lilly and Roche, this subsection analyzes observations on the variations in the rate of change observed within the firms, on the drivers of change observed within the firms, and on the timing of changes across various activities within each firm. Analysis of the rate of observed change is employed to investigate differences in the timing of adjustments across time and to provide insights into the nature of relations between adjustments in any one time period and those periods preceding and following it. Analysis of variations in the drivers of change, reflected in the objective behind adjustments in each period, is employed to investigate both the variations in the drivers of change and the nature of change that cccurs during each individual period. Analysis of the variations in the timing of adjustments across activities is employed to investigate patterns in the direction of change over time.

Important variations in the *rate of change* within the firms are apparent throughout the study period. Figure 10.4 is a plot of the range of observed globality levels within each firm across activities and firm means between 1980 and 1994. Table 10.4 reports the percentage of total change accounted for during each period. The data indicate that the transition at both firms was an accelerating process, with early changes in globality being relatively minor. The 1980-1985 period accounts for 5.75% of the total change in globality at Lilly and 3.43% of that at Roche. The 1985-1990 period accounts for 14.14% of the total change at Lilly and 12.66% of that at Roche. Finally, the 1990-1994 period accounts for 80.11% of the total change at Lilly and 83.90% of that at Roche. The firms' rates of observed change are similar despite differences in initial starting points and in the extent of total change observed. The processes of change within the two firms have similar patterns in terms of accelerating internal adjustment.

In terms of the *drivers of change* during each period, reference to field data provides insights as to the accelerating nature of this process based on changes in the objectives for globalization process within each firm. Over time, the managers of each firm altered how they characterized the objectives of the globalization effort. During the early 1980s, Lilly managers emphasized expanding sales of

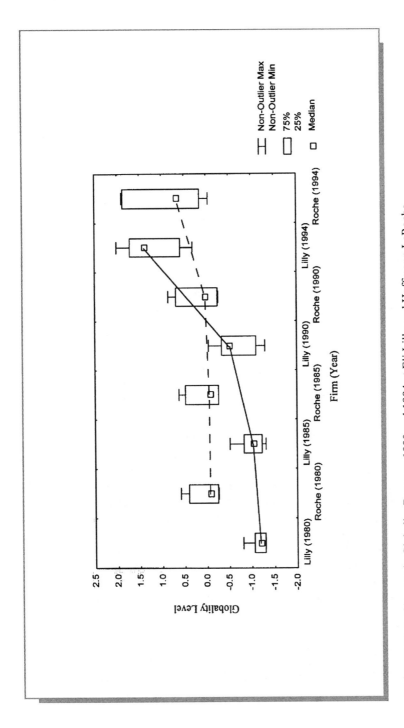

FIGURE 10.4. Changes in Globality Between 1980 and 1994 at Eli Lilly and Hoffmann LaRoche

NOTE: The figure is a plot of firm median globality level and activity globality level ranges over time. Globality levels represent positions on the horizontal dimension of the multidimensional scaling plot in Figure 10.2.

TABLE 10.4

Firm-Level Changes in Globality by Period

	Eli Lilly	*Hoffmann LaRoche*
Firm average globality		
1980	−1.14	0.09
1985	−1.01	0.12
1990	−0.67	0.22
1994	1.22	0.86
Total change in globality	2.36	0.76
Percentage of total change by period		
1980-1985	5.75	3.43
1985-1990	14.14	12.66
1990-1994	80.11	83.90

NOTE: Globality measures are based on the horizontal dimension of the multidimensional scaling scatter diagram in Figure 10.2. Firm average globality is the average across the 11 activities for each firm during each time period.

current products as well as products in development. Given that two thirds of company sales were in the United States, which represented one third of the total world market, international markets were considered important sources of untapped opportunity. During the late 1980s, company managers described the need to minimize duplication of operations to increase worldwide efficiency and enhance the firm's ability to use dispersed operations in meeting global, as opposed to just local, objectives. Finally, during the early 1990s, Lilly's managers characterized globalization as the movement toward a single, integrated worldwide organization to strengthen not only international operations but also domestic operations.

At Roche, before the mid-1980s, most initiatives to alter the firm's traditional worldwide organizational structure involved expanding communication across still autonomous affiliates, often through meetings among staff from around the world. The outcome of those exchanges was characterized as having little impact on ongoing operations. During the late 1980s, Roche's globalization effort was based on a notion of building a "shared organization," a recommendation arising from a 1986 consulting study, to create formal international teams to coordinate and align operations across affiliates. During the early 1990s, after a 1991 consulting study, the direction of the firm's globalization effort shifted toward the global "optimization" of individual functions or operations.

The shifting objectives were reflected in patterns of adjustments across individual activities, with significant variations in the *timing of changes* across activities. Table 10.5 details the percentage of total change observed within each activity over time, and Table 10.6 categorizes activities on the basis of similarities in patterns of adjustments. Four categories can be distinguished. Some activities had higher degrees of change early in the process than did others, essentially *leading* the overall change process. A total of five such activities were observed (four at Lilly and one at Roche), averaging 15.2% of their total change during the initial period, 17.2% during the second period, and 67.6% during the third period. Other activities closely followed average firm-level rates of change. A total of four such activities were observed (two at each firm), averaging 5.5% of their total change during the first period, 14.7% during the second, and 79.8% during the final period. A third category had little change in the initial period followed by accelerating change, essentially *following* the overall change process. A total of four such activities were observed (two at each firm), averaging 0.6% of their total change during the first period, 26.4% during the second period, and 72.8% during the final period. Finally, a fourth category had change concentrated in the final period, representing *late followers* of the overall process. A total of nine such activities were observed (three at Lilly and six at Roche), averaging −0.4% of their total change during the first period, 2.1% during the second period, and 98.3% during the final period.

In terms of identifying overall patterns of organizational change within Lilly and Roche, the findings suggest an initial *focusing* of adjustments within a limited number of activities, then a gradual *acceleration* in both the number of activities affected and the rate of change within individual activities over time. Reference to the changing objectives of the globalization process highlights some factors behind these empirical findings. At Lilly, early adjustments were in downstream or delivery-related activities and were associated with an initial expansion of resources outside a domestic operation. At Roche, which had accomplished such a buildup early in its history, early expansion of resources in downstream activities was not observed. Rather, adjustments in downstream activities were relatively minor and concentrated late in the study period.

The field data provide one further potential explanation for the initial focusing of changes. Managers at both firms emphasized the risks of disrupting ongoing operations within discovery (*DISC*), regulatory approval (*IRA*), bulk chemical production (*BC*), and marketing (*MKTG*), four activities in which adjustments generally were concentrated later in the overall process but also activities that eventually had the highest levels of globality. For initial regulatory approval, managers spoke of a need to meet strict regulatory standards including a need to

TABLE 10.5

Percentages of Total Change in Activity Globality by Period

	Eli Lilly			Hoffmann LaRoche		
Activity	1980-1985	1985-1990	1990-1994	1980-1985	1985-1990	1990-1994
Compound discovery (DISC)	−86.00	4.19	96.67	2.68	17.79	79.54
Initial product development (DPRO)	1.25	3.99	94.67	16.48	29.63	53.89
Develop product extensions (EXT)	3.33	0.01	96.66	−0.49	1.54	98.95
Local (clinical) marketing support (LMS)	19.00	28.53	52.47	−0.66	0.24	100.43
Bulk chemical production (BC)	0.95	32.09	66.96	4.45	6.22	89.33
Bulk formulation production (BF)	12.29	5.62	82.10	−0.05	6.60	93.45
Fill and finish production (F1)	15.59	9.35	75.06	−1.05	0.15	100.90
Product marketing (MKTG)	−0.49	27.52	72.97	0.14	28.09	71.77
Sales in major markets (S1)	7.99	37.88	54.13	−0.38	1.35	99.04
Sales in minor markets (S2)	−0.09	0.03	100.06	−1.51	1.01	100.50
Firm average	5.75	14.14	80.11	3.43	12.66	83.90

TABLE 10.6

Activity-Level Change Patterns at Eli Lilly and Hoffmann LaRoche

Activity Category	Percentage of Total Activity Globality Change During Period			Activities			
				Eli Lilly		Hoffmann LaRoche	
	1980-1985	1985-1990	1990-1994	Activities With Less Than Average Total Change	Activities With Greater Than Average Total Change	Activities With Less Than Average Total Change	Activities With Greater Than Average Total Change
Change leaders	15.2	17.2	67.6	LMS BF F1	IRA	DPRO	**IRA** **DISC** **MKTG**
Average	5.5	14.7	79.8	S1	EXT BC MKTG		
Followers	0.6	26.4	72.8				
Late followers	−0.4	2.1	98.3	S2	DISC DPRO	EXT LMS F1 S1 S2	BF

NOTE: Activities in bold are ones moving toward global operating structures.

maintain tight controls over internal processes. Initial international expansion within that activity, therefore, was used to generate supplemental data, primarily to meet specific local requirements. For compound discovery, managers at both firms spoke of the time and cost of setting up new research facilities and attracting leading scientists. For bulk chemical production, firm managers spoke of the tight regulatory controls over the production process. Finally, for marketing, managers described the traditional success of the activity based on either strong domestic (for Lilly) or local (for Roche) autonomy, the importance of maximizing sales of current products, and the risk of disrupting successful established systems and procedures. For each the activities, managers generally had been reluctant to disrupt ongoing operations that were considered instrumental to both firms' traditional success.

Variations in the Nature of Adjustments Over Time

Analysis of the internal change process revealed patterns of variations in the mix of organizational variables affected at each phase of the change process. Of 1,254 potential changes (19 variables × two firms × 11 activities × three adjustment periods), 322 (25.7%) individual variable adjustments were observed. The 1980-1985 period accounted for 9.9% of the changes, the 1985-1990 period accounted for 22.7%, and the 1990-1995 period accounted for 67.4%. The periods differed in the mix of organizational variables affected by the change process, as shown in Table 10.7.

During the 1980-1985 period, 54% of total observed changes were in variables related to planning and communication systems, with the majority of the changes (8 of the 14 observed changes) being in informal or off-line communication mechanisms. The adjustments generally were associated with the formation of task forces and committees crossing traditional organizational units or supplemental planning systems. In addition, 23% of observed changes during the initial period were in resource configuration, primarily associated with a buildup of international operations in line with the perspective developed in traditional IB research. Fewer adjustments (19%) were made in formal systems (i.e., authority and procedures), where the changes observed were related primarily to decentralization of operating authority and procedures. Of the total changes observed during the 1980-1985 period, the majority (about 64%) were observed in activities categorized as change leaders.

During the 1985-1990 period, 53% of observed changes were in variables related to planning and communication systems. However, the changes were increasingly associated with adjustments to the formal communication and planning systems, reflected in the formalization of ongoing committees, meetings, and other similar mechanisms. At the same time, there was a growing emphasis on changes to authority and procedures, with 31% of observed changes affecting

TABLE 10.7

Observed Changes in Organizational Variables by Period

Period	Resource Configuration (2 Variables)	Resource Grouping (3 Variables)	Authority, Procedures (6 Variables)	Planning, Communication Systems (6 Variables)	Cultural Variables (2 Variables)	Total Observed Changes (19 Variables)
1980-1985	**6**	**4**	**5**	**14**	**3**	**2**
Percentage Period Changes	23.08	15.38	19.23	53.85	11.54	—
Percentage Total Changes	1.86	1.24	1.55	4.35	0.93	9.94
1985-1990	**5**	**5**	**21**	**36**	**6**	**73**
Percentage Period Changes	7.35	7.35	30.88	52.94	8.82	—
Percentage Total Changes	1.55	1.55	6.52	11.18	1.86	22.67
1990-1994	**19**	**16**	**81**	**81**	**20**	**217**
Percentage Period Changes	9.60	8.08	40.91	40.91	10.10	—
Percentage Total Changes	5.90	4.97	25.16	25.16	6.21	67.39

those variables. Initially, adjustments to decision authority and procedures emphasized tactical or operating control systems. During this period, 29% of changes observed during the period were in activities categorized as change leaders, 19% in activities following the firm average changes, 37% in follower activities, and 15% in late follower activities.

During the 1990-1994 period, adjustments were comprehensive in terms of both the number of activities and the number of organizational variables affected by the change process. Specifically, the change process had a significant impact on a wide range of organizational variables, fundamentally altering how each activity was structured and managed. A majority of these changes (80%) involved authority and procedures as well as planning and communication systems, formalizing changes made during earlier periods. Adjustments were made in 52% of all observed organizational variables during this period (67.5% if activities not significantly affected by the overall globalization process are excluded). Those findings highlight the comprehensive nature of the changes that occurred during the 1990-1994 period.

Overall, these patterns suggest that early organizational adjustments primarily affected informal or off-line communication-related variables, with some additional adjustments to resource locations, operating decision authority, and standards and procedures. Adjustments during the second period continued to be concentrated in the communication variables, formalizing previous adjustments, but also affected tactical decision authority and standards and procedures. During the final observation period, fundamental change occurred across all organizational variables. Those findings suggest that at the two firms studied, one element of the accelerating change process was an initial focus on both a search for new organizational alternatives and a gradual expansion of nondomestic resources. Those adjustments can be associated not only with determining direction but also with building resources required for subsequent adjustments.

TOWARD A MODEL OF ACCELERATING CHANGE

In terms of the process of fundamental organizational change observed at Lilly and Roche, the findings of this study identify important differences from both the incremental change and punctuated equilibrium models, as outlined in Figure 10.5.

Globalization at Lilly and Roche was accomplished through an accelerating process of adjustments both at the firm level and within individual activities. The change process involved a high degree of interdependence in adjustments across time periods, reflecting an initially focused but gradually expanding pattern of

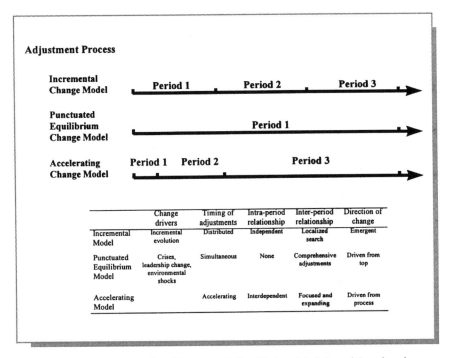

FIGURE 10.5. Incremental and Punctuated Equilibrium Models and Accelerating Change Model

adjustment within activities and across the organization. The initial focusing of adjustments was important both in limiting the impact of the adjustments on ongoing and still highly profitable current operations and in facilitating subsequent adjustments by expanding operations globally. A further difference from prior models is that determination of the direction of change was an integral element of the process and was particularly important given the movement toward previously unknown and complex organizational models. Among activities initially affected by the change process, informal or off-line communication was an important focus of adjustments, with subsequent changes affecting an expanding array of organizational variables. The findings indicate that the change process initially involved maintaining the firm's traditional success by focusing and minimizing initial organizational disruptions while simultaneously expanding new operations and using off-line communication mechanisms to identify and focus subsequent adjustments. Hence, the process involved balancing the competing pressures for change and continuity, long highlighted in research on organizational change, as the organization moves toward initially unknown organizational states.

Although limited by the study's focus on two firms within a single industry, the findings differ from those of prior research on the process of fundamental organizational change as projected in the punctuated equilibrium or incremental change models. For example, Romanelli and Tushman (1994) posited that organizations overwhelmingly accomplish fundamental transformations within a 2-year period (with a maximum range of 4.67 years), finding no evidence to support arguments that small changes over time accomplish fundamental organizational transformation. By focusing on the level of the activity and developing a comprehensive perspective on organizational structure, the research reported here identified important patterns of adjustments that resulted in fundamental transformations over longer periods of time. Research examining only the final period studied (1990-1994), representing a 4-year span and thus within the time projected by punctuated equilibrium models, would capture about 80% of the total changes in the two organizations. However, the findings suggest that the final acceleration of adjustments across the organization was related directly to earlier initiatives that made subsequent adjustments possible and provided direction for them. One factor potentially influencing the variation in the rate of change was the relative success of both organizations throughout the period studied. Whereas the punctuated equilibrium model posits change in response to organizational shocks, the study found change prior to the emergence of such organizational shocks, in response to gradually increasing competitive pressures over time.

It should be noted that one important limitation of this research is that observations are at 5-year intervals; thus, punctuated equilibrium-type change could well have occurred between observations. This study cannot eliminate that possibility. However, one element of the punctuated equilibrium model also is the movement between equilibrium states, where relative stability enables organizations to emphasize the efficiency of current operations. This study observed change continuing, and in fact escalating, across time periods. Thus, even if punctuated equilibrium-type change occurred among observations in this study, there are further issues that this model neglects within the context of dynamic environments and change processes associated with the movement toward previously unknown organizational models. One such change process investigated in this study involved firm responses to globalization and the introduction of new organizational models.

The findings also differ from those obtained with incremental models characterizing fundamental transformations as emerging (Mintzberg, 1979) from independent localized initiatives. Although both models reflect a process of path-dependent adjustments across an organization, the study findings suggest a process of accelerating and drastic organizational adjustments as opposed to gradual and incremental adjustments distributed over time as projected in traditional incremental change models. Hence, in the observed change process, adjustments were focused within a limited period of time rather than distributed over time as projected in the incremental change model.

Overall, whereas the punctuated equilibrium and incremental models of change emphasize response to pressures and risks associated with the need for either change or continuity, the observed change process suggests balancing of these pressures and risks over time. Specifically, the pressures for change in the observed process were sequential in their impact on the organization, resulting in focused and expanding patterns of adjustment over time. At the same time, the pressures for continuity within the organization fostered path-dependent adjustments that resulted in an expanding opportunity set within the organization over time.

The process of accelerating fundamental change, with its implications for the role of managers in guiding and directing the process, is likely to be predominant in dynamic environments. Firms that anticipate and adjust to external challenges rather than waiting for organizational crises to occur or randomly initiating localized initiatives, and that maintain internal stability to the extent possible, can simultaneously manage the conflicting pressures for change and continuity. Such firms would have the advantage of anticipating and thus avoiding competitive failures while also minimizing organizational disruptions through incremental but directed adjustments over time.

These findings suggest the need to consider a process of accelerating fundamental organizational change, particularly in dynamic environments where the ultimate direction of change might not be known at the outset. One important element of this process would be the important role of management and control systems in the change process. Whereas control systems have been described as *constraining* the organization to enhance efficiency and as promoting organizational inertia by limiting how organizations perceive their environments, what alternatives are considered, what decisions are made, and what actions are taken (Nelson & Winter, 1982), the findings highlight the need to investigate the role of management in facilitating and directing the change process. That insight is in line with research highlighting the role of control systems in promoting change by forcing organizations to question basic norms and assumptions and making visible new possibilities for organizational action (Argyris & Schon, 1978; Hopwood, 1974; Lorange et al., 1986). The study observed a process of adjustments based on initially altering off-line or informal communication variables, then altering formal communication and planning variables, and finally formalizing change across the organization. By emphasizing these patterns of adjustments across organizational variables, the findings suggest that adjustments in control systems can be instrumental in organizational learning by (a) providing new frames of reference for organizational action, (b) gradually altering the responsibilities of various units, (c) altering linkages to the firm's environment, and (d) helping to overcome inertial or administrative impediments to change.

Initial informal network building and focused organizational adjustments, followed by rapid and simultaneous organizational change, are generally in line with the perspective of strategic change developed by Bower (1970), Burgelman (1983, 1991), and Burgelman and Grove (1996). That research has emphasized the role of middle managers, with superior access to information, in shaping problem definition and defining the context for strategic and organizational change. Burgelman and Grove (1996) further suggested that growing divergence between traditional strategic intent and ongoing strategic action causes strategic dissonance in the organization. In the change process observed here, growing dissonance could be an important factor behind the rapid expansion late in the overall change process of organizational adjustments made possible by initial focused adjustments that both developed strategic and organizational alternatives (through informal networks) and put in place new operations and resources.

TOWARD A PROCESS MODEL
OF GLOBALIZATION

The study findings also have important potential implications for research on firm globalization. In general, the findings support projections of the movement within MNCs toward more globally oriented strategies and organizations including the emergence of internal network-based structures (Bartlett and Ghoshal, 1989, 1990, 1994; Hedlund, 1986, 1994; Perlmutter, 1969). They also suggest a convergence across firms in degree of globality at both the firm and activity levels but indicate growing divergence within firms in degree of globality across activities. The findings support prior results indicating the movement toward a hybrid mix of organizational models within firms. The perspective developed here supports an integrated system view of MNCs as firms made up of integrated networks pursuing a widening array of advantages based on coordination of flows within and across a firm's worldwide network of operations (Kogut, 1984). That perspective emphasizes both the firm's idiosyncratic bundles of resources, or its capacity to access dispersed and location-embedded resources, and its organizational capacity to manage and integrate those resources effectively to develop competitive advantage within and across national markets. A key finding is that organizational variations occur at the level of the activity rather than at the level of the firm or geographic affiliate as projected in previous research (Bartlett & Ghoshal, 1986; Gupta & Govindarajan, 1991).

Given that only two firms and one industry were represented in the study, no claim can be made about the generalizability of the findings in terms of the frequency of accelerating change as opposed to punctuated or incremental change. A natural extension of the study would be to replicate it with other organizations, including some in other industries, or to contrast firms within the same industry that had the same starting organizational structure. In addition, research could examine how firms respond to pressures other than globalization. However, despite its limitations, the study is one of the first empirical and longitudinal studies of fundamental organizational change within and across organizations. The observation of organizational change as an accelerating process is an important potential perspective within the challenges of fundamental change within firms, and the findings provide evidence of the characteristics of the adjustment process associated with firm globalization.

Appendix

Organizational Variables and Coding

Building on prior research on MNCs, the study distinguished seven dimensions of an MNC's operations and 19 organizational variables for coordinating and controlling worldwide operations. One dimension was a firm's *resource configuration* or the location of its resources and operations, highlighted by several prior studies (Bartlett and Ghoshal, 1989; Hedlund, 1986; Kogut, 1984; Porter, 1986). Per Bartlett and Ghoshal (1989), a distinction was made between the structuring of primary strategic resources and that of supporting resources. A second dimension was *organizational orientation* associated with the grouping of activities (Simon, 1976) within distinctive units, a focus of a long stream of research on MNCs (e.g., Davidson & Haspeslagh, 1982; Stopford & Wells, 1972). Specifically, data characterized the presence and role of organizational units representing functional, product, and other (e.g., customer) elements of a firm's operations, as prior research has suggested that organizational units can have multiple roles (e.g., weak dotted line reporting, solid line reporting) and that MNCs are moving toward having multiple units simultaneously involved in various aspects of operations.

A third dimension was the locus of *decision-making authority* (Lawrence & Lorsch, 1967; Simon, 1976) as an important component of an MNC's formal control mechanisms (Brooke & Remmers, 1970). The study distinguished the location and orientation of decision-making authority in terms of primary or core strategic decision making (representing long-term strategic directions for each activity), short-term or tactical strategic decisions, and operating or implementation decision-making authority. A fourth dimension was standards *and procedures,* in line with research emphasizing standardized routines, procedures, or rules as important organizational variables (Lawrence & Lorsch, 1967; Nelson & Winter, 1982; Thompson, 1967). In literature on MNCs, such research has been associated with discussions on the extent of formalization. Specific variables distinguished primary or core strategic policies and standards (e.g., core product policies, investment policies), short-term or tactical strategic policies and standards, and operating policies and standards. The fifth organizational dimension was *planning and information systems* that plan, guide, and measure activities (Galbraith & Kazanjian, 1986; March & Simon, 1958; Thompson, 1967). Variables distinguished formal and informal or supplemental planning systems, which have been highlighted in literature on organizational change as important mechanisms in generating strategic alternatives outside the current organizational focus.

Finally, the sixth and seventh dimensions were less formal organizational mechanisms, lateral or *coalition-based integration mechanisms* and *firm culture*. Much research on MNC organizations has emphasized the role of supplemental communication mechanisms, including task forces, meetings, and committees crossing organizational lines, a topic also addressed by Lawrence and Lorsch (1967), Galbraith and Kazanjian (1986), and others. The research demonstrated the presence and status of three such mechanisms: temporary coalitions (e.g., task forces, meetings), regular and ongoing coalitions, and senior management cross-functional committees (overseeing activities). Finally, several researchers (Baliga & Jaeger, 1984; Johnson & Ouchi, 1974) also have emphasized firm culture as a control mechanism. Specific cultural control mechanisms include the use of expatriates, frequent visits, management transfer policies, and a strong socialization process as well as a company's style, ways of doing things, or values (Mintzberg, 1983; Selznick, 1957; Simon, 1976). The study incorporated two variables on cultural controls, one reflecting the general mind-set of management and the other reflecting the national origin of senior managers overseeing an activity.

The organizational variables and coding procedures are outlined in Table 10.A1.

NOTES

1. For example, one activity distinguished in the pharmaceutical industry is drug discovery, a process involving several functions with a goal of identifying new high-potential compounds.

2. Examples of activity definition in the field of management accounting include "a unit of work, or task, with a specific goal" (Atkinson et al., 1995, p. 607) and "a basic unit of work performed within an organization. It can also be defined as an aggregation of actions within an organization useful to managers for purposes of planning, controlling, and decision making" (Hansen & Mowen, 1995, p. 979).

3. Interdependence can be associated with environments in which significant differences are present across national markets in terms of resource endowments, market demand, and competitive characteristics (Kogut, 1993; Porter, 1990) but where competition within national markets is highly sensitive or vulnerable to variations or economic disturbances in other national markets. For firms competing within such environments, opportunities from operating globally include building efficiency and scale, accessing specialized resources, enhancing innovation through operation across different markets, and achieving flexibility to respond to multiple risks (e.g., exchange rates, differences in growth rates).

TABLE 10.A1
Organizational Variables and Coding

Dimension	Variable	Definition	Value	Interpretation
Resource configuration	Strategic resources	Location of strategic resources for performing an activity; strategic resources are ones that primarily influence the activity outcome	1	Resources exclusively concentrated within firm domestic market and oriented toward domestic market requirements
			2	Resources primarily concentrated within domestic market, with overseas resources oriented toward domestic market requirements
	Nonstrategic resources	Location of nonstrategic resources for performing an activity; nonstrategic resources are ones that support an activity but do not significantly and directly influence the activity outcome	3	Resources decentralized within local markets and oriented toward local market requirements
			4	Resources dispersed, centralized by region and oriented toward regional requirements
			5	Resources dispersed, centralized globally and oriented toward global market requirements
Organizational orientation	Functionally oriented units	Nature of functionally oriented organization units (e.g., grouping of resources) for performing activity	0	No organizational units (i.e., grouping of resources) to reflect the specified orientation
			1	Specified units present but informal and supplemental to primary activity organization (e.g., weak dotted-line reporting relations)

	Product-oriented units	Nature of product-oriented organization units (e.g., grouping of resources) for performing activity	2	Specified units present as formal units but supplemental to primary activity organization (e.g., strong dotted-line reporting relationships)
	Other units (e.g., customers)	Nature of other-oriented organization units (e.g., grouping of resources) for performing activity	3	Specified organization present and fully integrated in primary activity management (e.g., solid-line reporting relationships)
Decision authority	Core strategic decision authority	Location and orientation of decision authority for core activity strategies; core strategies reflect primary policies and typically affect what activities will be performed 3 to 5 years forward	1	Centralized at domestically oriented headquarters; decisions typically reflect domestic market factors
			2	Decentralized at geographically focused affiliates; decisions typically reflect local market factors
			3	Centralized at regionally focused headquarters; decisions typically reflect regional market factors
	Tactical strategic decision authority	Location and orientation of decision authority for tactical activity strategies; tactical strategies reflect short-term policies and typically affect what activities will be performed 1 to 3 years forward	4	Centralized at globally focused headquarters; decisions typically reflect global market factors
	Operating decision authority	Location and orientation of decision authority for implementing strategies within defined guidelines; tactical strategies reflect how activities are performed		

(Continued)

Table 10.A1 Continued

Dimension	Variable	Definition	Variable Coding		
				Value	Interpretation
Standards and procedures	Policies, standards (strategic)	Orientation of standardized routines, procedures, and rules that affect core strategic decisions		1	Centralized and primarily reflecting firm domestic market factors
				2	Decentralized and reflecting local market factors
				3	Centralized and reflecting regional market factors
				4	Centralized and reflecting global market factors
	Policies, standards (tactical)	Orientation of standardized routines, procedures, and rules that affect tactical strategic decisions			
	Policies, standards (operating)	Orientation of standardized routines, procedures, and rules that affect operating decisions			
Planning and information systems	Formal planning systems	Orientation of primary systems used to plan, guide, and measure activities		1	Centralized and primarily reflecting firm domestic market factors
				2	Decentralized and reflecting local market factors
	Supplemental planning systems	Presence and orientation of any supplemental systems to plan, guide, or measure activities		3	Centralized and reflecting regional market factors
	Information systems	Orientation of primary systems used to measure and evaluate activities		4	Centralized and reflecting global market factors

Coalition integration mechanisms	Temporary coalitions	Presence and nature of temporary task forces and meetings among staff from across units	0	Mechanisms not extensively used for specified activity
			1	Mechanisms extensively and informally used for specified activity
	Regular coalitions	Presence and nature of regular meetings and other forums among staff from across units	2	Mechanisms extensively and formally used for specified activity
	Senior executive committees	Presence of senior executive committees to oversee and manage an activity		
Firm culture	Mind-set	General orientation of company style, ways of doing things, values, or common practices	1	Primarily reflecting firm domestic practices and style
			2	Significant variations in style and practices across local markets
			3	Significant variations in style and practices across regional markets
			4	Centralized and reflecting common practices and styles incorporating worldwide practices and styles
	Senior executives	National origin of senior executives overseeing specified activity	1	Home country executives hold all senior posts
			2	Locally based executives hold key local posts
			3	Regionally based executives hold local posts
			4	Key senior executive positions held by executives from across worldwide operations

4. A frequently used framework for investigating these conflicting pressures is the global integration-national responsiveness framework (or IR grid) developed by Prahalad (1976) and subsequently expanded by others (Bartlett, 1986; Bartlett & Ghoshal, 1989; Doz, Bartlett, & Prahalad, 1981; Prahalad & Doz, 1987).

5. Ghoshal and Westney (1993) summarized key elements of projected internal organizational complexity as reflecting the simultaneous influence of the global dispersion of resources, high levels of interdependence across and tight coupling of subunits, the need for cross-unit learning, and structural flexibility. Prahalad and Doz (1993) emphasized that organizational challenges facing MNCs reflect the inherent multidimensionality of their operations, which span multiple national *markets* often providing a mix of *products* developed and produced through undertaking a number of *functional* operations.

6. Long streams of research in strategy (Mintzberg, 1979; Porter, 1980, 1985; Quinn, 1980) and organization theory (Pfeffer & Salancik, 1978; for a review of open systems perspectives, see also Scott, 1987) have emphasized the importance of a firm's fit with its external environment. Research emphasizing efficient strategies builds on the concepts of organizational inertia (Hannan & Freeman, 1989), institutionalization (Selznick, 1957), and strategic continuity (Miller & Friesen, 1980, 1984; Mintzberg, 1979; Pettigrew, 1985; Starbuck, Greve, & Herberg, 1978).

7. Support for punctuated equilibrium models has come from several directions. Miller and Friesen (1984) argued that if change were piecemeal and disjointed, then cross-sectional research would observe organizations in a large number of states or configurations. Further support has been based on firm-level case histories (Tushman, Newman, & Romanelli, 1986).

8. Some writers have emphasized the role of management in focusing and directing changes across organizations over time, positing the use of temporary or intermediate transition stages between equilibrium states (Beckhard & Harris, 1987; Lorange, Morton, & Ghoshal, 1986; Simons, 1995). However, little comprehensive empirical evidence supports a managed process of fundamental organizational change.

9. In general, the ethnocentric MNC model involves a strong domestic orientation, with the majority of important operations located within a firm's home market. In addition, the domestic headquarters exercises strong management control over operations outside its home market. The polycentric MNC model involves a strong host market orientation, with the firm operating as a network of largely autonomous national affiliates. Important operations generally are duplicated within major national markets, with national management having a high degree of autonomy and control. Primary controls from the domestic headquarters are through financial controls.

10. For examples of activity definition in the field of management accounting, see Note 1.

11. Discovery involves chemical, biological, and pharmacological activities to identify and synthesize new compounds for the treatment of various diseases. Ph.D. scientists and technicians work in many laboratories on specific and highly focused scientific issues. Regulatory approval is accomplished through preclinical and clinical testing activities investigating the safety and efficacy of new compounds and preparation of required new drug applications for those compounds. Production of pharmaceutical prod-

ucts involves a series of stages including the large-scale or bulk production of active ingredients, formulating the drugs, filling them into various delivery dosage forms, and packaging them for actual sale. Marketing and sales involve the development of marketing and promotion strategies as well as detailing and selling of products to doctors and other decision makers.

12. Stress values at various dimensions were as follows: one dimension, 11.5; two dimensions, 2.5; three dimensions, 1.1; four dimensions, 1.0.

13. The analysis reported here focuses on changes along the horizontal dimension, which are related to the geographic orientation of observed structures. Variations along the vertical dimension (not addressed here) are related to differences in the operating orientation in terms of functional, product, process, or other orientation.

REFERENCES

Argyris, C., & Schon, D. A. (1978). *Organizational learning: A theory of action perspective.* Reading, MA: Addison-Wesley.

Atkinson, A. A., Banker, R. D., Kaplan, R. S., & Young, S. M. (1995). *Management accounting.* Englewood Cliffs, NJ: Prentice Hall.

Baliga, B. R., & Jaeger, A. M. (1984). Multinational corporations: Control systems and delegation issues. *Journal of International Business Studies, 15*(2), 25-40.

Bartlett, C. A. (1986). Building and managing the transnational: The new organizational challenge. In M. E. Porter (Ed.), *Competition in global industries.* Boston: Harvard Business School Press.

Bartlett, C. A., & Ghoshal, S. (1986). Tap your subsidiaries for global reach. *Harvard Business Review, 64*(6), 87-94.

Bartlett, C. A., & Ghoshal, S. (1989). *Managing across borders: The transnational solution.* Boston: Harvard Business School Press.

Bartlett, C. A., & Ghoshal, S. (1990). The multinational corporation as an interorganizational network. *Academy of Management Review, 15,* 603-625.

Bartlett, C. A., & Ghoshal, S. (1994). Linking organizational context and managerial action: The dimensions of quality of management. *Strategic Management Journal, 15,* 91-112.

Beckhard, R., & Harris, R. T. (1987). *Organizational transitions: Managing complex change.* Reading, MA: Addison-Wesley.

Bower, J. L. (1970). *Managing the resource allocation process.* Boston: Harvard Business School Press.

Brooke, M. Z., & Remmers, H. L. (1970). *The strategy of multinational enterprise.* London: Longman.

Burgelman, R. A. (1983). A process model of internal corporate venturing in the diversified major firm. *Administrative Science Quarterly, 28,* 223-244.

Burgelman, R. A. (1991). Intraorganizational ecology of strategy making and organizational adaptation: Theory and field research. *Organizational Science, 2,* 239-262.

Burgelman, R. A., & Grove, A. S. (1996). Strategic dissonance. *California Management Review, 38*(2), 8-28.

Chandler, A. D., Jr. (1962). *Strategy and structure.* Cambridge, MA: MIT Press.

Cyert, R. M., & March, J. G. (1963). *A behavioral theory of the firm.* Englewood Cliffs, NJ: Prentice Hall.

Davidson, W. H., & Haspeslagh, P. (1982). Shaping a global product organization. *Harvard Business Review, 60*(4), 125-132.

Doz, Y., Bartlett, C. A., & Prahalad, C. K. (1981). Global competitive pressures and host country demands: Managing tensions in MNCs. *California Management Review, 23*(3), 63-74.

Egelhoff, W. G. (1982). Strategy and structure in multinational corporations: An information processing approach. *Administrative Science Quarterly, 27,* 435-458.

Franko, L. G. (1976). *The European multinationals: A renewed challenge to American and British big business.* Stamford, CT: Greylock.

Galbraith, J. R., & Kazanjian, R. K. (1986). *Strategy implementation: Structure, systems, and process.* St. Paul, MN: West.

Gersick, C. J. G. (1991). Revolutionary change theories: A multilevel exploration of the punctuated equilibrium paradigm. *Academy of Management Review, 16,* 10-36.

Ghoshal, S. (1987). Global strategy: An organizing framework. *Strategic Management Journal, 8,* 425-440.

Ghoshal, S., & Westney, D. E. (Eds.). (1993). *Organizational theory and the multinational corporation.* New York: St. Martin's.

Gupta, A. K., & Govindarajan, V. (1991). Knowledge flows and the structure of control within multinational corporations. *Academy of Management Review, 16,* 768-792.

Hannan, M. T., & Freeman, J. H. (1984). Structural inertia and organizational change. *American Sociological Review, 49,* 149-164.

Hannan, M. T., & Freeman, J. H. (1989). *Organizational ecology.* Cambridge, MA: Harvard University Press.

Hansen, D. R., & Mowen, M. M. (1995). *Cost management.* Cincinnati, OH: South-Western.

Haveman, H. A. (1992). Between a rock and a hard place: Organizational change and performance under conditions of fundamental environmental transformation. *Administrative Science Quarterly, 37,* 48-75.

Hedlund, G. (1981). Autonomy of subsidiaries and formalization of headquarters-subsidiary relations in Swedish MNCs. In L. Otterbeck (Ed.), *The management of headquarters-subsidiary relations in multinational corporations* (pp. 27-78). Hampshire, UK: Gower.

Hedlund, G. (1986). The hypermodern MNC: A heterarchy? *Human Resource Management, 25*(1), 9-35.

Hedlund, G. (1994). A model of knowledge management and the N-form corporation. *Strategic Management Journal, 15,* 73-90.

Hopwood, A. (1974). *Accounting and human behavior.* London: Haymarket.

Johnson, R. T., & Ouchi, W. G. (1974). Made in America (under Japanese management). *Harvard Business Review, 52*(5), 61-69.

Kindleberger, C. P. (1969). *American business abroad: Six lectures on direct investment.* New Haven, CT: Yale University Press.

Kobrin, S. J. (1991). An empirical analysis of the determinants of global integration. *Strategic Management Journal, 12,* 17-31.

Kogut, B. (1984). Normative observations on the international value-added chain and strategic groups. *Journal of International Business Studies, 15*(2), 151-168.

Kogut, B. (1989). A note on global strategies. *Strategic Management Journal, 10,* 383-389.

Kogut, B. (1993). *Country competitiveness: Technology and the organizing of work.* New York: Oxford University Press.

Kruskal, J. B., & Wish, M. (1978). *Multidimensional scaling.* Beverly Hills, CA: Sage.

Lawrence, P. R., & Lorsch, J. W. (1967). *Organization and environment.* Boston: Harvard Business School Press.

Lorange, P., Morton, M. F. S., & Ghoshal, S. (1986). *Strategic control systems.* St. Paul, MN: West.

Malnight, T. W. (1995). Globalization of an ethnocentric firm: An evolutionary perspective. *Strategic Management Journal, 16,* 119-142.

Malnight, T. W. (1996). The transition from decentralized to network-based MNC structures: An evolutionary perspective. *Journal of International Business Studies, 27*(1), 43-66.

March, J. G. (1991). Exploration and exploitation in organizational learning. *Organizational Science, 2,* 71-87.

March, J. G., & Simon, H. A. (1958). *Organizations.* New York: John Wiley.

Meyer, J. W., & Scott, W. R. (Eds.). (1983). *Organizational environments: Ritual and rationality.* Beverly Hills, CA: Sage.

Miller, D., & Friesen, P. H. (1980). Momentum and revolution in organizational adaptation. *Academy of Management Journal, 22,* 591-614.

Miller, D., & Friesen, P. H. (1984). *Organizations: A quantum view.* Englewood Cliffs, NJ: Prentice Hall.

Mintzberg, H. (1979). *The structuring of organizations.* Englewood Cliffs, NJ: Prentice Hall.

Mintzberg, H. (1983). *Power in and around organizations.* Englewood Cliffs, NJ: Prentice Hall.

Negandhi, A. R., & Baliga, B. R. (1981). *Tables are turning: German and Japanese multinational companies in the United States.* Cambridge, MA: Oelgeschlager, Gun, & Hain.

Nelson, R. R., & Winter, S. G. (1982). *An evolutionary theory of economic change.* Cambridge, MA: Belknap/Harvard University Press.

Ohmae, K. (1985). *Triad power.* New York: Free Press.

Perlmutter, H. V. (1969, January-February). The tortuous evolution of the multinational corporation. *Columbia Journal of World Business,* pp. 9-18.

Pettigrew, A. M. (1985). *The awakening giant: Continuity and change at ICI.* Oxford, UK: Basil Blackwell.

Pfeffer, J., & Salancik, G. R. (1978). *The external control of organizations.* New York: Harper & Row.

Porter, M. E. (1980). *Competitive strategy: Techniques for analyzing industries and competitors.* New York: Free Press.

Porter, M. E. (1985). *Competitive advantage.* New York: Free Press.

Porter, M. E. (1986). Competition in global industries: A conceptual framework. In M. E. Porter (Ed.), *Competition in global industries.* Boston: Harvard Business School Press.

Porter, M. E. (1990). *The competitive advantage of nations.* New York: Free Press.

Prahalad, C. K. (1976). *The strategic process in a multinational corporation.* Unpublished doctoral dissertation, Harvard Business School.

Prahalad, C. K., & Doz, Y. L. (1987). *The multinational mission: Balancing local demands and global vision.* New York: Free Press.

Prahalad, C. K., & Doz, Y. L. (1993). Managing DMNCs: A search for a new paradigm. In S. Ghoshal & D. E. Westney (Eds.), *Organizational theory and the multinational corporation.* New York: St. Martin's.

Quinn, J. B. (1980). *Strategies for change: Logical incrementalism.* Homewood, IL: Irwin.

Romanelli, E., & Tushman, M. L. (1994). Organizational transformation as punctuated equilibrium: An empirical test. *Academy of Management Journal, 37,* 1141-1166.

Schumpeter, J. A. (1934). *The theory of economic development.* Cambridge, MA: Harvard University Press.

Scott, W. R. (1987). *Organizations: Rational, natural, and open systems* (3rd ed.). Englewood Cliffs, NJ: Prentice Hall.

Selznick, P. (1957). *Leadership in administration.* New York: Harper & Row.

Simon, H. A. (1976). *Administrative behavior.* New York: Free Press.

Simons, R. (1995). Control in the age of empowerment. *Harvard Business Review, 73*(2), 80-88.

Singh, J. V., House, R. J., & Tucker, D. J. (1986). Organizational change and organizational mortality. *Administrative Science Quarterly, 31,* 587-611.

Starbuck, W. H., Greve, A., & Herberg, B. L. T. (1978). Responding to crisis. *Journal of Business Administration, 9*(2), 111-137.

StatSoft. (1995). *Statistica for Windows* [computer program manual]. Tulsa, OK: Author.

Stopford, J. M., & Wells, L. T. (1972). *Managing the multinational enterprise.* New York: Basic Books.

Thompson, J. D. (1967). *Organizations in action.* New York: McGraw-Hill.

Tushman, M. L., Newman, W. H., & Romanelli, E. (1986). Convergence and upheaval: Managing the unsteady pace of organizational evolution. *California Management Review, 28*(1), 29-44.

Tushman, M. L., & Romanelli, E. (1985). Organizational evolution: A metamorphosis model of convergence and reorientation. In L. L. Cummings & B. M. Staw (Eds.), *Research in organizational behavior* (Vol. 14, pp. 171-222). Greenwich, CT: JAI.

Vernon, R. (1979). The product cycle hypothesis in a new international environment. *Oxford Bulletin of Economics and Statistics, 4,* 255-267.

Winter, S. G. (1994). Organizing for continuous improvement: Evolutionary theory meets the quality revolution. In J. A. C. Baum & J. V. Singh (Eds.), *Evolutionary dynamics of organizations.* Oxford, UK: Oxford University Press.

Woodward, J. (1958). *Technology and organization.* London: Her Majesty's Printing Office.

Yoshino, M. Y. (1976). *Japan's multinational enterprises.* Cambridge, MA: Harvard University Press.

Zucker, L. G. (Ed.). (1988). *Institutional patterns and organizations: Culture and environment.* Cambridge, MA: Ballinger.

chapter 11

Strategic Colonialism in Unfamiliar Cultures

Overcoming Extreme Forms of Causal Ambiguity Internationally

ELAINE MOSAKOWSKI

How do managers formulate strategy when they do not understand which factors contribute to their firms' success? Although recent strategic management research emphasizes firm experimentation under extreme forms of uncertainty (Bourgeois & Eisenhardt, 1988; Burgelman, 1990; Eisenhardt, 1989; Eisenhardt & Brown, 1998, 1999; Eisenhardt & Tabrizi, 1995; Galunic & Eisenhardt, 1996; Hamel & Prahalad, 1989, 1993, 1994; Hedlund, 1994; Madsen & McKelvey, 1996; Miyazaki, 1994; Mosakowski, 1997; Prahalad & Hamel, 1990; Stopford & Baden-Fuller, 1994), experimentation has its limits. A manager might never be able to understand very complex, embedded, and subtle relationships.

This chapter discusses a manager's strategic possibilities when establishing an operation in a foreign culture. The difficulty of understanding cultures has been widely discussed. Hymer (1976) suggested that developing cultural under-

AUTHOR'S NOTE: I would like to thank the following: Myrdene Anderson, Chris Earley, Kent Miller, John Prescott, Harbir Singh, Jose de la Torre, Srilata Zaheer, and two anonymous reviewers from the Academy of Management 1999 meetings for comments on this paper; the Center for International Business Education Research (CIBER) at UCLA for funding; and Sport for teaching me a new game.

standing is a significant cost of doing business abroad. Although some suggest that foreign managers can acquire cultural knowledge only through cultural immersion and experience (Johanson & Vahlne, 1977), much attention has been directed at shortcuts to cultural learning. Hiring local managers, tapping into local networks, and partnering with local firms (Barkema, Bell, & Pennings, 1996; Kogut & Singh, 1988) are recommended. Yet, in an article that argued for an end to "corporate imperialism," where multinational corporations (MNCs) export their business models around the world, Prahalad and Lieberthal (1998) highlighted the difficulty of overcoming cultural barriers. With regard to hiring local managers, they pointed out that "MNCs frequently lack the cultural understanding to get the mix of expatriate and local leaders right" (p. 75). They suggested problems that arise in incorporating local managers' input into strategic decisions including the diminished voice of local managers at corporate headquarters and the limited firm experience of local managers. Prahalad and Lieberthal also pointed out that joint venturing with local partners to overcome cultural barriers often creates tensions that divert management attention away from learning about the local market, and many local partners do not have adequate market knowledge (p. 76).

This chapter offers a different approach to an MNC entering an unfamiliar culture. I assume that foreign operation managers might not be able to learn the culture to any sophisticated degree, unlearn their own culture (Vaill, 1989), or adopt any of the shortcuts to cultural learning discussed earlier. Therefore, operating in a foreign culture often means making decisions under causal ambiguity, where managers cannot specify the causal link between strategic choices and their firms' performance. This does not necessarily suggest, however, that managerial actions must be random. Instead, under irreducible causal ambiguity, a manager in a foreign culture might be able to change the rules of the game for competition and/or cooperation within an industry. Simply put, if you can't join them, you might want to change them.

This chapter argues that, under certain circumstances, firms expanding abroad should engage in strategic colonialism, where they export their rules for competitive or cooperative interaction from established markets.[1] The chapter's goal is to describe how firms can purposefully use unfamiliarity with a cultural context to their strategic advantage. This is a form of ethnocentrism (Perlmutter, 1969), where firms rely on their domestic strategy abroad. Strategic colonialism is proposed as a way for firms to exploit cultural unfamiliarity for competitive advantage, and I emphasize a foreign entrant's intention to alter local firms' behavior rather than adapt to local rules of the game.

The next section introduces causal ambiguity and describes why managers in culturally unfamiliar countries experience it. This argument is based on the idea that strategy formulation may differ across cultures, everything else being equal, in ways that are difficult to understand. The subsequent section discusses how a manager creates a new causal model. Finally, I discuss the implications of strategic colonialism for international management and strategic management research.

CULTURAL UNFAMILIARITY AND CAUSAL AMBIGUITY

Basic Ideas

This subsection discusses strategic choices available to managers charged with entering a culturally unfamiliar country and who, in the process, experience an overwhelming feeling of disorientation that parallels "culture shock."

My theoretical approach focuses on the challenge of managing an operation without a causal model to tie managerial choices to firm performance. One metaphor is that of an infant unable to recognize what he needs to survive on his own. Another is that of an entrepreneurial firm unable to recognize important financing or marketing opportunities that determine its ultimate success. A similar situation might exist with a newly established foreign operation. An unfamiliar cultural context might serve as a great source of confusion about which factors contribute to the foreign operation's success or failure.

I distinguish among several types of factors that influence firm performance. To discuss how managers experience causal ambiguity, my earlier article (Mosakowski, 1997) draws on distinctions proposed by Winter (1987). Winter (1987) distinguished among control, state, and environmental variables. He defined state variables as aspects of the system not subject to choice over a short time span but rather subject to managerial influence over the long run, control variables as aspects of a system subject to change over a short time span, and environmental variables as not subject to managerial influence over any reasonable time span (Nelson & Winter, 1982).

Based on this distinction, one might characterize a typical managerial task as twofold: (a) developing a causal model that links control and state variables, contingent on environmental variables, to firm outcomes and (b) manipulating the control variables in the short run and the state variables in the long run, contingent on the environmental variables, to maximize a firm's performance. The critical questions then become whether managers can distinguish among control, state, environmental, and extraneous variables and whether they can ascertain causal relations among these variables and firm outcomes. *Causal ambiguity* exists if either condition is unmet.

This chapter asserts that distinguishing among types of variables and descriptions of causal relations will be considerably more difficult, if not impossible, in an unfamiliar culture than in a familiar one. The next subsection discusses why. I emphasize strategic choices such as whether the firm should enter an industry or how it should compete on entry.

Cultural Differences in Strategic Behavior

This subsection argues that firms' strategic behaviors differ across cultures. By *culture,* I refer to a "shared meaning system" (Shweder & LeVine, 1984), such that members of the same culture share their worldview. Culture can be deeply embedded in an individual's and society's consciousness, being "the collective programming of the mind which distinguished members of one group or category of people from another" (Hofstede, 1991, p. 5). Thus, culture frames how individuals perceive themselves, others, and the world around them. The effect of culture on behavior can be so complex and subtle that some scholars of culture argue against a reductionist approach to the construct. Brett, Tinsley, Janssens, Barsness, and Lytle (1997) and Geertz (1973) approach a group's culture as a gestalt. There can be so many levels to culture that a deep understanding of culture is extremely difficult (Hofstede, 1980, 1991).

Although cultural effects are not nationally bounded and appear at different levels of analysis (e.g., regional, professional, organizational), I emphasize a society's broad cultural context. This is appropriate given my interest in foreign firm entry.[2] In addition, I link societal culture to individual decision-maker behavior. I focus on the individual as firm strategist. Although this simplifying assumption ignores how multiple organizational factors and actors contribute to firm strategy, I avoid anthropomorphizing the firm. (The chapter's conclusion discusses this simplification.)

Hofstede's (1980) study of national values argued that moving from the nation-state to the individual level can lead to an "ecological fallacy." This refers to a false assumption that relationships among variables at one level of analysis necessarily hold at another level of analysis. Findings at the nation-state or aggregate level cannot be assumed to apply directly to individuals. Instead, to understand individual behavior, some cross-cultural research argues that individual behavior will be shaped by both cultural- and individual-level factors (Bond, 1988; Earley, 1994; Earley & Mosakowski, 1996; Triandis, 1989). Following this tradition, I assume that, within any given society, an individual's behavior is affected by shared (cultural) factors and factors unique to the individual's experiences. Because this chapter's focus is not on underlying psychological processes that link cultural characteristics to individual behavior, I refer readers to relevant cross-cultural psychological research. For example, Erez and Earley (1993) used a schema-based approach to describe cultural effects on individual behavior. Triandis's (1972) process model of subjective culture suggested that culture maps onto individual behavior through attitudes, habits, and norms.

The individual is central to my argument because I tie societal culture to an individual's utility in the following way. Strategic choices have observable and unobservable consequences such as monetary rewards and feelings of self-enhancement. This chapter focuses on the observable economic consequences of a firm's strategic choices. These economic consequences can affect the firm's owners, managers, employees, and other stakeholders such as customers, suppliers, and the local community. My view is that *culture determines how the economic consequences of a firm's strategic choices are translated into pay-offs to the individual strategist.* Pay-offs "indicate the utility that each player receives if a particular combination of strategies is chosen" (Varian, 1993). When these pay-offs vary across cultures, different strategic choices may be taken.

Interest in how pay-offs determine strategic choices underlies game theory applied to strategic management problems (Brandenburger & Nalebuff, 1995, 1996; Camerer, 1991; Dixit & Nalebuff, 1991; Ghemawat, 1997; Postrel, 1991; Shapiro, 1991). To illustrate how culture could affect pay-offs, consider experimental economic research on games. Although experimental economic research tends toward domestic participant pools, a few multicountry studies suggest cultural differences. For example, Roth, Prasnikar, Okuno-Fujiwara, and Zamir (1991) presented a multicountry experiment that distinguished country differences that were not cultural in nature from cultural differences. With a two-person bargaining and multiperson markets experiment in the United States, Japan, Israel, and Yugoslavia, their study associated market outcomes (which may be based on currencies, languages, or experimenter differences) with country differences and bargaining outcomes (which the authors attributed to cultural differences). Their findings support the importance of cultural, instead of market, differences.

The view of culture as translating economic consequences to pay-offs is relevant given behavioral game research such as Harnett and Cummings' (1980) study of how game solutions vary across cultures. They suggested that pay-offs are more important than cultural differences. What Harnett and Cummings called "pay-offs," however, are not individual utility (as defined previously) but rather economic consequences for the individual. If culture affects pay-offs (defined as individual utility), then culture can influence game solutions in a way consistent with their empirical findings. That is, culture can translate individual economic consequences to individual utility. In addition, I allow for cultural influences on the relation between *firm* economic consequences and individual utility.

Certainly, factors other than culture affect how a firm's economic consequences translate to an individual's pay-offs. For example, the principal-agency relationship between the firm's owners and the individual strategist also determines the link between the firm's economic consequences and the individual strategist's pay-offs. Whereas my argument allows for differences at the level of societal culture, the firm, and the individual in how a firm's economic consequences translate to an individual's pay-offs,[3] I focus on societal culture's effects.

From this view of culture flow two premises. The first is that culture's translation role can affect strategy formulation. In an identical situation with identical economic consequences associated with choices, the strategic choices taken by a firm and/or its competitors can vary across cultures. Because of this effect, the relationship between strategic choices and firm performance also can differ across cultures, everything else being equal. The second premise is that understanding the translation of economic consequences to pay-offs process can be extremely difficult, if not impossible, for an individual outside a culture. This translation can cloud causal relations because, whereas economic consequences might be observable, pay-offs are not and are embedded in the cultural context. To use game theoretical language, a decision maker must describe the game being played, calculate associated economic consequences, translate these consequences into players' utility, and determine the solution. Cultural unfamiliarity can obscure the penultimate step to the point that choices cannot be predicted.

Consider the example of a simple game with well-specified economic consequences—a noncooperative game in an industry with one incumbent and many potential entrants. Limit pricing models have been proposed to address this situation, where the incumbent prices somewhere between the monopolist's price and the price under perfect competition (Gaskins, 1971; Kamien & Schwartz, 1971; Milgrom & Roberts, 1982; Pyatt, 1971; Salop, 1979). The equilibrium price balances forgone profits in the near term against benefits of entry deterrence in future periods (Milgrom & Roberts, 1982). Although various limit pricing models (some of which are game theoretical) incorporate different assumptions about the incumbent firm and entrants, such as whether they are acting with complete information, the price decision always depends on the discount rate because of the trade-off between short- and long-term rents. Thus, rent streams over time yield a single pay-off number that depends on the discount rate.

Culture can affect a manager's discount rate. The temporal orientation of the incumbent firm's manager might depend on his or her culture. One aspect of time orientation highlighted by cross-cultural research is a future, present, or past emphasis (Adler, 1991; Hampden-Turner & Trompenaars, 1993; Kluckholn & Strodtbeck, 1961). Individuals in future-oriented cultures are more likely to exhibit what psychological research refers to as a future time perspective at the individual level (De Volder, 1979; Gjesme, 1983; Gorman & Wessman, 1977; Wallace & Rabin, 1960). Everything else being equal, individuals with a future time perspective assign a lower discount rate to future rents than do present- or past-oriented individuals. A low discount rate causes the future-oriented manager to price the product lower than do present- or past-oriented managers.

Managers' discount rates might depend on other cultural dimensions including uncertainty avoidance. This describes the extent to which individuals in a society use rules, standard procedures, and laws to avoid ambiguity in their environment (Hofstede, 1991). The individual-level characteristic most closely associated with the societal-level construct of uncertainty avoidance is risk aversion.

Risk aversion affects the discount rate used because future returns are riskier and of less value for risk-averse individuals. When a manager is both future oriented and risk averse, these effects work in opposite directions (Harnett & Cummings, 1980). It is unclear which factor will dominate. A foreign entrant might be unable to predict a local manager's discount rate and ultimately the price the local manager chooses.

Although this limit pricing example illustrates how cultural effects make strategic prediction difficult, it obviously is simplistic. It also is conservative. This example assumes a known model of behavior (limit pricing), only one focal competitor (the incumbent firm), and only one choice (the discount rate that determines price). Obviously, cultural effects on competitors' behaviors might be more widespread, increasing an entrant's causal ambiguity about factors that affect incumbents' behavior and ultimately firm performance.

I use the term "rules of the game" to encompass the broad set of parameters that describes competitive and/or cooperative behavior in an industry. One might think of this as analogous to *structure* and *conduct* in the structure-conduct-performance paradigm of industrial organization economics. Thus, rules of the game represent firms' choices, where industry structure is one of many endogenous factors (Ghemawat, 1997). Dimensions of these rules include, for example, the following. Are firms price takers or price setters? Is competition solely on the basis of price or also on the basis of other dimensions? How intense is price competition? How intense is competition to innovate? What types of cooperative behavior are exhibited? Where do innovations come from in this industry? How likely is the imitation of innovations? What role does government play in setting the rules of the game? Thus, the rules of the game describe the nature of competition and cooperation within an industry. They are a set of heuristics that simplify firm interaction similar to what Spender (1989) called "industry recipes" and Brandenburger and Nalebuff (1995) called "rules of engagement" in rule-based games.

I suggest that culture can affect the rules of the game. There are two possibilities in the limit pricing model. One is that culture moderates the model, such that the entrants in a high-power distance or hierarchical culture, for example, might be slower to challenge the dominant incumbent. In this case, the limit price set will be higher in high-power distance cultures than in low-power ones, but the model still applies. Another possibility is that cultural effects completely invalidate a model and a different model applies. In a high-power distance culture, the incumbent's position can forestall entry regardless of price. A basic premise of the model—that entry rates and price are related—would be invalid in this example.

Foa and Foa (1974) suggested that individuals in different cultures prefer different types of rewards or what they called "resources." Consider status as a resource. Foa and Foa noted that the "loss of face," or the loss of status, is more important among Asian workers than among American workers. They argued that, although American managers expect criticism to improve Asian workers' performance, it actually deteriorates the relationships between American managers and Asian workers. Thus, Foa and Foa proposed different models of criticism and performance enhancement that apply across cultures. Earley (1997), however, emphasized that the loss of face is significant in all cultures and argued for managing face in a way that is compatible with a culture (p. 329). Compared to Foa and Foa's (1974) arguments, Earley's (1997) approach implied greater similarity across cultures in how the loss of face influences worker motivation, commitment, performance, and the like.

The previous discount rate example illustrates preferences for reward allocation over time. Similar cross-cultural differences can arise for reward allocation across a group's members. Different reward allocation patterns within a group can affect an individual's utility. Cultures differ in their rules for distributing rewards within society. Cross-cultural research on distributive justice (James, 1993; Leung & Bond, 1982) suggests that equity-based distributions will be most valued in individualist cultures, whereas equal distributions might be preferred in collectivist cultures. Cultural differences in distributional preferences suggest one way in which culture can influence the cross-level relation between firm outcomes and individual pay-offs.

Recent economic game theoretical research has incorporated the impact of distributions within a group affecting an individual's utility. Although this research does not offer clear distinctions among fairness, equity, altruism, and manners or between envy and spite (Camerer & Thaler, 1995), these articles share a focus on reward allocation across players. Rabin (1993) considered how fairness affects behavior, even going so far as to introduce a new equilibrium concept, a "fairness equilibrium."[4] Recent interest lies in how game structure affects altruistic or spiteful solutions—how group size (e.g., two-person vs. four-person groups) affects altruism/spitefulness; whether opponents' total, average, or maximum utility matters; and how important the number of rounds of play is (for a discussion, see Levine, 1998). To date, however, the economic game theoretical literature has forged neither a theoretical link nor an empirical link between these concepts and the culture of its experimental participants (for an empirical exception, see Roth et al.'s [1991] cross-national study of altruistic and spiteful behaviors).

My focus on the strategist's cultural context differs from extant cross-cultural strategy research. The dominant view is that culture influences the strategic *situation,* not the *strategist.* This occurs because culture affects a firm's employees, management practices, financial constraints, and the like. For example, the issues involved in strategic alliances or buyer-supplier relationships are presumed to vary across countries. In essence, the dominant view is that culture dictates the situation facing the strategist.

This type of argument has been applied to diverse and multilayered situational elements. At the *individual* level, culture affects the extent to which employees are willing to take risks or trust others (Shane, 1994; Shane, Venkataraman, & MacMillan, 1995). Hofstede (1991) proposed that individuals from certain cultures are suited for different tasks or environments. He argued that individuals from feminine cultures, where roles are not directly linked to gender, are better suited to personal services, custom-made products, and biochemistry, whereas individuals from masculine cultures are better suited to mass production, efficiency, heavy industry, and bulk chemistry.

At the organizational level of analysis, certain *managerial practices, structures, and systems* are more or less available in different cultures (Hofstede, 1980). Organizational and human resource practices found in certain cultures might discourage the dissension necessary to innovate; in these cultures, strategies dependent on radical innovations will be rare (Shane, 1995). Cross-cultural or cross-national research has demonstrated differences in human resource practices (Child, 1981; Milliman, Nason, Gallagher, Huo, & Von Glinow, 1999; Pascale & Maguire, 1980; Teagarden et al., 1995), leadership styles (Smith, Misumi, Tayeb, Peterson, & Bond, 1989; Smith & Peterson, 1988; Smith, Wang, & Leung, 1997), organizational structure (Chandler, 1986; Lachman, Albert, & Hinings, 1994), and control systems (Bartlett & Ghoshal, 1989; Calori, Lubatkin, & Very, 1994; Redding & Pugh, 1986; Zaheer, 1995). Also at the organizational level of analysis, firms can draw on *organizational routines, repertoires,* and *capabilities* embedded in different national cultures (Morosini, Shane, & Singh, 1998), creating different national administrative heritages (Bartlett & Ghoshal, 1989; Calori, Lubatkin, Very, & Veiga, 1997; Zaheer, 1995).

This chapter's alternative view of cultural effects on strategy formulation highlights the strategist's choices. To explain cross-cultural strategy differences, I consider both shared (cultural) and idiosyncratic (individual) characteristics of the strategist. For an identical strategic situation—a firm employing workers with the same individual characteristics, using the same portfolio of available management practices, and possessing identical organizational routines—two strategic decision makers in different cultures may make different choices (for a similar perspective, see Schneider, 1989, and Schneider & DeMeyer, 1991).

Although my argument emphasizes cultural differences, I acknowledge that countervailing forces can homogenize the rules of the game across cultures. An obvious counterargument to the earlier discount rate example is that investors in international financial markets link the costs of capital across countries. Increasing globalization implies greater multinational influence in many, if not all, domestic markets. Whether the net effect of foreign entry is to homogenize strategies across cultures or to introduce novel variations is difficult to say. Thus, forces for global divergence or convergence in rules of the game might coexist. As in the debate about whether cultures are converging or diverging over time

(Boyacigiller & Adler, 1991; Smith & Bond, 1999; Weber, 1969), it is impossible to offer a general answer as to which force dominates.

The next subsection discusses how cultural differences in strategy formulation affect a foreign entrant.

Implications of Cross-Cultural Differences

Considerable cross-cultural research is available to assist managers in unfamiliar cultures, sometimes emphasizing individual country knowledge (Cooper & Cooper, 1982; Craig, 1979; Wei & Li, 1995) and sometimes general cross-cultural understanding (Earley & Erez, 1997; Schneider & Barsoux, 1997). Is international strategic management research developed well enough to advise multinational managers in specific strategies for each country that their firms might enter? Although certain patterns have been identified, such as how MNCs' entry modes depend on the cultural distance between home and host countries (Kogut & Singh, 1988), this literature has not developed to the point of offering guidance specific to home and host cultures. For example, Root (1982, 1987) offered general entry advice. Yet, culture is, by definition, deeply embedded in a group's consciousness. It has a "taken-for-granted" nature (Rohner, 1984). Cultural effects may be quite subtle, manifest in nuances of language or gesture that embody significant meaning (Geertz, 1973). Culture also is extremely complex, both in terms of what it is and what its causes and consequences are.

Why can't a promising student of culture untangle its effects on firm strategy? Whereas Weick (1985) took the position that organizational culture and strategy are virtually synonymous, societal culture and firm strategy also may be inextricably linked, and understanding these links can be extremely difficult. Relating societal culture to firm strategy poses many cross-level problems (Klein, Dansereau, & Hall, 1994). How can an observer distinguish the pervasive influence of societal culture from other broad forces affecting actors at different levels of analysis such as individuals, groups, divisions, firms, networks, industries, and economies? Also, the complexity of interactions among competitors, customers, suppliers, employees, and other forces such as government agencies—with culture potentially affecting any or all of these—makes the development of a general model of cultural effects on firm strategy nearly impossible.

To respond to the daunting question of how firms will adapt their strategic choices to an unfamiliar culture, practicing managers may adopt an evolutionary approach (Burgelman, 1988). This approach allows foreign operation managers to modify extant models of business practices piecemeal as they gain *experience* in the unfamiliar culture. They also can make adjustments based on *expected* cultural effects, as the earlier discussion did with the limit pricing model. As the number of adjustments increases, however, the usefulness of the initial model declines. Thus, managers operating in an unfamiliar culture are likely to be at a competitive disadvantage vis-à-vis firms with more complete causal models such as local or foreign firms that have significant cultural experience. This is one source of the liabilities of "foreignness" (Zaheer, 1995; Zaheer & Mosakowski, 1997).

In addition to the complexity of widespread cultural influences, idiosyncratic characteristics of actors increase causal ambiguity. Although it is difficult to describe how individualism versus collectivism generally affects firms' propensity to internalize technological externalities, for example, it might be virtually impossible to predict how specific firms with a specific technology will behave in their domestic market. Moving away from cultural averages substantially complicates causal model development. In an unfamiliar culture, it might be especially difficult to distinguish what is typical from what is not typical. Thus, in addition to cultural knowledge, one cannot ignore learning specific to individuals and situations.

I conclude that managers in unfamiliar cultures will operate with very incomplete causal models, both in terms of identifying control, state, environmental, and extraneous variables and in terms of drawing causal linkages. Because managers' causal models are so incomplete, one might take the extreme position that behavior is random. Although my position is not this extreme, I assume that cultural learning is extremely difficult because of the nature of cultural knowledge and the complex relationship between culture and specific strategic choices.

Therefore, I propose an alternative to attempted cultural assimilation: A manager in an unfamiliar culture should act to create a new causal model. This serves two purposes: instituting a more desirable causal model for the entrant and putting the entrant at a competitive advantage through superior causal understanding of the industry context.

CREATING A NEW CAUSAL MODEL

Sources of New Causal Models

There are many examples of foreign entry changing the rules of a local game. Japanese firms entering the U.S. automobile market during the early 1970s moved competition away from styling and design proliferation to reliability and fuel efficiency. Globally, American fast-food franchises have emphasized uniformity and reliability in an industry where novelty and creativity have natural places. Michelin's entry into the U.S. tire market shifted the focus from cost to differentiation. Sotheby's and Christie's entry into the U.S. auction market transformed a fragmented market into one with two dominant firms. Are these examples of foreign entrants carefully studying the rules of the game in unknown cultures and adopting strategies suited to extant rules? Are these examples random behaviors? Or do they illustrate how firms can strategically alter the rules of the game to their own advantage?

Take the example of Honda entering foreign motorcycle markets such as the United States and the United Kingdom. This case is perhaps the most widely discussed example of a successful entry strategy by a foreign firm (Boston Consulting Group, 1975; Pascale, 1984, 1996; Prahalad & Hamel, 1990; Rumelt, 1996). Various authors disagree as to whether the entry strategy was devised with foresight and calculation or whether it emerged from a highly chaotic process (Rumelt, 1996). The Boston Consulting Group (1975) study suggested that the entry strategy was intentional and obtained from a cost advantage tied to scale and learning unnoticed by myopic incumbents. Prahalad and Hamel (1990) also proposed that the strategy was intentional. They focused on Honda's "stretch" for global leadership and exploitation of "loose bricks" as success factors. Pascale (1984, 1996), however, interpreted Honda's strategy as emerging from a chaotic process. The inability of Honda's managers to see, understand, and exploit the opportunities available in the U.S. market played a major role in his explanation.

Given extant diverse perspectives on one entry case, what new insights derive from strategic colonialism and causal ambiguity? On entering foreign markets, Honda either intentionally or accidentally altered the rules of the game from those where Honda was at a competitive disadvantage to those where Honda was at a competitive advantage. How Honda entered the U.S. motorcycle industry offers several examples of entry changing the rules of the game. The target customer changed from a motorcycle aficionado (the "black leather jacket customer") to an "average American" seeking low-cost transportation (Pascale, 1984). Along with this, the product shifted from motorcycles with substantial horsepower to low-cost and lightweight ones. Honda changed the channels of distribution. Retailing shifted from motorcycle retailers to sporting goods stores. Honda also sold directly to retailers instead of distributors and changed payments from sales-on-consignment to cash-on-delivery. Honda's entry into the U.S. motorcycle market also affected credit policies, away from dealer credit to bank credit (Pascale, 1984). Given these differences between Honda's and incumbents' strategies, it is clear that Honda played its own game.

Where did this game come from? I suggest that it came from Honda's strategy in the Japanese motorcycle industry. The low-cost, lightweight Supercub was Honda's star product in the Japanese market, representing 168,000 of the 285,000 motorcycles sold in 1959 (Pascale, 1984). Typical Supercub customers were working people who used the motorcycle as their main form of transportation instead of trains and buses. In Japan, Honda circumvented distributors, selling directly to retailers, primarily bicycle shops. Honda also implemented a cash-on-delivery system in Japan, against the industry practice of sales-on-consignment. Therefore, many key differences between Honda's and U.S. incumbents' strategies can be traced back to Honda's strategy in Japan. Note that Honda's Japanese strategy was not consistently shared with other Japanese motorcycle manufacturers. Other manufacturers used distributors; Honda was forced to sell directly to retailers in Japan because it was a late entrant and a second line for many distributions (Pascale, 1984). Other aspects of Honda's strategy were shared with other Japanese manufacturers such as target customers and the low-cost, lightweight product.

Honda's entry process did not emphasize learning about U.S. culture and extant practices in the U.S. motorcycle industry. From an interview with Kihachiro Kawashima, who was soon to be the president of American Honda, Pascale (1984) described Kawashima's first U.S. experience:

> My first reaction after traveling across the United States was: How could we have been so stupid as to start a war with such a vast and wealthy country! My second reaction was discomfort. I spoke poor English. We dropped in on motorcycle dealers who treated us discourteously and, in addition, gave the general impression of being motorcycle enthusiasts who, secondarily, were in business.

Thus, it would not be unreasonable to characterize this experience as strategic culture shock. To respond to this, Kawashima and his assistant did not immerse themselves in American culture, hire local managers, or partner with local firms. Instead, they arrived on U.S. shores with a strategy based on Honda's Japanese strategy.

Rumelt (1996) suggested that the answer to whether Honda's entry strategy was intentional or its managers were lucky is indeterminate. Whether intentionally or unintentionally, Honda did change the rules of the game to its own advantage. In particular, the current discussion highlights how Honda exported practices common in established foreign markets. Why base a new entry strategy on past successes? First, this approach economizes on resources. Firms can rely on existing routines (Nelson & Winter, 1982) to orchestrate the entry strategy. A second reason is perhaps as important as the first: Competitors will expect the new foreign entrant to behave in this way. To some extent, local incumbents can anticipate the foreign entrant's strategy and accommodate it.

My position is that some moderate level of transparency is desirable. This will help industry incumbents to react to the entrant and move quicker to the new game's steady-state, yet it also will allow the entrant to have a superior causal understanding of the new game. Even with moderate transparency, the foreign entrant will appear as an odd competitor. Therefore, the next subsection discusses how the foreign entrant can "teach" local incumbents the rules of the new game under strategic colonialism.

Teaching Rules to a New Game

Colonizing a new market often requires considerable adaptation by incumbents. What processes can a foreign entrant use to transform the rules of the game? I suggest general insights from game theory and operant conditioning.

The metaphor I use is that of a dog trying to train a person how to play a new game—"I'm going to get you."[5] In this game, the person throws a stick, and the dog catches it and runs away. The person then chases the dog until the person grabs the stick, throws the stick, and the game begins again. The dog's fun is being chased. This example assumes that the person does not know the new game; the person only knows "fetch." "I'm going to get you" is much preferred by the dog over fetch. It involves much more work by the person and much less by the dog, and it asserts the dominance of the dog over the person instead of the reverse.

How does a dog teach an old person this new game? The person throws the stick, expecting the dog to fetch it. The dog grabs it and begins to run away with it. The dog runs back and forth in front of the person in a tight circle, always in danger of having the person grab the stick. The person begins to chase the dog. So long as this continues, the game continues. A critical decision is when to let the person have the stick given that the stick must stay in motion to continue the game.[6] When a very stubborn person captures the stick, the person will continue to throw it to initiate fetch. A very adaptive person grabbing the stick also might throw it to initiate "I'm going to get you." The person most likely to drop out of the game is one who is between the two extremes; such a person still wants to play fetch but recognizes that the dog is doing something else. Eventually, the game will fail or the dog will train the person.

What are the elements of this transformation? First, the dog need not understand the owner's game (fetch) for the transformation to succeed. Instead, the dog must understand only the person's basic motivation. Two possible motivations are that (a) if a person lets go of something, the person wants it back, and (b) the person wants to interact with the dog. Depending on the person's motivation, the dog should or should not let the person grab the stick after the game has begun. In other words, the dog must have a general idea of the pay-offs associated with different choices of how to behave.

Similar to the importance of motivation is the idea that player type also affects how the dog behaves. The person's stubbornness versus adaptability affects whether and how often the dog lets the person have the stick. One sees the importance of player type in many game theoretical models of incomplete information (Gibbons, 1997). One party might not know what type of player he or she faces and must choose a course of action based on prior beliefs, signals (Cho & Kreps, 1987; Spence, 1973), and/or credible communication (Farrell & Rabin, 1996).

Third, this example illustrates the stimulus-response framework of operant conditioning (Luthans & Kreitner, 1985). The dog creates an antecedent condition—wagging the stick in front of the person. The desired stimulus is the person chasing the dog, and the response to this stimulus is the dog either playing with the person or letting the person have the stick. Operant conditioning techniques can generate the desired stimulus from the person. The dog can respond to successive approximations of the desired stimulus and use intermittent reinforcements. Clear messages also are important. If the dog sometimes played fetch and brought the stick right back, sometimes ran over into the bushes and dropped the stick, and sometimes played "I'm going to get you," then it would be very difficult for the person to learn the game.

Neither game theoretical reasoning nor traditional operant conditioning alone specifies a process for changing the rules of the game. Both theoretical perspectives talk about the interaction of actors and how one actor's behavior affects another actor's behavior. Traditional operant conditioning, however, does not take into account how actors vary in their motivation or represent types to be dealt with differently. Game theoretical logic specifies the motivation behind actors' choices and allows for distinct actor types. In addition, game theory can portray this interaction as a "supergame" during which players can choose between subgames at certain points. It is at these points where the rules of the game become endogenous.

Game theoretical logic does not, however, specify the process by which players get to the game's solution—whether it is through pure introspection/ calculation, evolution, adaptation, or some other process (Camerer, 1991). Operant conditioning describes a process by which the student of the game moves to the game theoretical solution. This well-delineated learning process is a specific case of what Camerer (1991) generally called adaptation.

This discussion of teaching a new game highlights two observations. First, a complex understanding of the old rules of the game is not needed. Instead, a basic understanding of the motivation of a potential student of the new game is critical to designing the learning process and engaging the student's interest during the learning process. This requires some cultural understanding, but the new game teacher need not immerse himself or herself in nuances of past games. Second, teaching a new game requires behaviors whose timing is critical. This further reinforces the idea that the teacher not try to learn the old game; attempts at learning the old game could signal inconsistent behavior and a lack of commitment to the new game.

The preceding example has suggested a general process for introducing the new game. The next subsection considers under what conditions incumbents will accept a new game.

When a New Game Strategy Is Likely to Work

Incumbents facing a "blank slate" will be more accepting of a new game than will entrenched incumbents. Depending on its size and resources, the entrant may create a blank slate through the act of entry. Microsoft's entry into Internet businesses raised more questions about the future of the industry than it answered. Also, pathbreaking changes among incumbents may facilitate a change in the rules of the game. Competitors may exit or consolidate. Recent radical changes in the global automobile industry, such as the merger between Chrysler and Mercedes Benz, may create a blank slate in this industry.

The breaking of industry recipes (Spender, 1989) is more likely to occur after significant industry change. Radical innovations, major shifts in customer demand, and changes in government regulations facilitate a new game introduction. Although still on a small scale, General Motors' and Honda's electric cars could lead to a new game in how cars are sold; customers were offered only leases, not purchases.[7] Not allowing customers to buy a car is an obvious departure from past sales practices.

Can *any* firm teach competitors a new game under these conditions? As noted earlier, moderate transparency of a firm's past strategies might help competitors to anticipate its behavior in a new market. Also, rewarding competitors to change is important. This can occur directly or indirectly. A firm can directly reward its competitors for playing a new game by helping them to achieve their goals if they play the new game. To get other videocassette recorder (VCR) producers to play the game of JVC and Matsushita (JVC's parent and ally) by adopting the VHS format, JVC and Matsushita widely licensed this format to competing VCR manufacturers. They also rewarded the cooperation of these manufacturers in a number of ways. Cusumano, Mylonadis, and Rosenbloom (1992) described this as follows:

> In addition, to entice other firms to support VHS, JVC was willing to let other companies participate in refining the standard, such as moving from two hours to longer recording times or adding new features. JVC also provided considerable assistance in manufacturing and marketing. Yet another important difference from Sony proved to be style: JVC managers approached prospective partners in an exceedingly "polite and gentle" manner and encouraged them to adopt as the common VCR standard "the best system we are all working on" rather than the VHS per se. One outcome of JVC's approach was that prospective manufacturing partners truly believed they would have some stake in the future evolution of VHS features. (pp. 72-74)

While this occurred, Sony was playing a game based on technological superiority that did not attempt to align the behavior of other VCR manufacturers with its strategy.

Rewards from someone other than the teacher of the new game also can encourage competitors to adopt it. Customers might favor the new game over the old game. After the energy crisis during the early 1970s, U.S. car buyers demanded fuel-efficient cars, and Japanese exports skyrocketed. The U.S. firms generally were more profitable if they developed fuel-efficient cars than if they did not. However, rewards for adopting this new product definition came from customers, not from Japanese entrants.

Finally, a teacher's irreversible investments may cause student firms to adopt a new game because of the teacher's commitment to the game. For example, Arco's then chief executive officer, Robert O. Anderson, staged a campaign to "blow up the credit card" in 1982. After Arco moved to a cash-only basis, many competitors attempted to lure Arco customers by accepting the Arco credit card. To respond to this market share threat, Arco invested heavily in advertising to stage a price promotion campaign and lowered its wholesale price an average of 2.8 cents per gallon (Davis, 1982). After this investment was made, it represented sunk costs. Because Arco was committed to this campaign, competitors were forced to respond to a novel strategy—a branded low-cost strategy.

To summarize, not all firms should attempt to colonize an industry. This subsection proposed that the probability of success will be increased if (a) a blank slate situation is created by a major industry upheaval; (b) the rules of the new game are somewhat transparent; (c) students are rewarded to adopt the game, either from the teacher or others (e.g., customers); and/or (d) the teacher is committed to the game, either because of its history or because of recent sunk investments.

The final section concludes this discussion by putting strategic colonialism into broader context.

CONCLUSION

Strategic colonialism relates to extant strategic thinking at many levels. A widely held belief is that a firm must develop a *unique* strategy to succeed. The resource-based view of strategy (Amit & Schoemaker, 1993; Barney, 1986a, 1986b, 1991; Conner, 1991; Dierickx & Cool, 1989; Lippman & Rumelt, 1982; Mahoney & Pandian, 1992; Mosakowski, 1993; Penrose, 1959; Peteraf, 1993; Rubin, 1973; Rumelt, 1984, 1991; Wernerfelt, 1984, 1995) emphasizes resource uniqueness or scarcity as critical to economic rent generation. Porter's (1980) discussion of entry and mobility barriers also suggested that the fewer, the merrier. Hamel (1996) went so far as to describe strategy as revolution. Game theorists working in the strategic management tradition mention the importance of creating a new game (Brandenburger & Nalebuff, 1995, 1996). Porter (1990) argued that firms from countries with intense rivalries may export their rules of the game abroad. Thus, there is precedent for the argument that doing something novel, such as creating a new game, is critical to strategic success.

This chapter is distinct in several ways, that is, its emphasis on cultural learning and on how causal ambiguity dictates a firm's choices. Causal ambiguity about the rules of the game can arise out of cultural unfamiliarity, and causal ambiguity makes it extremely costly, if not impossible, to learn existing rules of the game. Creating a new game can be a source of competitive advantage for two reasons. The first is that the new game might be more desirable for the foreign entrant than will the old game, and the second is that the creator of a new game will have more complete causal understanding than will incumbents. The first reason is similar to the arguments of Brandenburger and Nalebuff (1995, 1996), Hamel (1996), and Porter (1990), and the second differentiates my arguments from existing ones.

Strategic colonialism emphasizes causal understanding obtained through a firm manipulating its competitive environment (Hamel & Prahalad, 1994). Instead of emphasizing experience and learning by doing as ways in which firms develop causal understanding, my approach endogenizes causal understanding by suggesting that firms' strategic choices affect the causal model in operation. Initiating a new causal model enhances a firm's relative strategic position because the initiator of the new causal model is more likely to understand it even when competitors have considerably more experience. In fact, a colonial strategy suggests that the new game creator *not* gain experience of previous rules for strategic interaction; attempts at learning the old game might be detrimental.

To develop these arguments, I assume that cultural effects on firm strategy are necessarily complex and difficult to understand. This chapter purposefully does not address all the ways in which culture can affect firms' strategic choices and performance. One could detail and perhaps categorize distinct ways in which culture affects strategy formulation and/or implementation. This chapter narrows its sights by focusing on economic consequences of strategic choices and by highlighting the individual decision maker. I do not disallow, however, that cultural effects may be broader, more diverse, and more complex than discussed.

The context considered was that of the MNC entering a culturally unfamiliar country. Entering an unfamiliar culture offers an ideal example of a situation in which learning might be extremely slow, and my arguments might be broadened to general entry situations. Entrants might be able to play a form of strategic judo (Brandenburger & Nalebuff, 1996) by using incumbents' accumulated experience against them. Incumbents often are locked into taken-for-granted business models. This lock-in occurs from experience; causal understanding; and sunk investments in plant, equipment, distribution channels, and the like. If an entrant can introduce a new business model that its competitors do not completely understand, then it might be able to convert what formerly were incumbent strengths into weaknesses.

Although this chapter takes the position that cultural adaptation to an incumbent's strategies is not always desirable, this does not necessarily apply to management practices. The strategic colonizing firm might be required to adapt to a country's local management practices. Firms might need to adopt local personnel and human resource practices, appropriate organizational structures, control and information systems, and the like. Successful implementation of strategic colonialism also might dictate some understanding of the motives and types of competitors in the local market. Thus, although I discuss the extreme view that cultural familiarity might be extremely costly and difficult to develop, firms pursuing a colonial strategy cannot completely ignore cultural effects. This tension between strategic colonialism and culturally embedded management/ implementation practices offers another possible interpretation of Percy Barnevik's motto for Asea Brown Boveri: "Think global, act local" (Taylor, 1991).

My focus on the individual brings together psychological, cross-cultural, and economic research to inform the discussion. In many but not all cases, psychological characteristics of individuals relate to cultural values (Schwartz, 1992; Triandis, 1989), and I allow for individuals to be affected by shared and idiosyncratic factors. Both types of individual characteristics translate economic consequences to individual pay-offs. The link between the individual and the firm is not, however, well developed here. For example, the individual decision maker acts as an agent of the firm's owners, and I do not consider how agency relationships can affect the translation process.

Future research on the effectiveness of strategic colonialism might want to take into account multiple individuals or groups as contributors to firm strategy and consider how causal ambiguity is experienced and acted on by them. Cultural influences on firm strategy also may arise through culture's effects on group or organizational interactions. This chapter does not consider how the agency relationship, for example, might be affected by societal culture or individual differences (Roth & Donnell, 1996). Research on incentive contracts has considered the latter (Harris and Raviv, 1979; Hart, 1983) but not the former. Discussion of cultural effects on organizational phenomena may provide a different perspective from that considered here as to how culture influences strategic choices.

To advance research on strategic colonialism, I suggest that an important next step is integrating this chapter's arguments with a discussion of internal management practices. This is particularly salient because of the tension noted earlier between locally embedded management practices and global strategic choices. In the long run, will this tension be sustainable, or will it lead to the cross-fertilization and ultimate homogenization of management practices and strategic choices across cultures? Further discussion of the dynamics of strategic colonialism might shed light on waves of global revolutions and evolutions in strategic and management practice.

NOTES

1. I do not distinguish exporting rules for competitive or cooperative interaction from the MNC's home country versus other established markets. This distinction, in part,

underlies Prahalad and Lieberthal's (1998) argument against corporate imperialism, where the MNC exports primarily home country practices.

2. Barkema et al. (1996) linked national and organizational culture together for the foreign entry decision. They examined the effect of cultural differences at the country and organizational levels in international partnerships.

3. For example, Mitchell and Mickel (1999) reviewed research on individual differences in the meanings that people attach to money.

4. I do not mean to imply that economic game theory research has embraced distributional effects without question. Some suggest that these concepts are unnecessary and that the obtained results can be explained otherwise. Weg and Zwick (1994) argued that strategic behavior may motivate what appear to be results driven by a concern for fairness.

5. Although some readers might ask whether dogs have the cognitive abilities to use operant conditioning without the benefit of introductory psychology classes, my own experience suggests that this example will ring true to many pet owners as well as to parents of 2-year-olds.

6. I am indebted to Myrdene Anderson for highlighting the importance of staying in the game. She pointed me to Slobodkin's (1968) suggestion that the point of evolution and other dynamic systems is not to win the game but rather to stay in the game.

7. In part, this was done because the automobile manufacturers did not want to develop the reputation of selling what was soon to be obsolete battery technology. A lease reduces customers' risk of technological obsolescence and concerns with long-term reliability. Also, leases reduced the amount of expertise about local regulations and the electric car technology that customers needed because General Motors and Honda include local tax incentives for zero-emissions vehicles, maintenance, charger installation, and roadside assistance into one monthly payment (Murphy, 1997).

REFERENCES

Adler, N. J. (1991). *International dimensions of organizational behavior* (2nd ed.). Boston: PWS Kent.

Amit, R., & Schoemaker, P. J. H. (1993). Strategic assets and organizational rent. *Strategic Management Journal, 14,* 33-36.

Barkema, H. G., Bell, J. H. J., & Pennings, J. M. (1996). Foreign entry, cultural barriers, and learning. *Strategic Management Journal, 17,* 151-166.

Barney, J. B. (1986a). Organizational culture: Can it be a source of sustained competitive advantage? *Academy of Management Review, 11,* 656-665.

Barney, J. B. (1986b). Strategic factor markets: Expectations, luck, and business strategy. *Management Science, 32,* 1231-1241.

Barney, J. B. (1991). Firm resources and sustained competitive advantage. *Journal of Management, 17,* 99-120.

Bartlett, C., & Ghoshal, S. (1989). *Managing across borders: The transnational solution.* Boston: Harvard Business School Press.

Bond, M. H. (1988). Finding universal dimensions of individual variation in multicultural studies of values: The Rokeach and Chinese value surveys. *Journal of Personality and Social Psychology, 55,* 1009-1015.

Boston Consulting Group. (1975). *Strategy alternatives for the British motorcycle industry.* London: Her Majesty's Stationery Office.

Bourgeois, L. J., III, & Eisenhardt, K. M. (1988). Strategic decision processes in high velocity environments: Four cases in the microcomputer industry. *Management Science, 34,* 816-835.

Boyacigiller, N. A., & Adler, N. J. (1991). The parochial dinosaur: Organizational science in a global context. *Academy of Management Review, 16,* 262-290.

Brandenburger, A. M., & Nalebuff, B. J. (1995). The right game: Using game theory to shape strategy. *Harvard Business Review, 73*(4), 57-71.

Brandenburger, A. M., & Nalebuff, B. J. (1996). *Coopetition.* New York: Doubleday.

Brett, J. M., Tinsley, C. H., Janssens, M., Barsness, Z. I., & Lytle, A. L. (1997). New approaches to the study of culture in industrial/organizational psychology. In P. C. Earley & M. Erez (Eds.), *New perspectives on international industrial/organizational psychology* (pp. 75-129). San Francisco: New Lexington Press/Jossey-Bass.

Burgelman, R. A. (1988). A comparative evolutionary perspective on strategy making: Advantages and limitations of the Japanese approach. In K. Urabe, J. Child, & T. Kagono (Eds.), *Innovation and management: International comparisons* (pp. 63-80). Berlin: Walter de Gruyter.

Burgelman, R. A. (1990). Strategy-making and organizational ecology: A conceptual integration. In J. V. Singh (Ed.), *Organizational evolution: New directions* (pp. 164-181). Newbury Park, CA: Sage.

Calori, R., Lubatkin, M., & Very, P. (1994). Control mechanisms in cross-border acquisitions: An international comparison. *Organization Studies, 15,* 361-379.

Calori, R., Lubatkin, M., Very, P., & Veiga, J. F. (1997). Modeling the origins of nationally bound administrative heritages: A historical institutional analysis of French and British firms. *Organization Science, 8,* 681-696.

Camerer, C. F. (1991). Does strategy research need game theory? *Strategic Management Journal, 12,* 137-152.

Camerer, C., & Thaler, R. H. (1995). Anomalies: Ultimatums, dictators, and manners. *Journal of Economic Perspectives, 2,* 209-219.

Chandler, A. D. (1986). The evolution of modern global competition. In M. E. Porter (Ed.), *Competition in global industries* (pp. 405-448). Boston: Harvard Business School Press.

Child, J. (1981). Culture, contingency, and capitalism in the cross-national study of organizations. In B. M. Staw & L. L. Cummings (Eds.), *Research in organizational behavior* (Vol. 3, pp. 303-356). Greenwich, CT: JAI.

Cho, I-K., & Kreps, D. (1987). Signaling games and stable equilibria. *Quarterly Journal of Economics, 102,* 179-222.

Conner, K. R. (1991). A historical comparison of resource-based theory and five schools of thought within industrial organization economics. *Journal of Management, 17,* 121-154.

Cooper, R., & Cooper, N. (1982). *Culture shock! Thailand and how to survive it.* Singapore: Times Books.

Craig, J. (1979). *Culture shock! Malaysia and Singapore.* Singapore: Times Books.

Cusumano, M. A., Mylonadis, Y., & Rosenbloom, R. S. (1992). Strategic maneuvering and mass-market dynamics: The triumph of VHS over beta. *Business History Review, 66*(1), 51-94.

Davis, B. J. (1982, May). Arco one of few not honoring its card. *National Petroleum News,* pp. 31-32.

De Volder, M. (1979). Time orientation: A review. *Psychologica Belgica, 19,* 61-79.

Dierickx, I., & Cool, K. (1989). Asset stock accumulation and sustainability of competitive advantage. *Management Science, 35,* 1504-1511.

Dixit, A., & Nalebuff, B. (1991). *Thinking strategically: The competitive edge in business, politics, and everyday life.* New York: Norton.

Earley, P. C. (1994). Self or group? Cultural effects of training on self-efficacy and performance. *Administrative Science Quarterly, 39,* 89-117.

Earley, P. C. (1997). *Face, harmony, and social structure.* New York: Oxford University Press.

Earley, P. C., & Erez, M. (1997). *The transplanted executive.* New York: Oxford University Press.

Earley, P. C., & Mosakowski, E. (1996). Experimental international management research. In B. J. Punnett & O. Shenkar (Eds.), *Handbook of international management research* (pp. 83-114). London: Blackwell.

Eisenhardt, K. M. (1989). Making fast strategic decisions in high-velocity environments. *Academy of Management Journal, 32,* 543-576.

Eisenhardt, K. M., & Brown, S. L. (1998). Time pacing: Competing in markets that won't stand still. *Harvard Business Review, 76*(2), 59-69.

Eisenhardt, K. M., & Brown, S. L. (1999). Patching: Restitching business portfolios in dynamic markets. *Harvard Business Review, 77*(3), 72-82.

Eisenhardt, K., & Tabrizi, B. N. (1995). Accelerating adaptive processes: Product innovation in the global computer industry. *Administrative Science Quarterly, 40,* 84-110.

Erez, M., & Earley, P. C. (1993). *Culture, self-identity, and work.* New York: Oxford University Press.

Farrell, J., & Rabin, M. (1996). Cheap talk. *Journal of Economic Perspectives, 10*(3), 103-118.

Foa, U. G., & Foa, E. B. (1974). *Societal structures of the mind.* Springfield, IL: Charles C Thomas.

Galunic, D. C., & Eisenhardt, K. M. (1996). The evolution of intracorporate domains: Divisional charter losses in high-technology, multidivisional corporations. *Organization Science, 7,* 255-282.

Gaskins, D. (1971). Dynamic limit pricing: Optimal pricing under threat of entry. *Journal of Economic Theory, 2,* 306-322.

Geertz, C. (1973). *The interpretation of culture.* New York: Basic Books.

Ghemawat, P. (1997). *Games businesses play.* Cambridge, MA: MIT Press.

Gibbons, R. (1997). Introduction to applicable game theory. *Journal of Economic Perspectives, 11,* 127-149.

Gjesme, T. (1983). On the concept of future time orientation: Considerations of some functions' and measurements' implications. *International Journal of Psychology, 18,* 443-461.

Gorman, B. S., & Wessman, A. E. (Eds.). (1977). *The personal experience of time.* New York: Plenum.

Hamel, G. (1996). Strategy as revolution. *Harvard Business Review, 74*(4), 69-82.

Hamel, G., & Prahalad, C. K. (1989). Strategic intent. *Harvard Business Review, 67*(3), 63-76.

Hamel, G., & Prahalad, C. K. (1993). Strategy as stretch and leverage. *Harvard Business Review, 71*(2), 75-84.

Hamel, G., & Prahalad, C. K. (1994). *Competing for the future.* Boston: Harvard Business School Press.

Hampden-Turner, C., & Trompenaars, A. (1993). *The seven cultures of capitalism: Value systems for creating wealth in the United States, Japan, Germany, France, Britain, Sweden, and the Netherlands.* New York: Doubleday.

Harnett, D. L., & Cummings, L. L. (1980). *Bargaining behavior: An international study.* Houston, TX: Dame Publishers.

Harris, M., & Raviv, A. (1979). Optimal incentive contracts with imperfect information. *Journal of Economic Theory, 20,* 231-259.

Hart, O. D. (1983). Optimal labour contracts under asymmetric information: An introduction. *Review of Economic Studies, 50,* 3-35.

Hedlund, G. (1994). A model of knowledge management and the N-form corporation. *Strategic Management Journal, 15,* 73-90.

Hofstede, G. (1980). *Culture's consequences.* Beverly Hills, CA: Sage.

Hofstede, G. (1991). *Cultures and organizations: Software of the mind.* New York: McGraw-Hill.

Hymer, S. H. (1976). *The international operations of national firms: A study of direct investment.* Cambridge, MA: MIT Press.

James, K. (1993). The social context of organizational justice: Cultural, intergroup, and structural effects on justice behaviors and perceptions. In R. Cropanzano (Ed.), *Justice in the workplace: Approaching fairness in human resource management* (pp. 21-50). Hillsdale, NJ: Lawrence Erlbaum.

Johanson, J., & Vahlne, J-E. (1977). The internalization process of the firm: A model of knowledge development and increasing foreign market commitments. *Journal of International Business Studies, 8*(1), 23-32.

Kamien, M. I., & Schwartz, N. (1971). Limit pricing and uncertain entry. *Econometrica, 39,* 441-454.

Klein, K. J., Dansereau, F., & Hall, R. J. (1994). Levels issues in theory development, data collection, and analysis. *Academy of Management Review, 19,* 195-229.

Kluckholn, F. R., & Strodtbeck, F. L. (1961). *Variations in value orientations.* Evanston, IL: Row, Peterson.

Kogut, B., & Singh, H. (1988). The effect of national culture on the choice of entry model. *Journal of International Business Studies, 19,* 411-432.

Lachman, R., Albert, N., & Hinings, B. (1994). Analyzing cross-national management and organizations: A theoretical framework. *Management Science, 40,* 40-55.

Leung, K., & Bond, M. H. (1982). How Chinese and Americans reward task-related contributions: A preliminary study. *Psychologia, 25,* 32-39.

Levine, D. K. (1998). Modeling altruism and spitefulness in experiments. *Review of Economic Dynamics, 1,* 593-622.

Lippman, S. A., & Rumelt, R. P. (1982). Uncertain imitability: An analysis of interfirm differences in efficiency under competition. *Bell Journal of Economics, 13,* 418-438.

Luthans, F., & Kreitner, R. (1985). *Organizational behavior modification and beyond: An operant conditional and social learning approach.* Glenview, IL: Scott, Foresman.

Madsen, T., & McKelvey, B. (1996). Darwinian dynamic capability: Performance effects of balanced intrafirm selection processes. In *Proceedings of the Academy of Management* (pp. 26-30). Cincinnati, OH: Academy of Management.

Mahoney, J. T., & Pandian, J. R. (1992). The resource-based view within the conversation of strategic management. *Strategic Management Journal, 13,* 363-380.

Milgrom, P., & Roberts, J. (1982). Limit pricing and entry under incomplete information: An equilibrium analysis. *Econometrica, 50,* 443-459.

Milliman, J., Nason, S., Gallagher, E., Huo, P., & Von Glinow, M. A. (1999). The impact of national culture on human resource management practices: The case of performance appraisal. In J. L. C. Cheng & R. B. Peterson (Eds.), *Advances in international comparative management* (Vol. 12, pp. 147-183). Greenwich, CT: JAI.

Mitchell, T. R., & Mickel, A. E. (1999). The meaning of money: An individual difference perspective. *Academy of Management Review, 24,* 568-578.

Miyazaki, K. (1994). Search, learning, and accumulation of technological competences: The case of optoelectronics. *Industrial and Corporate Change, 3,* 631-654.

Morosini, P., Shane, S., & Singh, H. (1998). National cultural distance and cross-border acquisition performance. *Journal of International Business Studies, 29*(1), 137-158.

Mosakowski, E. (1993). A resource-based perspective on the dynamic strategy-performance relationship. *Journal of Management, 19,* 819-839.

Mosakowski, E. (1997). Strategy making under causal ambiguity: Conceptual issues and empirical evidence. *Organization Science, 8,* 414-442.

Murphy, I. P. (1997, August 18). Charged up: Electric cars get jolt of marketing. *Marketing News,* pp. 1-7.

Nelson, R. R., & Winter, S. G. (1982). *An evolutionary theory of economic change.* Cambridge, MA: Belknap.

Pascale, R. T. (1984). Perspectives on strategy: The real story behind Honda's success. *California Management Review, 26*(3), 47-72.

Pascale, R. T. (1996). Reflections on Honda. *California Management Review, 38*(4), 112-117.

Pascale, R. T., & Maguire, M. A. (1980). Comparison of selected work factors in Japan and the United States. *Human Relations, 33,* 433-455.

Penrose, E. T. (1959). *The theory of growth of the firm.* London: Blackwell.

Perlmutter, H. (1969). The tortuous evolution of the multinational corporation. *Columbia Journal of World Business, 4,* 9-18.

Peteraf, M. A. (1993). The cornerstones of competitive advantage: A resource-based view. *Strategic Management Journal, 14,* 179-191.

Porter, M. (1980). *Competitive strategy: Techniques for analyzing industries and companies.* New York: Free Press.

Porter, M. E. (1990). *Competitive advantage of nations.* New York: Free Press.

Postrel, S. (1991). Burning your britches behind you: Can policy scholars bank on game theory? *Strategic Management Journal, 12,* 153-155.

Prahalad, C. K., & Hamel, G. (1990). The core competence of the corporation. *Harvard Business Review, 68*(3), 79-91.

Prahalad, C. K., & Lieberthal, K. (1998). The end of corporate imperialism. *Harvard Business Review, 76*(4), 69-79.

Pyatt, G. (1971). Profit maximization and the threat of new entry. *Economic Journal, 81,* 242-255.

Rabin, M. (1993). Incorporating fairness into game theory. *American Economic Review, 83,* 1281-1302.

Redding, S. G., & Pugh, D. S. (1986). The formal and the informal: Japanese and Chinese organization structures. In S. R. Clegg, D. C. Dunphy, & S. G. Redding (Eds.), *The enterprise and management in East Asia* (pp. 153-167). Hong Kong: University of Hong Kong, Centre for Asian Studies.

Rohner, R. P. (1984). Toward a conception of culture for cross-cultural psychology. *Journal of Cross-Cultural Psychology, 15,* 111-138.

Root, F. R. (1982). *Foreign market entry strategies.* New York: AMACOM.

Root, F. R. (1987). *Entry strategies for international markets.* Lexington, MA: Lexington Books.

Roth, A., Prasnikar, V., Okuno-Fujiwara, M., & Zamir, S. (1991). Bargaining and market behavior in Jerusalem, Ljubljana, Pittsburgh, and Tokyo: An experiment. *American Economic Review, 81,* 1068-1095.

Roth, K., & Donnell, S. O. (1996). Foreign subsidiary compensation strategy: An agency theory perspective. *Academy of Management Journal, 39,* 678-703.

Rubin, P. H. (1973). The expansion of firms. *Journal of Political Economy, 81,* 936-949.

Rumelt, R. P. (1984). Toward a strategic theory of the firm. In R. Lamb (Ed.), *Competitive strategic management* (pp. 556-570). Englewood Cliffs, NJ: Prentice Hall.

Rumelt, R. P. (1991). How much does industry matter? *Strategic Management Journal, 12,* 167-185.

Rumelt, R. P. (1996). The many faces of Honda. *California Management Review, 38*(4), 103-111.

Salop, S. C. (1979). Strategic entry deterrence. *American Economic Review, 69,* 335-338.

Schneider, S. (1989). Strategy formulation: The impact of national culture. *Organization Studies, 10,* 149-168.

Schneider, S., & Barsoux, J-L. (1997). *Managing across cultures.* Englewood Cliffs, NJ: Prentice Hall.

Schneider, S. C., & DeMeyer, A. (1991). Interpreting and responding to strategic issues: The impact of national culture. *Strategic Management Journal, 12,* 307-320.

Schwartz, S. (1992). Universals in the content and structure of values: Theoretical advances and empirical tests in 20 countries. In M. Zanna (Ed.), *Advances in experimental social psychology* (Vol. 25, pp. 1-65). San Diego: Academic Press.

Shane, S. (1994). The effect of national culture on the choice between licensing and direct foreign investment. *Strategic Management Journal, 15,* 627-642.

Shane, S. (1995). Uncertainty avoidance and the preference for innovation championing roles. *Journal of International Business Studies, 26*(1), 47-68.

Shane, S., Venkataraman, S., & MacMillan, I. (1995). Cultural difference in innovation championing strategies. *Journal of Management, 21,* 931-952.

Shapiro, C. (1991). The theory of business strategy. *Rand Journal of Economics, 20,* 125-137.

Shweder, R. A., & LeVine, R. A. (1984). *Culture theory: Essays on mind, self, and emotion.* New York: Cambridge University Press.

Slobodkin, L. B. (1968). Toward a predictive theory of evolution. In R. C. Lewontin (Ed.), *Population biology and evolution: Proceedings of the international symposium, June 7-9, 1967* (pp. 187-205). Syracuse, NY: Syracuse University Press.

Smith, P. B., & Bond, M. H. (1999). *Social psychology: Across cultures* (2nd ed.). Boston: Allyn & Bacon.

Smith, P. B., Misumi, J., Tayeb, M., Peterson, M., & Bond, M. (1989). On the generality of leadership style measures across cultures. *Journal of Occupational Psychology, 62,* 97-109.

Smith, P. B., & Peterson, M. F. (1988). *Leadership, organizations, and culture.* London: Sage.

Smith, P. B., Wang, Z. M., & Leung, K. (1997). Leadership, decision-making, and cultural context: Event management within Chinese joint ventures. *Leadership Quarterly, 8,* 413-431.

Spence, A. M. (1973). Job market signaling. *Quarterly Journal of Economics, 97,* 355-374.

Spender, J.-C. (1989). *Industry recipes: An enquiry into the nature and sources of managerial judgement.* Oxford, UK: Basil Blackwell.

Stopford, J. M., & Baden-Fuller, C. W. F. (1994). Creating corporate entrepreneurship. *Strategic Management Journal, 15,* 521-536.

Taylor, W. (1991). The logic of global business: An interview with ABB's Percy Barnevik. *Harvard Business Review, 69*(2), 90-105.

Teagarden, M. B., Von Glinow, M. A., Bowen, D. E., Frayne, C. A., Nason, S., Huo, Y. P., Milliman, J., Arias, M. E., Butler, M. C., Geringer, J. M., Kim, N-H., Scullion, H., Lowe, K. B., & Drost, E. A. (1995). Toward a theory of comparative management research: An idiographic case study of the best international human resources management project. *Academy of Management Journal, 38,* 1261-1287.

Triandis, H. C. (1972). *The analysis of subjective culture.* New York: Wiley Interscience.

Triandis, H. C. (1989). The self and social behavior in differing cultural context. *Psychological Review, 96,* 506-520.

Vaill, P. B. (1989). *Managing as a performing art: New ideas for a world of chaotic change.* San Francisco: Jossey-Bass.

Varian, H. R. (1993). *Intermediate microeconomics: A modern approach* (3rd ed.). New York: Norton.

Wallace, M., & Rabin, A. I. (1960). Temporal experience. *Psychological Bulletin, 57,* 213-236.

Weber, R. H. (1969). Convergence or divergence? *Columbia Journal of World Business, 4*(3), 75-83.

Weg, E., & Zwick, R. (1994). Toward the settlement of the fairness issues in ultimatum games: A bargaining approach. *Journal of Economic Behavior and Organization, 24,* 19-34.

Wei, B-P-T., & Li, E. (1995). *Culture shock! Hong Kong.* Portland, OR: Graphic Arts Center Publishing.

Weick, K. E. (1985). The significance of corporate culture. in P. Frost, L. F. Moore, M. R. Louis, C. C. Lundberg, & J. Martin (Eds.), *Organizational culture* (pp. 381-390). Beverly Hills, CA: Sage.

Wernerfelt, B. (1984). A resource-based view of the firm. *Strategic Management Journal, 5,* 171-180.

Wernerfelt, B. (1995). The resource-based view of the firm: Ten years after. *Strategic Management Journal, 16,* 171-174.

Winter, S. G. (1987). Knowledge and competence as strategic assets. In D. J. Teece (Ed.), *The competitive challenge* (pp. 159-184). Cambridge, MA: Ballinger.

Zaheer, S. (1995). Overcoming the liability of foreignness. *Academy of Management Journal, 38,* 341-363.

Zaheer, S., & Mosakowski, E. (1997). The dynamics of the liability of foreignness: A global study of survival in financial services. *Strategic Management Journal, 18,* 439-464.

chapter **12**

Time Zone Economies and Managerial Work in a Global World

SRILATA ZAHEER

Many companies find that they can obtain a competitive edge by using the differences in time zones between countries to obtain a 24-hour per day workday.

—Quinn (1992, p. 53)

Reports of the value added for firms from configuration and coordination (Porter, 1986) across different global time zones have begun to proliferate recently. Engineering companies claim to have structured their value-adding activities around the world in such a way as to be able to hand off projects from office to office so as to obtain efficiency benefits by "following the sun." For example, Fluor Corporation, an engineering firm located in Irvine, California, has set up engineering design offices around the world. On time-critical projects, a team in the California location can complete a full day of design on the project and, at the end of the day, pass the project on to a design team in the Philippines, which, after working on the project, can in turn send it over to structural engineers in Calgary and Houston, from where it is sent back to Irvine. In effect, the project gets the benefit of nearly 3 days of effort within a single 24-hour period. By following this global relay strategy, in this case of the *responsibility* for development work,[1] Fluor maintains that it has cut as much as 3 months out of a 14-month engineering design cycle. Similarly, Bechtel Corporation, working on

339

the expansion of the airport in Dubai, United Arab Emirates, passed the plans on among dozens of architects and engineers working round-the-clock in San Francisco, New Delhi, Dubai, and London. As a Bechtel official pointed out, "This project never sleeps" ("Work Week," 1997, p. A1). Software firms, telephone hotline services, and even banks and law firms have been cited as setting up offices in different time zones so that software development, hotline services, and legal research can continue round-the-clock in a world where time zones might "matter more than miles" (Cairncross, 1997).

Apart from these reports in the press, there has been some research on the presence of time zone effects, especially in the financial services industry. Research in finance on foreign exchange markets has demonstrated time zone effects in that, as the day progresses, trading may be transmitted from one trading center to another (Baillie & Bollerslev, 1991; Engle, Ito, & Lin, 1990; Hogan & Melvin, 1994). Without a firm's operations spanning the time zones associated with the major markets, a firm in such an industry will not be able to coordinate its trading to match the circadian rhythms of the market. In an organizational study that involved interviewing managers with international business (IB) responsibility in the financial services industry (Zaheer, 1995), the issue of distributing value-adding activity across global time zones, and the implications of coordinating activity across these time zones both for the competitive advantage of the firm and for managerial work, were brought up by several respondents. In that article, the economies that arise from spanning time zones were referred to as "economies of diachronic scope."

However, it is not immediately obvious why there should be any economic benefits at all from spanning time zones that cannot be achieved through operating round-the-clock in one geographic location. Furthermore, to what extent the reported time zone economies are truly dependent on location or coordination across time zones, as opposed to location and coordination to take advantage of differential factor costs across geographic space, needs to be resolved. This chapter is an attempt to disentangle these issues and examine what types of economies firms might reap by distributing value-adding activity across different time zones and what the implications of such distributed value-adding activity are for managerial work in a global world. This is an exploratory piece meant to begin a conversation about how work, and in particular managerial work, is being transformed by the global information revolution, focusing on issues of configuration and coordination across time zones. It also is a tentative attempt to draw on research rooted in biology and the natural sciences to explain phenomena in the social sciences in the spirit of Wilson (1998), who suggested that there is a fundamental unity underlying all forms of knowledge and called for a move away from the narrow specialization and fragmentation into which researchers have fallen.

This chapter begins with a brief discussion of research on the biology of human circadian rhythms, which has shown that individual alertness, efficiency, and performance tend to vary throughout the day (Folkard, 1997; Smith,

Guilleminault, & Efron, 1997; Smith-Coggins, Rosekind, Buccino, Dinges, & Moser, 1997). Along with the social rhythms that emerge with the light-dark cycle, these circadian rhythms influence both the efficiency and the social desirability of night work (Hamermesh, in press).

This is followed by an assessment of the *efficiency* benefits realizable through coordination across time zones that is one outcome of these rhythms. A key element in the realization of economies of scale and scope is the ability of the firm to increase its rate of "throughput" (Chandler, 1990; Hammer & Champy, 1993) through its value-adding system. The matching of individual circadian rhythms, as well as social rhythms, with the rhythm of work that is obtainable from handing off responsibility across time zones in a relay strategy can make a difference to throughput, thus contributing to potential economies of scale and scope. This is especially possible in industries where value-adding activity is costlessly fungible across borders, as is the case with the engineering design, software, and legal firms discussed in the examples.

The chapter also explores the benefits that arise from locating across time zones in the *speed of response* (Eisenhardt, 1989; Nayyar & Bantel, 1994; Stalk, 1988) when there is need for managerial coordination across a global value-adding network. The true realization of economies of scale or scope across a global value chain relies on rapid, real-time managerial coordination (Chandler, 1990; Porter, 1986). Speed of response not only contributes to increasing throughput but also is likely to facilitate coordination by fostering good relationships and building social capital with supplier and customer networks.

The chapter ends with an evaluation of the *information advantages* that can accrue to firms that locate and coordinate across time zones, when the market is globally integrated, and when prices and market information are determined by patterns of demand and supply that shift across time zones throughout the day. It concludes with a discussion of the implications of these suggestions for theory and for the managers of the multinational corporation (MNC).

CIRCADIAN RHYTHMS, SOCIAL RHYTHMS, AND THE RHYTHMS OF WORK

Many cycles in living organisms, including humans, recur with an approximately 24-hour periodicity. These cycles are called *circadian rhythms,* from the Latin words *circa diem* (Halberg, 1959). These circadian rhythms match an individual's functions to what is appropriate for that hour of the day and represent perhaps one of the most fundamental biological adaptations to the environment—the adaptation of living organisms to light and dark.

A human has more than 100 different circadian rhythms, each of which affects a different aspect of how the individual functions at different times during the day—from heart rate, to hormone production, to pain tolerance, to body temperature. The human brain relies on outside influences called *zeitgebers* (literally, *time givers*) to provide the signals that keep it on a 24-hour schedule. Such zeitgebers that send time cues to the brain include elements in nature, in particular daylight, but they also can include social elements such as the last meal of the day and contact with coworkers. A change in some element of the daily schedule, or any disruption that causes a mismatch between the schedule required by a person's environment and his or her circadian rhythms (most readily observable in mismatched sleep-wake cycles), can cause "clinically significant distress and/or impairment in social/occupational or other important areas of functioning" (American Psychiatric Association, 1994).

There is a significant amount of research interest in the causes and effects of circadian rhythms (Campbell & Murphy, 1998; Dijk, Shanahan, Duffy, Ronda, & Czeisler, 1997; Jewett et al., 1997). The work ranges from studies at molecular and biochemical levels to empirical work at more macro levels of analysis. Examples of the latter include the effects of night work or work at different times of the day on alertness, effectiveness, and performance in a wide variety of areas, from accidents and transport safety (Folkard, 1997), to night-shift physicians' alertness and speed of reaction (Smith-Coggins et al., 1997), to the "circadian advantage" held by National Football League teams located on the West Coast when they play night games on the East Coast (Smith et al., 1997). The conclusions of these empirical studies inevitably have been that night work is associated with lower performance efficiency, decreased alertness, and up to an 80% higher accident rate (Folkard, 1997).

Added to these well-documented individual-level effects, there is some evidence of a societywide decline in night work, especially with increasing incomes. Hamermesh (in press) found a sharp decline in the proportion of evening and night work in the United States over the past 20 years. The decline was greatest in the highest wage brackets and late at night. This suggests that evening/night work is viewed "as a disamenity, with rising real earnings leading workers to shift away from such work." Therefore, night work seems to be associated both with diminished performance and a degree of social undesirability.

LOCATION ACROSS TIME ZONES AND ECONOMIES OF SCALE AND SCOPE

The Role of Throughput in Economies of Scale and Scope

An important element in capturing economies of scale and scope is simply to increase throughput (Chandler, 1990; Hammer & Champy, 1993) or the speed at which value-added output moves through the system. In essence, increasing the rate of throughput enables the distribution of fixed costs over larger volumes of output by increasing the speed of processing rather than the size of processing capacity. Furthermore, realizing economies of scale and scope through increasing throughput is essentially an organizational capability that relies heavily on managerial coordination. Chandler (1990) captured this idea succinctly when he stated, "The actual economies of scale or of scope, as determined by throughput, are organizational" (p. 24). Chandler also commented, "The throughput needed to maintain minimum efficient scale requires careful coordination not only of the flow through the processes of production but also of *the flow of inputs from suppliers and the flow of outputs to intermediaries and final users.* Such coordination . . . demanded the *constant attention* of a managerial team or *hierarchy*" (p. 24, emphases added).

These comments suggest that there might be economies associated with location across time zones and coordination across these locations within the firm by their effect on increasing throughput. Although coordination across time zones is not costless and sometimes can be inefficient, I submit that there are situations in which location in multiple time zones can actually be more efficient for the firm, in terms of increasing the rate of throughput, than working round-the-clock in one location. There are possibly at least two different situations in which locating activity across time zones could contribute to economies of scale and scope through improving throughput through coordination. One involves increasing the speed of processing within the firm itself, and the other involves increasing throughput in the firm's value-adding system through coordination with its network of buyers and suppliers.

Throughput and Coordination Within the Firm

Examples of relay strategies across time zones often involve improving the rate of throughput within the firm, whether it is Fluor's ability to cut down design time or the ability of a law firm in New York to have its Hong Kong office continue research on legal precedents for a case during its night so that the partners will have more background material to work with when they return fresh in the morning in New York. Increasingly, this type of global relay strategy, involving the handing off of work within the firm, is becoming required in industries such as software, where it is not uncommon for code to pass from Auckland, New Zealand; to Bangalore, India; to Dublin, Ireland; to Palo Alto, California; and back to Auckland in the course of one 24-hour day.[2] Although some of the benefits of distributing value-added activity in this manner in industries where engineering designs or software are costlessly fungible across borders clearly are the ability to exploit traditional factor cost advantages (e.g., the low cost of programming labor in India or Ireland), examples such as Fluor's cutting down of development *time* through such practices clearly suggest that there is more than just traditional factor cost advantage at work.

Entrained work. There are perhaps at least two factors (and the interaction between them) that might contribute to the increased rate of throughput or shortened cycle time that appears to result from this process of handing off responsibility for work across time zones *within* the firm. One factor is just the entrainment or synchronization of the individual circadian rhythms, social rhythms, and work rhythms mentioned earlier. It is a well-documented fact that night workers typically are paid more and that night supervisors typically are less senior and less experienced than their daytime counterparts.[3] As for managers, it is rare to find a manager working a night shift. The decline over time in the proportion of work done at night, especially among high-income groups, speaks to the social undesirability of night work, for which even the premium paid for such work does not appear to compensate (Hamermesh, in press). Furthermore, empirical research clearly has established that night work is associated with lower efficiency, lower alertness, and higher accident rates. As such, the cost of night work, and especially the quality of night work, might be one reason why handing off work to other time zones that are operating during their "day" might be better for throughput in certain types of industries than is working multiple shifts at one location. Locations going through their day benefit from the entrainment (Ancona & Chong, 1996) of the rhythms of work with the rhythms of social life and individual circadian rhythms.

Overlapping work. The other factor that can lead to time zone economies in internal firm coordination arises from the fact that handing off work across time zones might involve overlapping work times in both locations. How throughput may be enhanced in such a situation is best understood by referring to the relay analogy, where the second runner already is running at full speed when the baton is passed. Although firms could attempt to replicate this effect by running overlapping shifts in one location, there are likely to be physical constraints (e.g., office space, equipment) to truly making a system of overlapping shifts operational in one location. Firms might find it more worthwhile to install the necessary additional physical capacity to achieve this in a different time zone location. As such, they could obtain the interaction benefits of *both* overlapping work and entrained work.

Obviously, such hand-off strategies could not work in all industries. The businesses that would benefit clearly are those in which activities are costlessly transmittable across borders, those that rely on information (discussed later), those operating with codified rather than tacit knowledge (Zander & Kogut, 1995) given that codified knowledge would be easier to hand off in a relay strategy, and those in which the throughput requirements are *not* tied to a particular piece of capital equipment. An example of handing off responsibility that improves throughput, and perhaps also reduces risk, can be found in foreign exchange trading. Callier (1986) argued that a presence across time zones may enable multinational banks to take speculative positions in the foreign exchange market without increasing the overnight risk of their portfolios because being located in multiple time zones enables them to pass their open positions on to branches further west, which will be in a position to execute better deals in more liquid markets.

Throughput, Responsiveness, and Social Capital

Another factor contributing to time zone economies could be the increased coordination demands that arise when suppliers and customers are distributed across time zones around the world (Quinn, 1992). A classic example of the increasingly geographically dispersed structure of global value-adding activity is the global component network for Ford's European manufacturing of the Escort (Daniels & Radebaugh, 1998, p. 761), where parts and components used in its assembly plants in the United Kingdom and Germany come from at least 15 different countries.

Coordination, both within the firm and across its network of suppliers and customers, is a fundamental feature of the transnational corporation (Bartlett & Ghoshal, 1989). Good coordination across a global network requires quick responses (especially in crisis situations), constant communication, and the ability to build social capital with the other parties over time. Such speed of response, communication, and relationship building, even if at a distance, require that one party is active and working when the other party is active and working. It is likely to be much easier to communicate and build interpersonal relationships within the same time zone than across time zones.[4] Even if face-to face contact is not possible (e.g., two people in the same time zone could be located in Canada and Argentina), it is possible to pick up a phone at any time during the workday and know that there is a good chance that the person one is trying to reach also will be at work. Furthermore, it is nearly impossible to shorten response cycle times and to deal with queries or crises in real time unless both parties are located in the same time zone. Even a simple response to a simple query, which could be handled instantaneously within the same time zone, might have to wait for the next workday if handled across time zones. As before, the critical assumption here is the fact that managers with the capability and responsibility to handle these relationships are likely to be unwilling to work nights in another time zone. As mentioned earlier, the existence of individual circadian rhythms, as well as the social rhythms of family life and events, results in individuals both having more energy and tending to prefer working during the day when these rhythms are entrained or synchronized with the rhythms of their work lives (Ancona & Chong, 1996).

A key issue that has to be considered is that, because this coordination is between the firm and the market, it appears that the firm needs an *internalized* coordination team to work across time zones. In other words, a critical assumption is that *co-location in the same time zone is more important for coordination with the market than for coordination within the firm;* that is, it will be easier to communicate, build relationships, and coordinate within the firm (among members of the coordination team, even though they are located in different time zones) than to coordinate with external actors in other time zones. This assumption, that coordination within a hierarchy across time zones will be easier than coordination with external actors across time zones, appears to be a reasonable assumption to make given that firms are likely to have multiple mechanisms to support and encourage internal communication and coordination.

Given this combination of factors, it is likely that firms that internalize coordination activities with the global market by physically locating offices in different time zones are likely to be better able to respond rapidly to the demands of their global supplier and customer networks. This rapid response capability is likely to speed throughput through the value-adding system, thereby allowing these firms to capture economies of scale. Such responsiveness also is likely to influence the quality of relationships with these global networks, thus laying a stronger foundation for smooth coordination. Speed of response (Eisenhardt, 1989; Nayyar & Bantel, 1994; Stalk, 1988; Zaheer & Zaheer, 1997) has been identified as a critical organizational capability that can provide a firm with competitive advantage. With the spread of customers and suppliers worldwide, location across time zones may facilitate such responsiveness and, therefore, act as a further source of competitive advantage to the firm.

INFORMATION ADVANTAGE AND TIME ZONES

Apart from the efficiency benefits of increasing throughput and responsiveness, the idea of information as one of the assets which the firm might benefit by internalizing is briefly developed in this section[5], to show how internalizing information across time zones (which requires both location and coordination across time zones) can also result in economies of scope to the firm.

Indivisible Assets and Economies of Scope

Basic theories of the economies of scope were centered on the idea that these economies exist when the cost of joint production of multiple products is less than the cost of producing each of these products separately (Baumol, Panzar, & Willig, 1982; Panzar & Willig, 1981). The fundamental driver behind these theories is that the products can *share physical assets in production or in distribution* that the firm cannot make available to the market due to its indivisibility or specialization. Teece (1980) further extended the idea of economies of scope to suggest that the presumptions of market failure for these assets (which leads to economies of scope by allowing joint production costs within the firm to be lower than separate production costs) rests *critically* on the indivisibility of the assets and is particularly salient when the shared assets take the form of proprietary knowledge, which, *due to its public goods nature,* is lost to the firm if shared with another firm.

Information as an Indivisible Asset

The creation of shared indivisible assets within the firm through internalization of the market for the asset is a key determinant of whether there are any potential economies of scope that the firm can exploit. As Teece (1980) pointed out, knowledge assets are one of the assets that are prone to market failure and, therefore, benefit the firm that internalizes the market for knowledge. I have suggested elsewhere (Mosakowski & Zaheer, 1999) that information assets have similar properties.

Although information assets share many of the public goods characteristics of knowledge assets (Teece, 1982), they differ from knowledge assets in that they tend to be at the explicit end of the tacit-explicit spectrum (where knowledge assets might not always be). Although their explicitness might argue for the possibility of market transactions in information, what leads to a market failure for certain information assets (Arrow, 1962; Teece, 1982) is that they are of value only so long as they are "private" rather than public and act as advance information on the state of the world to come. For example, information on likely government actions related to interest rates or the economy, or on likely trends in demand for certain currencies, is valuable to a firm only if it has the information in advance of everyone else in the market. As such, information assets tend to have a very short "shelf life" (i.e., the length of time they remain private and are truly valuable to the firm).

The value of such private information arises from the "foreknowledge" it provides to the firm that the firm can trade on and exploit (Hirshleifer, 1971; Mosakowski, 1998; Mosakowski & Zaheer, 1999). Foreknowledge is forward looking and refers to becoming better informed about the states of the world that will, at some time in the future, be revealed. It is this foreknowledge or private information on *what is to come* that acts as an indivisible asset that a firm can exploit in many fast-moving industries (e.g., financial trading). Location in different time zones and coordination across time zones play a role in *creating* foreknowledge in many information-intensive industries, and this is just one of the ways in which firms can benefit from time zone economies.

Location Across Time Zones and Information Advantage

What role can location and coordination across time zones play in creating an information advantage for the firm? In many industries, an offshoot of globalization is the emergence of a circadian (24-hour) rhythm of global activity, whereby industry participants, no matter where they are located, are influenced by the patterns of supply and demand faced by the industry throughout the global day. The most obvious manifestation of the emergence of the global day is in a variety of trading activities, whether in commodities, currencies, ship-broking or the booking of airline cargo. In these industries, the global day tends to follow the sun, beginning at about 5 p.m. Eastern Standard Time, as activity in New Zealand and the Far East begins to pick up, and continuing westward through Europe to the Americas. What is interesting about these circadian rhythms is that activity levels are not constant around the world through the entire period; rather, peak activity levels shift from time zone to time zone (Zaheer, 1995).

In terms of information assets, I suggest that the best information on demand and supply, on market expectations of price trends, and on patterns of buying and selling tends to be focused through this global day in the time zone where activity levels currently are at their peak. These are the time zones where there are the maximum numbers of buyers and sellers operating at a particular point in the global day, where the market is most liquid, and where fast-breaking developments first emerge. Firms needing to stay ahead of the curve on foreknowledge need to be active when different time zones around the world are most active and perhaps need to locate activity in these time zones and coordinate activity across them. Thus, I suggest that to be *alert* to information in such industries (Zaheer & Zaheer, 1997), it is necessary for firms to be able to synchronize their activities with the activity patterns in the global day. This is perhaps easiest to do by physically locating offices in the most active time zones at different times of the day, thereby internalizing information seeking across time zones.

There is some empirical work to support the idea that synchronization of firm activity and market activity across time zones, as well as location in more than one global time zone, matters in certain industries. In a study of patterns of information seeking among 4,088 banks in the global currency market (Zaheer & Zaheer, 1997), it was found that synchronization of firm activity across time zones with market activity was positively correlated to measures of a firm's alertness to information including its ability to bridge structural holes ($r = .37$, $p < .01$) in the information network (Burt, 1992), the extensiveness of its information seeking ($r = .18$, $p < .01$), and its ability to maintain a large number of weak ties for information ($r = .16$, $p < .01$). In another study of the global configuration of banks' currency-trading operations over a 20-year period (Mosakowski & Zaheer, 1999), it was clear that presence in all three major time zones (Asia, Europe, and America) appeared to provide the banks with access to information on required changes to their global configuration in ways that being present in just one or two of the time zones did not. The effects of location in multiple time zones were some of the strongest effects in this study.

Although the benefits of synchronizing firm activity with the circadian rhythms of global activity in information-intensive industries in order to develop good information and foreknowledge are fairly obvious, what is not so obvious is why firms need to actually physically locate operations in multiple time zones to capture these information assets. I suggest that physically locating operations in multiple time zones, rather than operating multiple shifts in one geographic location (from where the firm can stay in touch with the currently most active time zone), is required for many of the same reasons suggested in the discussion of efficiency benefits. These include the importance of interpersonal networks in the information-gathering process (Burt, 1992; Granovetter, 1973, 1985) and the entrainment (Ancona & Chong, 1996) of individual circadian rhythms (Halberg, 1959) and social rhythms with the rhythms of work life.

DISCUSSION AND IMPLICATIONS

Although there is no doubt that there are increased costs for a firm to locate and coordinate activity across time zones, I suggest that the value of synchronizing individual circadian rhythms and work rhythms, as well as the nature of global activity in certain industries, may prove sufficient to generate economies for a firm from the institution of global relay strategies across time zones. Such economies might be particularly realizable in industries where the activity is costlessly fungible across borders by the effect of increasing throughput within the firm to achieve economies of scale and scope. A further necessary condition for these economies to be realized is that they are not tied to throughput through particular location-specific capital assets.

There also are economies to be gained from increasing the speed of response to a global network of suppliers and customers, both through its effect on throughput through the value-adding system and through its effect on relationship quality and social capital, which can further facilitate coordination. Finally, another benefit from location across time zones could arise from the creation of an information advantage through the acquisition of private information or foreknowledge that is facilitated from such location.

Managerial Work in a Global World

The existence of such time zone economies, and the managerial coordination required to realize them, poses some special issues for managerial work in a global world. Increasingly, managers with IB responsibilities are going to have to work to a global circadian rhythm. This is particularly true of the "meta-coordinators" within the firm, that is, those who have to coordinate the coordinators who are located in different time zones. Working to a global circadian rhythm also has become a requirement in globally integrated industries, especially those in which information is a key asset, such that for a currency trader in New York, the workday begins at 7 p.m. when Tokyo is beginning to become active (Zaheer, 1995) and continues through to 3 p.m. the next day when traders in the United States are slowing down their activities. The desynchronizing of individual circadian rhythms and social rhythms with the rhythm of work can lead to stress and physiological and psychological effects, a fact of which biologists working on human circadian rhythms are acutely aware (Folkard, 1997; Halberg, 1959; Smith-Coggins et al., 1997).

In assessing the effects of globalization on work, the forces of globalization appear to counter, to some extent, the beneficial effects of automation that, in the optimistic view of Marcuse (1979), "renders possible the reversal of the relation between free time and working time: the possibility of working time becoming marginal and free time becoming full-time." At least for the meta-coordinators, this certainly is not true, and globalization is perhaps at least one of the major reasons why, despite the fact that American productivity has more than doubled since 1948, Americans are working longer hours (Schor, 1991).

The Privileged Position of Europe

These are issues that firms need to be aware of as they internationalize. In particular, the key role of managerial coordination in realizing economies of scale and scope globally requires round-the-clock coordination. A possible solution, and one that is likely to emerge even more strongly in the future, is *the location of such meta-coordination managerial roles in Europe,* which enjoys a privileged position in the global day, with the centrality of its time zone.[6] A manager located in Europe can, without too much disruption to his or her circadian and social rhythms, coordinate with Asia in the European morning and with the United States in the European afternoon. In MNCs, using their offices in Europe as a center for global coordination would greatly facilitate the realization of global economies of scale and scope. The emergence of London as the major financial center in the world is at least partly due to the privileged position it occupies in terms of time zone centrality. That MNCs are particularly well equipped to take advantage of such temporal location choices comes as no surprise. As Rifkin (1995) put it, "Global corporations are by their very nature temporal rather than spatial institutions" (p. 237).

NOTES

1. The informational aspects of such global relay strategies are dealt with in a working paper by Mosakowski (1998).

2. This information was gleaned from an interview with software managers in Minneapolis, Minnesota.

3. For example, it is common practice to have the junior-most residents staff the "graveyard shift" in most hospitals.

4. Of course, even closer proximity such as being in the same country, the same city, or even the same office building would be better for the development of personal relationships.

5. For a more thorough exposition of the informational aspects of location across time zones, see Mosakowski (1998) and Mosakowski and Zaheer (1999).

6. Although countries in Africa also occupy a similarly privileged time zone position, the absence of good communications infrastructure and managerial resources in many African countries might negatively affect the location of meta-coordination roles there.

REFERENCES

American Psychiatric Association. (1994). *Diagnostic and statistical manual of mental disorders* (4th ed.). Washington, DC: Author.

Ancona, D., & Chong, C-L. (1996). Entrainment: Pace, cycle, and rhythm in organizational behavior. In B. M. Staw & L. L. Cummings (Eds.), *Research in organizational behavior* (Vol. 18, pp. 251-284). Greenwich, CT: JAI.

Arrow, K. J. (1962). Economic welfare and the allocation of resources of invention. In National Bureau of Economic Research (Ed.), *The rate and direction of inventive activity: Economic and social factors* (pp. 609-625). Princeton, NJ: Princeton University Press.

Baillie, R., & Bollerslev, T. (1991). Intra-day and inter-market volatility in foreign exchange rates. *Review of Economic Studies, 58,* 565-585.

Bartlett, C., & Ghoshal, S. (1989). *Managing across borders: The transnational solution.* Boston: Harvard Business School Press.

Baumol, W. J., Panzar, J. C., & Willig, R. D. (1982). *Contestable markets and the theory of industry structure.* San Diego: Harcourt Brace Jovanovich.

Burt, R. S. (1992). *Structural holes: The social structure of competition.* Cambridge, MA: Harvard University Press.

Cairncross, F. (1997). *The death of distance.* London: Orion Business Books.

Callier, P. (1986). "Professional trading," exchange rate risk, and the growth of international banking: A note. *Banca Nazionale del Lavoro Quarterly Review, 159,* 423-428.

Campbell, S., & Murphy, P. J. (1998). Extraocular circadian phototransduction in humans. *Science, 279,* 396-399.

Chandler, A. D., Jr. (1990). *Scale and scope: The dynamics of industrial capitalism.* Cambridge, MA: Belknap/Harvard University Press.

Daniels, J. D., & Radebaugh, L. H. (1998). *International business: Environments and operations* (8th ed.). Reading, MA: Addison-Wesley.

Dijk, D. J., Shanahan, T. I., Duffy, J. F., Ronda, J. M., & Czeisler, C. A. (1997). Variation of electroencephalographic activity during non-rapid eye and rapid eye movement sleep with phase of circadian melatonin rhythm in humans. *Journal of Physiology, 505,* 851-858.

Eisenhardt, K. (1989). Making fast strategic decisions in high-velocity environments. *Academy of Management Journal, 32,* 543-576.

Engle, R. T., Ito, T., & Lin, W. (1990). Meteor showers or heat waves? Heteroskedastic intra-daily volatility in the foreign exchange market. *Econometrica, 58,* 525-542.

Folkard, S. (1997). Black times: Temporal determinants of transport safety. *Accident Analysis and Prevention, 29,* 417-430.

Granovetter, M. (1973). The strength of weak ties. *American Journal of Sociology, 78,* 1360-1380.

Granovetter, M. (1985). Economic action, social structure, and embeddedness. *American Journal of Sociology, 91,* 481-510.

Halberg, F. (1959). Physiologic 24-hour periodicity: General and procedural considerations with reference to the adrenal cycle. *Z. Vitamin-Hormon-Fermentforsch, 10,* 225-296.

Hamermesh, D. S. (in press). The timing of work over time. *Economic Journal.*

Hammer, M., & Champy, J. (1993). *Reengineering the corporation: A manifesto for business revolution.* New York: Harper Business.

Hirshleifer, J. (1971). The private and social value of information and the reward to inventive activity. *American Economic Review, 61,* 561-574.

Hogan, K., & Melvin, M. (1994). Sources of meteor showers and heat waves in the foreign exchange market. *Journal of International Economics, 37,* 239-247.

Jewett, M. E., Rimmer, D. W., Duffy, J. F., Klerman, E. B., Kronauer, R. E., & Czeisler, C. A. (1997). Human circadian pacemaker is sensitive to light throughout subjective day without evidence of transients. *American Journal of Physiology, 273,* 1800-1809.

Marcuse, H. (1979). *Eros and civilization.* Frankfurt, Germany: Suhrkamp.

Mosakowski, E. (1998). *Global relay strategies: Using informational assets dynamically.* Working paper, Purdue University.

Mosakowski, E., & Zaheer, S. (1999). The global configuration of a speculative trading operation: An empirical study of foreign exchange trading. *Organization Science, 10,* 401-423.

Nayyar, P. R., & Bantel, K. A. (1994). Competitive agility: A source of competitive advantage based on speed and variety. In P. Shrivastava, A. S. Huff, & J. E. Dutton (Eds.), *Advances in strategic management: Resource-based view of the firm* (Vol. 10, pp. 193-222). Greenwich, CT: JAI.

Panzar, J., & Willig, R. (1981). Economies of scope. *American Economic Review, 71,* 268-272.

Porter, M. E. (1986). Competition in global industries: A conceptual framework. In M. E. Porter (Ed.), *Competition in global industries* (pp. 15-60). Boston: Harvard Business School Press.

Quinn, J. B. (1992). The intelligent enterprise: A new paradigm. *Academy of Management Executive, 6*(4), 48-63.

Rifkin, J. (1995). *The end of work: The decline of the global labor force and the dawn of the post-market era.* New York: Jeremy P. Tarcher/Putnam.

Schor, J. (1991). *The overworked American: The unexpected decline of leisure.* New York: Basic Books.

Smith, R. S., Guilleminault, C., & Efron, B. (1997). Circadian rhythms and enhanced athletic performance in the National Football League. *Sleep, 20,* 362-365.

Smith-Coggins, R., Rosekind, M. R., Buccino, K. R., Dinges, D. F., & Moser, R. P. (1997). Rotating shiftwork schedules: Can we enhance physician adaptation to night shifts? *Academy of Emergency Medicine, 4,* 951-961.

Stalk, G. (1988). Time: The next source of competitive advantage. *Harvard Business Review, 66*(4), 41-51.

Teece, D. J. (1980). Economies of scope and the scope of the enterprise. *Journal of Economic Behavior and Organization, 1,* 223-247.

Teece, D. J. (1982). Towards an economic theory of the multiproduct firm. *Journal of Economic Behavior and Organization, 3,* 39-63.

Wilson, E. O. (1998). *Consilience: The unity of knowledge.* New York: Knopf.

Work week: A special news report about life on the job—and trends taking shape there. (1997, October 28). *The Wall Street Journal,* p. A1.

Zaheer, S. (1995). Circadian rhythms: The effects of global market integration in the currency trading industry. *Journal of International Business Studies, 26*(4), 699-728.

Zaheer, A., & Zaheer, S. (1997). Catching the wave: Alertness, responsiveness, and market influence in global electronic networks. *Management Science, 43,* 1493-1509.

Zander, U., & Kogut, B. (1995). Knowledge and the speed of the transfer and imitation of organizational capabilities: An empirical test. *Organization Science, 6,* 76-92.

Author Index

Adler, N. J., 17
Agrawal, A., 154
Albanese, R., 133
Alder, N. J., 176
Anacona, D., 344, 345
Anderson, E., 117-118
Anderson, J. C., 225
Andrews, K. R., 121, 183-184
Aoki, M., 245-246, 250
Argyle, M., 219

Baliga, B. R., 114, 121
Barley, S. R., 5
Bartlett, C. A., 345
Benedict, R., 54
Berry, J. W., 36
Bird, A., 132
Black, J. S., 146
Blalock, H. M., 31, 35
Bowie, N.E., 189
Boynton, L. L., 187
Brandenburger, A. M., 328
Burgelman, R. A., 320
Burgelman, R. A., 298

Cairncross, F., 340
Callier, P., 345
Camerer, C. F., 318
Cantwell, J., 148
Casson, M., 221
Caves, R. E., 150, 246
Chandler, A. D., 343
Cox, D. R., 257
Cusumano, M. A., 326
Cyert, R. M., 271

Daft, R., 219
Daniels, J. D., 345
Davidson, W. H., 118
Davis, B. J., 327
Denis, D. J., 151
DiMaggio, P., 264
Dodwell Marketing Associates, 253-255
Donaldson, T., 134
Durkheim, E., 99
Dyer, J. H., 215-239, 220

Earley, P. C., 6-7, 33, 56, 318
Earley, P. C., 1-12, 208
Egelhoff, W. G., 121
Eisenhardt, K. M., 131, 134, 174-175
Enz, C. A., 183-209
Erez, M., 5-6
Erez, M., 38
Etzioni, E., 188-189

Ferguson, C., 263
Fischer, C. S., 53, 59
Fiske, A. D., 64
Florida, R., 246
Foa, U. G., 317-318
Frayne, C. A., 112, 115-116, 118
Friedman, M., 185
Fujimoto, H., 264

Gannon, M. J., 91-105
Garfinkel, H., 63
Geertz, C., 92, 320
Geringer, J. M., 107-124
Gerlach, M., 222

Gersick, C. J. G., 272
Gerth, H., 83
Ghemawat, P., 317
Gibbons, R, 324
Giddens, A., 79
Gilmore, D. D., 80
Glaser, B., 93-94
Gorer, G., 55
Gouldner, A. W., 221, 235
Granovetter, M., 218, 219, 235
Greenwood, D., 187
Gupta, A. K., 270

Hackman, J. R., 21
Hadley, E., 249
Haire, M., 2, 32-3
Hall, E., 92, 103
Hall, R. H., 187
Hamel, G., 327
Hamel, G., 328
Handy, C., 208
Harnett, D. L., 315, 316
Harrison, D., 187
Haveman, H. A., 272
Hofstede, G., 2, 3, 19, 55, 94, 99-100, 103,
    143, 143t, 145, 153, 314, 316, 319
Howard, C. G., 117
Hymer, S., 246
Hymer, S. H., 311

Imai, K., 249
Inkeles, A., 58

Jackson, S. E., 22
Jehn, K., 38-39
Jensen, M. C., 112
Johanson, J., 311

Kanter, R. M., 26, 183
Kerr, J. L., 112
Kimura, Y., 255
Kimura, Y., 248
Kogut, B., 3, 268
Kogut, B., 145
Krafcik, J., 246
Kroeber, A. L., 18

Lakoff, G., 92
Lasserre, P., 118
Lawrence, P. R., 268
Leung, K., 56, 59, 81
Lewellan, T. C., 187-188
Lewin, K., 76
Lincoln, J. R., 6
Londono, 148-149, 153, 158
Lorange, P., 280

Marcuse, E., 350
Martin, X., 246, 264
Martinez, Z. L., 114
Marx, K., 58
Maznevski, M., 135
McClelland, D., 99
McGrath, J. E., 22
Mead, M., 54
Meglino, B. M., 19
Merton, R. K., 80
Milgrom, P., 316
Miller, D., 268
Mintzberg, H., 272, 296
Morris, M. W., 52-85, 80
Mosakomwski, E., 311-330
Mullen, B., 27
Murphy, M., 80

Nelson, R. R., 297, 313, 322-323

Oppermann, M., 185
Ouchi, W. G., 219

Parsons, T., 62-64
Pascale, R. T., 322-323
Perlmutter, H., 312
Perrow, C., 134, 162
Peterson, M. F., 135, 137, 147, 151, 175
Peterson, M. F., 131-177
Piaget, J., 135, 137
Pondy, L. R., 20
Porter, M. E., 121, 268, 327-328
Powell, W., 188
Prahalad, C. K., 312

Quinn, J. B., 339, 345

Rabin, M., 318
Ravlin, E. C., 17-43
Reich, R. B., 185
Rifkin, J., 351
Roethlisberger, F. J., 79-80
Rohner, R. P., 320
Rokeach, M., 19
Romanelli, E., 296
Root, F. R., 320
Rosaldo, R., 1
Roth, A., 315
Rousseau, D., 185
Rumelt, R. P., 322-323

Sako, M., 217
Sampson, E. E., 35-36
Schor, J., 350
Schwartz, S., 8, 57, 100
Schwartz, S., 7-8, 38
Scott, W. R., 160
Shane, S., 185, 319
Sharma, A., 132
Shaw, J. B., 146
Sheahan, J., 187, 199
Shleifer, A., 150, 154
Shrivastava, P., 187, 189
Singelis, T. M., 57
Smith, P. B., 35-36, 132, 135, 138, 139, 144-145, 157
Smith, R. S., 342
Sohn, J. H. D., 219
Steiner, I. D., 22
Strauss, A., 93-94
Suchman, M. C., 32-33
Swidler, A., 63-64

Tajfel, H., 40-41

Teece, D. J., 347
Terpstra, V., 255
Thomas, D. C., 40
Thomas, D. C., 37
Thompson, J. D., 272
Ting-Toomey, S., 27
Tonnies, F., 99
Tornblom, K. Y., 6-7
Triandis, H. C., 100, 142
Triandis, H. C., 56, 57, 68-69
Trompenaars, F., 104
Tushman, M. L., 189

Uzzi, B., 236

Vaill, P. B., 312
Van Maanen, J., 7

Wall, J. A., 19-20
Warren, R. P., 52
Weber, M., 58, 79, 83
Weick, K. E., 135, 175, 320
Wheeler, L., 59-60
White, H. C., 59
Williamson, O., 193, 222
Wilson, E. O., 340
Winter, S. G., 313
Wrong, D. H., 55

Zaheer, A., 220
Zaheer, S., 339-351, 350
Zander, U., 344
Zarate, M. A., 26
Zucker, L., 221

Subject Index

Accelerated change model, for organizational change, 294-298, 295(figure)
Achievement, ascription versus, 62-63
Activity-level analysis:
in organizations, 178, 179(table), 275-277
organizational change and, 285-286
Administrative processes, study of, 3
Aerial Tram, Costa Rican development, 202-203
Affect, development of, 37-39
Affectivity, in networks, 60-61, 76, 78(figure)
Affiliative orientation, in work relationships, 67-68
Agency theory, 131, 133-135
improving, 174-175
modifications of, 176
risk and shirking, 174
Agent-principal relations. See Principal-agent relations
Agent(s):
agency theory, 133
Brazil as, 162-171
business experience of, 163
challenges of, 166(table)
expectations of, 164-165
responsibilities of, 166(table)
sources of meaning, 146-147, 167-168
upbringing of, 163-164
American. See United States
Ascription, achievement versus, 62-63
Assistance, trust and, 227, 229(table), 230(table), 232
Automotive industry, interfirm trust study, 223-239

Banana republics, in Costa Rica, 199-201

Banking regulation/receptivity rationale, for foreign direct investment, 149, 156-158
Bechtel Corporation, time zone economies and, 339-340
Behavior, influences on, 79-82, 82(figure)
Beliefs, group members and, 25-28, 28-30
Brazil:
as agent, 162-171
challenges of investing in, 172-174
cultural comparison, 142-145
financial growth of, 140
Brazilian financial market, 139-151
overview, 139-141
Business transactions, keiretsu and, 252-253, 256-257

Career development, in international joint ventures, 120-121
Categorization process, for group interaction, 25-28
Causal ambiguity, 327-328
cultural unfamiliarity and, 313-321
Causal model, for strategic colonialism, 321-327
China, cross-national comparison, 68-82
Chinese:
cultural metaphor of, 102-103
network density of, 59-60
work relationships, 66
Circadian rhythms, and work, 341-342
Circumvention challenges, in strategic partnerships, 173
Citibank, cross-national comparison, 68-82
Cluster analysis, in subjectivist approach, 55

Coalition-based integration mechanisms, organizational variable, 301, 305(table)
Cognitive influences, on group interaction, 25, 26-27
Cognitive legitimacy, 33
Cognitive moral development, legitimacy and, 36
Collectivism, 100
    cultural differences and, 143, 143(table)
    cultural metaphor and, 104
    economic, 70, 72(figure)
    expressive, 70, 72(figure)
    subjectivist approach and, 55-57
Commercial development, banking related event, 169-170
Communication, face-to-face, 226, 229(table), 230(table), 232
Communication challenges, in strategic partnerships, 172-173
Compensation and reward, in international joint ventures, 119-120
Competition, cross-national comparison, 70, 71(figure)
Composition:
    cultural, 23-29, 24(figure)
    group, 22-23
Comprehensive survey, cultural research, 98-101
Conflict, 19-20
    cultural composition and, 23-29, 24(figure)
    defined, 19-20
    development of, 36-39
    felt, 37-39, 39
    group effectiveness and, 21-22
    latent, 20
    manifest, 39
    multiculturalism and, 20-21
Conflict resolution processes, 39-42
    dyadic interaction, 40-41
    interaction process, 40
    multiple value systems, 42
    status of group, 41-42
Contractual exchange:
    in Costa Rica, 199-201
    in strategic partnerships, 191-193, 194(figure)
Convergence thesis, 58
Corporate governance mechanisms, 146-151, 152(table), 154

Costa Rica:
    contractual exchanges, 199-201
    integrated social covenants, 204-205, 206(figure), 207
    joint partnerships, 203-204
    limited social covenants, 202-203
    strategic partnerships in, 199-209
Cross-cultural differences, implications of, 320-321
Cross-national comparison:
    social relations measure, 73-79
    social values measure, 69-70, 71(figure), 72(figure)
    workplace culture, 68-82
Cultural difference(s):
    individual behavior and, 314-320
    relative, 145
Cultural metaphor(s), 94-98
    application of, 103-105
    defined, 91
    evolution of, 101-103
    grounded, 91, 100-101
Cultural research:
    challenges for, 8-9
    comprehensive survey, 98-101
    cultural metaphors, 94-98
    general framework, 4-8
    hybrid form, 9-10
    overview, 1-4
    socialcultural systems approach, 61-64
    structuralist approach, 53, 58-61
    subjectivist approach, 53, 54-58
Cultural unfamiliarity, causal ambiguity and, 313-321
Culture:
    affect on rules of the game, 317-318
    belief systems and, 25-28
    defined, 18, 314
    effect on management tasks, 315-317
    firm, 301, 305(table)
    multicultural interaction, 18-19

Decision-making authority, organizational variable, 300, 303(table)
Democracy, economic development and, 198
Developing countries:
    anticipating changes, 189-191, 190(figure)
    economic development, 184-188
    future research, 207-209

global economy, 183-184
    social contracts and, 188-189, 190(figure)
Development:
    activity-level analysis, 178, 179(table),
        275-277
    sustainable, 187-188
Diversification/hubris rationale:
    agent responsibility, 166(table)
    for foreign direct investment, 151,
        152(table), 161-162
    passions, 161
    temptations, 161
    tempters, 161-162
Diversity, valuing, 35
Duration, in networks, 60-61, 76, 78(figure)
Dyadic interaction, conflict resolution and,
    40-41

Economic collectivism:
    cross-national comparison, 70, 72(figure)
    of Chinese, 66
Economic development, 184-188, 198
Economic individualism:
    cross-national comparison, 69-70, 71(figure)
    of North Americans, 65
Economies of diachronic scope, 340
Economies of scale and scope:
    information assets, 346-347
    throughput, 342-343
    time zone economies, 342-346
Ecotourism, Costa Rican development,
    204-205
Eli Lilly, organizational change study,
    274-294
Emic research approach, defined, 5
Employee recruitment, 115-116
Environment, Costa Rica development and, 201
Ethnocentrism, legitimacy and, 35-36
Europe, time zone economies and, 350-351
Event management:
    agency theory, 135, 137-138
    sensemaking and, 175
Event(s):
    banking related, 169-171
    defined, 135

Factor analysis, in subjectivist approach, 55
Familial orientation, in work relationships, 66

Femininity, cultural differences and, 143,
    143(table)
Financial support, keiretsu and, 251-252, 256
Fluor Corporation, time zone economies and,
    339
Follow-the-client rationale:
    agent responsibility, 166(table)
    for foreign direct investment, 149-150,
        152(table), 158-159
    passions, 158-159
    temptations, 159
    tempters, 159
Follow-the-leader rationale:
    agent responsibility, 166(table)
    for foreign direct investment, 150,
        152(table), 159-160
    passions, 159-160
    temptations, 160
    tempters, 160
Foreign direct investment (FDI):
    reasons for, 146-151, 152(table)
    work patterns of, 3
Foreign direct investment theory, 148, 176
Foreknowledge, time zone economies and,
    347-248
Formal structure, friendships and, 76,
    77(figure)
French, cultural metaphor of, 104
Friendships, formal structure and, 76,
    77(figure)

Game theory, 315-327
    new game strategy, 325-327
    new rules, 323-325
    payoffs, 315-320
    role of culture in, 315-318
    rules of game, 317-318
German:
    cultural metaphor of, 104
    work relationships, 66-67
Germany, cross-national comparison, 68-82
Gestalt form, research approach, 5-6
Global economy, developing countries,
    183-184
Global markets, 170-171
Globality:
    activity-level analysis, 283-287, 290(table),
        291(table)
    changes in, 283-294

firm level, 283, 286, 288-289
    measure of, 283
Globalization:
    organizational change and, 267, 294-298
    process model for, 298-299
    time zone economies, 350-351
Grounded theory method, 93-94
Group effectiveness, 21
    conflict and, 21-22
    group composition and, 22-23

Hackman's group effectiveness model, 21
Hoffman LaRoche, organizational change
    study, 274-294
Honda, strategic colonialism and, 322-323
Hubris hypothesis, 151
    See also Diversification/Hubris rationale
Human resource management (HRM):
    components of, 108-109
    role of, 108
Human resource management international
    joint ventures:
    challenges for, 122-123
    components of, 111-122
    role of, 111
Human resource planning, in international
    joint ventures, 112, 113(figure), 114
Hybrid form, of cultural research, 7-10

Incremental change models, for organizational
    change, 272-273, 273(figure)
Individual behavior, cultural differences and,
    314-320
Individualism, 100
    cultural differences and, 143, 143(table)
    cultural metaphor and, 104
    subjectivist approach and, 55-57
Indivisible assets, information assets, 347-348
Industrial Groupings in Japan, 253-255
Industrialization, cultural differences and, 58
Influence challenges, in strategic partnerships,
    173
Information assets:
    economies of scale and scope, 346-347
    indivisible assets, 347-348
    time zone economies, 346-349
Information processing approach:
    conflict and, 37

group interaction and, 26-27
    status and, 29-30
Integrated social covenant, in strategic partner-
    ships, 192(figure), 194(figure), 197-198
Integrated social covenants, in Costa Rica,
    204-205, 206(figure), 207
Intel, Costa Rican development, 202
Interaction process, conflict resolution and, 40
International business (IB) research, 268-271
International competition/industry rivalry
    rationale:
    agent responsibility, 166(table)
    for foreign direct investment, 150-151,
        152(table), 159-160
International joint venture (IJV)
    challenges of, 107-108
Interpersonal perception, and group inter-
    action, 25
Italy, 101
    cultural metaphor of, 96, 97

Japan, interfirm trust study, 223-239
Japanese automakers, trust and, 233, 235
Joint partnerships:
    in Costa Rica, 203-204
    strategic partnerships, 192(figure),
        194(figure), 196-197
Joint ventures, defined, 107

Keiretsu:
    effect on overseas investment, 248-253,
        262-264
    factors for investment, 259-262
    firm demographics, 255-256
    in Japan, 245, 248-250
    investment in U.S., 245-246, 247(figure),
        248
    types of, 249-250
Keiretsu in U.S. study, 253-264
    measurement, 255-259
    model for, 257-259
    results, 259-262
    sample, 253-255
Korea, interfirm trust study, 223-239

Learning/options rationale:
    agent responsibility, 166(table)

for foreign direct investment, 152(table),
156-168
passions, 156
temptations, 156-157
tempters, 157-158
Legal-bureaucratic orientation, in work relationships, 66-67
Legitimacy, 32-36
challenges to, 33-36
defined, 32
self-identity and, 32-33
Limited social covenants:
in Costa Rica, 202-203
in strategic partnerships, 192(figure),
194(figure), 195-196
Logico-deductive theory, 93
Loyalty, cross-national comparison, 70,
72(figure)

Macro-level variables, in structuralist approach, 58
Majority/minority representation, legitimacy
and, 35
Management tasks:
causal ambiguity and, 313
cross-cultural differences, 320-321
time zone economies and, 339-351
Managerial values, cross-cultural, 2-3
Market imperfections/internationalization
rationale, for foreign direct investment,
148-150
Market orientation, in work relationships, 65
Marketing and sales, activity-level analysis,
178, 179(table), 275-277
Marriott Hotels, Costa Rican development,
203-204
Masculinity, cultural differences and, 143,
143(table)
Meaning:
agency theory and, 135-138
agent sources of, 167-168
principal sources of, 146-151, 152(table)
sources of, 138-139
Metacoordinators:
Europe and, 350-351
time zone economies, 350
Metaphors:
as conceptual models, 92
See also Cultural metaphor(s)

Micro-level social structures, in structuralist
approach, 58
Mixed-motive relationship, agency theory,
133
Model of Japanese investment, 257
Moral legitimacy, 32-33
Motivational influences, group interaction
and, 25-27
Multiculturalism, 18-19
conflict and, 20-21
Multinational corporations (MNCs):
globalization and, 298-299
organizational evolution of, 269-271
organizational variables of, 278, 280, 300-
305
Multiple value systems, integration of, 42
Multiplexity, in networks, 60, 73-76

National culture, concepts, 141-142
Network analysis, 59
Network density, 59-60
cross-national comparison, 73, 74(table)
obligation and, 82, 82(figure)
Networking, 65
Network(s), 59-61
advice exchange, 73, 75(figure)
cross-national comparison, 73-79
multiplexity of, 73-76
power-dependence in, 73, 75(figure)
Nightwork, 344
effect of, 342
Norms:
affiliative, 67
defined, 62
development of, 64
in workplace, 53-54
legal-bureaucratic, 67
of Chinese, 66
of Germans, 66-67
of Spanish, 67

Obligation, work behavior and, 79-80
Operant conditioning, game theory and, 324-
325
Options rationale, for foreign direct investment, 149
Organizational change:
accelerated change model, 294-298

incremental change models, 272-273, 294, 295(figure)
punctuated equilibrium models, 271-273, 294, 295(figure)
research on, 268
Organizational change study:
data analysis, 281
data collection, 280-281
findings, 281-294
methods, 274-281
research sites, 274-275
Organizational evolution, of multinational corporations, 269-271
Organizational orientation, organizational variable, 300, 302(table), 303(table)
Organizational theory (OT) research, 268-269
Organizational variables, 278, 280, 300-305
Ownership controls, keiretsu and, 250-251, 256

Parsonsian construct, for cultural research, 62-64
Particularism, universalism versus, 62-63
Particularism-achievement orientation, cultural tradition and, 63
Particularism-ascription orientation, cultural tradition and, 63
Passions:
agency theory, 138-139
diversification/hubris rationale, 161
follow-the-client rationale, 158-159
follow-the-leader rationale, 159-160
in banking, 155
learning/options rationale, 156
Payoffs, in game theory, 315-320
Performance appraisal, in international joint ventures, 116-118
Pharmaceutical firms:
activity-level analysis, 178, 179(table), 275-277
organizational change study, 274-294
Planning and information systems, organizational variable, 300-301, 304(table)
Power distance, cultural differences and, 143, 143(table)
Pragmatic legitimacy, 32
Principal-agent relations:
circumvention challenges, 173
communication challenges, 172-173

influence challenges, 173
misunderstandings, 165-166
symbolic challenges, 173-174
Principal(s):
agency theory, 133
American banker as, 153-162
sources of meaning, 146-151, 152(table)
Processed based perspective, of trust, 220-222
Production, activity-level analysis, 178, 179(table), 275-277
Punctuated equilibrium models, for organizational change, 271-273, 273(figure)

Reduced form, research approach, 6-7
Regulatory approval, activity-level analysis, 178, 179(table), 275-277
Relational constructs, in structuralist approach, 59
Relations:
horizontal, 79-80
vertical, 79-80
See also Network(s)
Relationship(s):
continuity of, 226-227, 229(table), 230(table), 232
length of, 226, 229(table), 230(table), 232
trust and, 215-239
Research approach:
gestalt form, 5-6
hybrid form, 7-8
reduced form, 6-7
unitary form, 5
Resource configuration, organizational variable, 300, 302(table)
Risk, agency theory and, 174

Self-identity, legitimacy and, 32-33
Self-interest, economic development, 185, 190(figure), 192(figure)
Sensemaking:
agency theory, 135, 137-138
event management theory and, 175
Sensemaking theory, 176
Shirking, agency theory and, 174
Similarity-attraction paradigm:
conflict and, 37-38
legitimacy and, 33
status and, 29-30

Social contracts, developing countries and, 188-190, 192(figure)
Social cultural systems approach, cultural research, 61-64
Social/embeddedness perspective, of trust, 218-220
Social identity and categorization theories:
  group interaction and, 27
  group status and, 41-42
  legitimacy and, 33
  status and, 29
Social relations:
  influence on behavior, 79-82, 82(figure)
  of Chinese, 66
  of Germans, 67
  of North Americans, 65
  of Spanish, 67-68
  structuralist approach and, 58-61
Social relations measure, 69
  cross-national comparison, 73-79
Social values:
  influence on behavior, 79-82, 82(figure)
  of Chinese, 66
  of Germans, 67
  of North Americans, 65
  of Spanish, 67
  subjectivist approach and, 54-58
Social values measure, 68-69
  cross-national comparison, 69-72
Spain:
  cross-national comparison, 68-82
  work relationships, 67-68
Staffing, in international joint ventures, 115-116
Standards and procedures, organizational variable, 300, 304(table)
Status characteristics theory, 29
Status hierarchy:
  agreement about, 30-32
  development of, 28-30
Status of group, conflict resolution and, 41-42
Status perceptions, legitimacy and, 34
Stewardship theory, of management, 134-135
Stock ownership, trust and, 227, 229(table), 230(table), 232
Strategic colonialism, 311-330
  causal ambiguity and, 313-321
  causal model, 321-327
  firm success and, 327-329
  future research, 329

Strategic partnerships:
  anticipating changes, 189-191
  contractual exchange, 191-194
  economic development, 184-188
  evolution of, 184-191
  future research, 207-209
  in Costa Rica, 199-209
  integrated social covenant, 192(figure), 194(figure), 197-198
  joint partnership, 192(figure), 194(figure), 196-197
  limited social covenant, 192(figure), 194-196
  models for, 191-199
  S-curve for, 189-191
  social contracts and, 188-189, 190(figure)
Structuralist approach:
  to cultural research, 53, 58-61
  See also Social relations
Subjective understandings
  in structuralist approach, 58
Subjectivist approach:
  to cultural research, 53, 54-58, 80-81
  See also Social values
Supplier-automaker relations, interfirm trust study, 223-239
Sweden, cultural metaphor of, 102
Symbolic challenges, in strategic partnerships, 173-174
System, defined, 4-5

Temptations:
  agency theory, 138-139
  diversification/hubris rationale, 161
  follow-the-client rationale, 159
  follow-the-leader rationale, 160
  in banking, 155
  learning/options rationale, 156-157
Tempters:
  agency theory, 138-139
  diversification/hubris rationale, 161-162
  follow-the-client rationale, 159
  follow-the-leader rationale, 160
  in banking, 155
  learning/options rationale, 157-158
Thailand, cultural metaphors, 94-95
Throughput:
  economies of scale and scope, 342-343

firm coordination and, 343-345
responsiveness and, 345-346
Time, conflict resolution and, 40
Time zone economies, 339-351
economies of scale and scope, 342-346
information assets, 346-349
management, 350-351
Tourism:
Costa Rican development, 204-205,
206(figure), 207
economic development, 186-187
Training and development, in international
joint ventures, 118-119
Trust:
defined, 217-218
determinants of, 218-223
economic perspective, 222-223
processed based perspective, 220-222
social/embeddedness perspective, 218-220
Trust, interfirm, 215-239
determinants of, 216-217
Trust, interfirm study, 223-239
data analysis, 227-228, 238-239
future research, 236-239
operational measures, 225-227
research setting, 223
results, 228-232
sample and data collection, 224-225, 237-238

Uncertainty avoidance, cultural differences
and, 143, 143(table)
Unitary form, research approach, 5

United States:
cross-national comparison, 68-82
cultural comparison, 142-145
interfirm trust study, 223-239
work relationships, 65
United States bankers:
as principal, 153-162
challenges in Brazil, 172-174
Universalism, particularism versus, 62-63
Universalist-achievement orientation, cultural
tradition and, 62-63
Universalist-ascription orientation, cultural
tradition and, 63

Value systems, multiple:
integration of, 42
Values:
managerial, 2-3
multicultural interaction and, 19
Values theory, conflict and, 38-39
Vision, shared:
human resource management and, 109-110, 113(figure)

Wealth maximization, economic development
and, 185
Work relationships:
Chinese, 66
German, 66-67
North American, 65
Spanish, 67-68

About the Editors

P. Christopher Earley is the Randall L. Tobias Chair of Global Leadership at the Kelley School of Business, Indiana University. His research interests include cross-cultural and international aspects of organizational behavior such as the relationship of cultural values to work group dynamics, the role of face and social structure in organizations, and motivation across cultures. He is the author of seven books and numerous articles and book chapters. His recent publications include *Culture, Self-Identity, and Work* and *The Transplanted Executive: Managing in Different Cultures* (both with Miriam Erez) (Oxford University Press); *Face, Harmony, and Social Structure: An Analysis of Behavior in Organizations* (Oxford University Press); and "East Meets West Meets Mideast: Further Explorations of Collectivistic and Individualistic Work Groups" (*Academy of Management Journal*). He received his Ph.D. in industrial and organizational psychology from the University of Illinois, Urbana-Champaign. He has taught on the faculties of London Business School, University of Arizona, University of Minnesota, and University of California, Irvine, and he has taught executives and consulted for companies in England, Hong Kong, Israel, People's Republic of China, Singapore, South Korea, and Thailand, among others.

Harbir Singh is Professor of Management and Chair of the Department of Management at the Wharton School, University of Pennsylvania. He has done extensive teaching and research in strategic management, particularly in the management of acquisitions and alliances. He has taught courses in strategic planning, competitive strategy, and corporate development via acquisitions and alliances. He joined the Wharton faculty in 1984 after receiving his Ph.D. from the University of Michigan. His research has encompassed many areas of strategic management such as competition in high-technology industries, management of emerging technologies, and management of acquisitions and alliances. He is chair of the Business Policy and Strategy division of the Academy of Management, the premier association for professionals interested in strategic management. He teaches extensively in Wharton's executive education programs. He has been academic director of Wharton's executive program on strategic thinking and management. He also is director of Wharton's executive program on strategic alliances. He has been a visiting professor at London Business School, Massachusetts Institute of Technology, and Bocconi University in Italy. He has consulted with several organizations including IBM, AT&T, Merck, and Bell Atlantic.

About the Contributors

Sheira Ariel is pursuing a Ph.D. in organizational behavior at Stanford University's Graduate School of Business. Her research interests include groups, distributed work, dispersed teams, networks, and culture. Before pursuing her Ph.D., she worked at IBM in San Jose, California. She received her B.S. in economics from the Wharton School and her B.A. from the College of Arts and Sciences, University of Pennsylvania.

Pino G. Audia is Assistant Professor of Organizational Behavior at London Business School. His research focuses on the inertial effect of success on strategic decision makers, multi-unit organizations, industrial clusters, the dynamics of technology organizations, responses to feedback, and cross-cultural management. His publications include articles in *Academy of Management Journal, American Journal of Sociology, Organization Science,* and *Journal of Applied Psychology.* He received his Ph.D. from the University of Maryland and his M.B.A. from Bocconi University in Italy.

Sea Jin Chang is Associate Professor at Korea University. He received his Ph.D. in management from the Wharton School, University of Pennsylvania. Previously, he was a faculty member at the Stern School of Business, New York University. He is primarily interested in the management of diversified multinational enterprises. His current research focuses on understanding the process of building a strong local organization after foreign entry. His other research interests include diversification, corporate restructuring, organizational learning, corporate growth through joint ventures and acquisitions, and comparative management studies of Japan and Korea.

Jeffrey H. Dyer is the Donald Staheli Professor of International Strategy at the Marriott School, Brigham Young University. Previously, he was a professor in the Department of Management at the Wharton School, University of Pennsylvania. His current research focuses on global strategy, strategic alliances, supplier management, and interorganizational learning. He is the author or coauthor of several articles that have appeared in publications such as *Strategic Management Journal, Harvard Business Review, Sloan Management Review, California Management Review, Organization Science,* and *Academy of Management Review.* He has a forthcoming book, *Collaborative Advantage: Winning Through Extended Enterprise Supplier Networks.*

Cathy A. Enz is the Lewis G. Schaeneman, Jr., Professor of Innovation and Dynamic Management at the School of Hotel Administration, Cornell University. She also is a research fellow at the Center for Hospitality Research and a past member of the center's board of directors. She received her Ph.D. in organization theory and behavior from The Ohio State University. She has written more than 40 articles and case studies as well as 2 books. Her most recent book presents the results of a study of best practices in the U.S. lodging industry. She currently serves on six editorial review boards and is a member of the board of directors for two private hotel companies.

Colette A. Frayne (B.S., University of Delaware; M.B.A., University of San Diego; Ph.D., University of Washington) is Professor of International and Human Resource Management at California Polytechnic University. She also is president of an international consulting company and is active in international management consulting and executive development activities in North America, Europe, and the Asia-Pacific region. Her teaching, research, and consulting interests have focused on issues of human resource management, self-management, international management, power and influence, and organizational change, particularly in international joint ventures and alliances. She has authored a book and approximately 65 articles and case studies published in journals such as *Journal of Applied Psychology, Academy of Management Journal,* and *Management International Review.*

Martin J. Gannon (Ph.D., Columbia University) is Professor of Management and Director of the Center for Global Business, Robert H. Smith School of Business, University of Maryland at College Park. He is the author or coauthor of 80 articles and 10 books including *Understanding Global Cultures* and *Ethical Dimensions of International Management.* He currently is under contract to co-edit the *Handbook of Cross-Cultural Management.* He has been a visiting professor at several European and Asian universities.

J. Michael Geringer (B.S., Indiana University; M.B.A. and Ph.D., University of Washington) is Professor of Strategy and International Management at California Polytechnic University. He has extensive executive development and consulting activities in Asia, Europe, Africa, Australia, and North America. His research focus has been on international strategic management, particularly strategies for developing and exploiting technical, human, and other competencies between organizations. He has authored more than 200 presentations, 35 case studies, 10 books and monographs, and more than 95 articles and chapters in journals and books including journals such as *Academy of Management Journal, Strategic Management Journal,* and *Journal of Applied Psychology.*

Arzu Ilsev is a Ph.D. candidate in business administration at the Darla Moore School of Business, University of South Carolina. Her research interests are organizational commitment, leader-member exchange, and cross-cultural organizational behavior. She currently is working on a longitudinal study of value change and congruence. She recently presented a paper at the Academy of International Business conference on cross-cultural issues in organizational commitment.

Crist Inman is Professor at INCAE and Director of the Tourism Project at the Center for Latin American Competitiveness and Sustainable Development, based in Costa Rica. In the latter capacity, he has been working on behalf of the presidents of Central America since 1996, creating and implementing a sustainable tourism development agenda for the region. His interests include organizational development and change, interorganizational cooperation, and action research, all focused on the global tourism industry. He received his Ph.D. from the School of Hotel Administration, Cornell University.

Melenie J. Lankau is Assistant Professor of Management at the Terry College of Business, University of Georgia. She received her Ph.D. in organizational behavior from the University of Miami. Her primary research interests are in mentoring, group process, workforce diversity, organizational development, work/family issues, and scale development and measurement. She has facilitated team-building seminars for students and organizational employees. Her research work has been published in a number of management journals such as *Journal of Management, Journal of Organizational Behavior, Journal of Vocational Behavior, Leadership Quarterly, International Journal of Public Administration,* and *Leadership and Organization Development Journal.*

Thomas W. Malnight is Professor of Strategy and International Management at the International Institute of Management Development, Lausanne, Switzerland, where he teaches in the M.B.A. and executive education programs. He researches and consults in the areas of global strategy and organization, focusing on the processes of strategic and organizational change in dynamic industries. Prior to returning to academics, he spent 10 years working at Mitsubishi International Corporation. He has authored more than 25 case studies and has had his work published in *Strategic Management Journal* and *Journal of International Business Studies.*

Michael W. Morris is Associate Professor of Organizational Behavior at the Graduate School of Business, Stanford University, and Research Affiliate of the Institute for Social and Personality Research at the University of California, Berkeley. His research interests include cultural influence on social cognition and action; interpersonal and intergroup conflict resolution; and individual perception, judgment, and decision making.

Elaine Mosakowski (Ph.D., University of California, Berkeley) is Associate Professor of Strategy at the Krannert School of Management, Purdue University. She is on leave from the Anderson School, University of California, Los Angeles, and previously was on the faculty at the Carlson School of Management, University of Minnesota. Her research focuses on the entrepreneur's role in firm strategy, strategy making under causal ambiguity, global organizations, firm evolution, corporate governance and innovation, and speculation as a source of firm profits.

Mark F. Peterson is Professor of Management and International Business at Florida Atlantic University. His principal interests are in developing a theory of event management concerning the way in which people in organizations make sense of work situations and in understanding the implications of national culture for organizations. He has published more than 60 articles and chapters as well as several books on topics such as these. The journal articles have appeared in *Administrative Science Quarterly, Academy of Management Journal, Journal of International Business Studies, Leadership Quarterly, Human Relations, Journal of Organizational Behavior,* and *Organization Science.* He currently is coediting (with Neal Ashkanasy and Celeste Wilderom) the *Handbook of Organizational Culture and Climate.*

Joel M. Podolny is Professor of Strategic Management and Organizational Behavior in the Graduate School of Business, Stanford University. His research interests include the importance of status and reputation in market competition, the role of personal networks in organizational mobility, and the organizational challenges posed by globalization. He has been at Stanford since receiving his Ph.D. in sociology from Harvard University.

Elizabeth C. Ravlin is Associate Professor of Organizational Behavior and Management at the Darla Moore School of Business, University of South Carolina. She received her Ph.D. in organizational behavior from Carnegie Mellon University. Her research interests include group process and effectiveness as well as work values and ethics. Her publications have appeared in journals and annuals such as *Journal of Applied Psychology, Organizational Behavior and Human Decision Processes, Personnel Psychology, Journal of Management,* and *Research in Organizational Behavior.* She currently is on the editorial boards of *Academy of Management Review* and *Human Resource Management Review.*

Carlos L. Rodriguez is a doctoral candidate in business/strategy at Florida Atlantic University. A Brazilian native, he received a B.S. in economics from the Federal University of Rio de Janeiro and a master of international business degree from the University of South Carolina. He has worked in Brazil in various finance-related positions. In his dissertation, he is studying the relative importance of factors influencing firm performance in transitional economies, examining in particular the interaction between institutional and competitive factors in the adoption of innovations. His other areas of interest are comparative management and competitive strategies in turbulent or fast-changing environments from a resource-based/dynamic capabilities perspective.

Peter B. Smith is Professor of Social Psychology at the University of Sussex, Brighton, United Kingdom. He also directs the Centre for Research Into Cross-Cultural Organization and Management at Sussex. He received his Ph.D. from the University of Cambridge. He is the author/coauthor of six books (most recently *Social Psychology Across Cultures* [with M. H. Bond]) and more than 90 other publications in the fields of social and organizational psychology. His current interest is in the effective handling of relations among managers from different cultures. This has led to studies in joint ventures and multinational corporations in China, Belarus, the United Kingdom, and the Netherlands. He currently is editor of *Journal of Cross-Cultural Psychology.*

David C. Thomas is Associate Professor in International Business at Simon Fraser University. A naturalized New Zealander, he was born and educated in the United States and received his Ph.D. from the University of South Carolina. Previously, he held positions at The Pennsylvania State University and the University of Auckland, New Zealand. He also has held visiting positions at the Chinese University of Hong Kong and the University of Hawaii. He serves on the editorial boards of *Journal of World Business* and *International Journal of Organizational Analysis.* His research interests center on cross-cultural interactions in organizational settings.

Srilata Zaheer (Ph.D., Massachusetts Institute of Technology) is Associate Professor of International Management at the Carlson School of Management, University of Minnesota. Her research interests include the effects of globalization in financial services, dynamic competitive advantage in multinational corporations, and temporal and spatial organizational networks. Her doctoral dissertation on currency trading in the United States and Japan won two awards for best dissertation in 1992 and was further recognized with the Eldridge Haynes Award for "the best interdisciplinary work in international business." From 1994 to 1996, she was a senior fellow at the Wharton School, University of Pennsylvania.